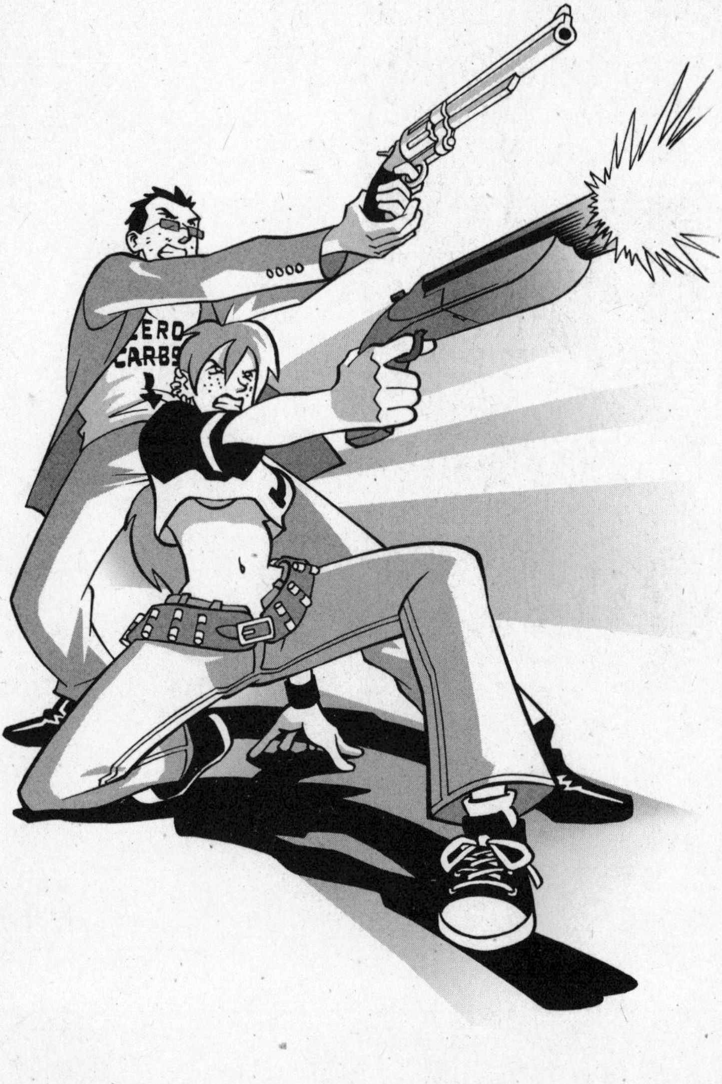

Riding Shotgun Vol. 1
story by Nate Bowden
art by Tracy Yardley

Lettering and Layout - Bowen Park
Production Artist - Alyson Stetz
Cover Art - Tracy Yardley
Tones - Nate Bowden and Tracy Yardley
Cover Color and Design - Gary Shum

Editor - Luis Reyes
Digital Imaging Manager - Chris Buford
Production Managers - Elisabeth Brizzi
Managing Editor - Lindsey Johnston
VP of Production - Ron Klamert
Editorial Director - Jeremy Ross
Editor-In-Chief - Rob Tokar
Publisher - Mike Kiley
President and C.O.O. - John Parker
C.E.O. and Chief Creative Officer - Stuart Levy

A **TOKYOPOP** Manga

TOKYOPOP Inc.
5900 Wilshire Blvd. Suite 2000
Los Angeles, CA 90036

E-mail: info@TOKYOPOP.com
Come visit us online at www.TOKYOPOP.com

ISBN: 1-59816-740-5

First TOKYOPOP printing: July 2006
10 9 8 7 6 5 4 3 2 1
Printed in the USA

RIDING SHOTGUN™

Volume 1

story by Nate Bowden
art by Tracy Yardley

HAMBURG // LONDON // LOS ANGELES // TOKYO

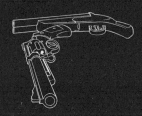

Contents

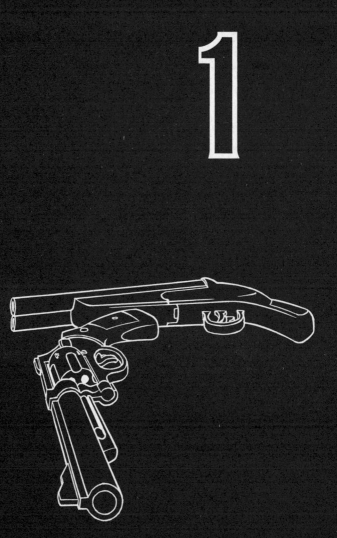

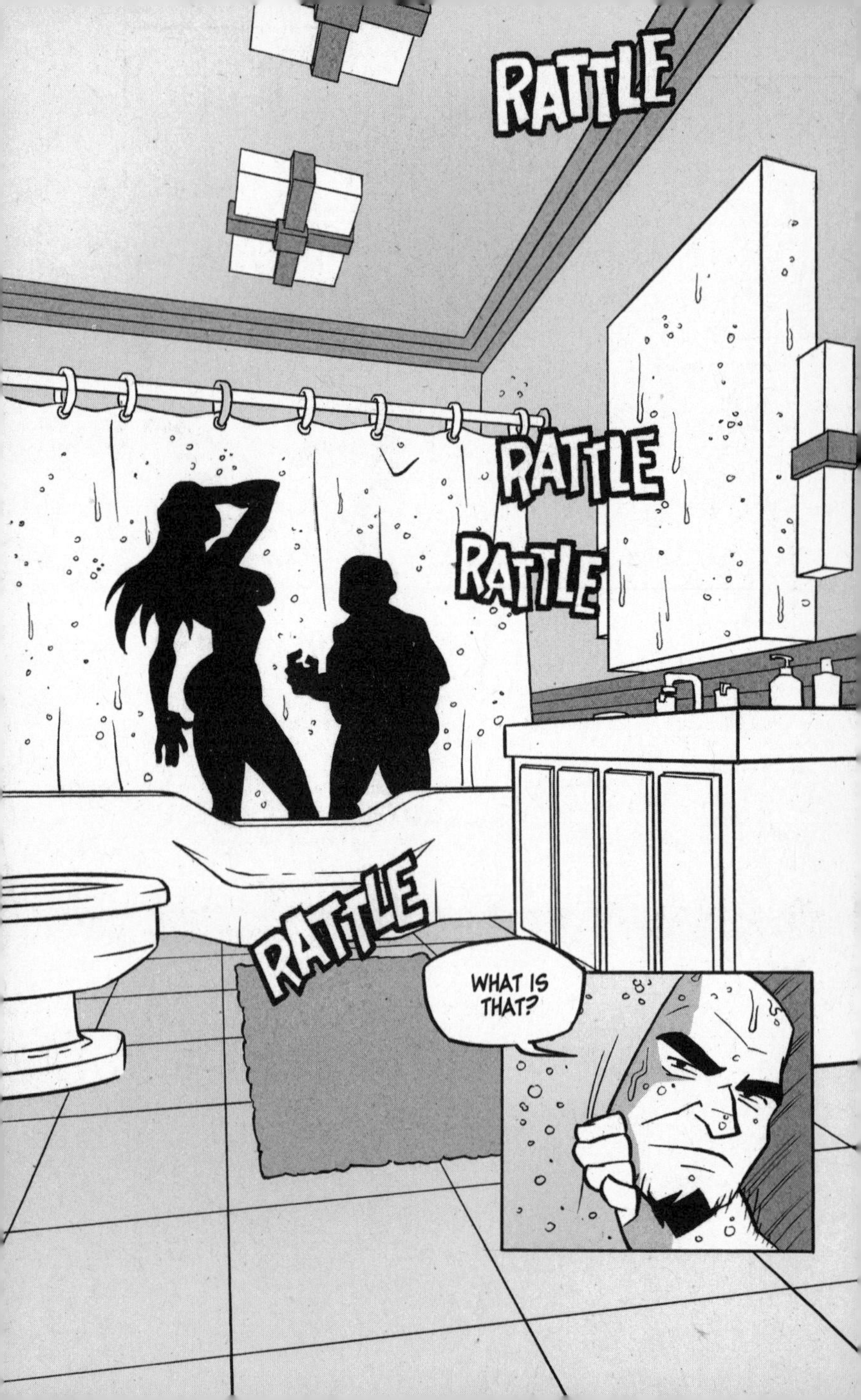
RATTLE
RATTLE
RATTLE
RATTLE
WHAT IS THAT?

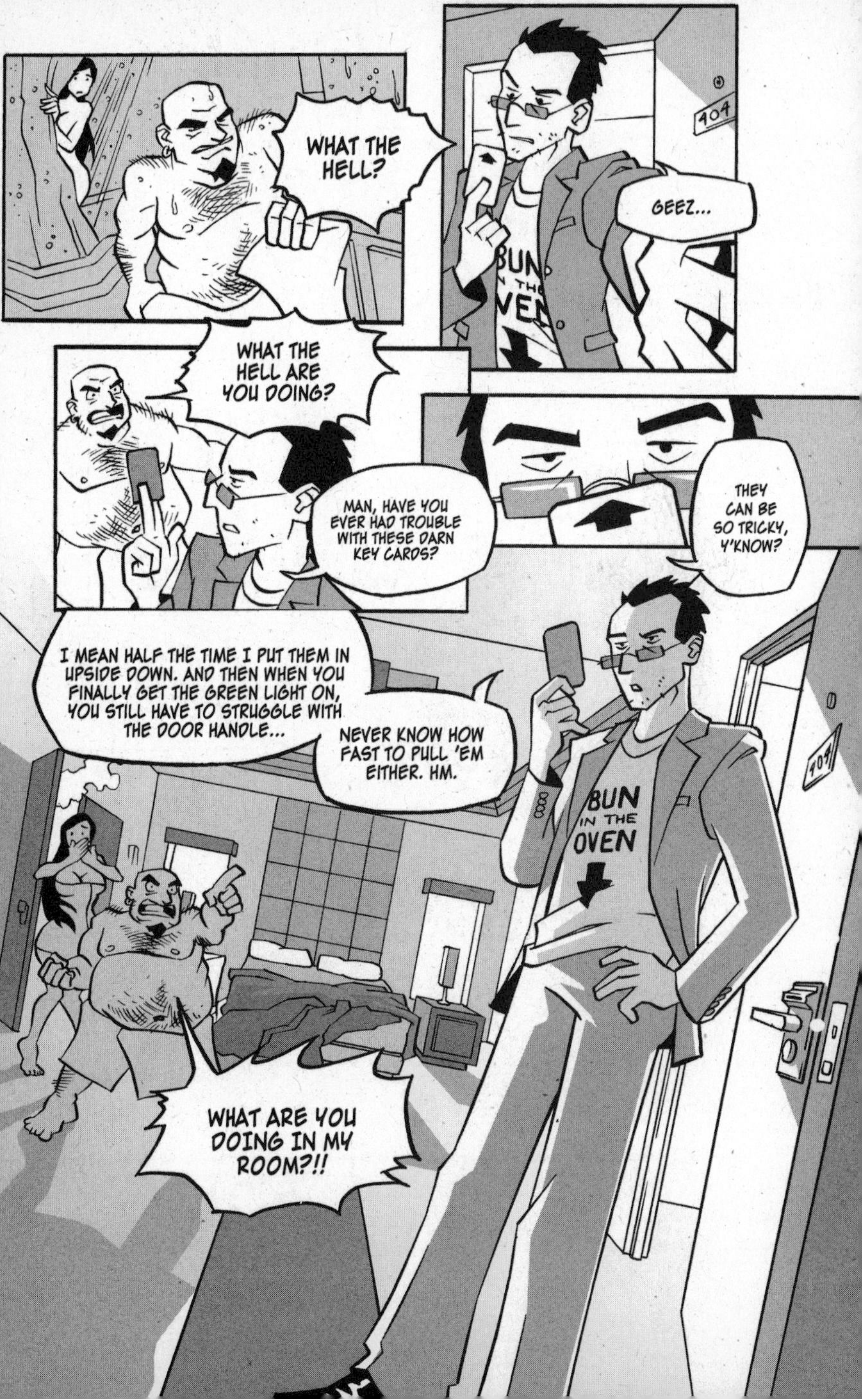

WHAT THE HELL?
GEEZ...
WHAT THE HELL ARE YOU DOING?
MAN, HAVE YOU EVER HAD TROUBLE WITH THESE DARN KEY CARDS?
THEY CAN BE SO TRICKY, Y'KNOW?
I MEAN HALF THE TIME I PUT THEM IN UPSIDE DOWN. AND THEN WHEN YOU FINALLY GET THE GREEN LIGHT ON, YOU STILL HAVE TO STRUGGLE WITH THE DOOR HANDLE...
NEVER KNOW HOW FAST TO PULL 'EM EITHER. HM.
WHAT ARE YOU DOING IN MY ROOM?!!

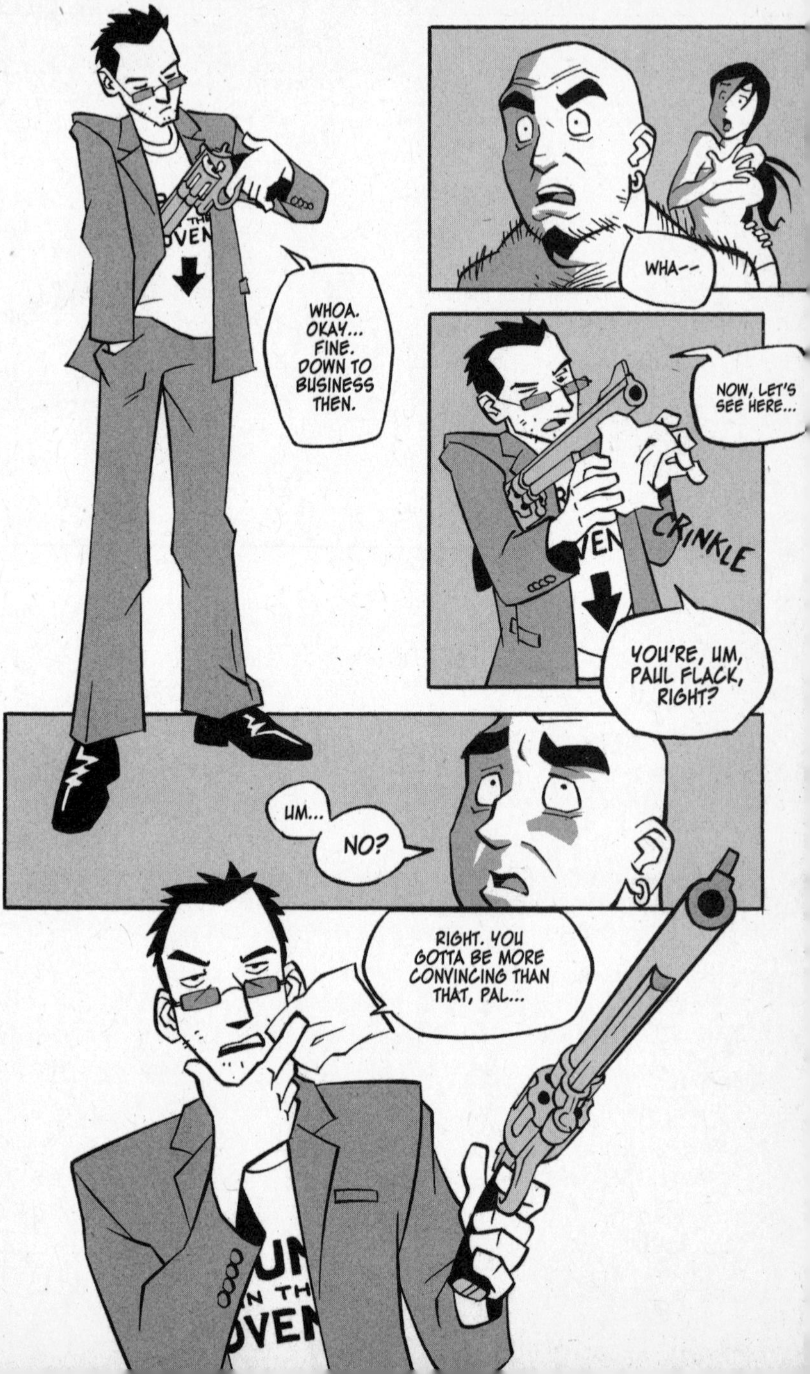
WHOA. OKAY... FINE. DOWN TO BUSINESS THEN.
WHA--
NOW, LET'S SEE HERE...
CRINKLE
YOU'RE, UM, PAUL FLACK, RIGHT?
UM...
NO?
RIGHT. YOU GOTTA BE MORE CONVINCING THAN THAT, PAL...

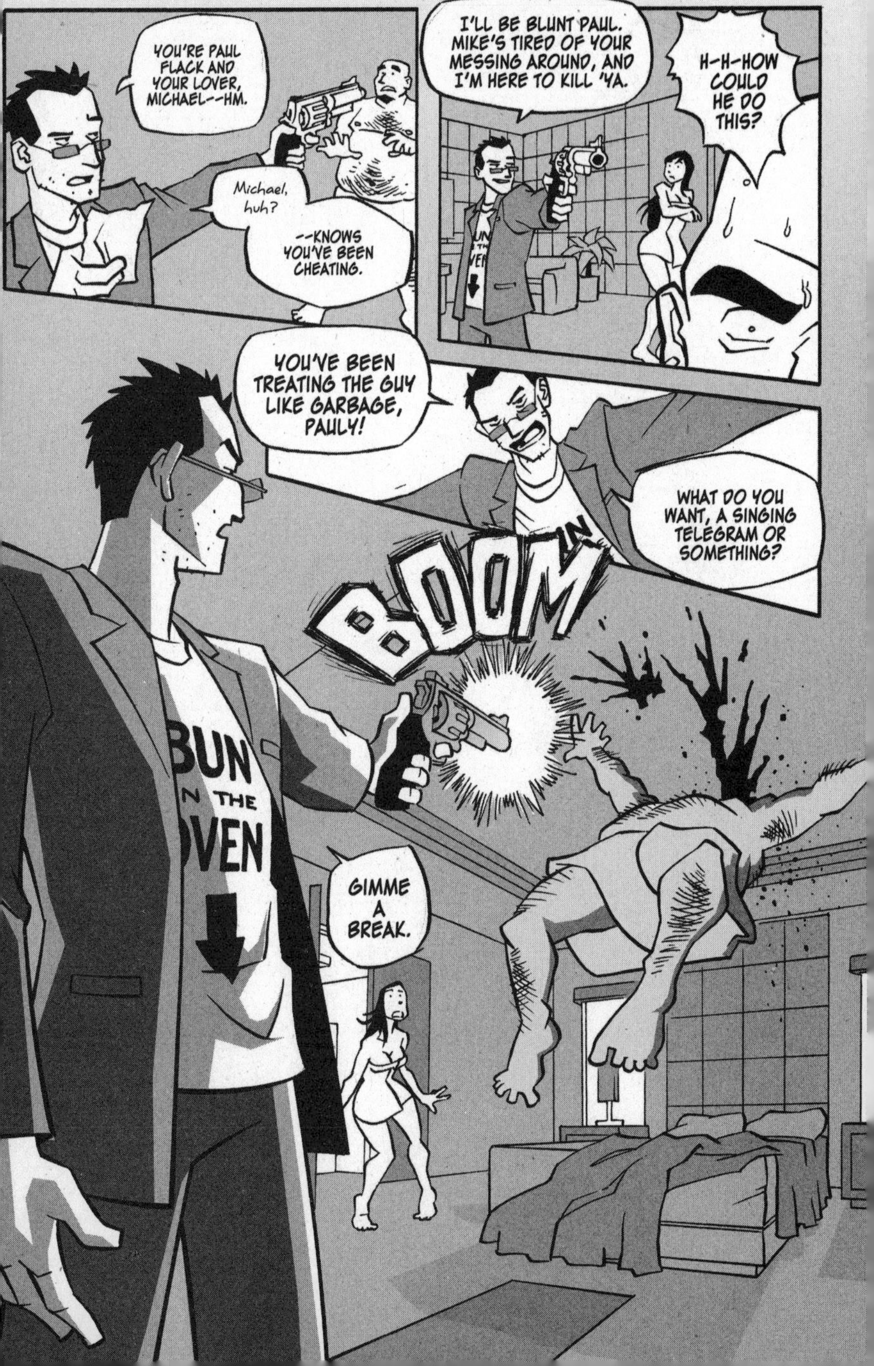
YOU'RE PAUL FLACK AND YOUR LOVER, MICHAEL--HM.
Michael, huh?
--KNOWS YOU'VE BEEN CHEATING.
I'LL BE BLUNT PAUL. MIKE'S TIRED OF YOUR MESSING AROUND, AND I'M HERE TO KILL 'YA.
H-H-HOW COULD HE DO THIS?
YOU'VE BEEN TREATING THE GUY LIKE GARBAGE, PAULY!
WHAT DO YOU WANT, A SINGING TELEGRAM OR SOMETHING?
BOOM
GIMME A BREAK.

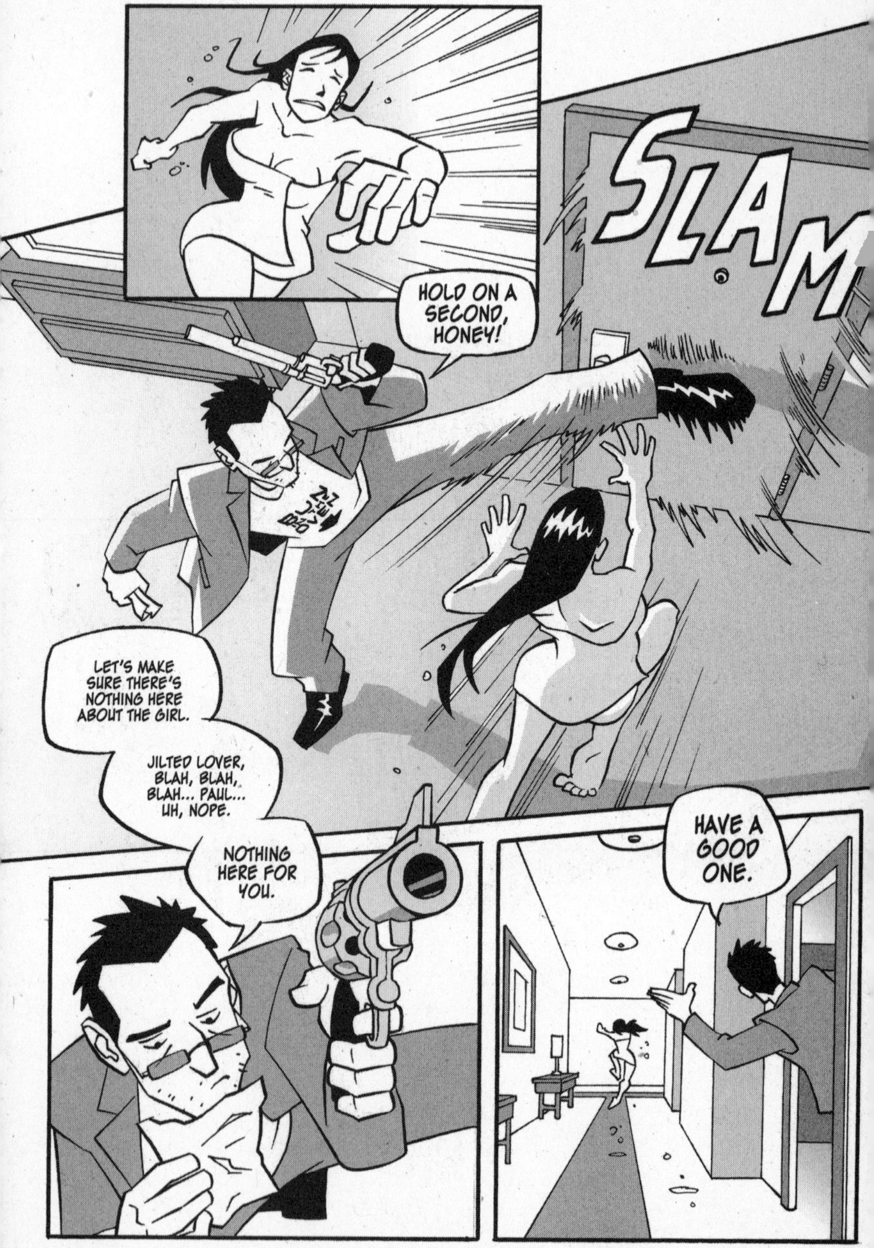
SLAM
HOLD ON A SECOND, HONEY!
LET'S MAKE SURE THERE'S NOTHING HERE ABOUT THE GIRL.
JILTED LOVER, BLAH, BLAH, BLAH... PAUL... UH, NOPE.
NOTHING HERE FOR YOU.
HAVE A GOOD ONE.

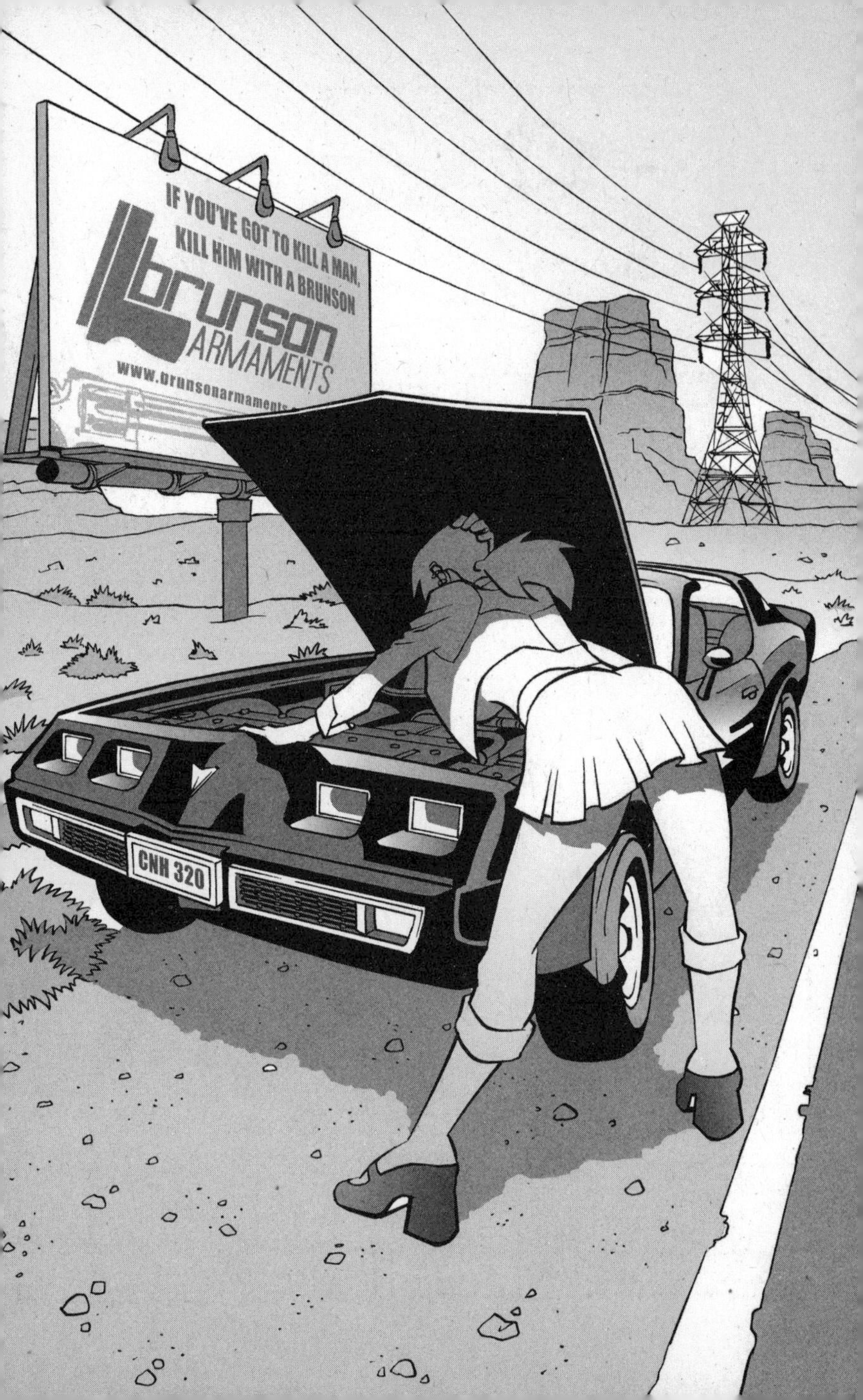
IF YOU'VE GOT TO KILL A MAN, KILL HIM WITH A BRUNSON
brunson ARMAMENTS
www.brunsonarmaments
CNH 320

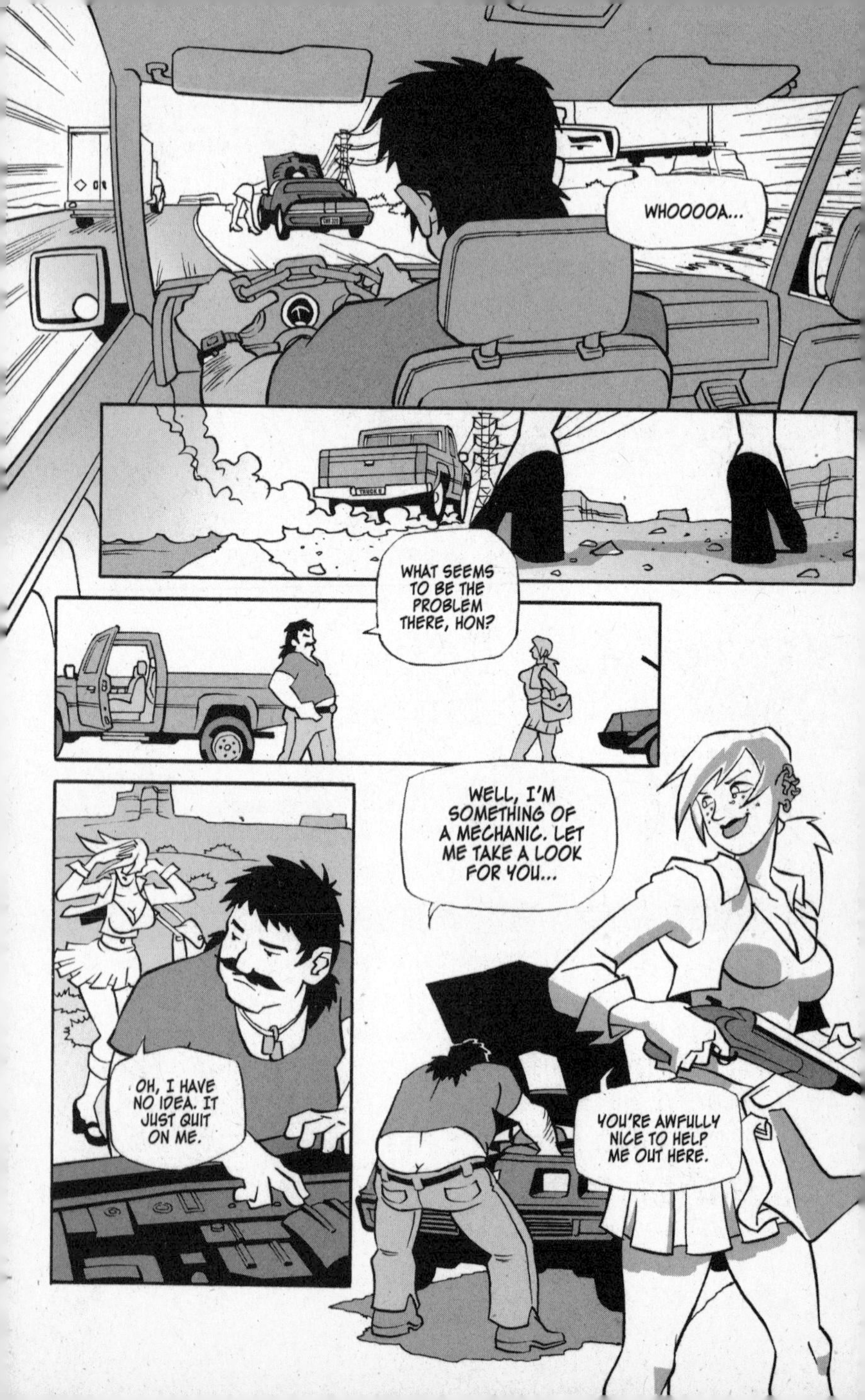
WHOOOOA...
WHAT SEEMS TO BE THE PROBLEM THERE, HON?
OH, I HAVE NO IDEA. IT JUST QUIT ON ME.
WELL, I'M SOMETHING OF A MECHANIC. LET ME TAKE A LOOK FOR YOU...
YOU'RE AWFULLY NICE TO HELP ME OUT HERE.

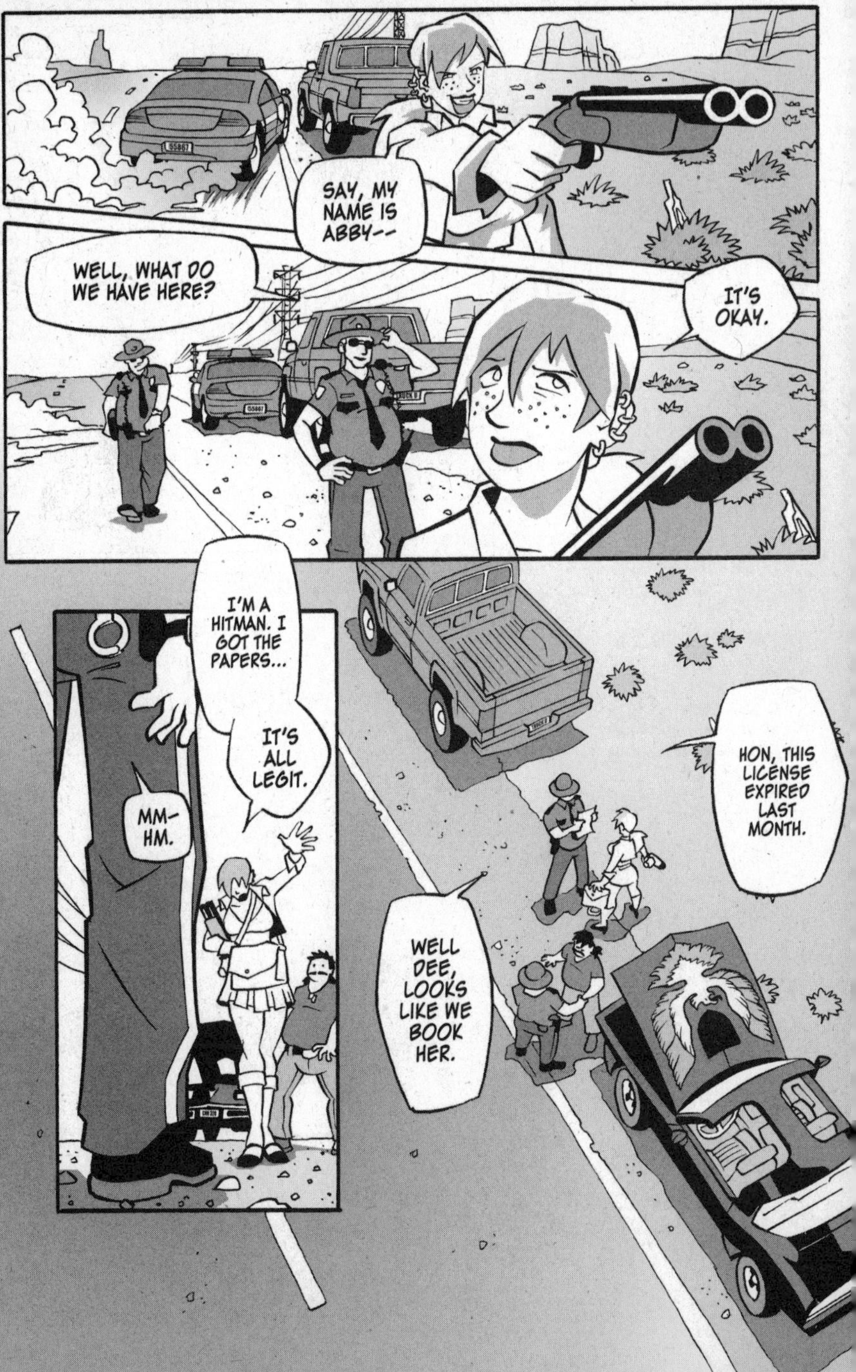
SAY, MY NAME IS ABBY--
WELL, WHAT DO WE HAVE HERE?
IT'S OKAY.
I'M A HITMAN. I GOT THE PAPERS...
IT'S ALL LEGIT.
MM-HM.
HON, THIS LICENSE EXPIRED LAST MONTH.
WELL DEE, LOOKS LIKE WE BOOK HER.

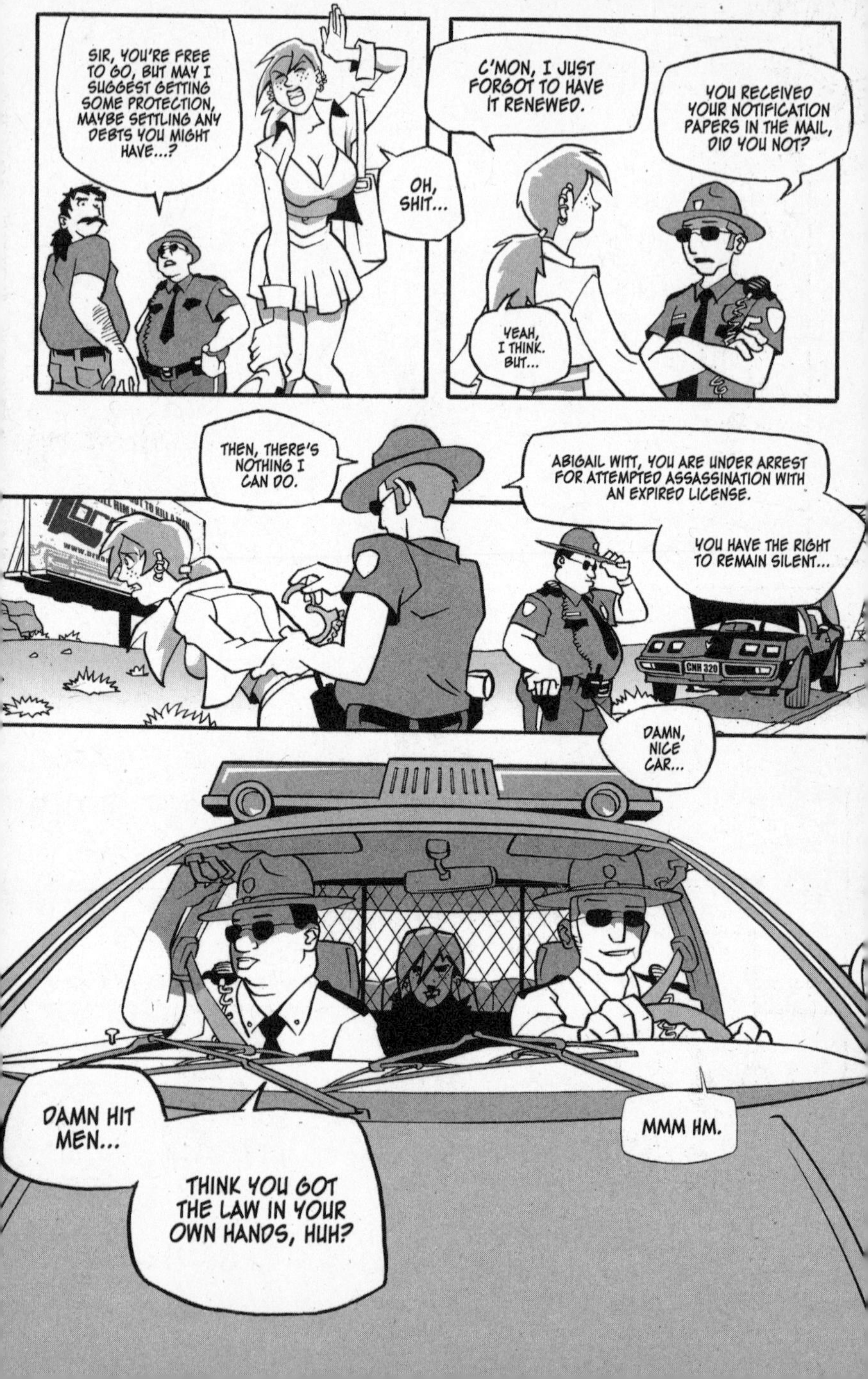
SIR, YOU'RE FREE TO GO, BUT MAY I SUGGEST GETTING SOME PROTECTION, MAYBE SETTLING ANY DEBTS YOU MIGHT HAVE...?
OH, SHIT...
C'MON, I JUST FORGOT TO HAVE IT RENEWED.
YOU RECEIVED YOUR NOTIFICATION PAPERS IN THE MAIL, DID YOU NOT?
YEAH, I THINK. BUT...
THEN, THERE'S NOTHING I CAN DO.
ABIGAIL WITT, YOU ARE UNDER ARREST FOR ATTEMPTED ASSASSINATION WITH AN EXPIRED LICENSE.
YOU HAVE THE RIGHT TO REMAIN SILENT...
CNR 320
DAMN, NICE CAR...
DAMN HIT MEN...
THINK YOU GOT THE LAW IN YOUR OWN HANDS, HUH?
MMM HM.

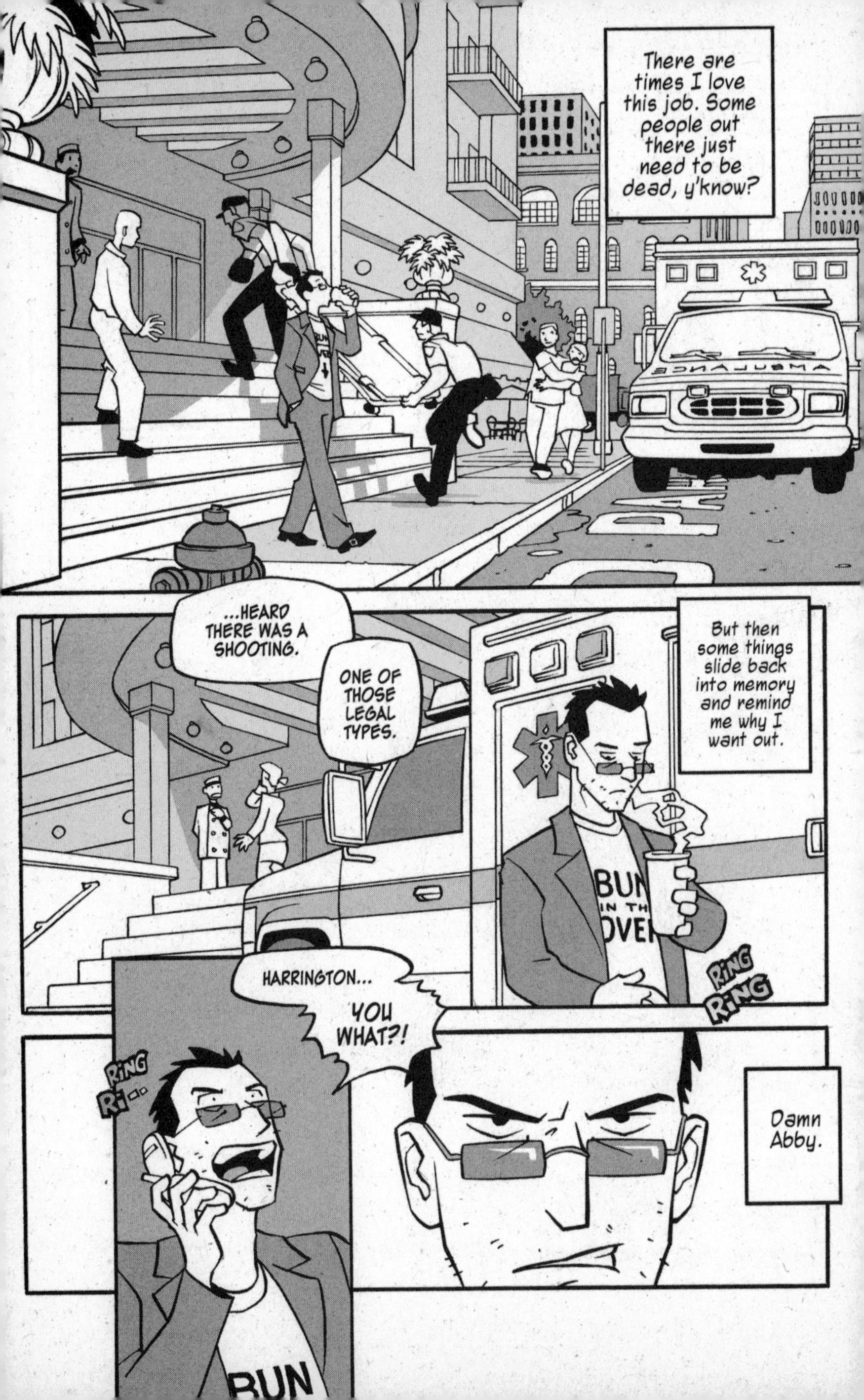
There are times I love this job. Some people out there just need to be dead, y'know?
...HEARD THERE WAS A SHOOTING.
ONE OF THOSE LEGAL TYPES.
But then some things slide back into memory and remind me why I want out.
RING RING
HARRINGTON...
YOU WHAT?!
RING Ri--
Damn Abby.

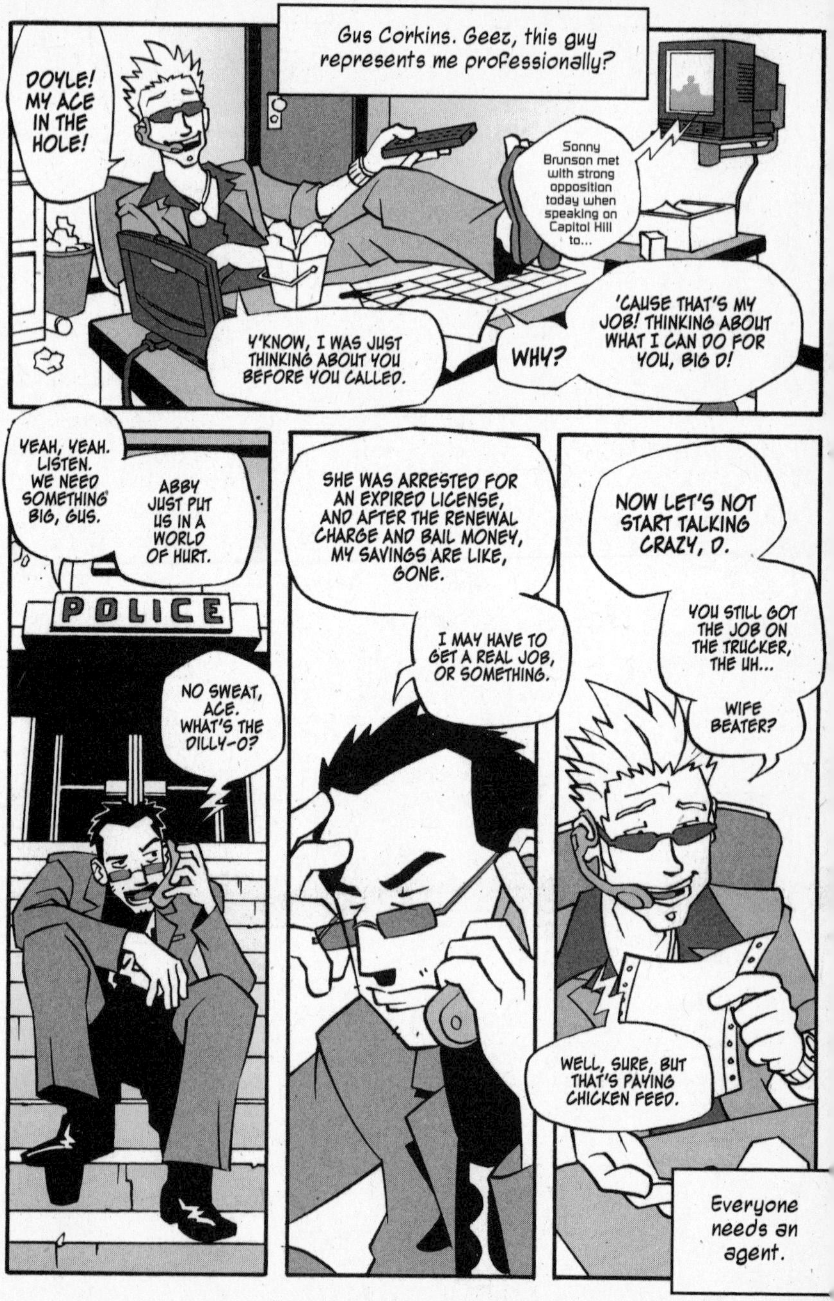
Gus Corkins. Geez, this guy represents me professionally?
DOYLE! MY ACE IN THE HOLE!
Sonny Brunson met with strong opposition today when speaking on Capitol Hill to...
Y'KNOW, I WAS JUST THINKING ABOUT YOU BEFORE YOU CALLED.
WHY?
'CAUSE THAT'S MY JOB! THINKING ABOUT WHAT I CAN DO FOR YOU, BIG D!
YEAH, YEAH. LISTEN. WE NEED SOMETHING BIG, GUS.
ABBY JUST PUT US IN A WORLD OF HURT.
POLICE
NO SWEAT, ACE. WHAT'S THE DILLY-O?
SHE WAS ARRESTED FOR AN EXPIRED LICENSE, AND AFTER THE RENEWAL CHARGE AND BAIL MONEY, MY SAVINGS ARE LIKE, GONE.
I MAY HAVE TO GET A REAL JOB, OR SOMETHING.
NOW LET'S NOT START TALKING CRAZY, D.
YOU STILL GOT THE JOB ON THE TRUCKER, THE UH...
WIFE BEATER?
WELL, SURE, BUT THAT'S PAYING CHICKEN FEED.
Everyone needs an agent.

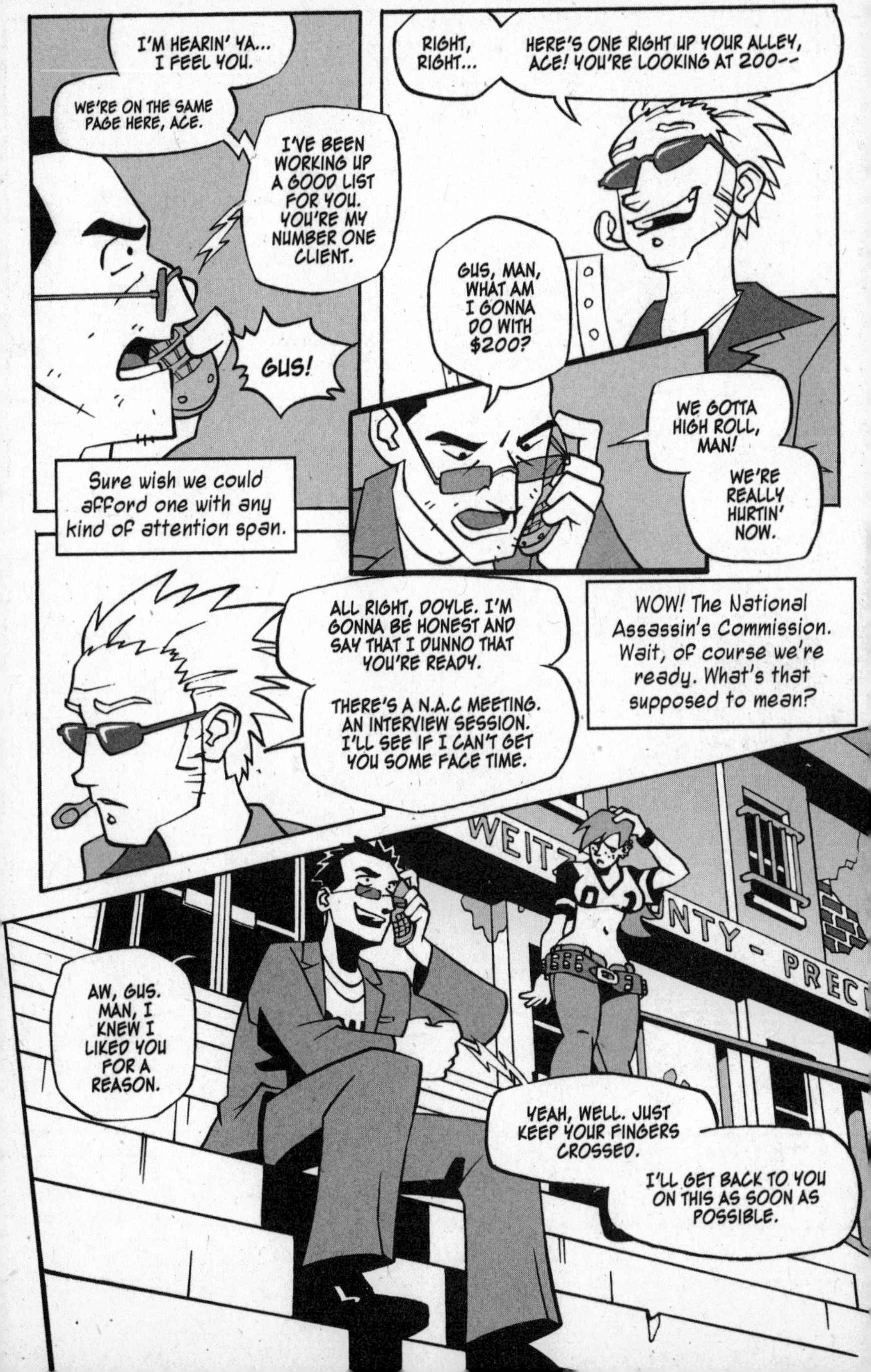
I'M HEARIN' YA... I FEEL YOU.
WE'RE ON THE SAME PAGE HERE, ACE.
I'VE BEEN WORKING UP A GOOD LIST FOR YOU. YOU'RE MY NUMBER ONE CLIENT.
GUS!
RIGHT, RIGHT...
HERE'S ONE RIGHT UP YOUR ALLEY, ACE! YOU'RE LOOKING AT 200--
GUS, MAN, WHAT AM I GONNA DO WITH $200?
Sure wish we could afford one with any kind of attention span.
WE GOTTA HIGH ROLL, MAN!
WE'RE REALLY HURTIN' NOW.
ALL RIGHT, DOYLE. I'M GONNA BE HONEST AND SAY THAT I DUNNO THAT YOU'RE READY.
THERE'S A N.A.C MEETING. AN INTERVIEW SESSION. I'LL SEE IF I CAN'T GET YOU SOME FACE TIME.
WOW! The National Assassin's Commission. Wait, of course we're ready. What's that supposed to mean?
AW, GUS. MAN, I KNEW I LIKED YOU FOR A REASON.
YEAH, WELL. JUST KEEP YOUR FINGERS CROSSED.
I'LL GET BACK TO YOU ON THIS AS SOON AS POSSIBLE.

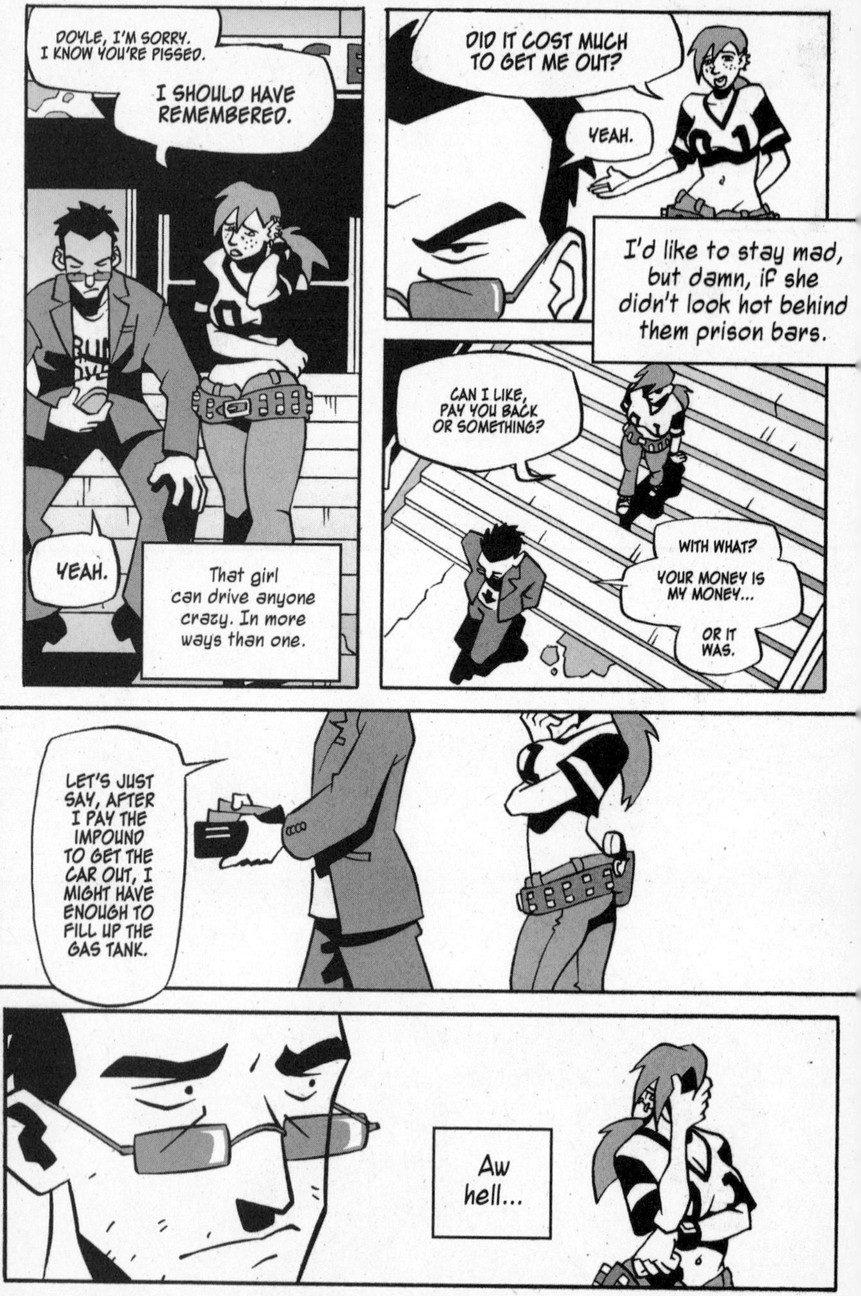
DOYLE, I'M SORRY. I KNOW YOU'RE PISSED.
I SHOULD HAVE REMEMBERED.
YEAH.
That girl can drive anyone crazy. In more ways than one.
DID IT COST MUCH TO GET ME OUT?
YEAH.
I'd like to stay mad, but damn, if she didn't look hot behind them prison bars.
CAN I LIKE, PAY YOU BACK OR SOMETHING?
WITH WHAT?
YOUR MONEY IS MY MONEY...
OR IT WAS.
LET'S JUST SAY, AFTER I PAY THE IMPOUND TO GET THE CAR OUT, I MIGHT HAVE ENOUGH TO FILL UP THE GAS TANK.
Aw hell...

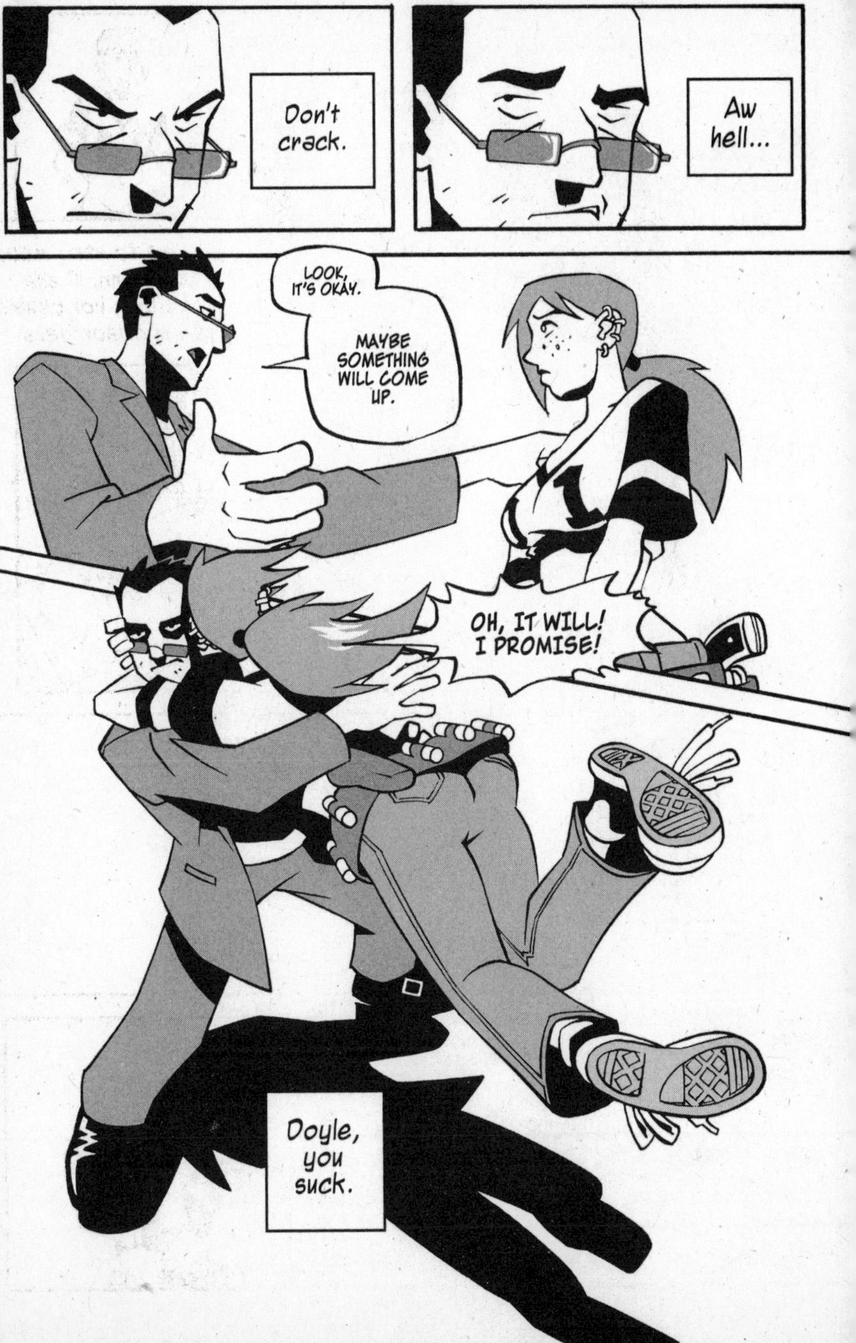
Don't crack.
Aw hell...
LOOK, IT'S OKAY.
MAYBE SOMETHING WILL COME UP.
OH, IT WILL! I PROMISE!
Doyle, you suck.

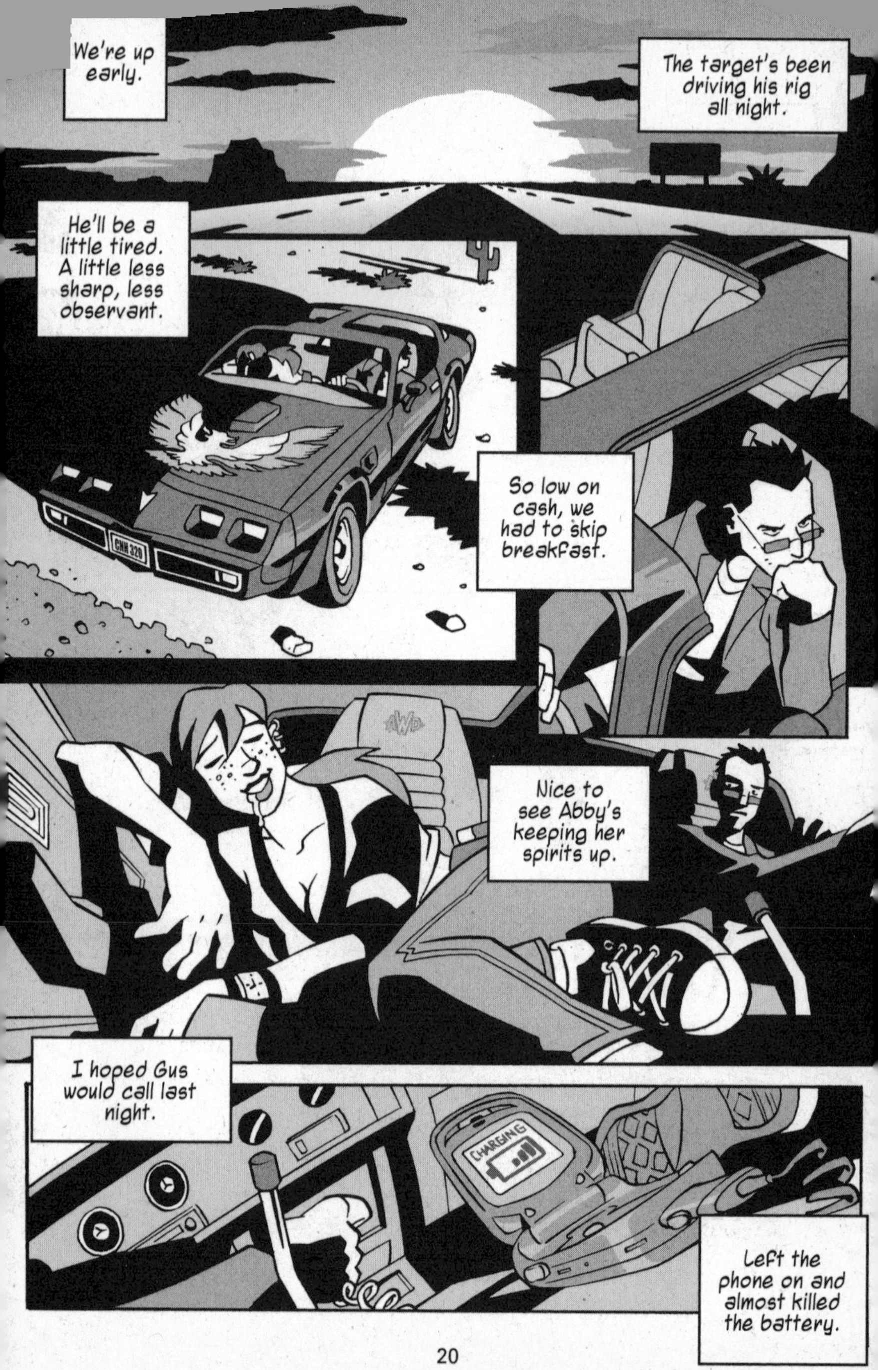
We're up early.
The target's been driving his rig all night.
He'll be a little tired. A little less sharp, less observant.
CNH 320
So low on cash, we had to skip breakfast.
Nice to see Abby's keeping her spirits up.
I hoped Gus would call last night.
CHARGING
Left the phone on and almost killed the battery.

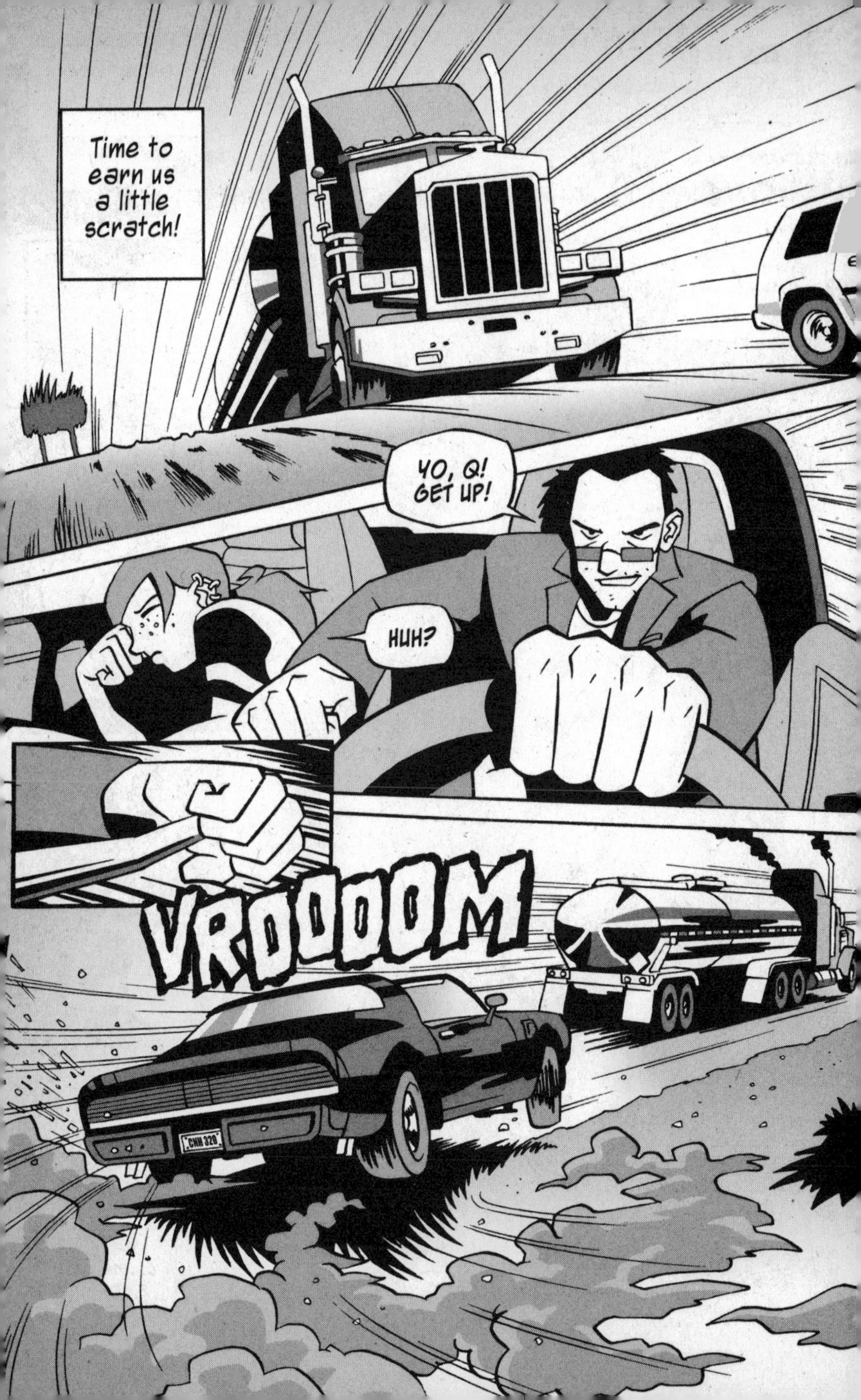
Time to earn us a little scratch!
YO, Q! GET UP!
HUH?
VROOOOM

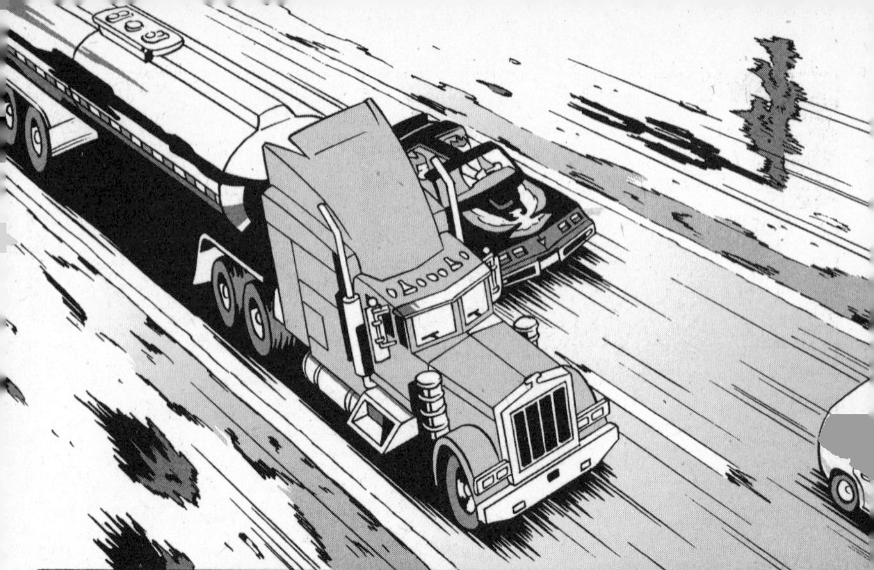

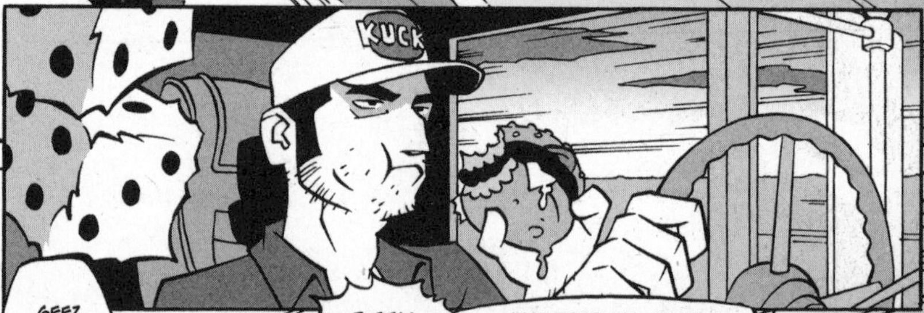
KUCK

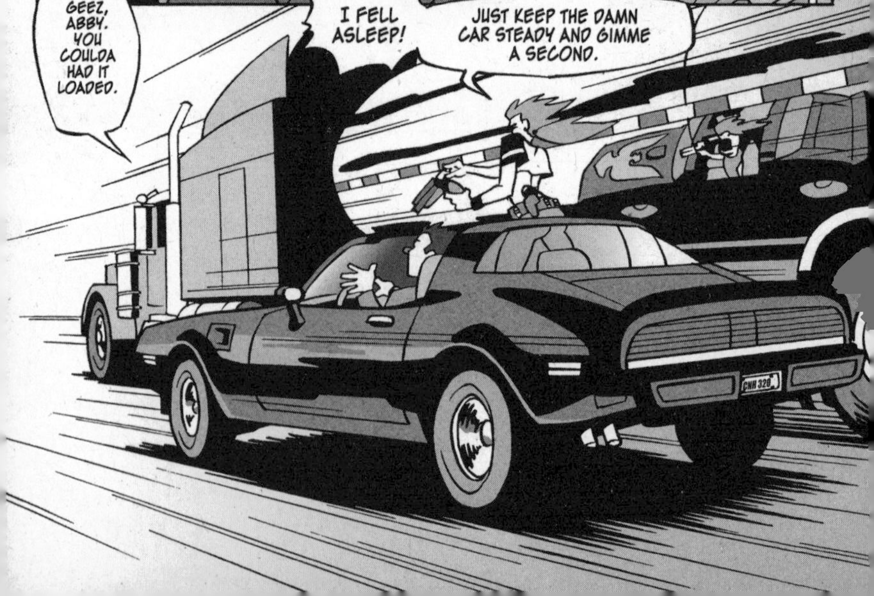
GEEZ, ABBY. YOU COULDA HAD IT LOADED.
I FELL ASLEEP!
JUST KEEP THE DAMN CAR STEADY AND GIMME A SECOND.
CNH 320

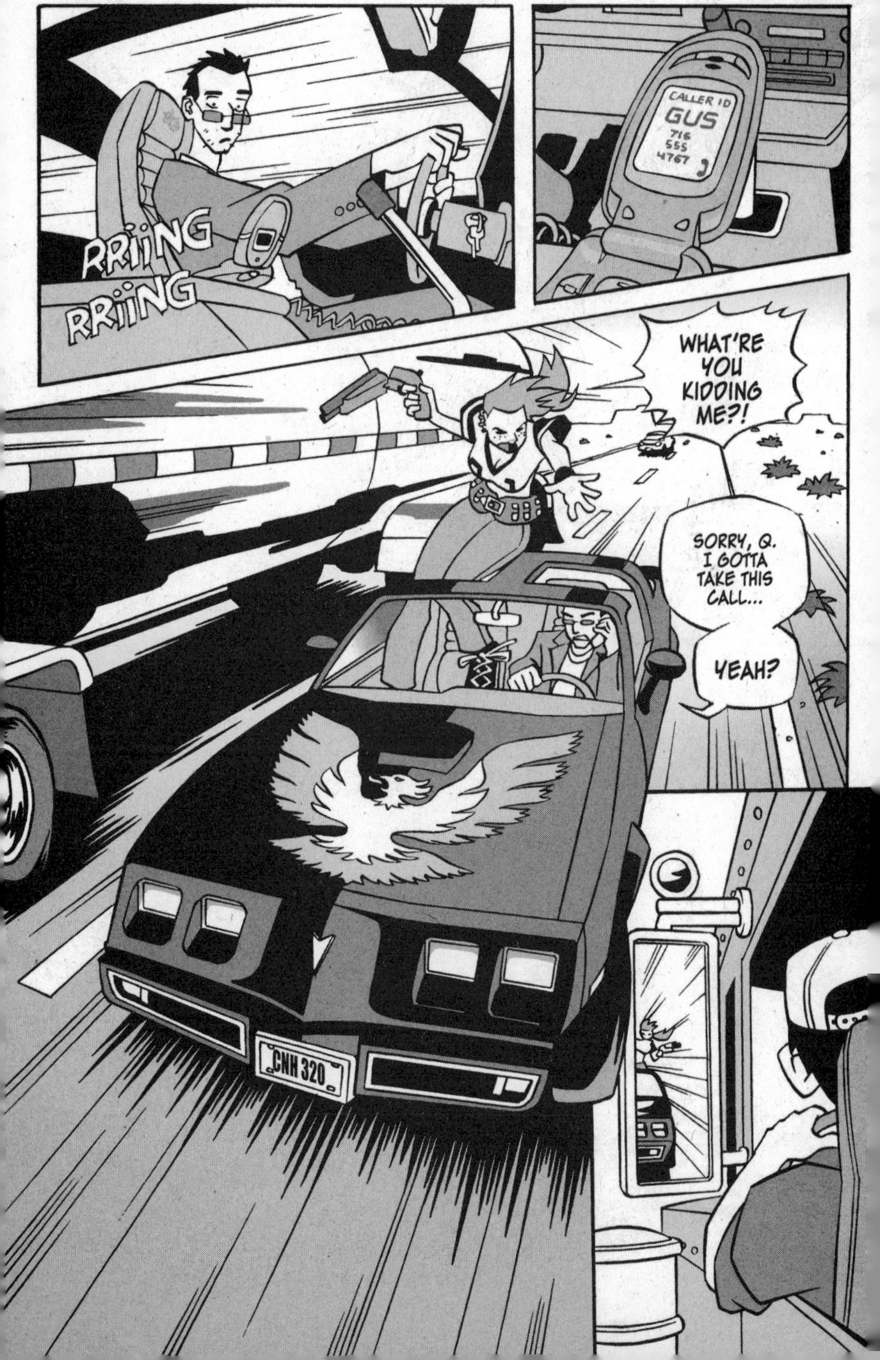
RRIING
RRIING
CALLER ID
GUS
716
555
4767
WHAT'RE YOU KIDDING ME?!
SORRY, Q. I GOTTA TAKE THIS CALL...
YEAH?
CNH 320

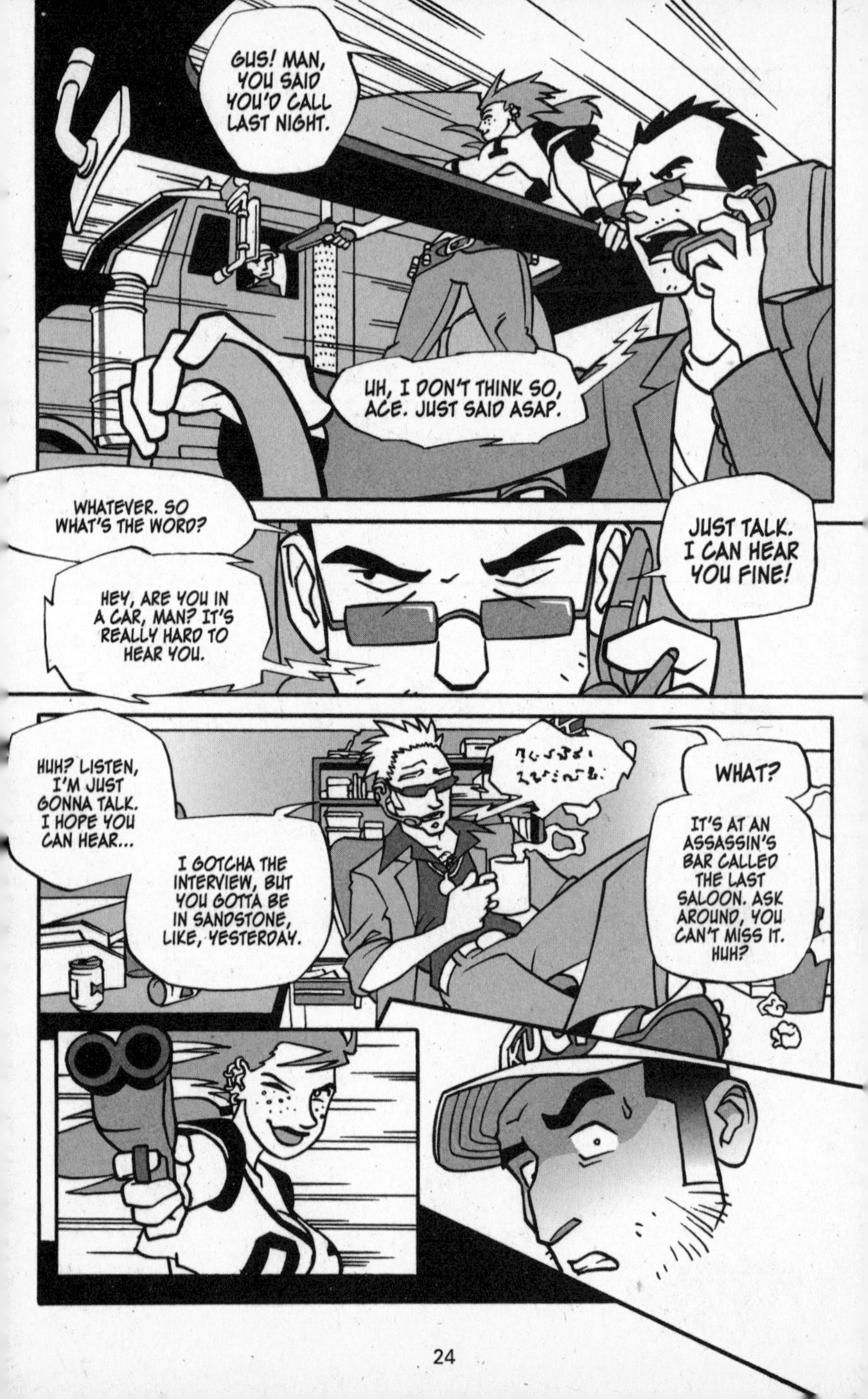
GUS! MAN, YOU SAID YOU'D CALL LAST NIGHT.
UH, I DON'T THINK SO, ACE. JUST SAID ASAP.
WHATEVER. SO WHAT'S THE WORD?
HEY, ARE YOU IN A CAR, MAN? IT'S REALLY HARD TO HEAR YOU.
JUST TALK. I CAN HEAR YOU FINE!
HUH? LISTEN, I'M JUST GONNA TALK. I HOPE YOU CAN HEAR...
I GOTCHA THE INTERVIEW, BUT YOU GOTTA BE IN SANDSTONE, LIKE, YESTERDAY.
WHAT?
IT'S AT AN ASSASSIN'S BAR CALLED THE LAST SALOON. ASK AROUND, YOU CAN'T MISS IT. HUH?

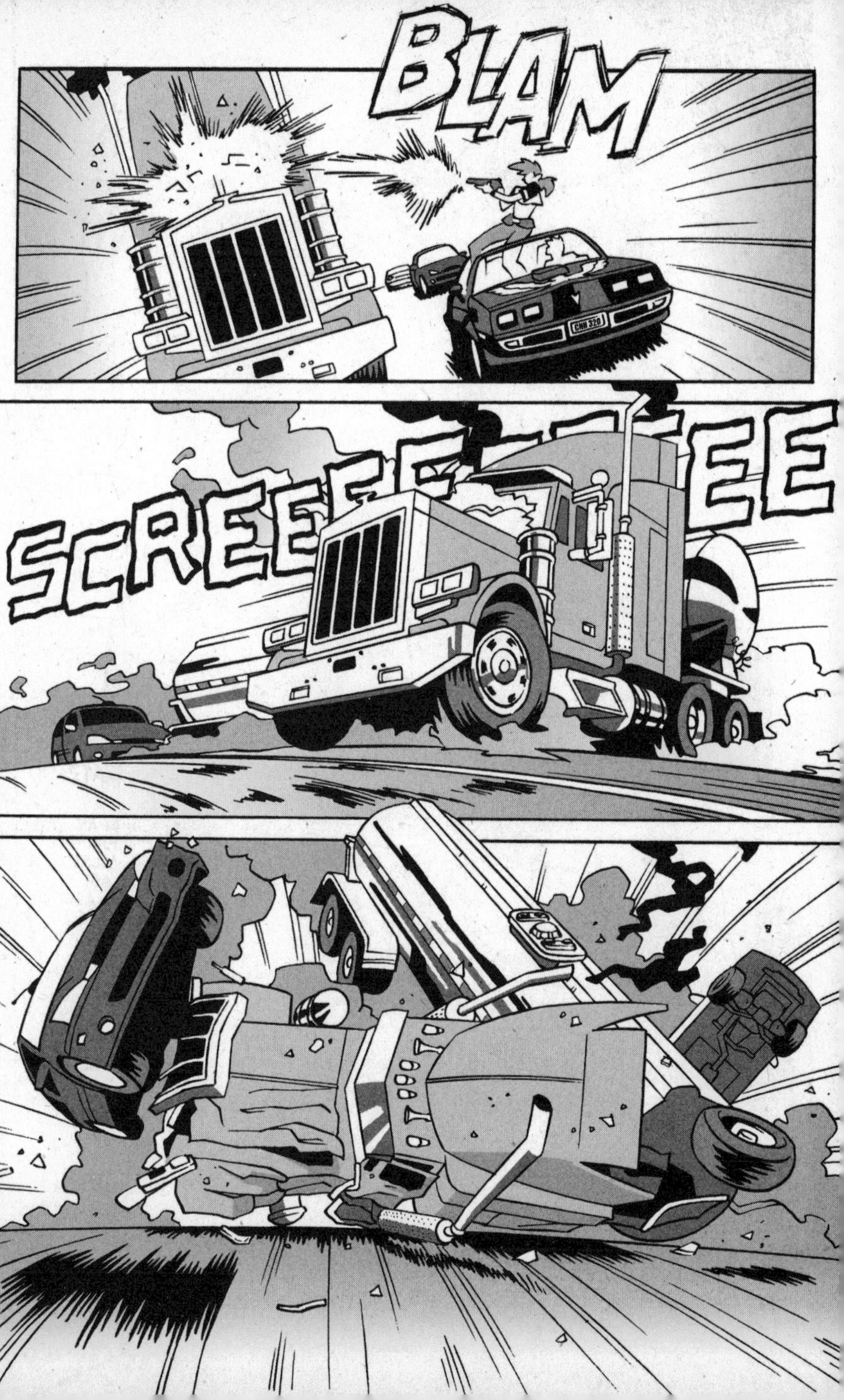
BLAM
SCREE
EE

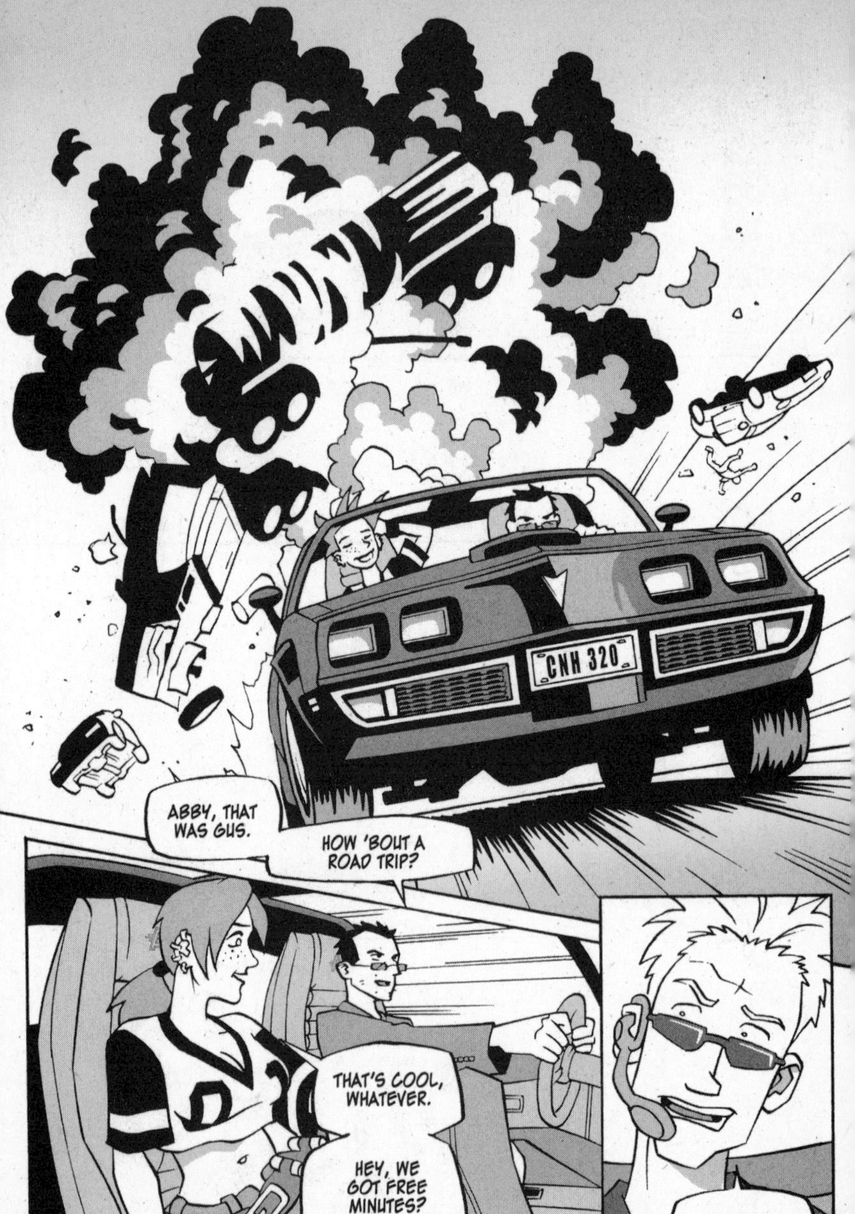
CNH 320
ABBY, THAT WAS GUS.
HOW 'BOUT A ROAD TRIP?
THAT'S COOL, WHATEVER.
HEY, WE GOT FREE MINUTES? LEMME USE THE PHONE?
HELLO?

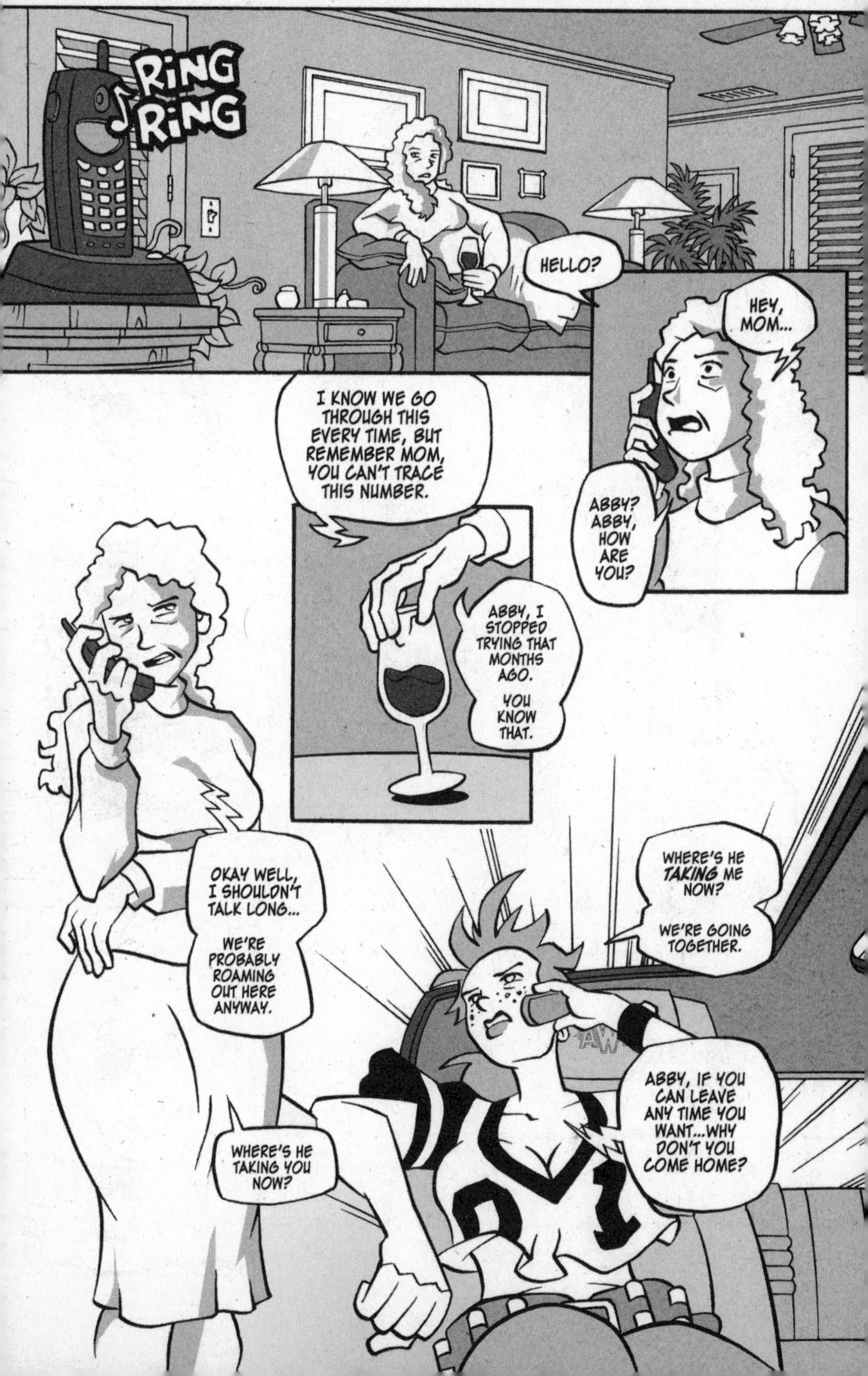
RING RING
HELLO?
HEY, MOM...
ABBY? ABBY, HOW ARE YOU?
I KNOW WE GO THROUGH THIS EVERY TIME, BUT REMEMBER MOM, YOU CAN'T TRACE THIS NUMBER.
ABBY, I STOPPED TRYING THAT MONTHS AGO.
YOU KNOW THAT.
OKAY WELL, I SHOULDN'T TALK LONG...
WE'RE PROBABLY ROAMING OUT HERE ANYWAY.
WHERE'S HE TAKING YOU NOW?
WHERE'S HE *TAKING* ME NOW?
WE'RE GOING TOGETHER.
ABBY, IF YOU CAN LEAVE ANY TIME YOU WANT...WHY DON'T YOU COME HOME?

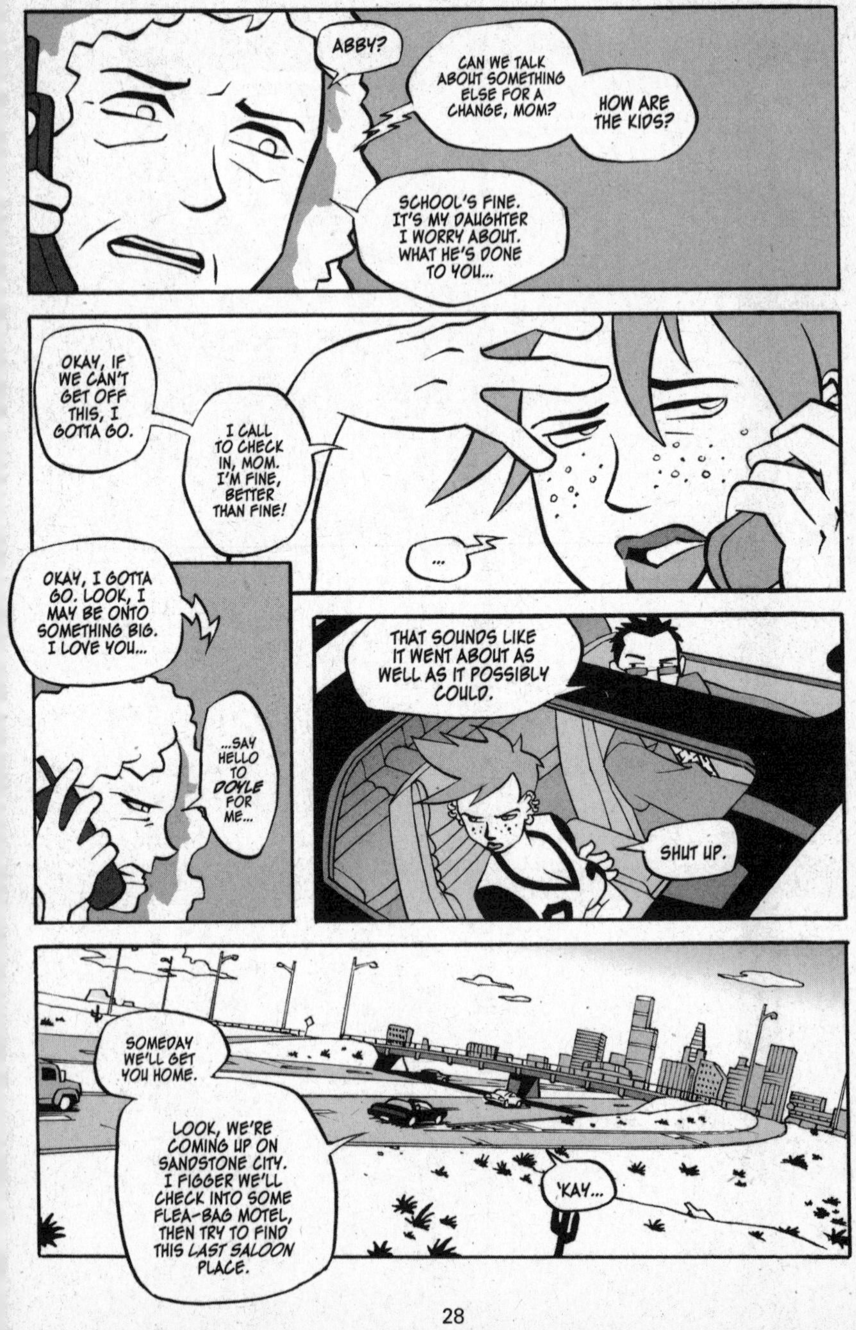
ABBY?
CAN WE TALK ABOUT SOMETHING ELSE FOR A CHANGE, MOM?
HOW ARE THE KIDS?
SCHOOL'S FINE. IT'S MY DAUGHTER I WORRY ABOUT. WHAT HE'S DONE TO YOU...
OKAY, IF WE CAN'T GET OFF THIS, I GOTTA GO.
I CALL TO CHECK IN, MOM. I'M FINE, BETTER THAN FINE!
...
OKAY, I GOTTA GO. LOOK, I MAY BE ONTO SOMETHING BIG. I LOVE YOU...
...SAY HELLO TO *DOYLE* FOR ME...
THAT SOUNDS LIKE IT WENT ABOUT AS WELL AS IT POSSIBLY COULD.
SHUT UP.
SOMEDAY WE'LL GET YOU HOME.
LOOK, WE'RE COMING UP ON SANDSTONE CITY. I FIGGER WE'LL CHECK INTO SOME FLEA-BAG MOTEL, THEN TRY TO FIND THIS *LAST SALOON* PLACE.
'KAY...

2

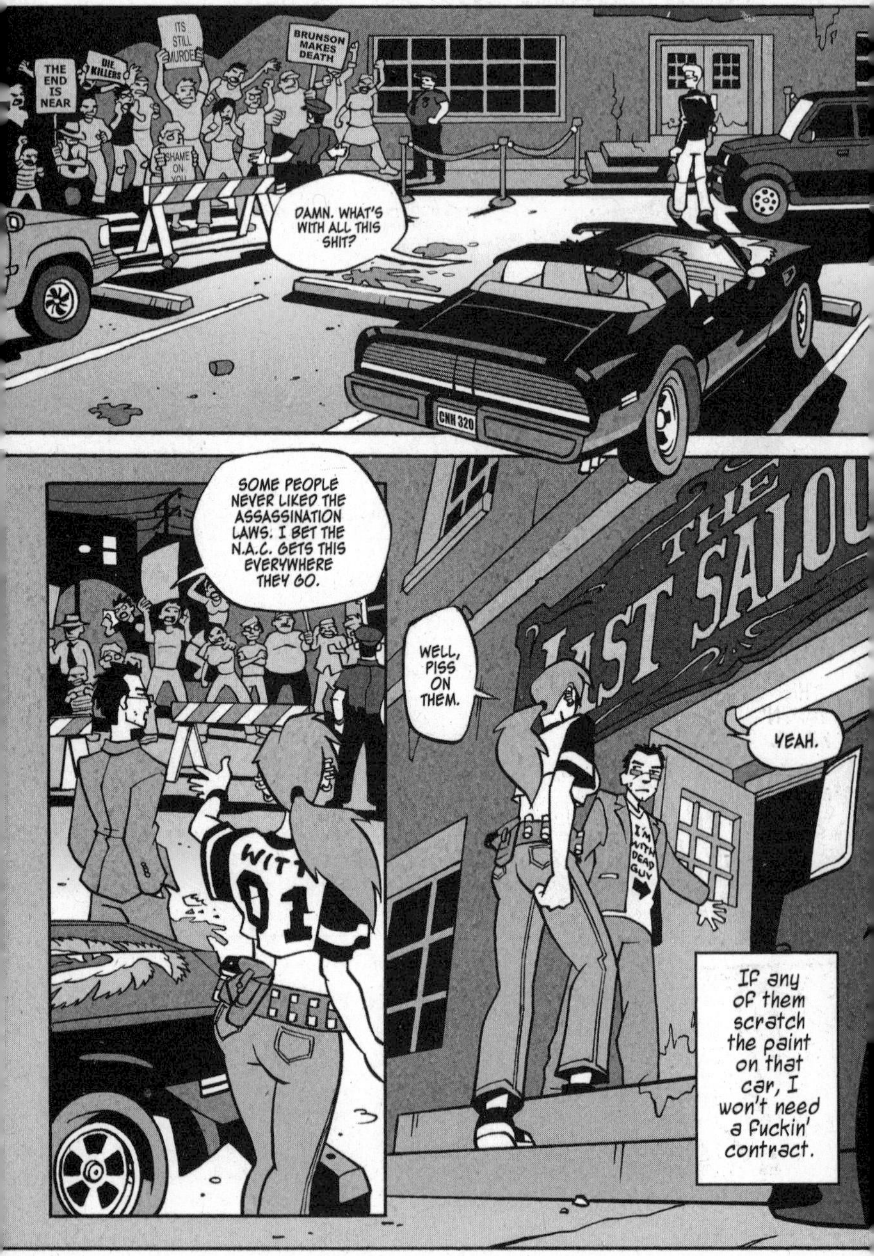
THE END IS NEAR
DIE KILLERS
ITS STILL MURDE
BRUNSON MAKES DEATH
SHAME ON
DAMN. WHAT'S WITH ALL THIS SHIT?
CNH 320
SOME PEOPLE NEVER LIKED THE ASSASSINATION LAWS. I BET THE N.A.C. GETS THIS EVERYWHERE THEY GO.
WELL, PISS ON THEM.
YEAH.
I'M WITH DEAD GUY
If any of them scratch the paint on that car, I won't need a fuckin' contract.

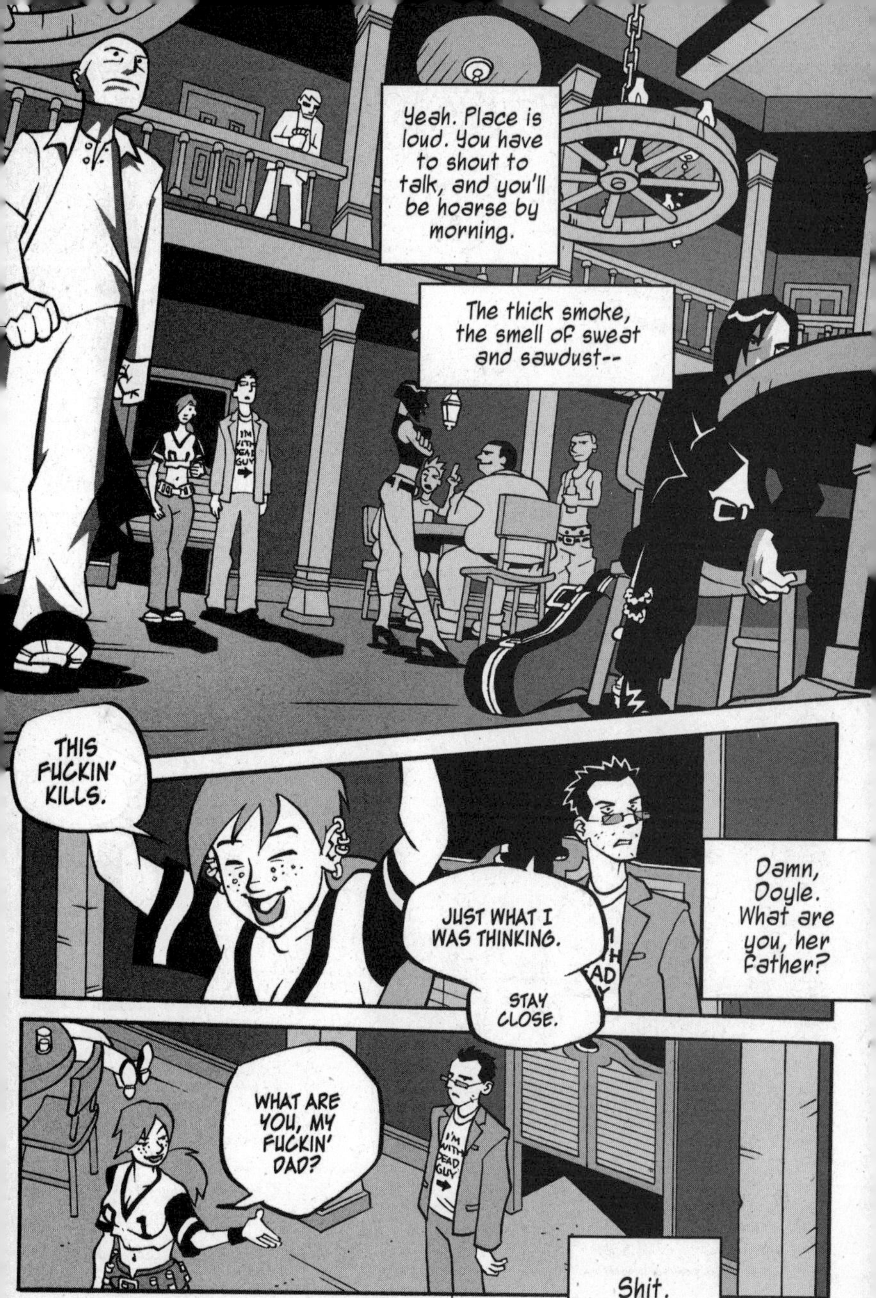
Yeah. Place is loud. You have to shout to talk, and you'll be hoarse by morning.
The thick smoke, the smell of sweat and sawdust--
I'M WITH DEAD GUY
THIS FUCKIN' KILLS.
JUST WHAT I WAS THINKING.
STAY CLOSE.
Damn, Doyle. What are you, her father?
WHAT ARE YOU, MY FUCKIN' DAD?
Shit.

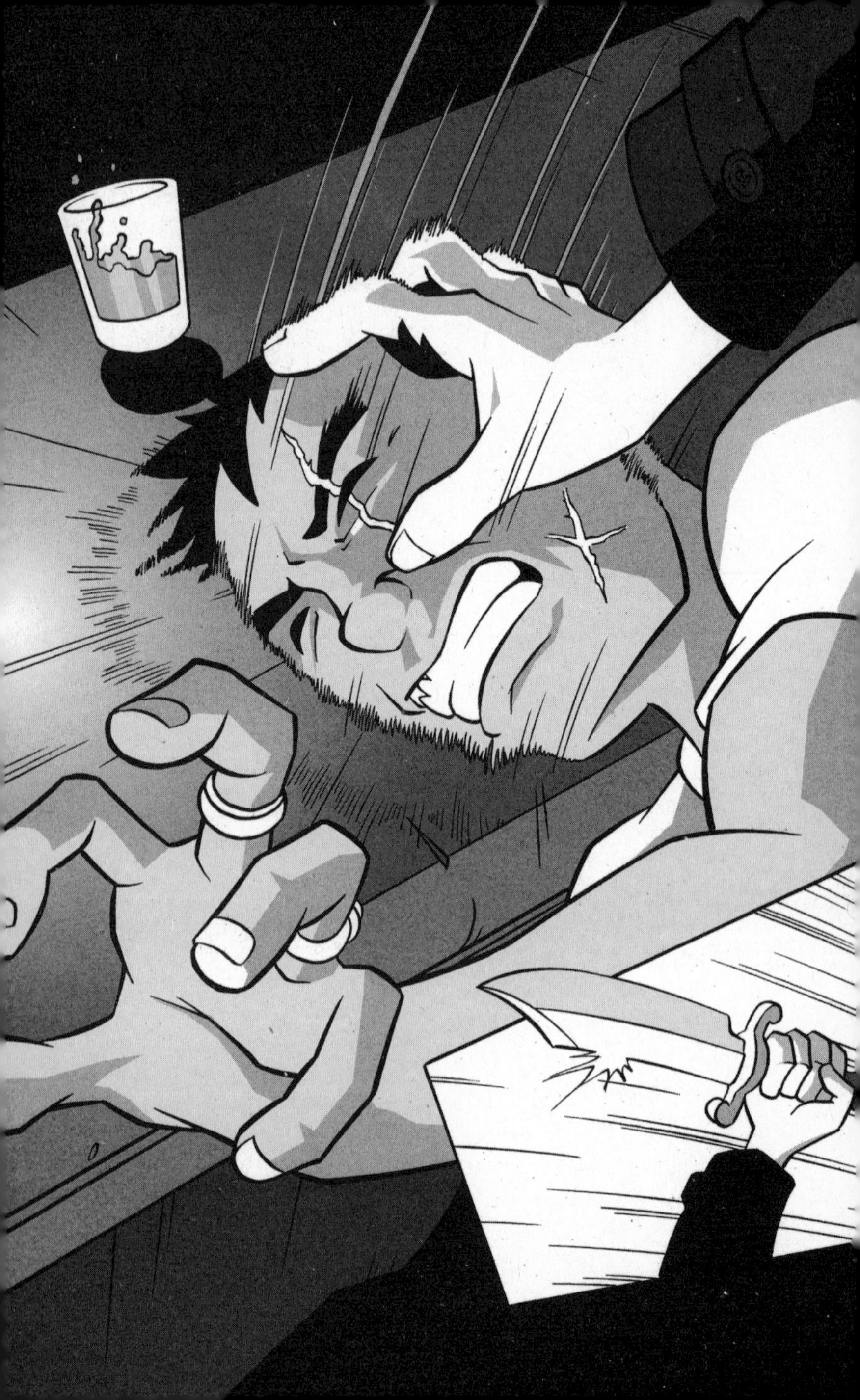

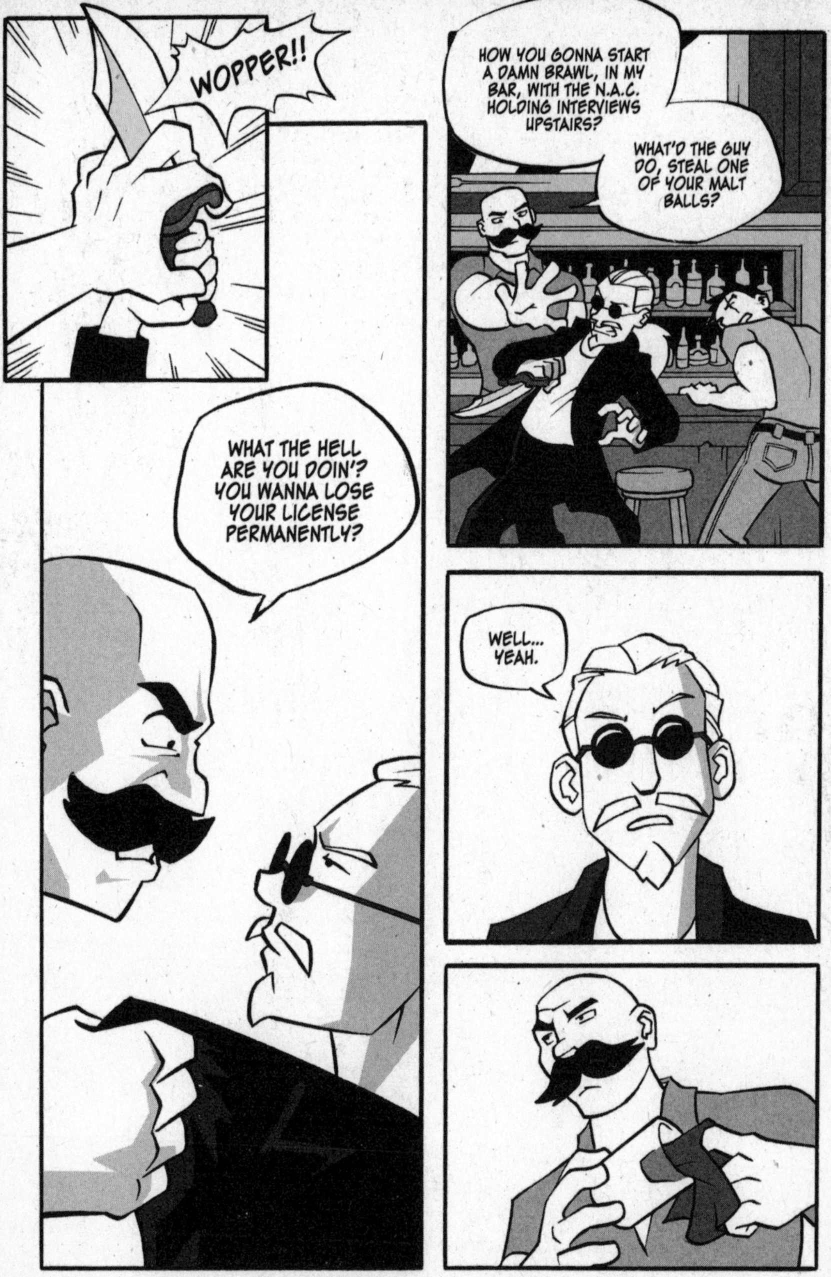
WOPPER!!
WHAT THE HELL ARE YOU DOIN'? YOU WANNA LOSE YOUR LICENSE PERMANENTLY?
HOW YOU GONNA START A DAMN BRAWL, IN MY BAR, WITH THE N.A.C. HOLDING INTERVIEWS UPSTAIRS?
WHAT'D THE GUY DO, STEAL ONE OF YOUR MALT BALLS?
WELL... YEAH.

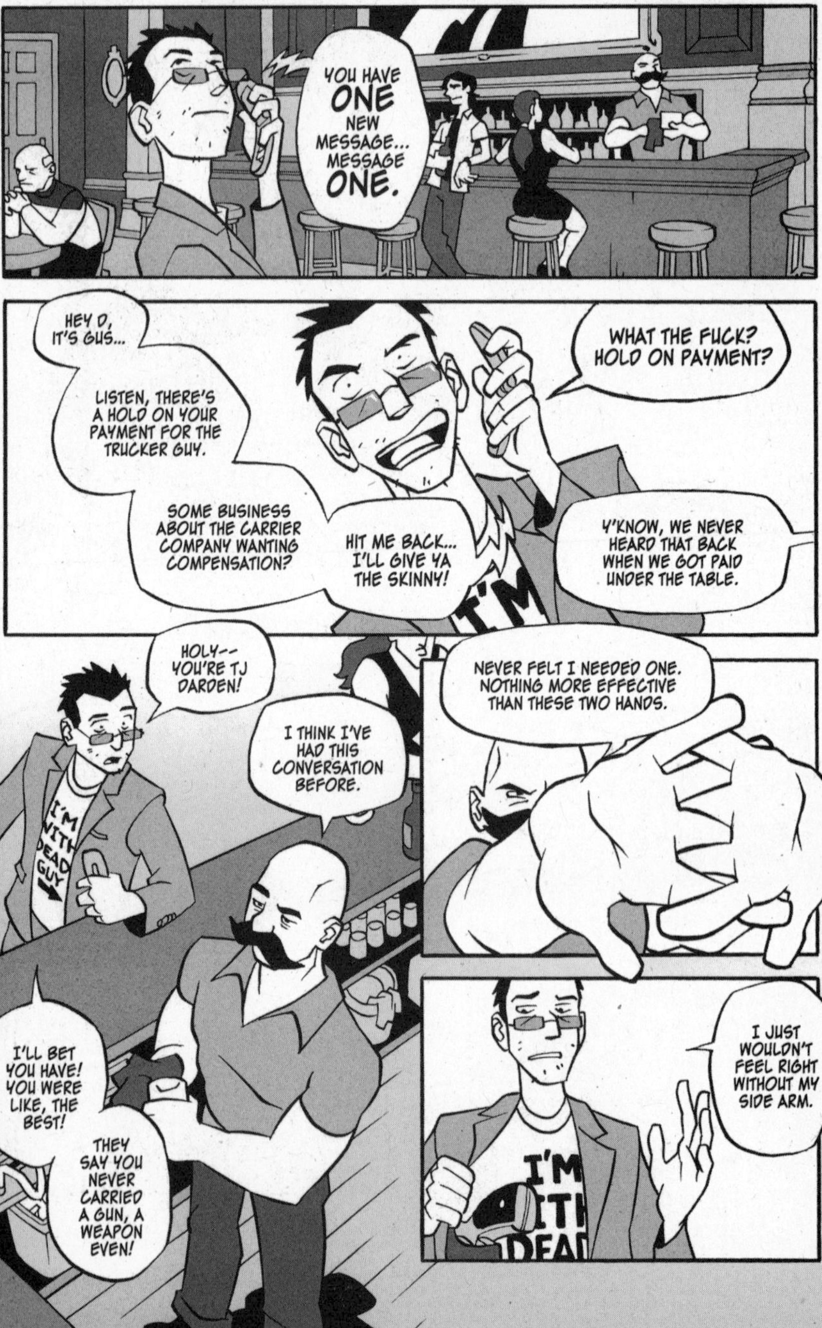
YOU HAVE ONE NEW MESSAGE... MESSAGE ONE.
HEY D, IT'S GUS...
LISTEN, THERE'S A HOLD ON YOUR PAYMENT FOR THE TRUCKER GUY.
SOME BUSINESS ABOUT THE CARRIER COMPANY WANTING COMPENSATION?
HIT ME BACK... I'LL GIVE YA THE SKINNY!
WHAT THE FUCK? HOLD ON PAYMENT?
Y'KNOW, WE NEVER HEARD THAT BACK WHEN WE GOT PAID UNDER THE TABLE.
HOLY-- YOU'RE TJ DARDEN!
I'M WITH DEAD GUY
I THINK I'VE HAD THIS CONVERSATION BEFORE.
I'LL BET YOU HAVE! YOU WERE LIKE, THE BEST!
THEY SAY YOU NEVER CARRIED A GUN, A WEAPON EVEN!
NEVER FELT I NEEDED ONE. NOTHING MORE EFFECTIVE THAN THESE TWO HANDS.
I JUST WOULDN'T FEEL RIGHT WITHOUT MY SIDE ARM.

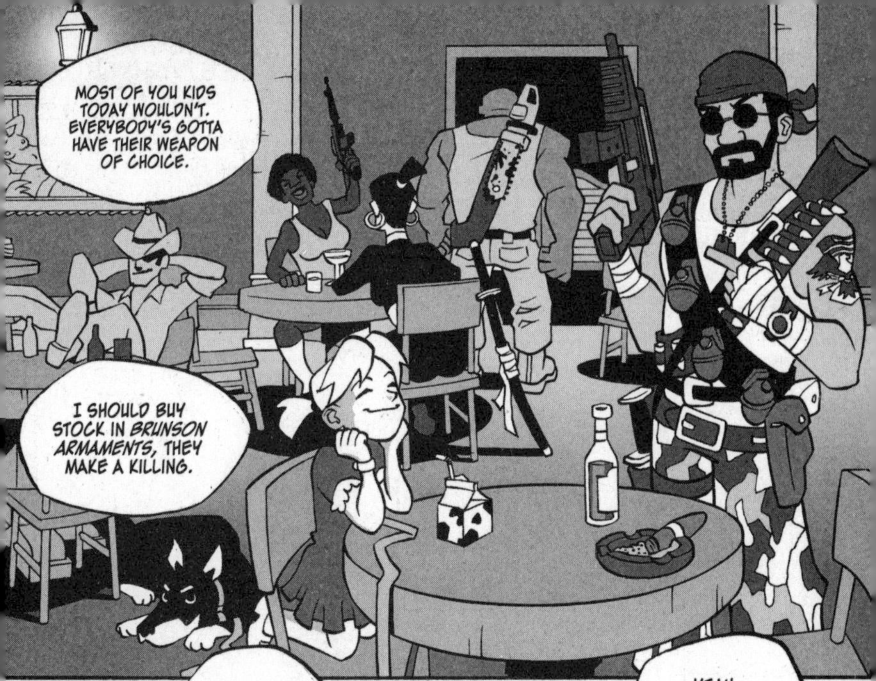
MOST OF YOU KIDS TODAY WOULDN'T. EVERYBODY'S GOTTA HAVE THEIR WEAPON OF CHOICE.
I SHOULD BUY STOCK IN *BRUNSON ARMAMENTS*, THEY MAKE A KILLING.
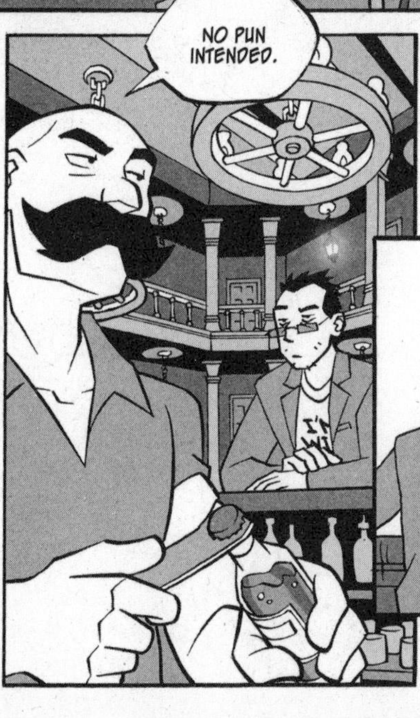
NO PUN INTENDED.
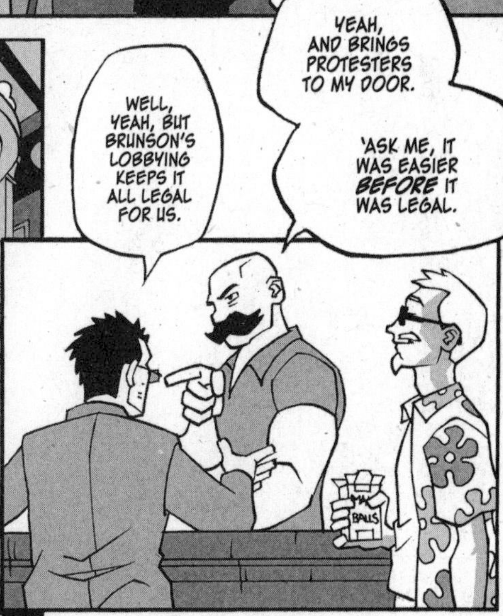
WELL, YEAH, BUT BRUNSON'S LOBBYING KEEPS IT ALL LEGAL FOR US.
YEAH, AND BRINGS PROTESTERS TO MY DOOR.
'ASK ME, IT WAS EASIER ***BEFORE*** IT WAS LEGAL.

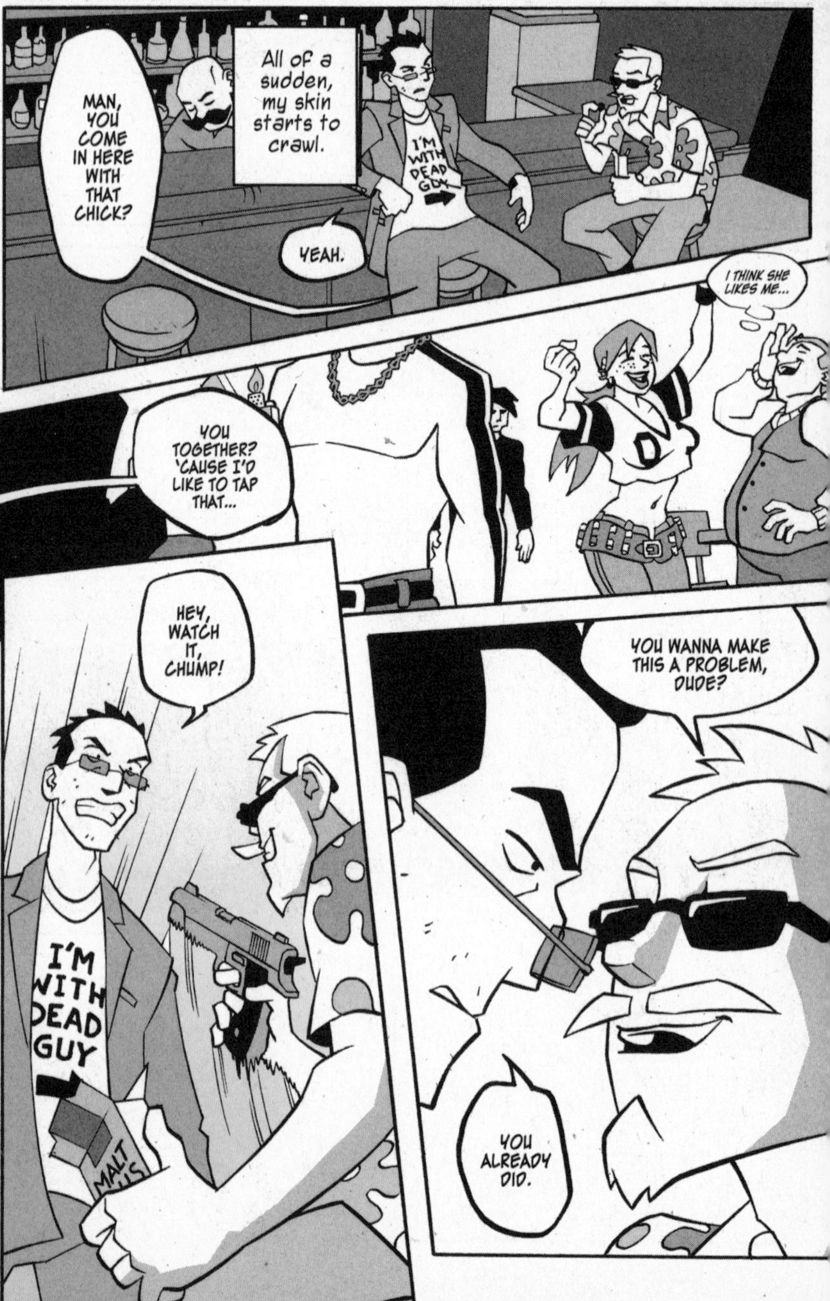
MAN, YOU COME IN HERE WITH THAT CHICK?
All of a sudden, my skin starts to crawl.
YEAH.
YOU TOGETHER? 'CAUSE I'D LIKE TO TAP THAT...
I THINK SHE LIKES ME...
HEY, WATCH IT, CHUMP!
I'M WITH DEAD GUY
YOU WANNA MAKE THIS A PROBLEM, DUDE?
YOU ALREADY DID.

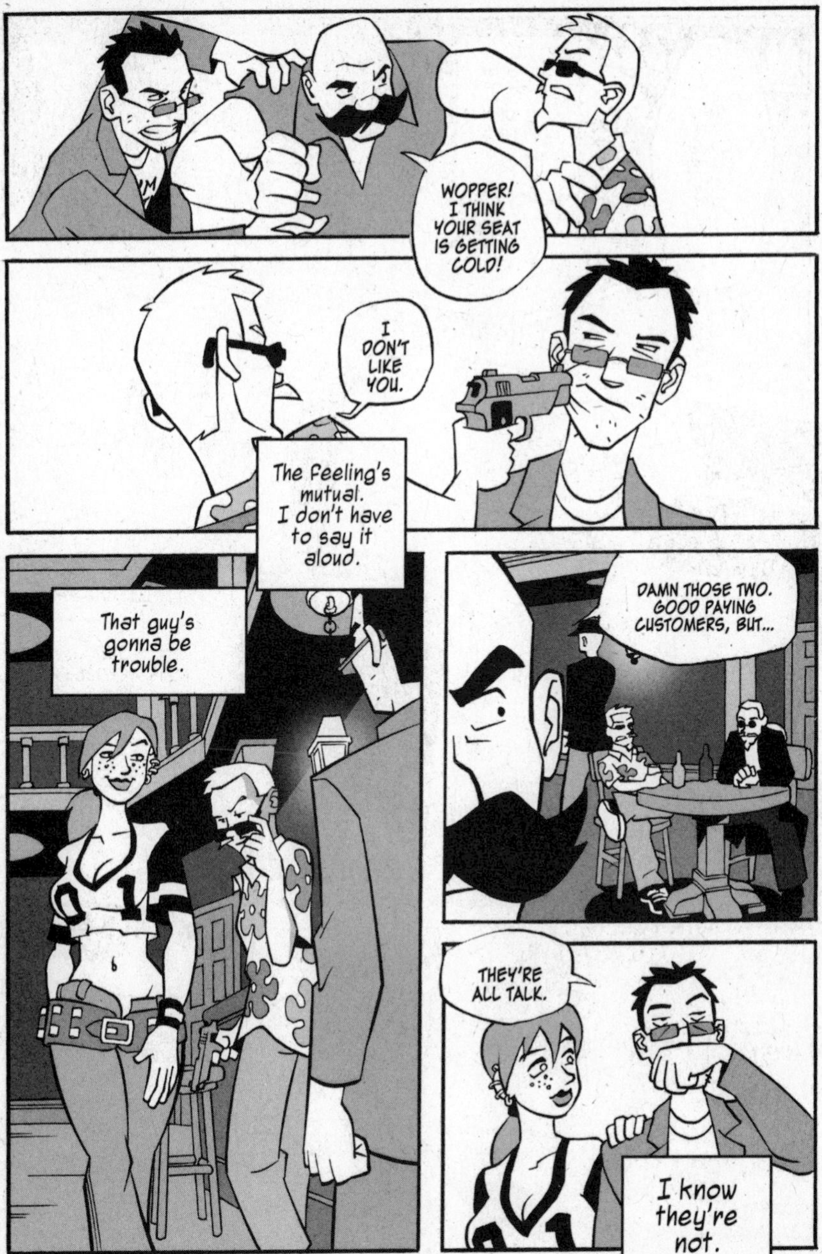
WOPPER! I THINK YOUR SEAT IS GETTING COLD!
I DON'T LIKE YOU.
The feeling's mutual. I don't have to say it aloud.
That guy's gonna be trouble.
DAMN THOSE TWO. GOOD PAYING CUSTOMERS, BUT...
THEY'RE ALL TALK.
I know they're not.

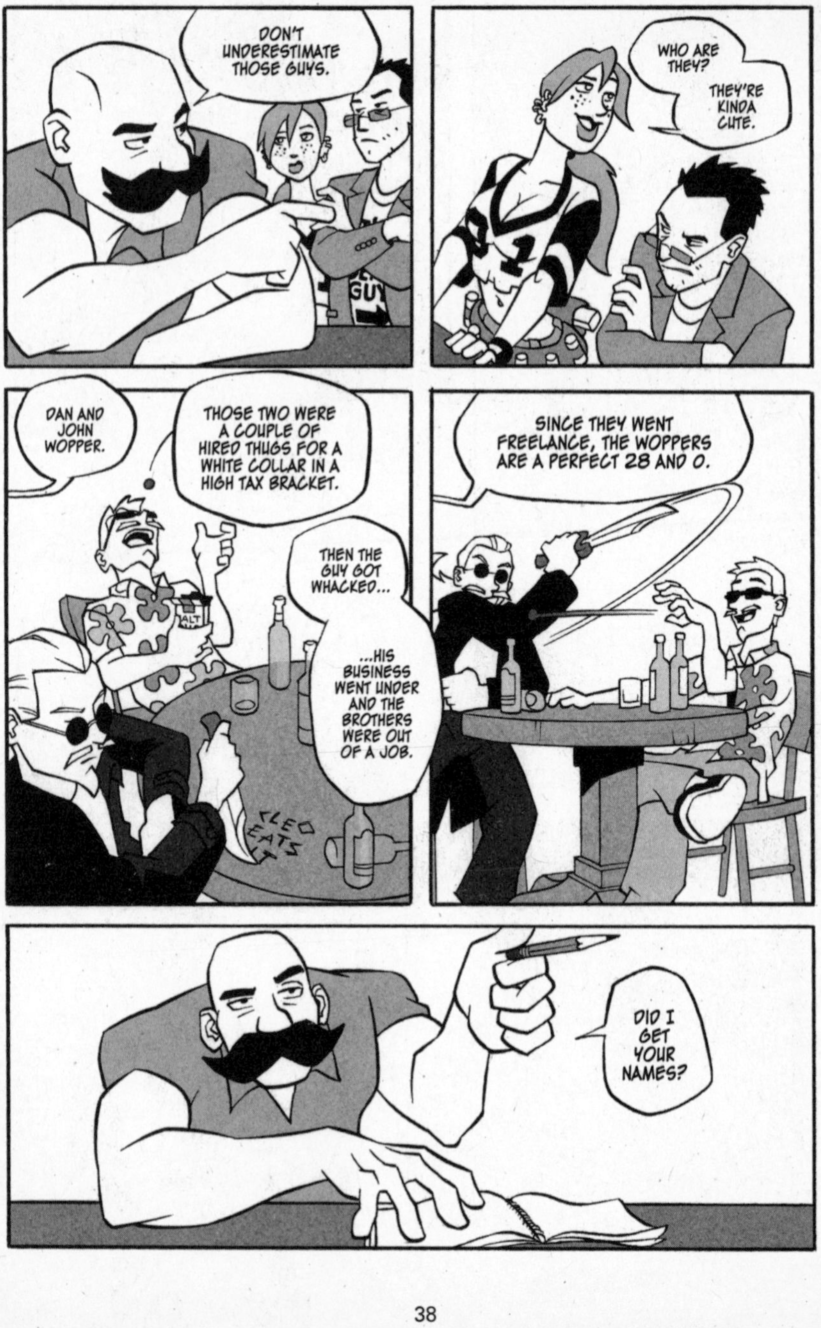
DON'T UNDERESTIMATE THOSE GUYS.
WHO ARE THEY?
THEY'RE KINDA CUTE.
DAN AND JOHN WOPPER.
THOSE TWO WERE A COUPLE OF HIRED THUGS FOR A WHITE COLLAR IN A HIGH TAX BRACKET.
THEN THE GUY GOT WHACKED...
...HIS BUSINESS WENT UNDER AND THE BROTHERS WERE OUT OF A JOB.
CLEO EATS
SINCE THEY WENT FREELANCE, THE WOPPERS ARE A PERFECT 28 AND 0.
DID I GET YOUR NAMES?

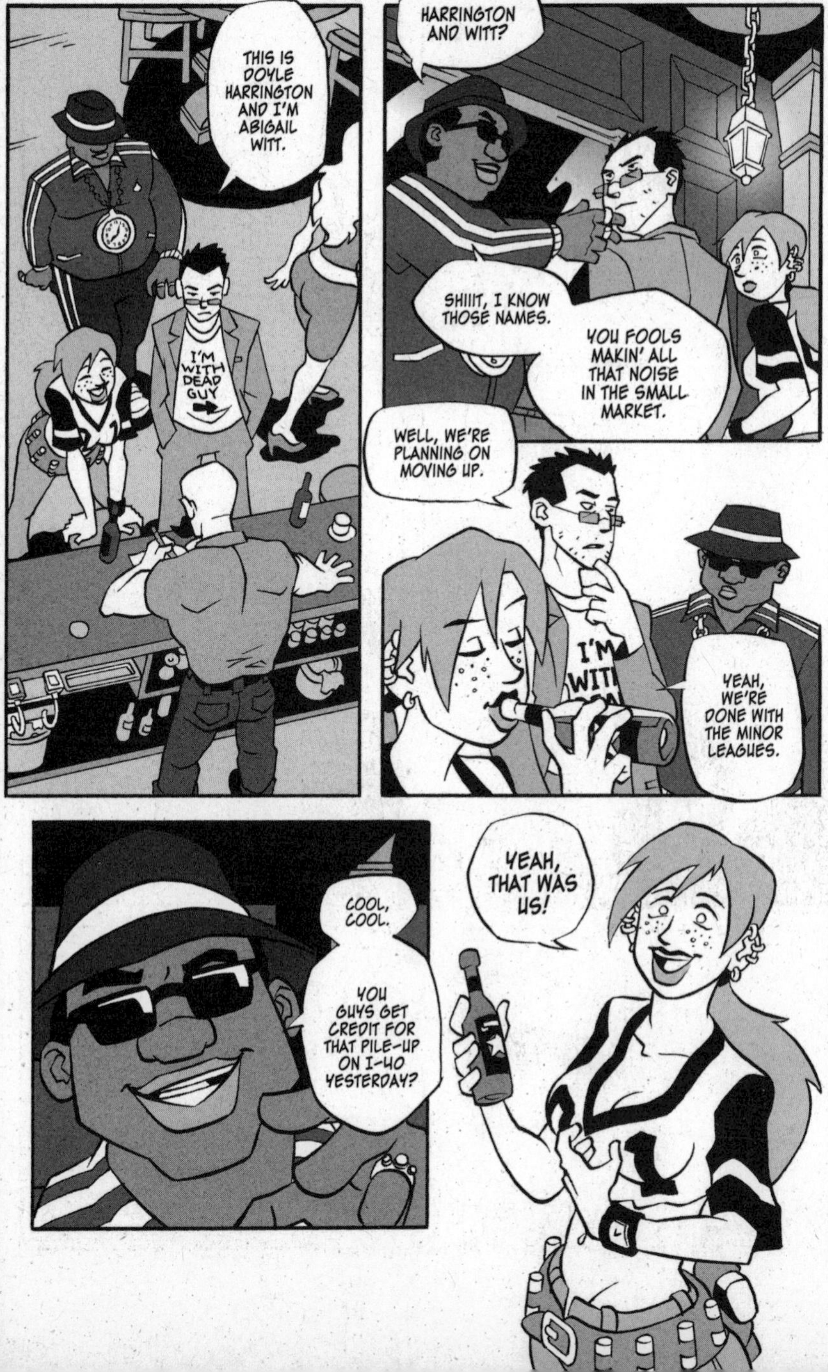
THIS IS DOYLE HARRINGTON AND I'M ABIGAIL WITT.
I'M WITH DEAD GUY
HARRINGTON AND WITT?
SHIIIT, I KNOW THOSE NAMES.
YOU FOOLS MAKIN' ALL THAT NOISE IN THE SMALL MARKET.
WELL, WE'RE PLANNING ON MOVING UP.
YEAH, WE'RE DONE WITH THE MINOR LEAGUES.
COOL, COOL.
YOU GUYS GET CREDIT FOR THAT PILE-UP ON I-40 YESTERDAY?
YEAH, THAT WAS US!

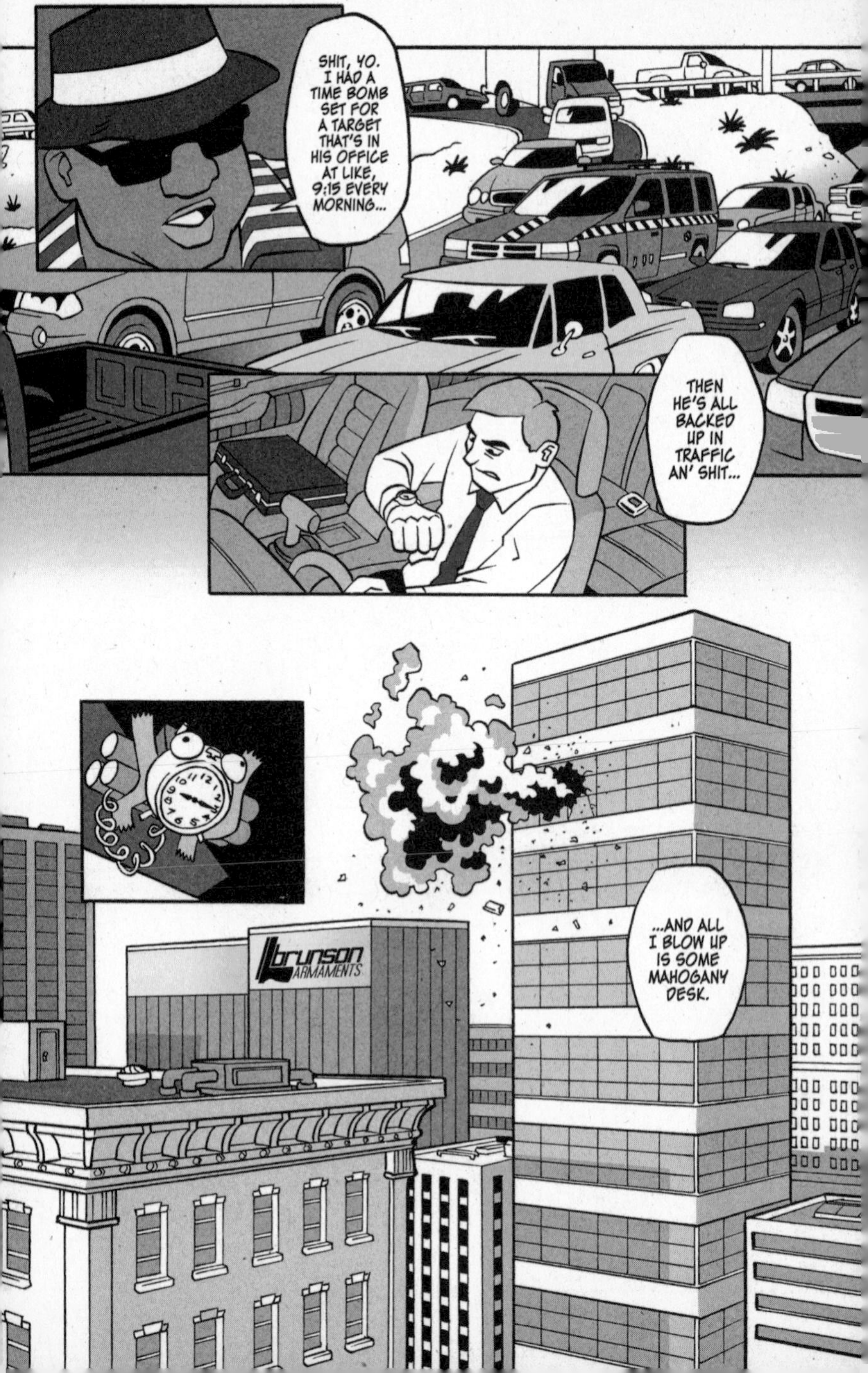
SHIT, YO. I HAD A TIME BOMB SET FOR A TARGET THAT'S IN HIS OFFICE AT LIKE, 9:15 EVERY MORNING...
THEN HE'S ALL BACKED UP IN TRAFFIC AN' SHIT...
brunson ARMAMENTS
...AND ALL I BLOW UP IS SOME MAHOGANY DESK.

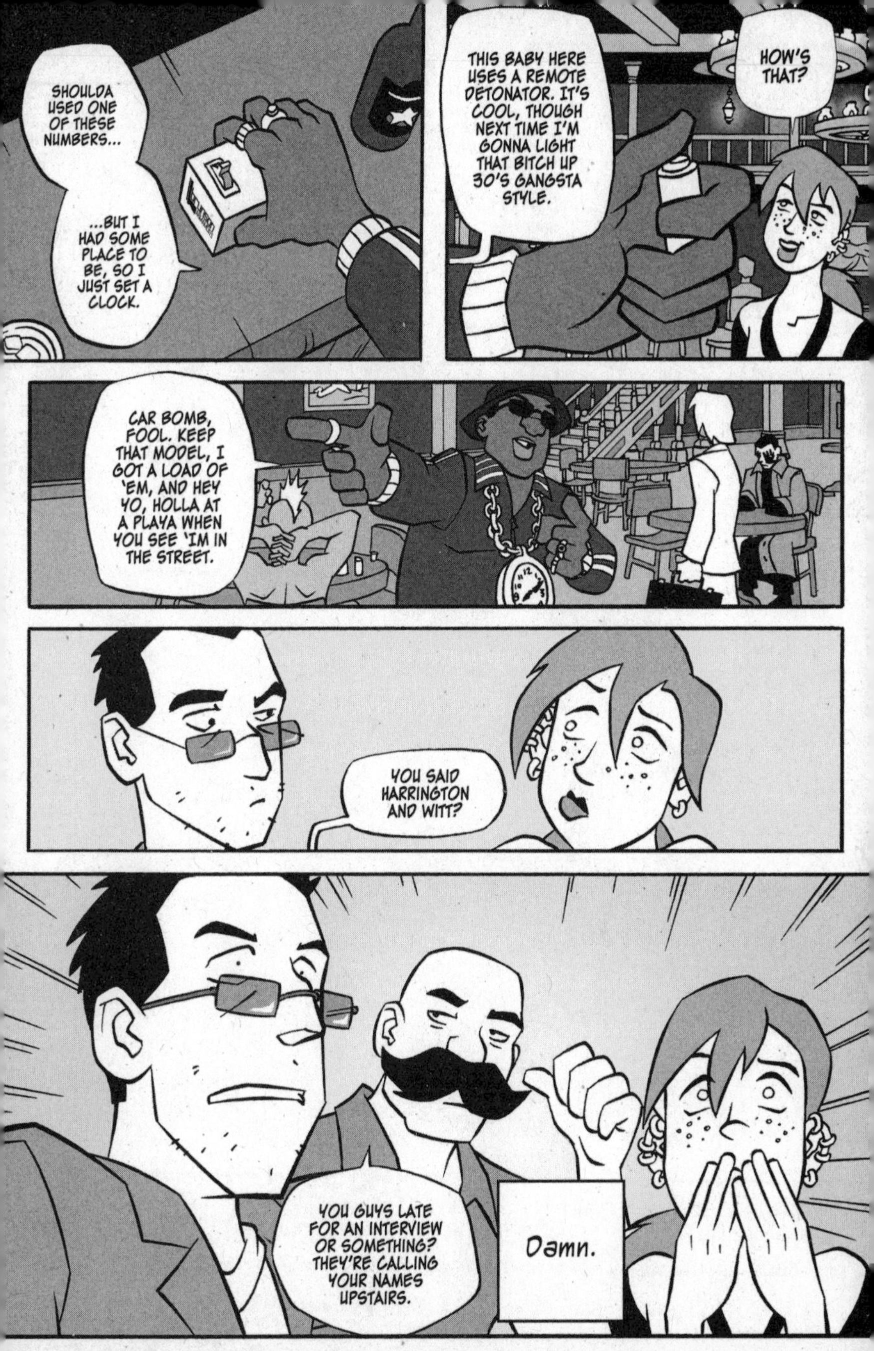
SHOULDA USED ONE OF THESE NUMBERS...
...BUT I HAD SOME PLACE TO BE, SO I JUST SET A CLOCK.
THIS BABY HERE USES A REMOTE DETONATOR. IT'S COOL, THOUGH NEXT TIME I'M GONNA LIGHT THAT BITCH UP 30'S GANGSTA STYLE.
HOW'S THAT?
CAR BOMB, FOOL. KEEP THAT MODEL, I GOT A LOAD OF 'EM, AND HEY YO, HOLLA AT A PLAYA WHEN YOU SEE 'IM IN THE STREET.
YOU SAID HARRINGTON AND WITT?
YOU GUYS LATE FOR AN INTERVIEW OR SOMETHING? THEY'RE CALLING YOUR NAMES UPSTAIRS.
Damn.

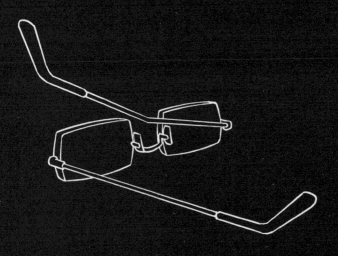

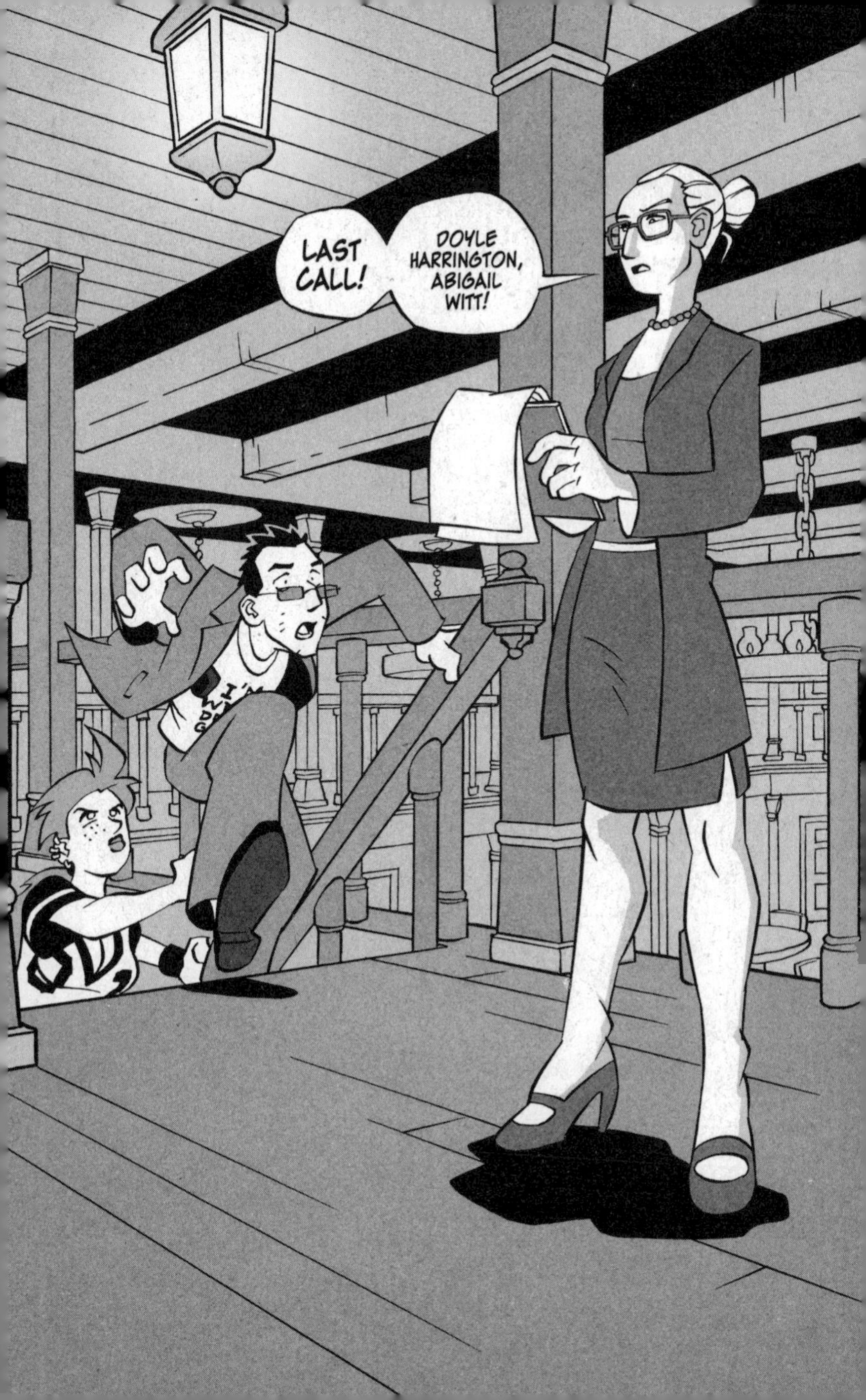
DOYLE HARRINGTON, ABIGAIL WITT!
LAST CALL!

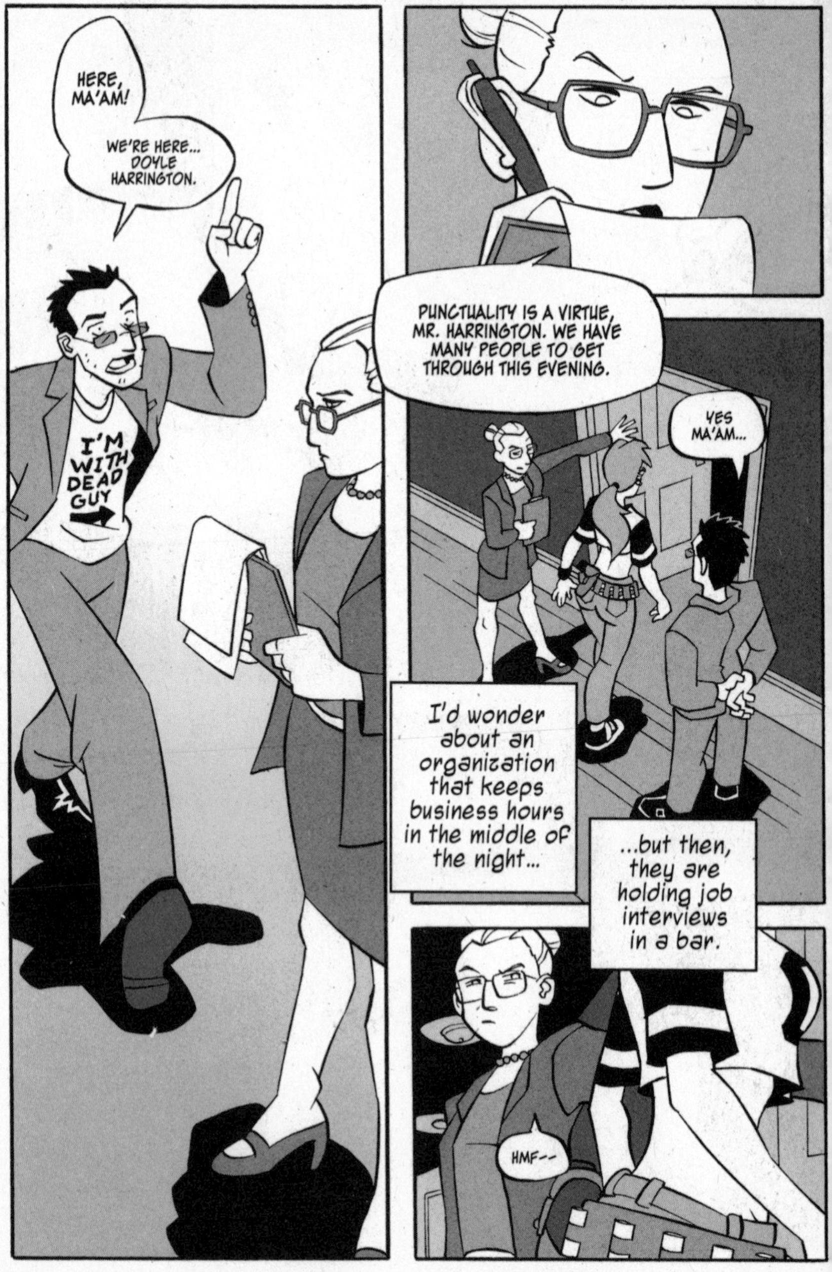
HERE, MA'AM!
WE'RE HERE... DOYLE HARRINGTON.
I'M WITH DEAD GUY
PUNCTUALITY IS A VIRTUE, MR. HARRINGTON. WE HAVE MANY PEOPLE TO GET THROUGH THIS EVENING.
YES MA'AM...
I'd wonder about an organization that keeps business hours in the middle of the night...
...but then, they are holding job interviews in a bar.
HMF--

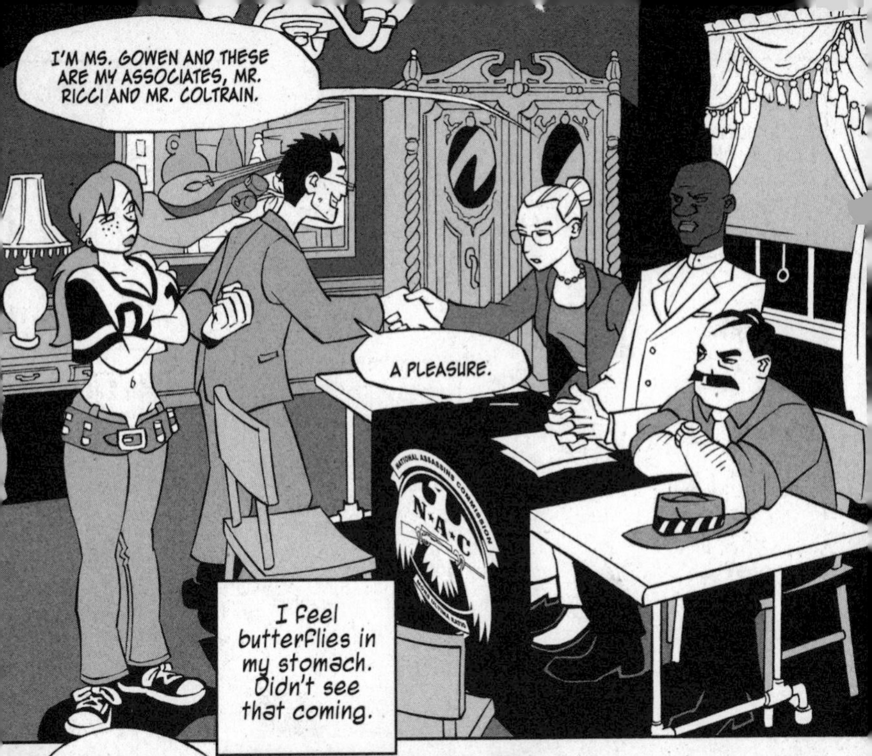
I'M MS. GOWEN AND THESE ARE MY ASSOCIATES, MR. RICCI AND MR. COLTRAIN.
A PLEASURE.
I feel butterflies in my stomach. Didn't see that coming.

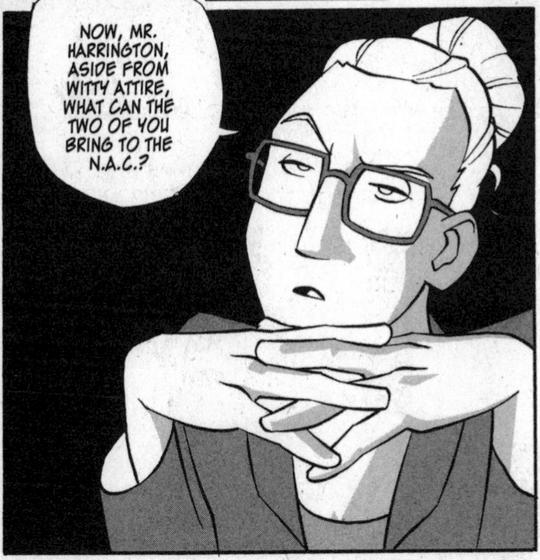
NOW, MR. HARRINGTON, ASIDE FROM WITTY ATTIRE, WHAT CAN THE TWO OF YOU BRING TO THE N.A.C.?

We talk for what seems like hours about the most trivial stuff. I have to search for answers and Abby's not saying a word.

I dunno why I thought this would be easy. Maybe because it's so easy to pull the trigger.

I have to admit my palms are sweaty, and I try not to let my voice shake.

I'm starting to think this game is a little bigger than we expected.

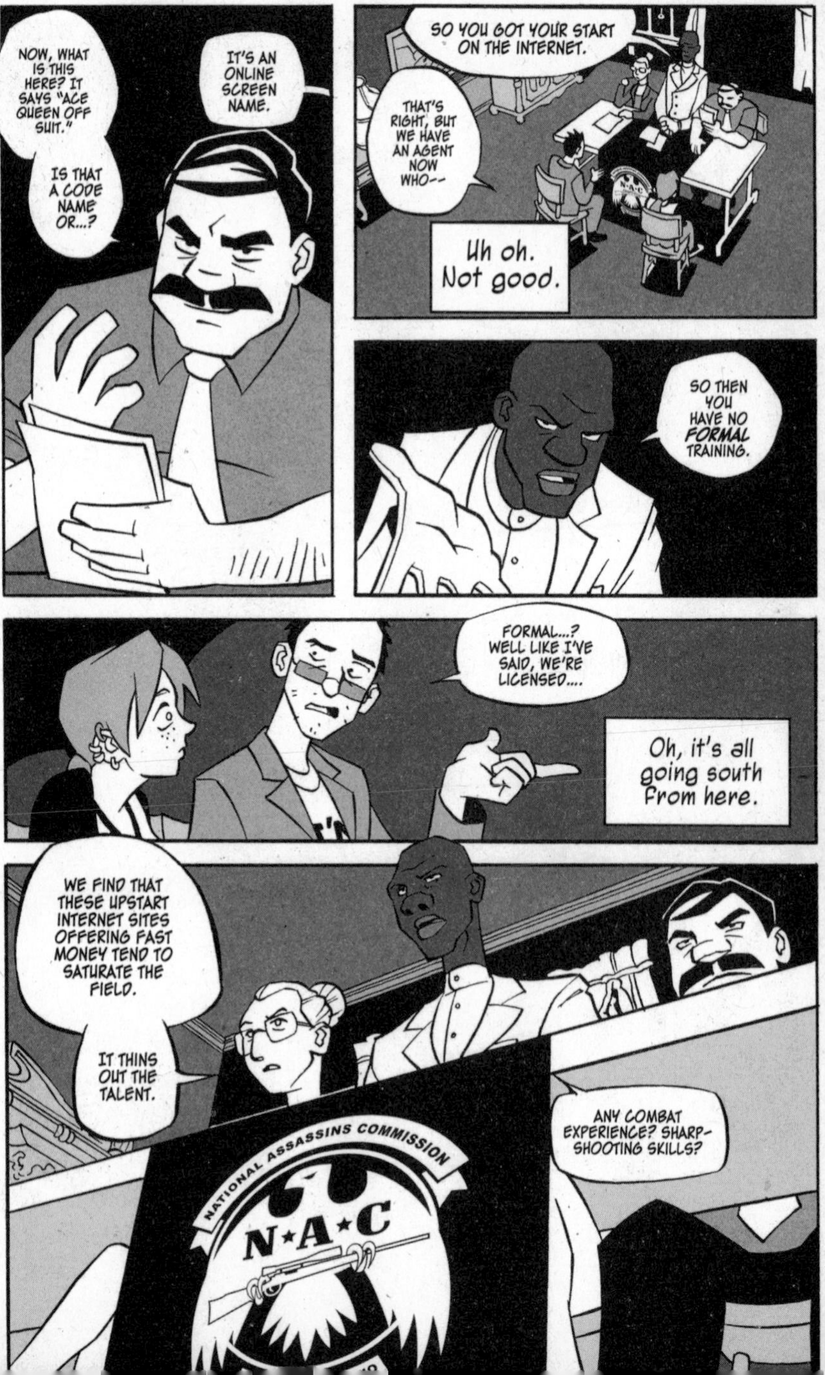
NOW, WHAT IS THIS HERE? IT SAYS "ACE QUEEN OFF SUIT."
IT'S AN ONLINE SCREEN NAME.
IS THAT A CODE NAME OR...?
SO YOU GOT YOUR START ON THE INTERNET.
THAT'S RIGHT, BUT WE HAVE AN AGENT NOW WHO--
Uh oh. Not good.
SO THEN YOU HAVE NO *FORMAL* TRAINING.
FORMAL...? WELL LIKE I'VE SAID, WE'RE LICENSED....
Oh, it's all going south from here.
WE FIND THAT THESE UPSTART INTERNET SITES OFFERING FAST MONEY TEND TO SATURATE THE FIELD.
IT THINS OUT THE TALENT.
ANY COMBAT EXPERIENCE? SHARP-SHOOTING SKILLS?
NATIONAL ASSASSINS COMMISSION
N·A·C

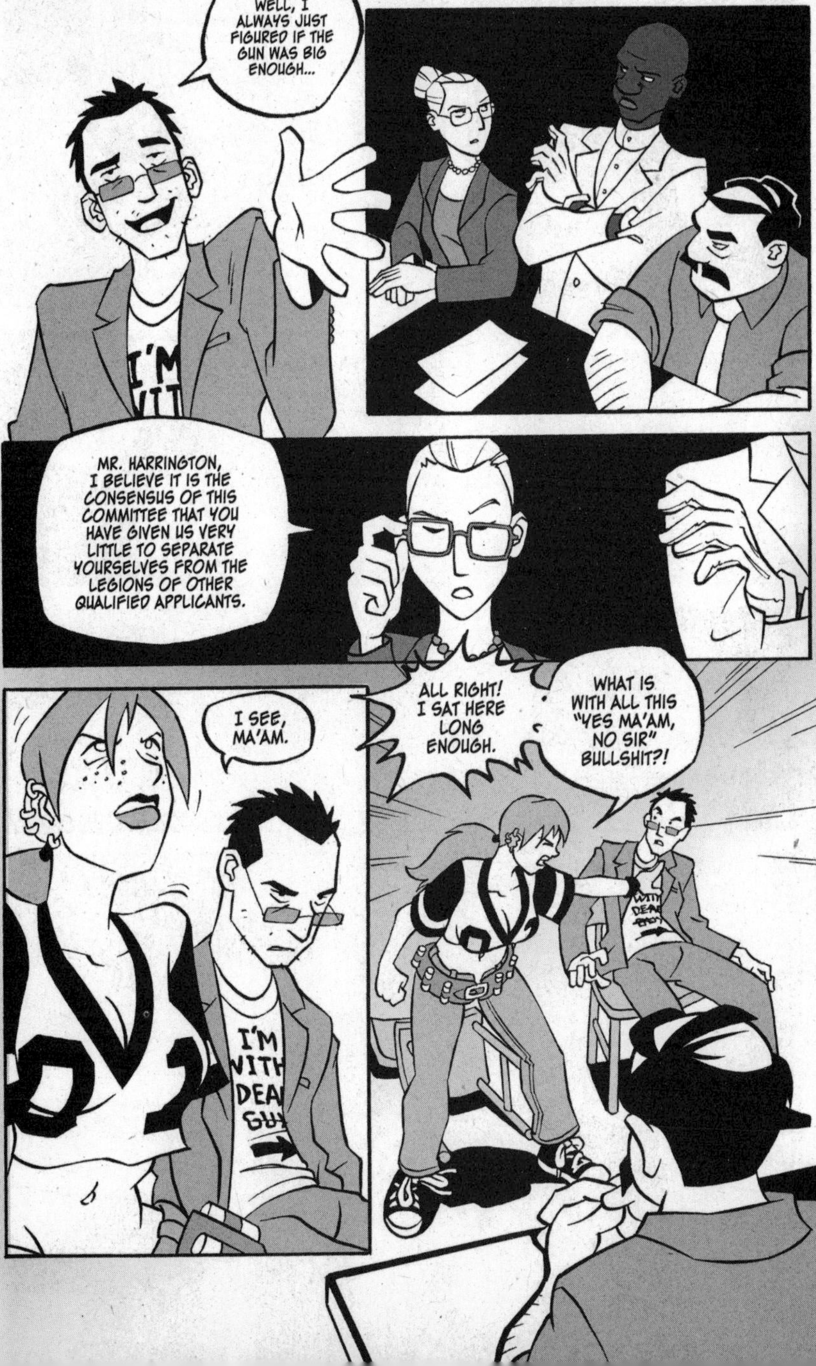
WELL, I ALWAYS JUST FIGURED IF THE GUN WAS BIG ENOUGH...
MR. HARRINGTON, I BELIEVE IT IS THE CONSENSUS OF THIS COMMITTEE THAT YOU HAVE GIVEN US VERY LITTLE TO SEPARATE YOURSELVES FROM THE LEGIONS OF OTHER QUALIFIED APPLICANTS.
I SEE, MA'AM.
ALL RIGHT! I SAT HERE LONG ENOUGH.
WHAT IS WITH ALL THIS "YES MA'AM, NO SIR" BULLSHIT?!

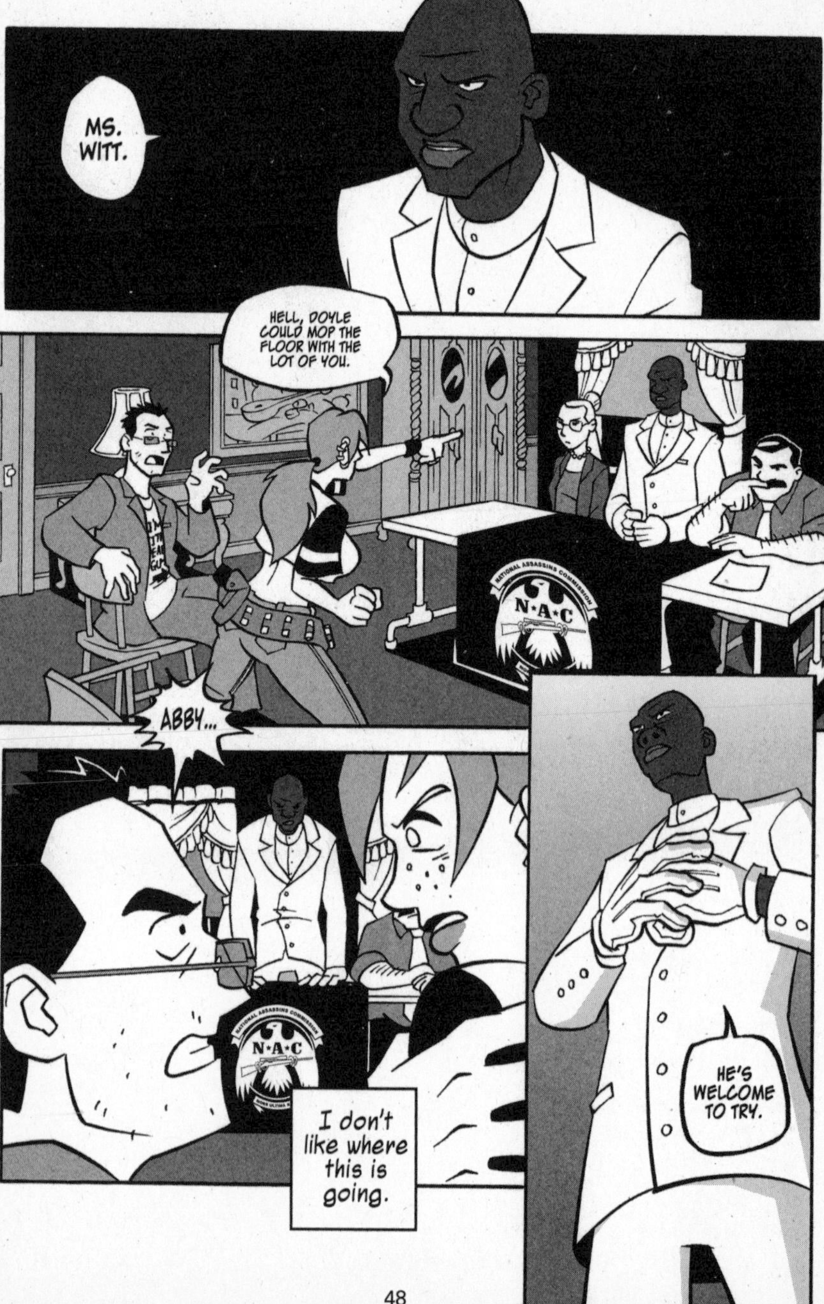
MS. WITT.
HELL, DOYLE COULD MOP THE FLOOR WITH THE LOT OF YOU.
ABBY...
I don't like where this is going.
HE'S WELCOME TO TRY.

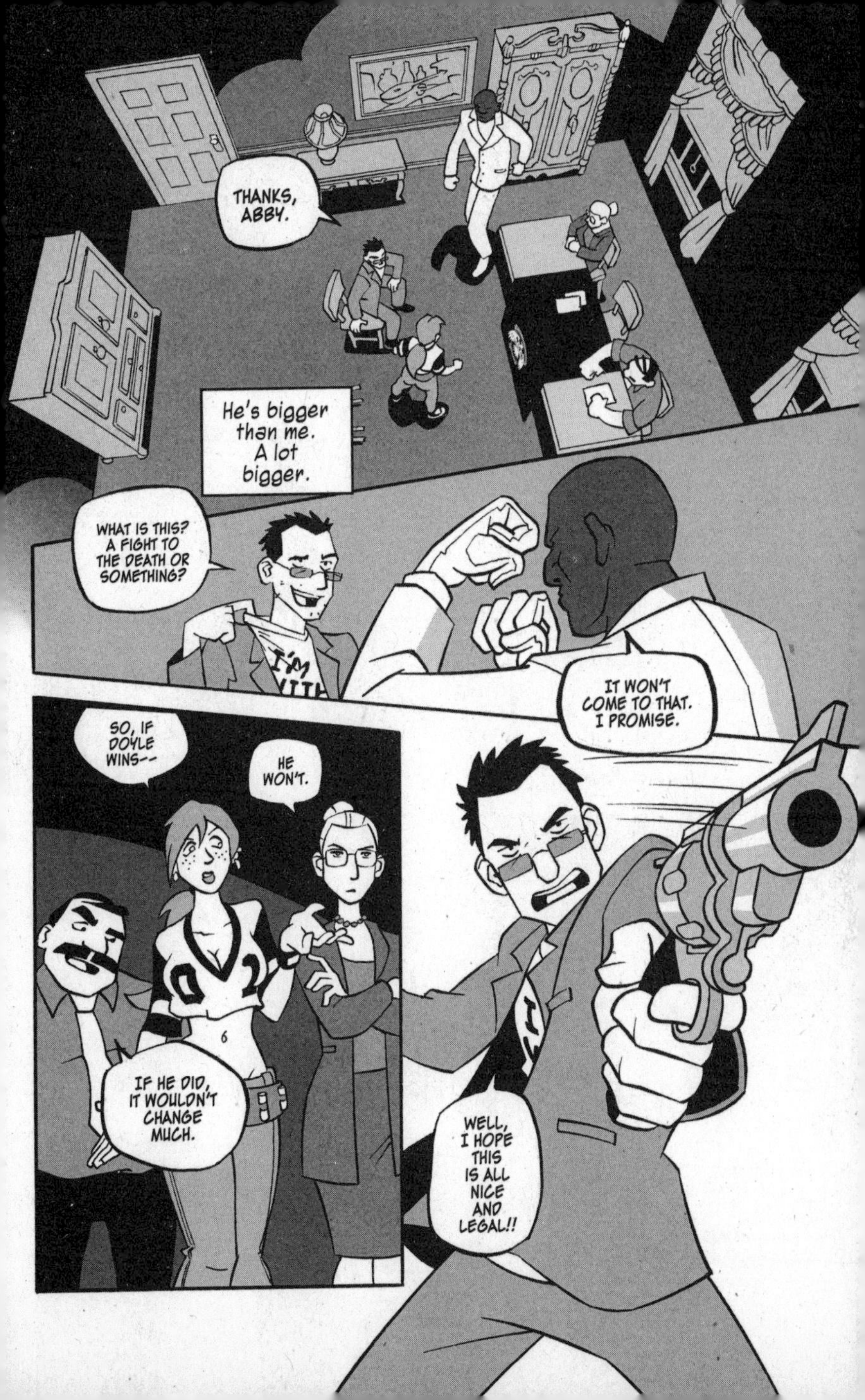
THANKS, ABBY.
He's bigger than me. A lot bigger.
WHAT IS THIS? A FIGHT TO THE DEATH OR SOMETHING?
IT WON'T COME TO THAT. I PROMISE.
SO, IF DOYLE WINS--
HE WON'T.
IF HE DID, IT WOULDN'T CHANGE MUCH.
WELL, I HOPE THIS IS ALL NICE AND LEGAL!!

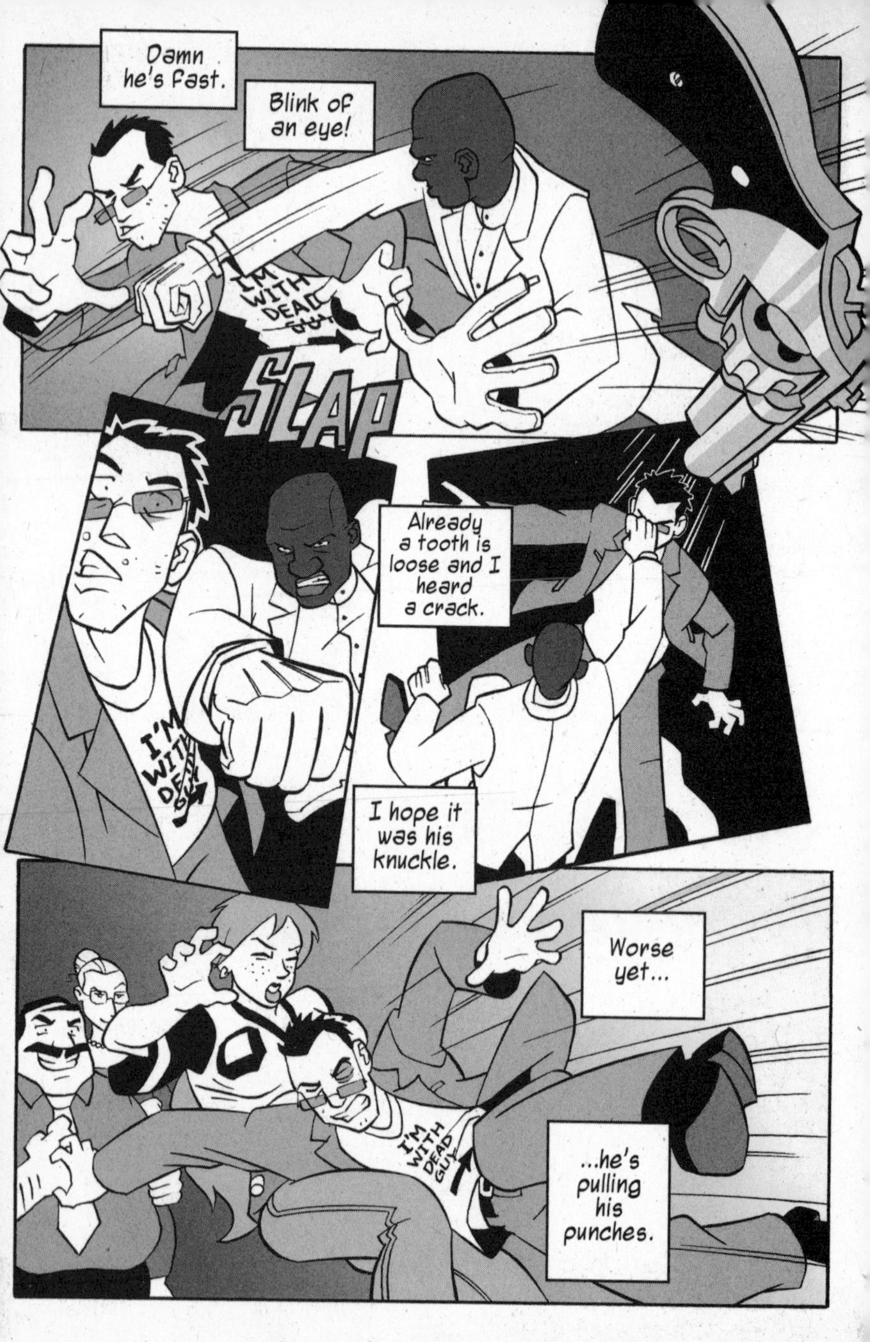
Damn he's fast.
Blink of an eye!
SLAP
Already a tooth is loose and I heard a crack.
I hope it was his knuckle.
Worse yet...
I'M WITH DEAD GUY
...he's pulling his punches.

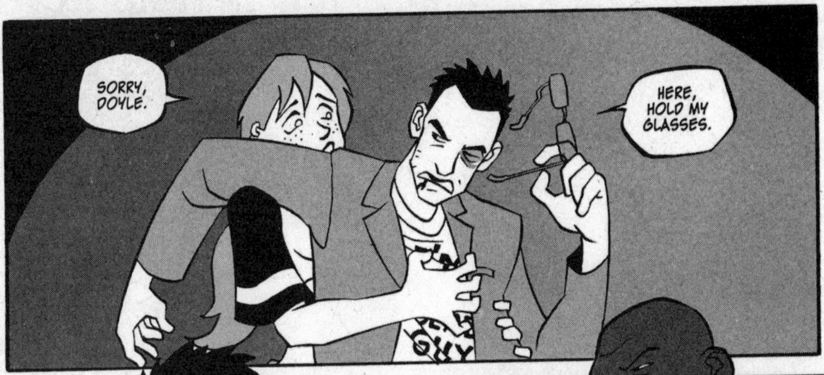
SORRY, DOYLE.
HERE, HOLD MY GLASSES.

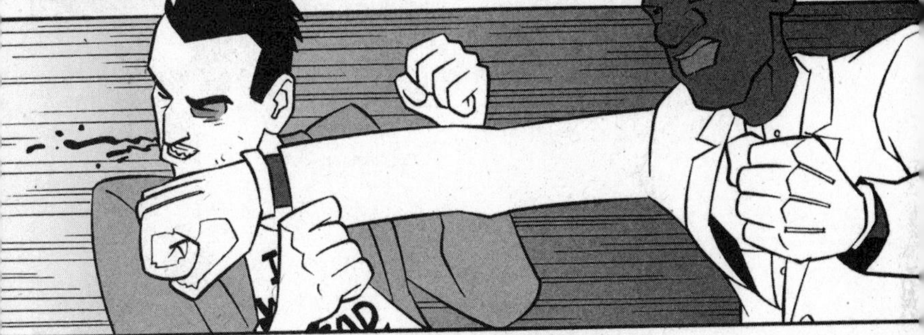

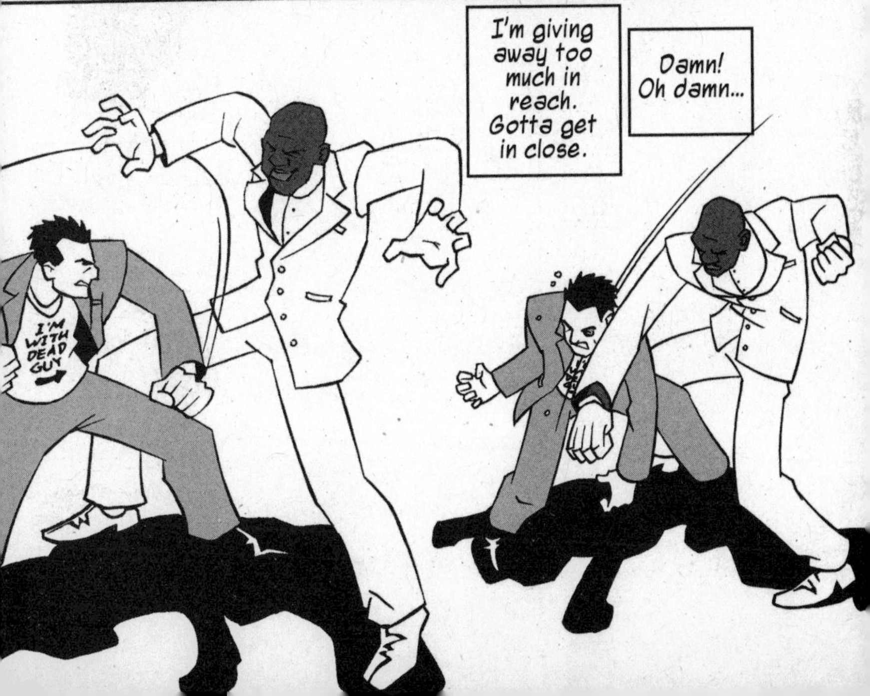
I'm giving away too much in reach. Gotta get in close.
Damn! Oh damn...
I'M WITH DEAD GUY

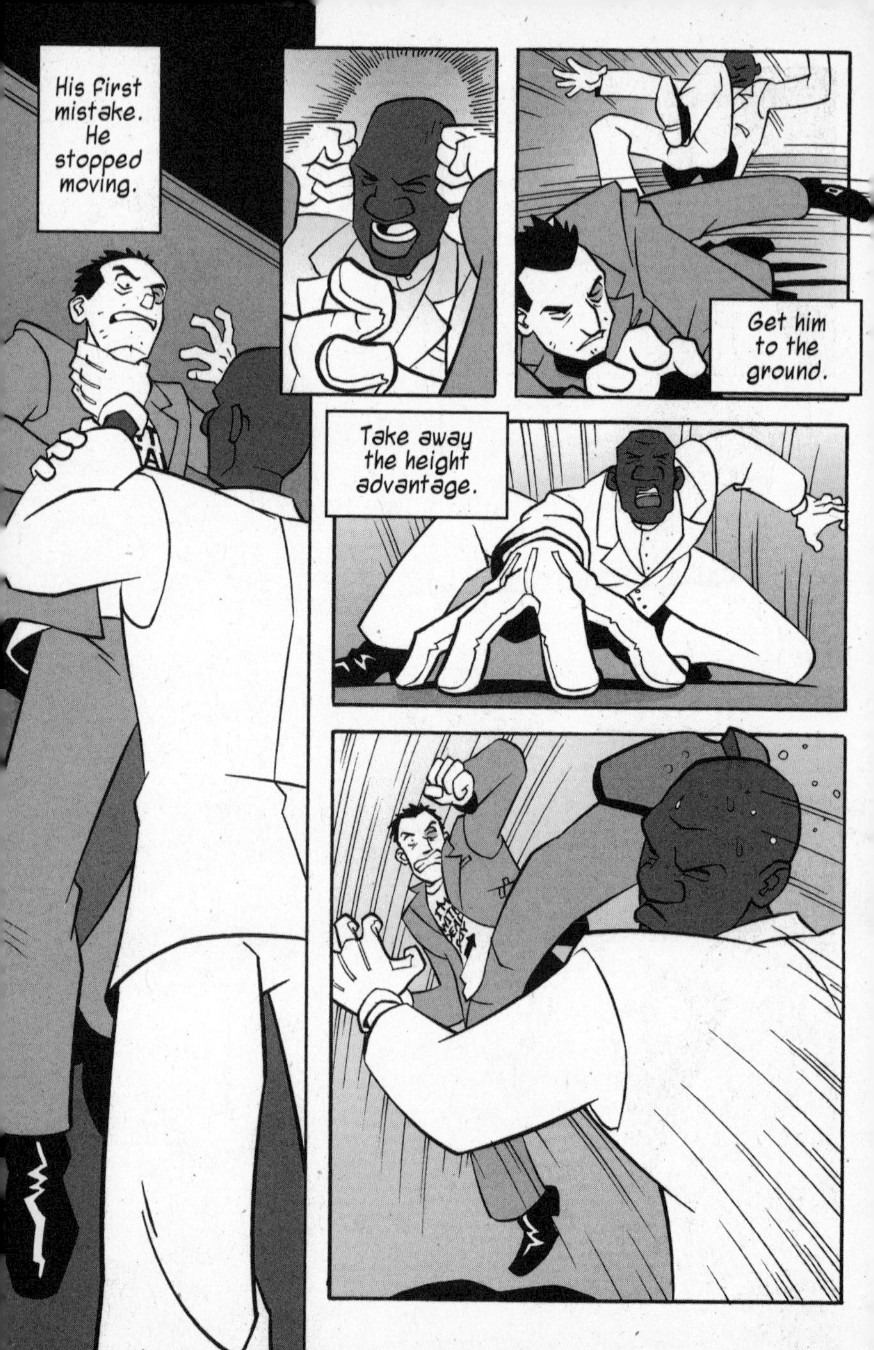
His first mistake. He stopped moving.
Get him to the ground.
Take away the height advantage.

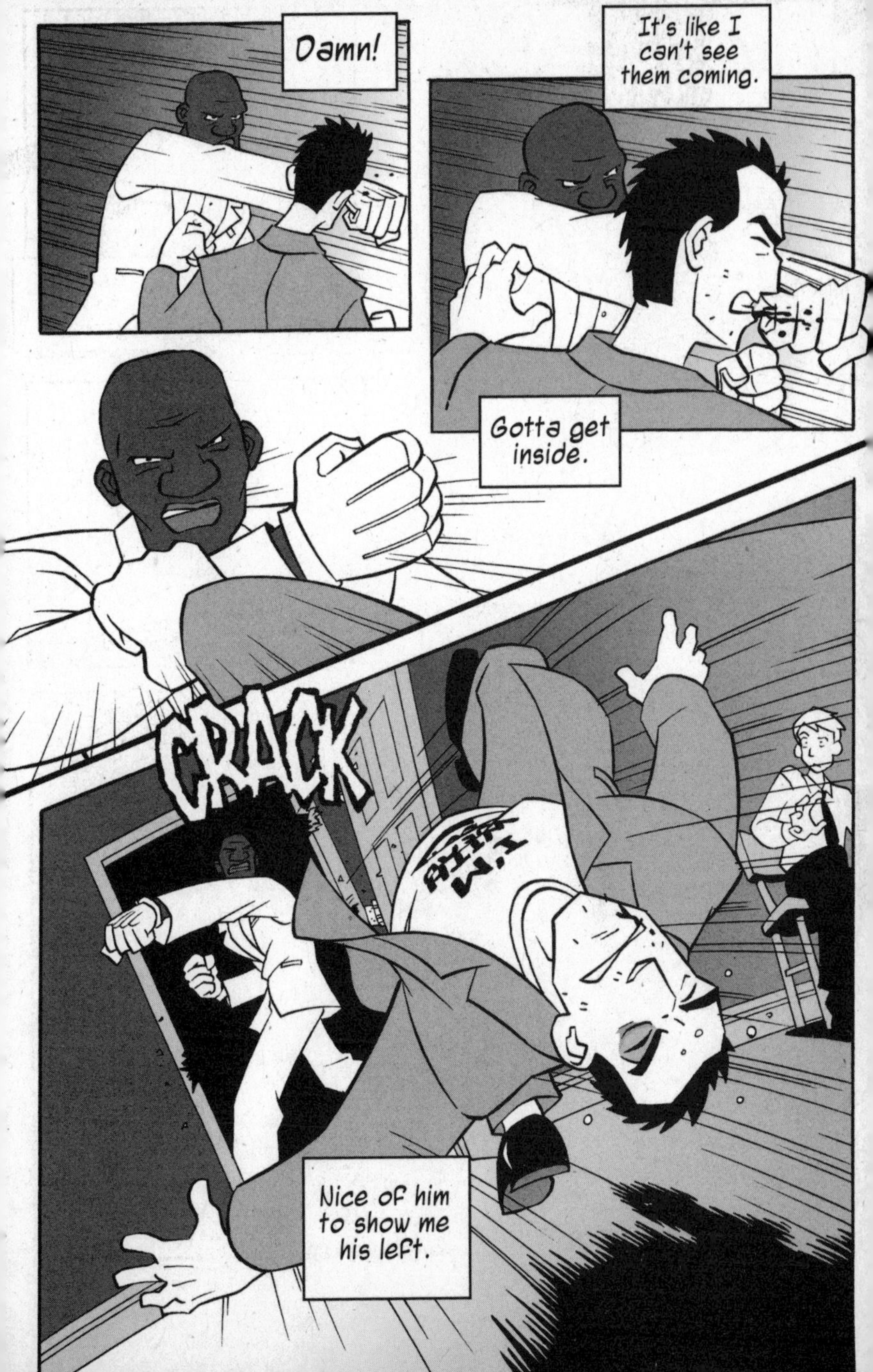
Damn!
It's like I can't see them coming.
Gotta get inside.
CRACK
Nice of him to show me his left.

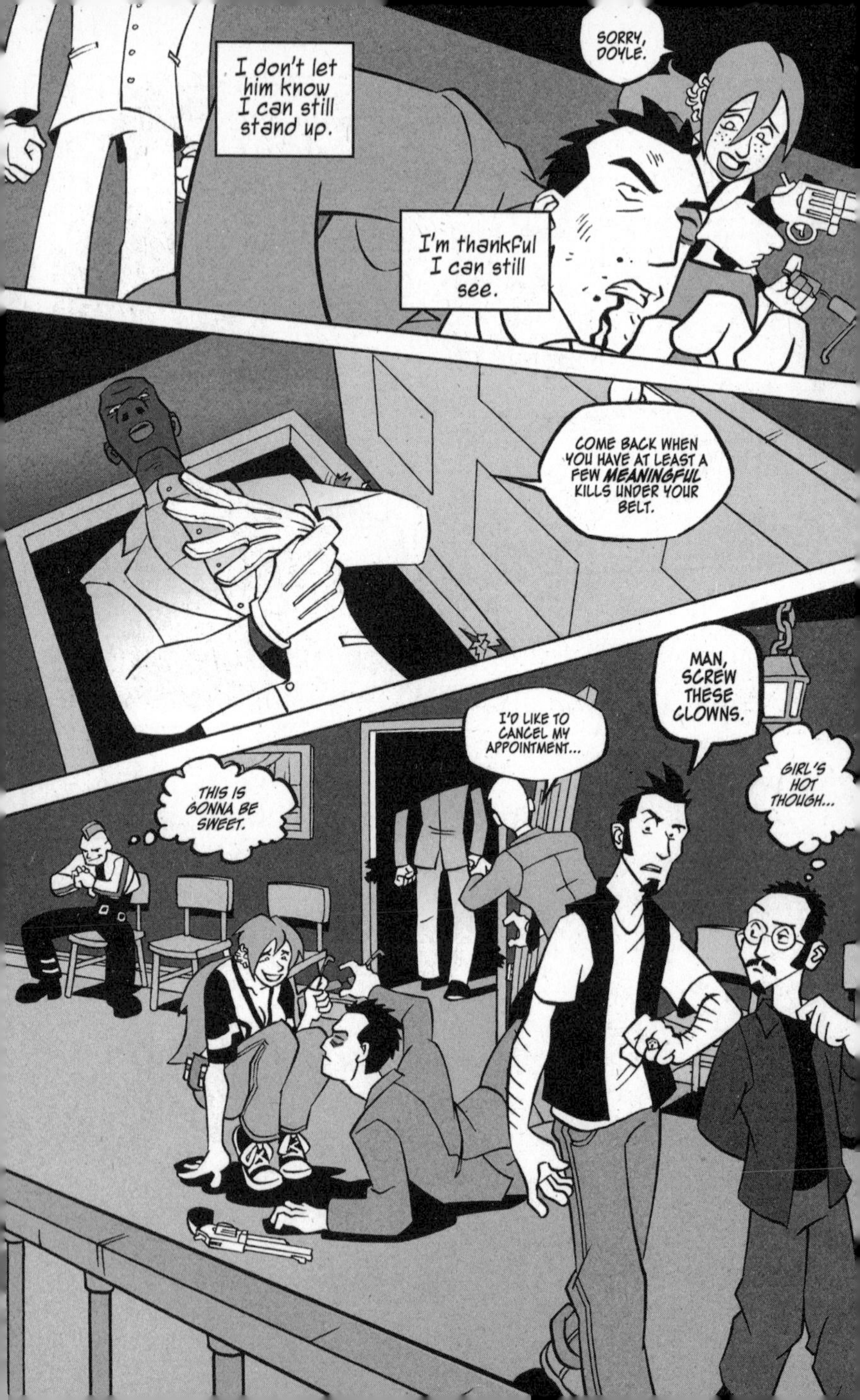
I don't let him know I can still stand up.
SORRY, DOYLE.
I'm thankful I can still see.
COME BACK WHEN YOU HAVE AT LEAST A FEW **MEANINGFUL** KILLS UNDER YOUR BELT.
THIS IS GONNA BE SWEET.
I'D LIKE TO CANCEL MY APPOINTMENT...
MAN, SCREW THESE CLOWNS.
GIRL'S HOT THOUGH...

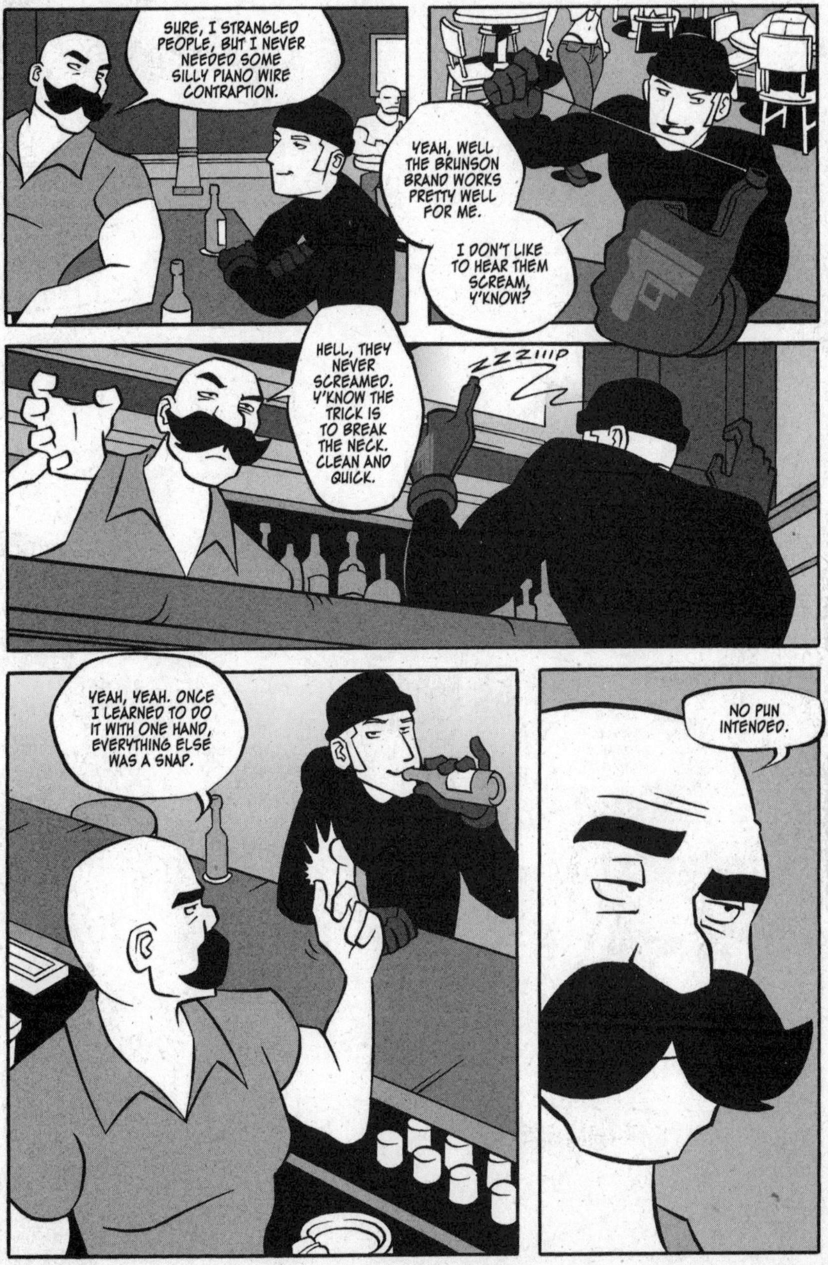
SURE, I STRANGLED PEOPLE, BUT I NEVER NEEDED SOME SILLY PIANO WIRE CONTRAPTION.
YEAH, WELL THE BRUNSON BRAND WORKS PRETTY WELL FOR ME.
I DON'T LIKE TO HEAR THEM SCREAM, Y'KNOW?
HELL, THEY NEVER SCREAMED. Y'KNOW THE TRICK IS TO BREAK THE NECK. CLEAN AND QUICK.
ZZZIIIP
YEAH, YEAH. ONCE I LEARNED TO DO IT WITH ONE HAND, EVERYTHING ELSE WAS A SNAP.
NO PUN INTENDED.

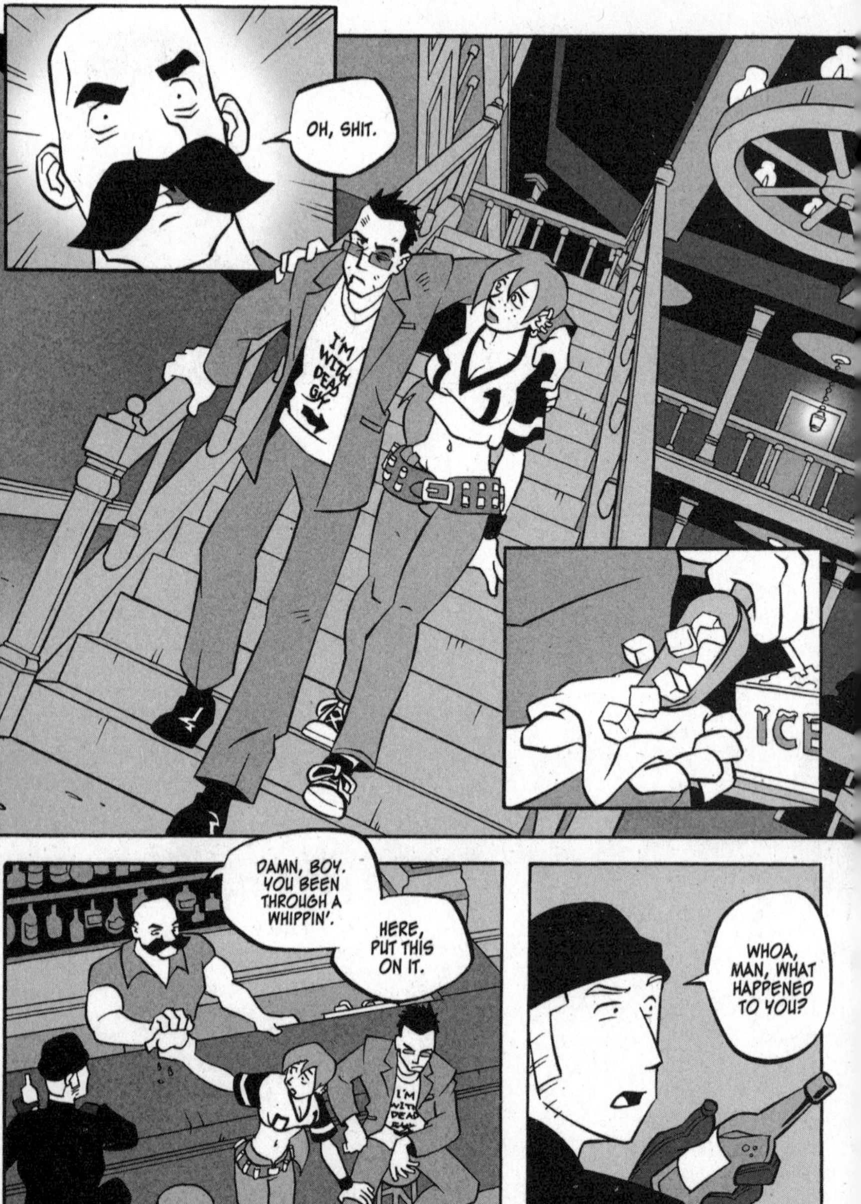
OH, SHIT.
I'M WITH DEAD GUY
ICE
DAMN, BOY. YOU BEEN THROUGH A WHIPPIN'.
HERE, PUT THIS ON IT.
WHOA, MAN, WHAT HAPPENED TO YOU?

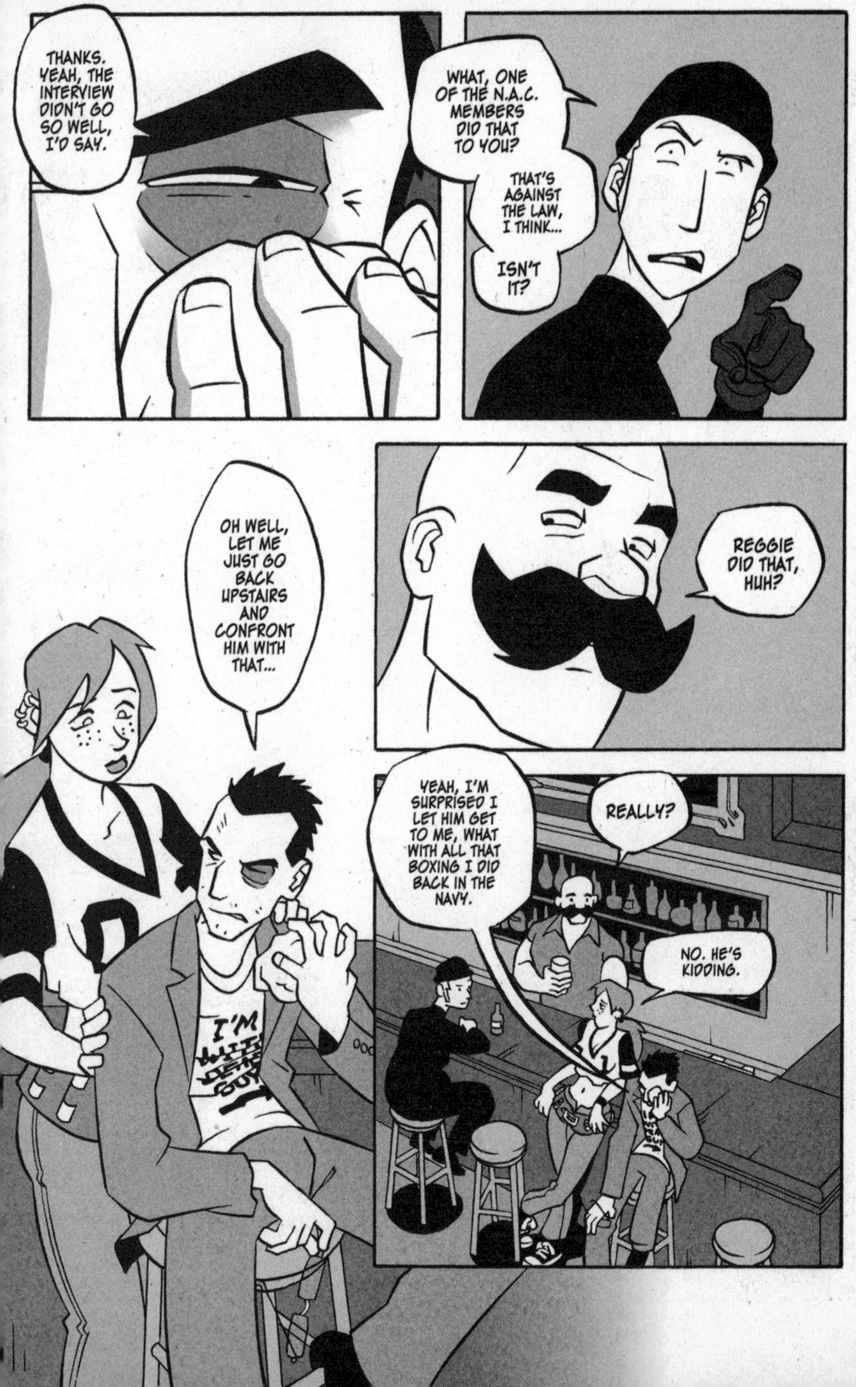
THANKS. YEAH, THE INTERVIEW DIDN'T GO SO WELL, I'D SAY.
WHAT, ONE OF THE N.A.C. MEMBERS DID THAT TO YOU?
THAT'S AGAINST THE LAW, I THINK...
ISN'T IT?
REGGIE DID THAT, HUH?
OH WELL, LET ME JUST GO BACK UPSTAIRS AND CONFRONT HIM WITH THAT...
YEAH, I'M SURPRISED I LET HIM GET TO ME, WHAT WITH ALL THAT BOXING I DID BACK IN THE NAVY.
REALLY?
NO. HE'S KIDDING.

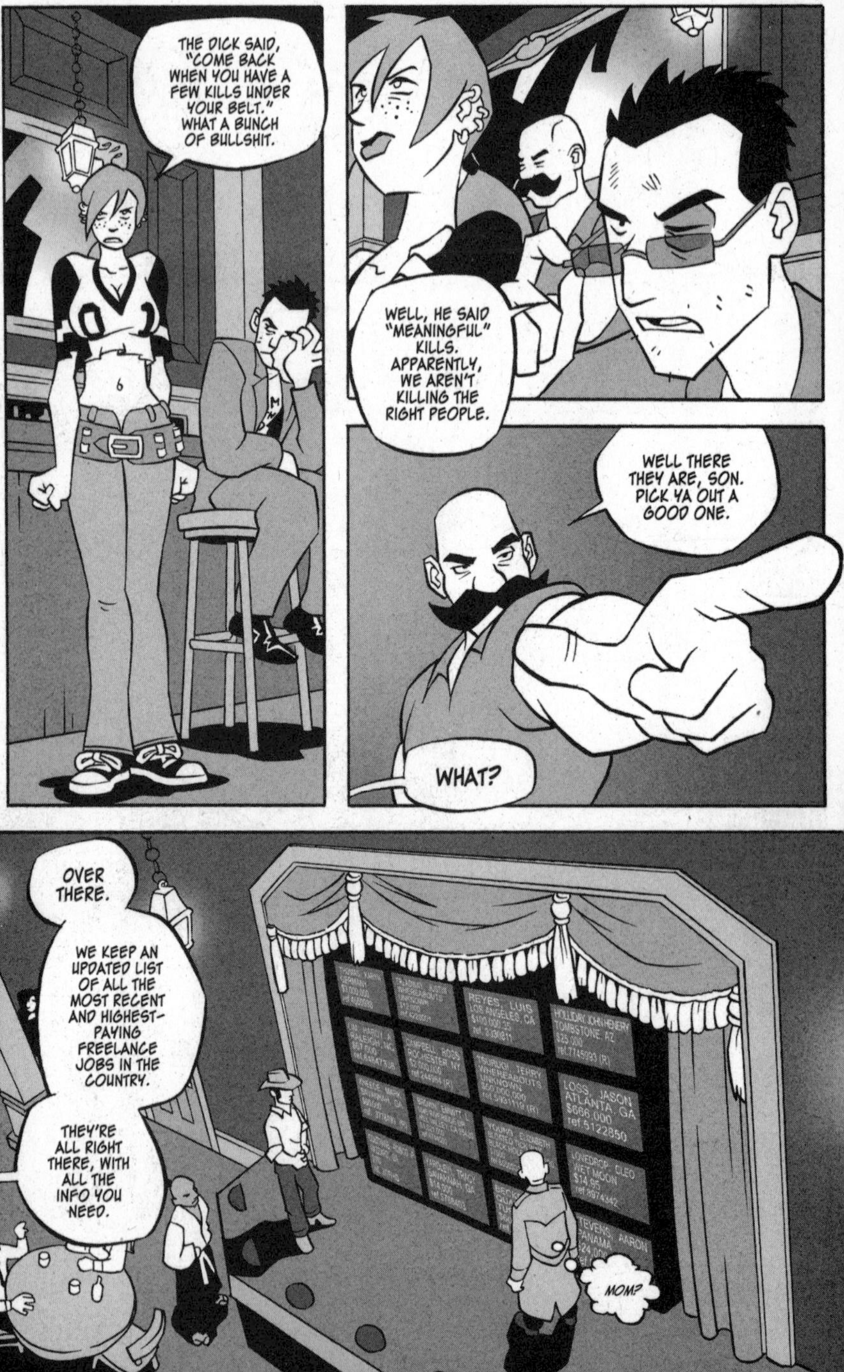
THE DICK SAID, "COME BACK WHEN YOU HAVE A FEW KILLS UNDER YOUR BELT." WHAT A BUNCH OF BULLSHIT.
WELL, HE SAID "MEANINGFUL" KILLS. APPARENTLY, WE AREN'T KILLING THE RIGHT PEOPLE.
WELL THERE THEY ARE, SON. PICK YA OUT A GOOD ONE.
WHAT?
OVER THERE.
WE KEEP AN UPDATED LIST OF ALL THE MOST RECENT AND HIGHEST-PAYING FREELANCE JOBS IN THE COUNTRY.
THEY'RE ALL RIGHT THERE, WITH ALL THE INFO YOU NEED.
REYES, LUIS LOS ANGELES, CA
HOLLIDAY, JOHN HENERY TOMBSTONE, AZ $25,000
LOSS, JASON ATLANTA, GA $666,000 ref.5122850
LOVEDROP, CLEO WET MOON $14.95
STEVENS, AARON PANAMA
MOM?

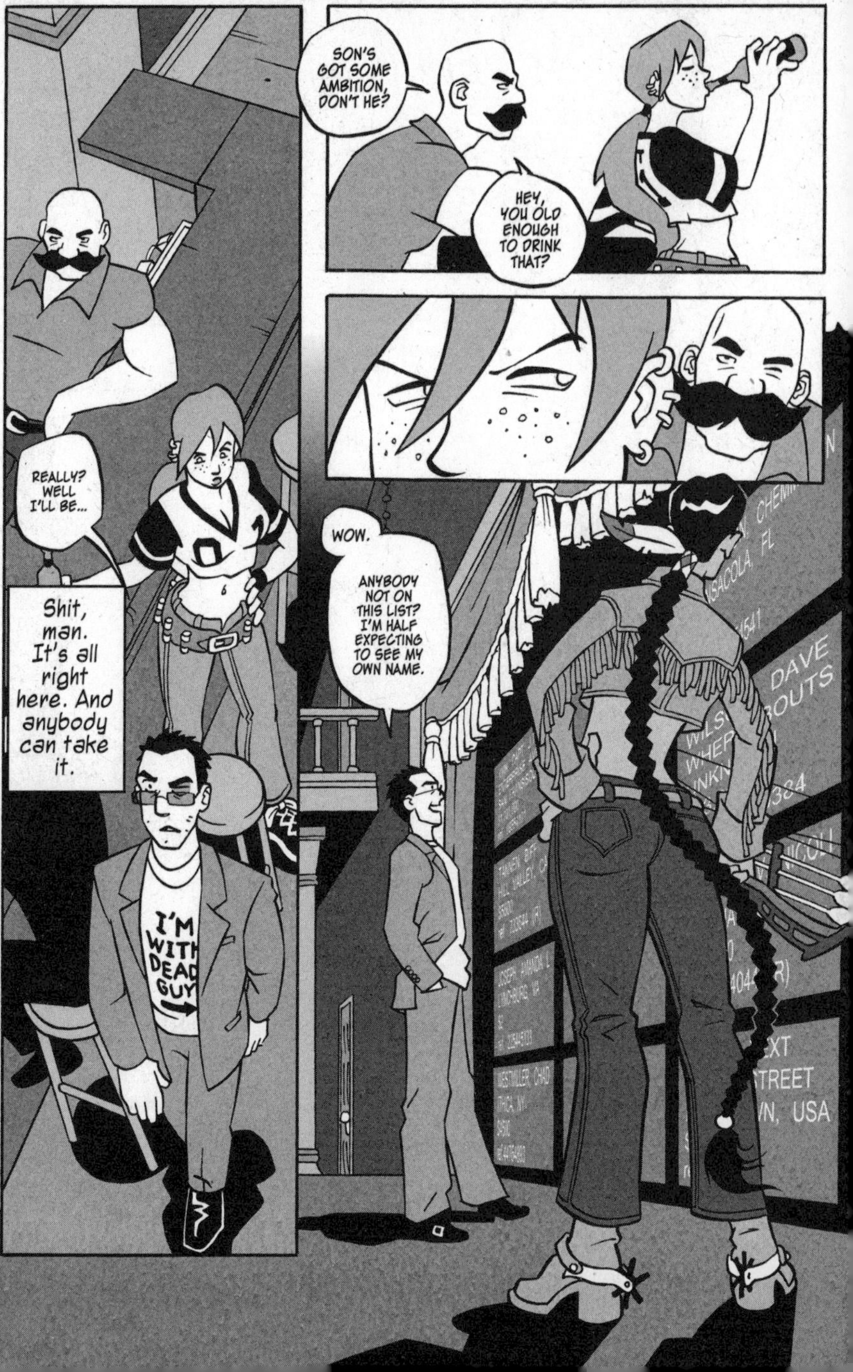
SON'S GOT SOME AMBITION, DON'T HE?
HEY, YOU OLD ENOUGH TO DRINK THAT?
WOW.
ANYBODY NOT ON THIS LIST? I'M HALF EXPECTING TO SEE MY OWN NAME.
REALLY? WELL I'LL BE...
Shit, man. It's all right here. And anybody can take it.
I'M WITH DEAD GUY

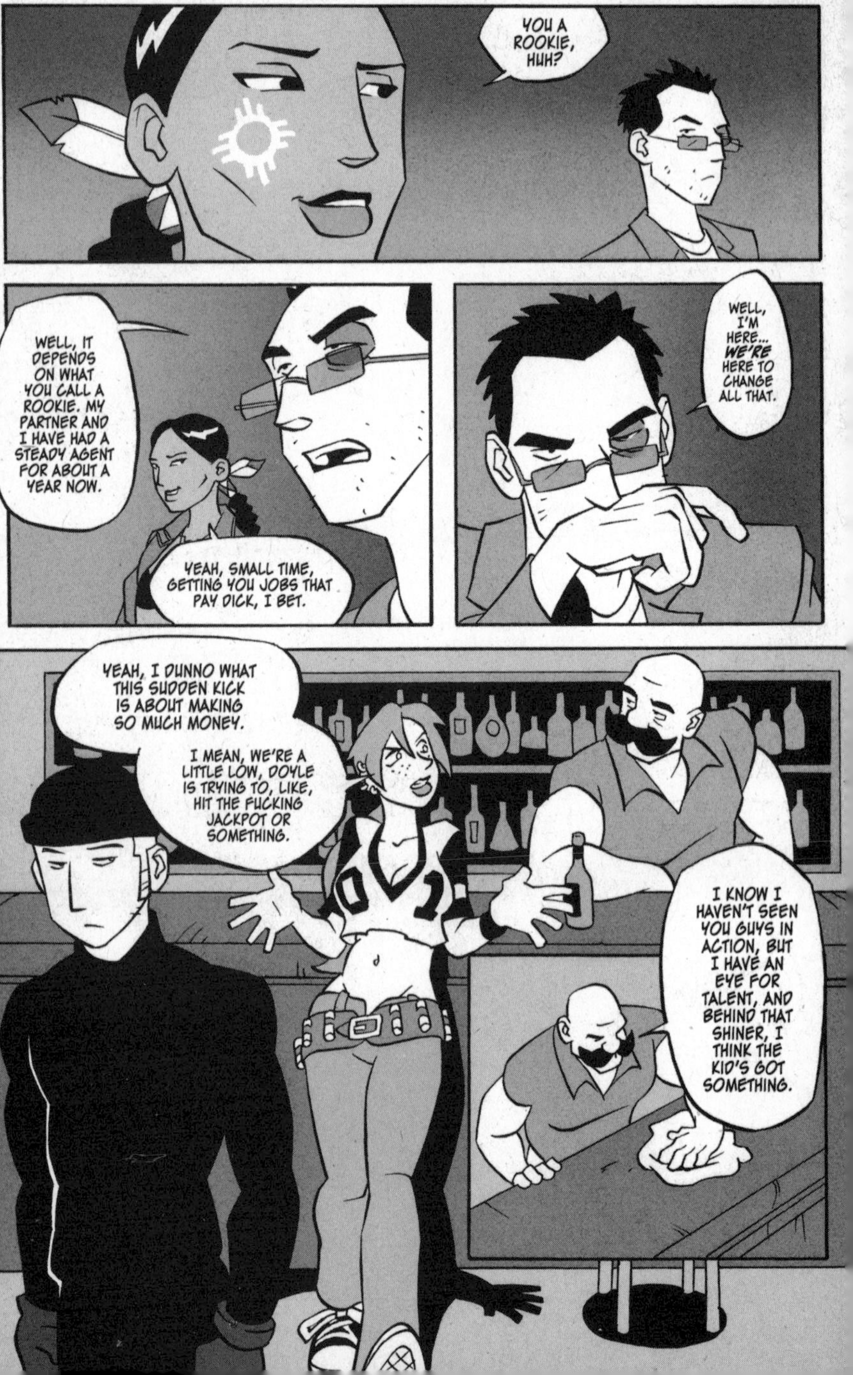
YOU A ROOKIE, HUH?
WELL, IT DEPENDS ON WHAT YOU CALL A ROOKIE. MY PARTNER AND I HAVE HAD A STEADY AGENT FOR ABOUT A YEAR NOW.
YEAH, SMALL TIME, GETTING YOU JOBS THAT PAY DICK, I BET.
WELL, I'M HERE... **WE'RE** HERE TO CHANGE ALL THAT.
YEAH, I DUNNO WHAT THIS SUDDEN KICK IS ABOUT MAKING SO MUCH MONEY.
I MEAN, WE'RE A LITTLE LOW, DOYLE IS TRYING TO, LIKE, HIT THE FUCKING JACKPOT OR SOMETHING.
I KNOW I HAVEN'T SEEN YOU GUYS IN ACTION, BUT I HAVE AN EYE FOR TALENT, AND BEHIND THAT SHINER, I THINK THE KID'S GOT SOMETHING.

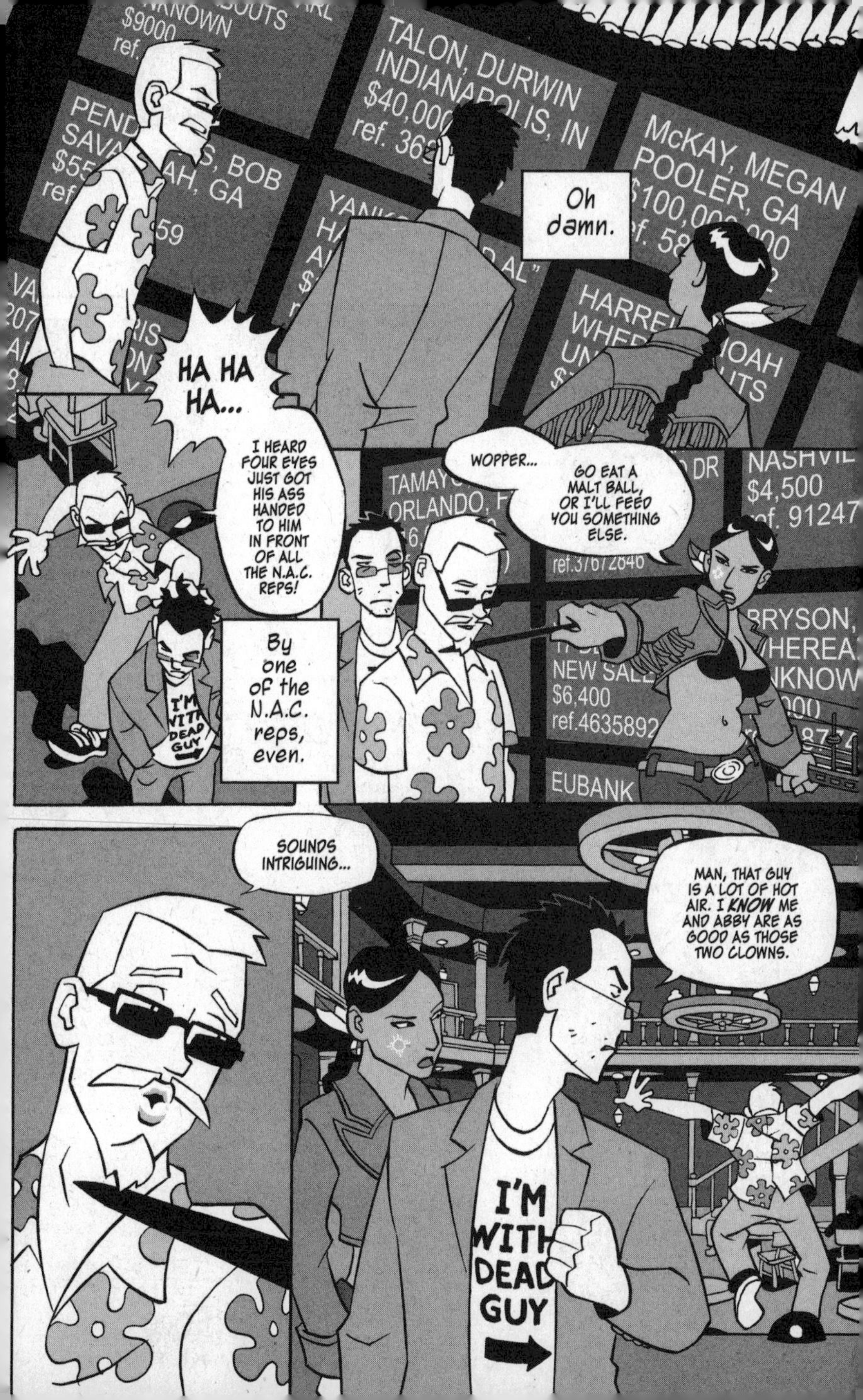
TALON, DURWIN
INDIANAPOLIS, IN
McKAY, MEGAN
POOLER, GA
Oh damn.
HA HA HA...
I HEARD FOUR EYES JUST GOT HIS ASS HANDED TO HIM IN FRONT OF ALL THE N.A.C. REPS!
By one of the N.A.C. reps, even.
WOPPER...
GO EAT A MALT BALL, OR I'LL FEED YOU SOMETHING ELSE.
SOUNDS INTRIGUING...
MAN, THAT GUY IS A LOT OF HOT AIR. I KNOW ME AND ABBY ARE AS GOOD AS THOSE TWO CLOWNS.
I'M WITH DEAD GUY

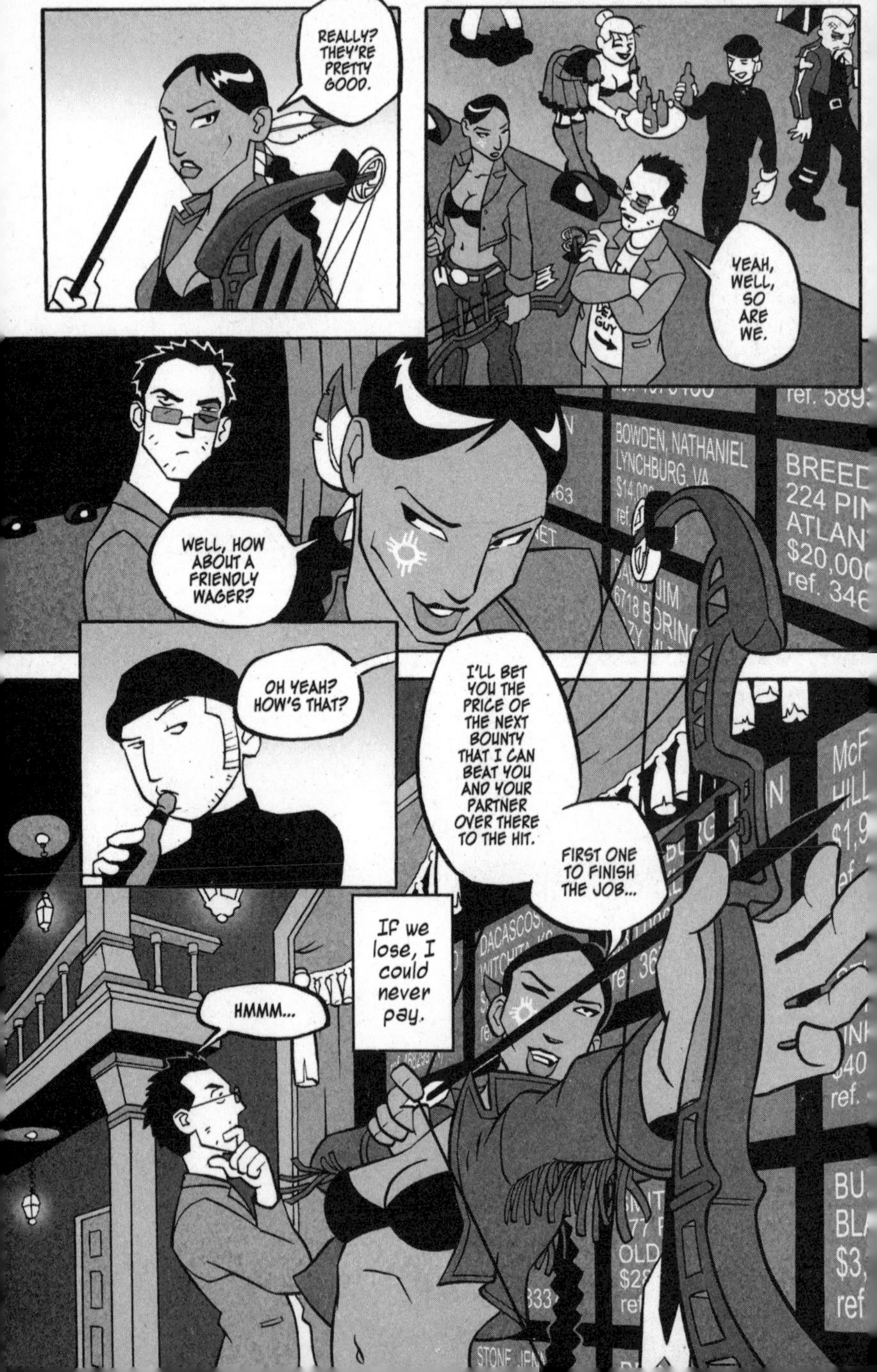
REALLY? THEY'RE PRETTY GOOD.
YEAH, WELL, SO ARE WE.
WELL, HOW ABOUT A FRIENDLY WAGER?
BOWDEN, NATHANIEL
LYNCHBURG, VA
OH YEAH? HOW'S THAT?
I'LL BET YOU THE PRICE OF THE NEXT BOUNTY THAT I CAN BEAT YOU AND YOUR PARTNER OVER THERE TO THE HIT.
FIRST ONE TO FINISH THE JOB...
If we lose, I could never pay.
HMMM...

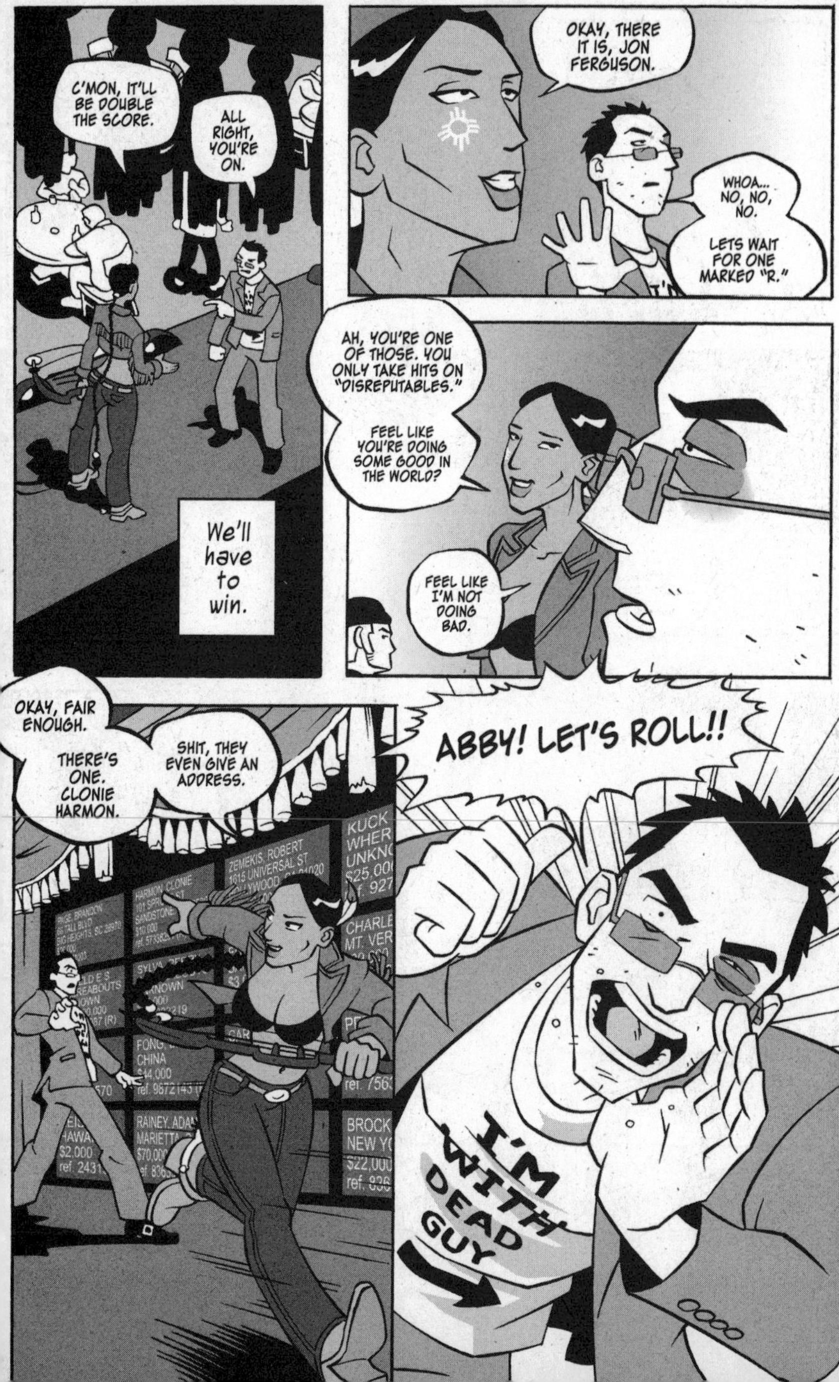
C'MON, IT'LL BE DOUBLE THE SCORE.
ALL RIGHT, YOU'RE ON.
We'll have to win.
OKAY, THERE IT IS, JON FERGUSON.
WHOA... NO, NO, NO.
LETS WAIT FOR ONE MARKED "R."
AH, YOU'RE ONE OF THOSE. YOU ONLY TAKE HITS ON "DISREPUTABLES."
FEEL LIKE YOU'RE DOING SOME GOOD IN THE WORLD?
FEEL LIKE I'M NOT DOING BAD.
OKAY, FAIR ENOUGH.
THERE'S ONE. CLONIE HARMON.
SHIT, THEY EVEN GIVE AN ADDRESS.
ABBY! LET'S ROLL!!
I'M WITH DEAD GUY

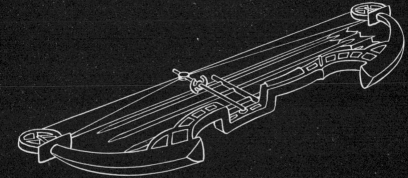

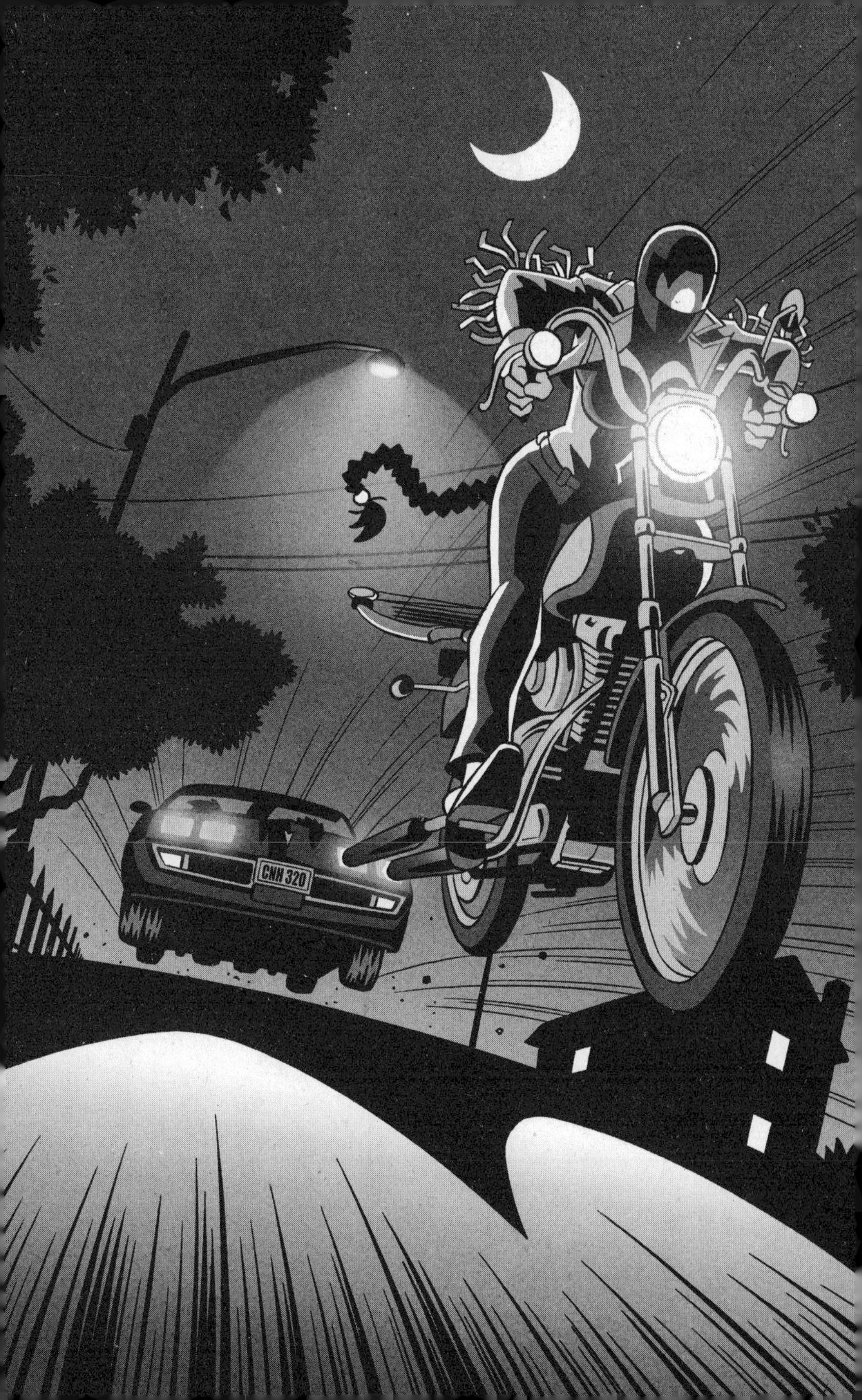
CNH 320

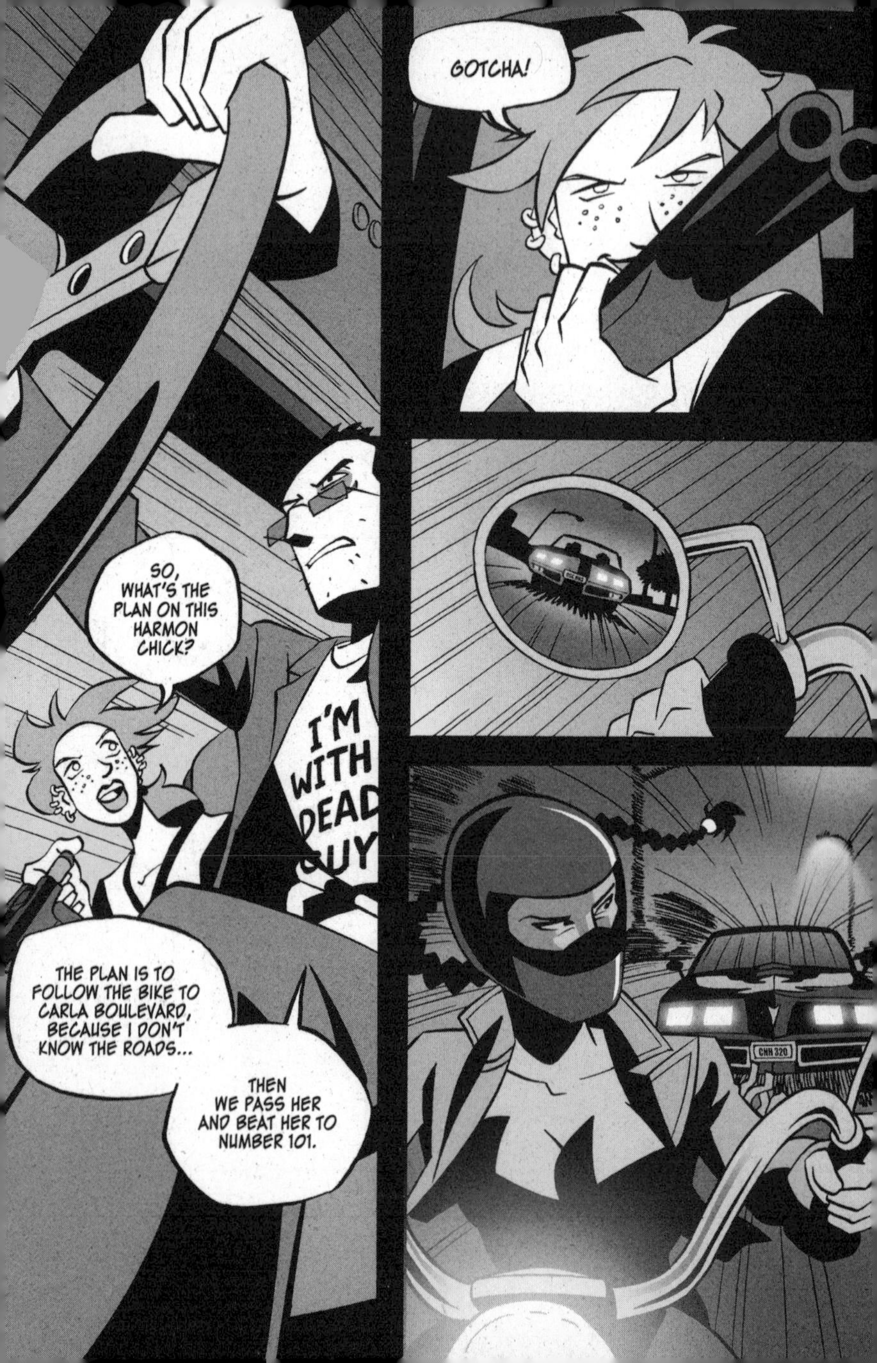
SO, WHAT'S THE PLAN ON THIS HARMON CHICK?
I'M WITH DEAD
THE PLAN IS TO FOLLOW THE BIKE TO CARLA BOULEVARD, BECAUSE I DON'T KNOW THE ROADS...
THEN WE PASS HER AND BEAT HER TO NUMBER 101.
GOTCHA!
CNH 320

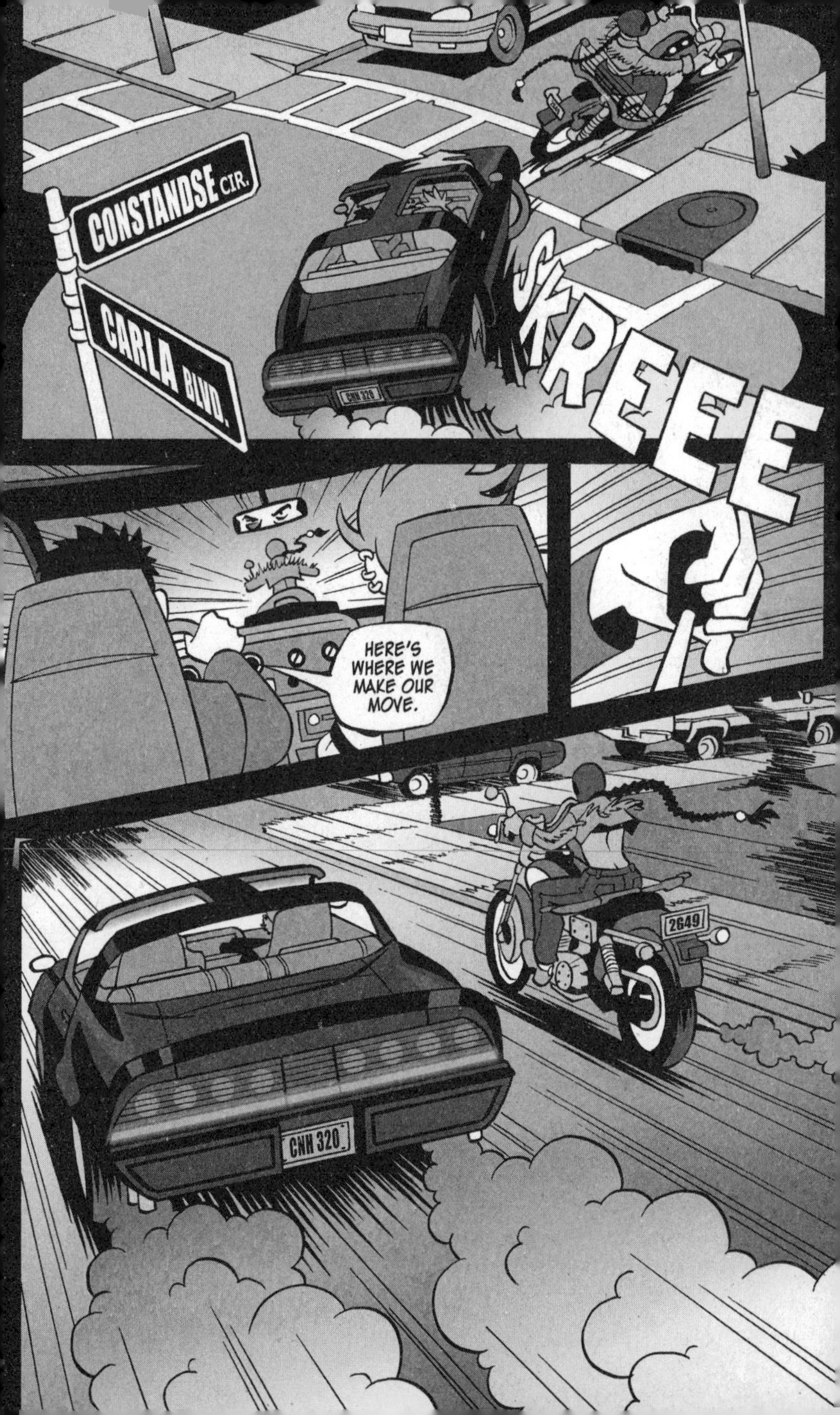CONSTANDSE CIR.
CARLA BLVD.
CNN 320
SKREEEE
HERE'S WHERE WE MAKE OUR MOVE.
2G49
CNN 320

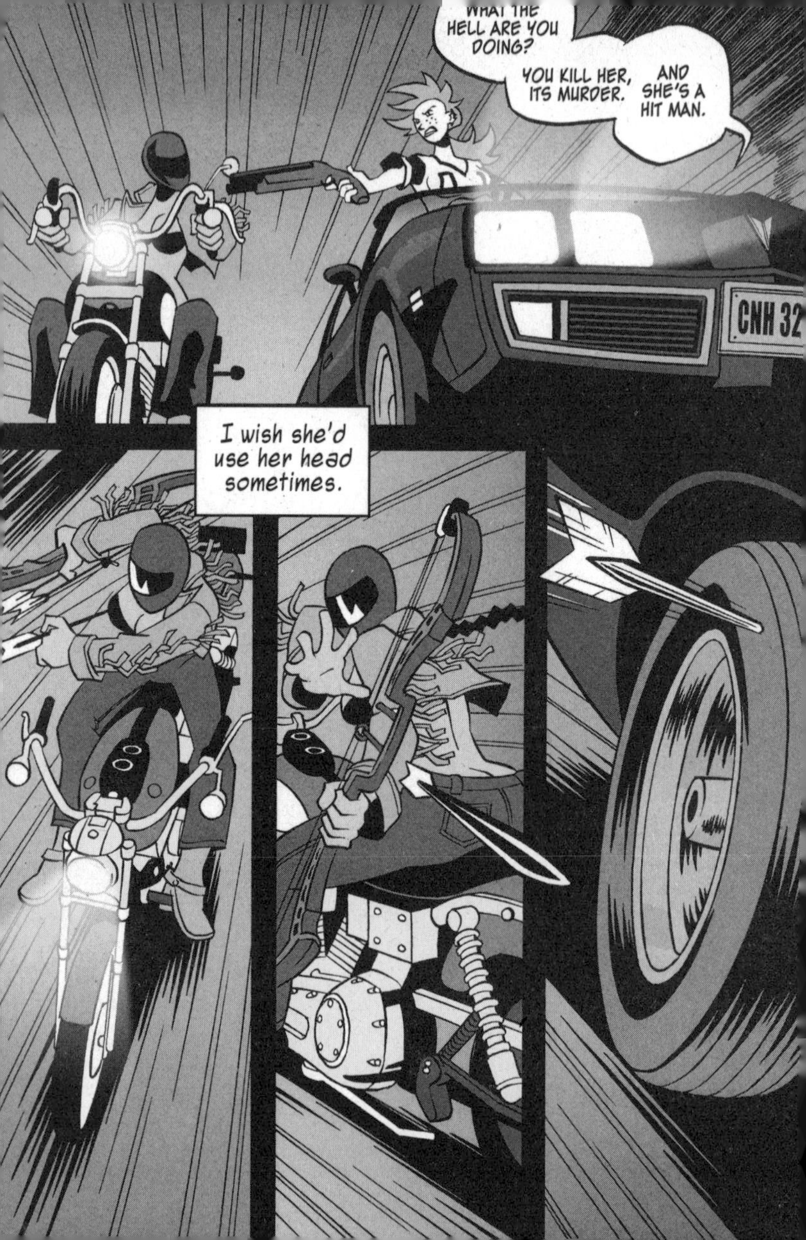
WHAT THE HELL ARE YOU DOING?
YOU KILL HER, ITS MURDER.
AND SHE'S A HIT MAN.
CNH 32
I wish she'd use her head sometimes.

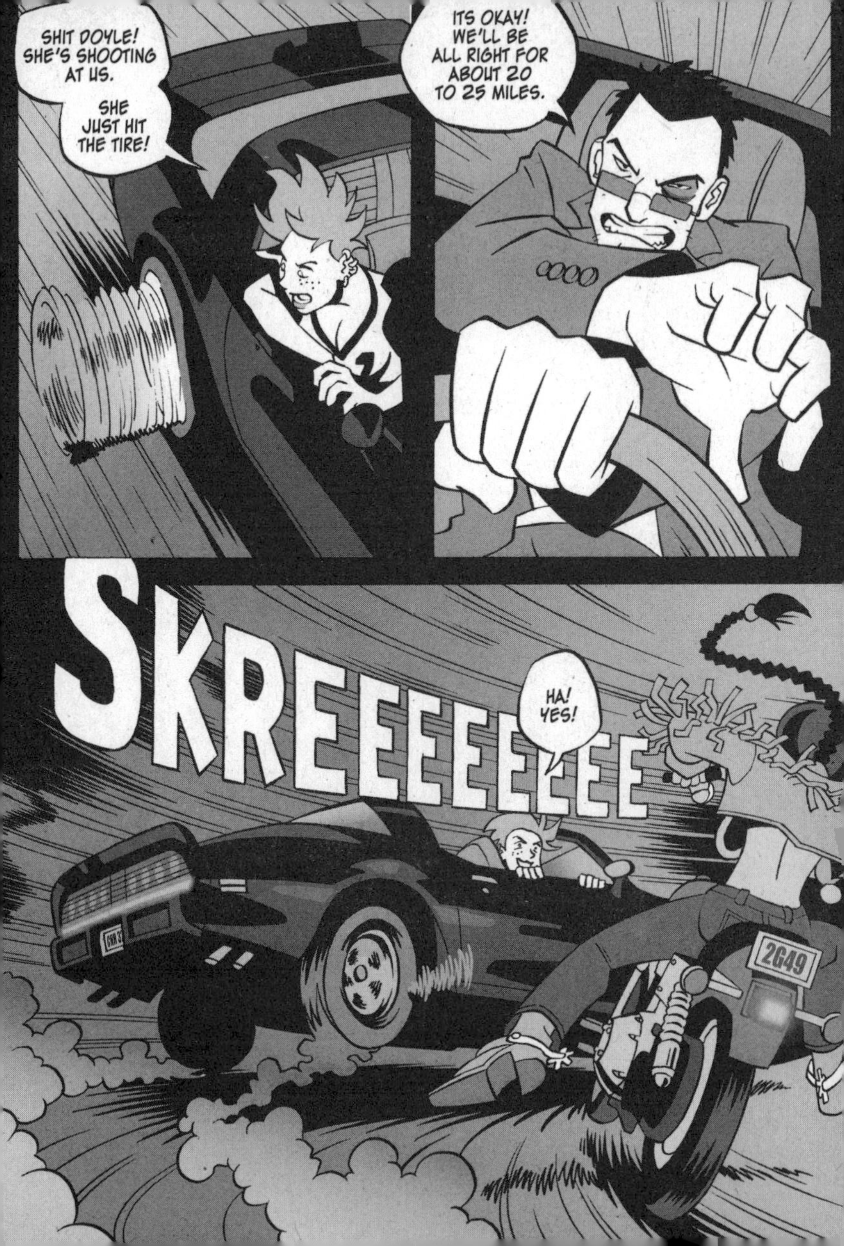
SHIT DOYLE! SHE'S SHOOTING AT US.
SHE JUST HIT THE TIRE!
ITS OKAY! WE'LL BE ALL RIGHT FOR ABOUT 20 TO 25 MILES.
SKREEEEEEEEE
HA! YES!
2G49

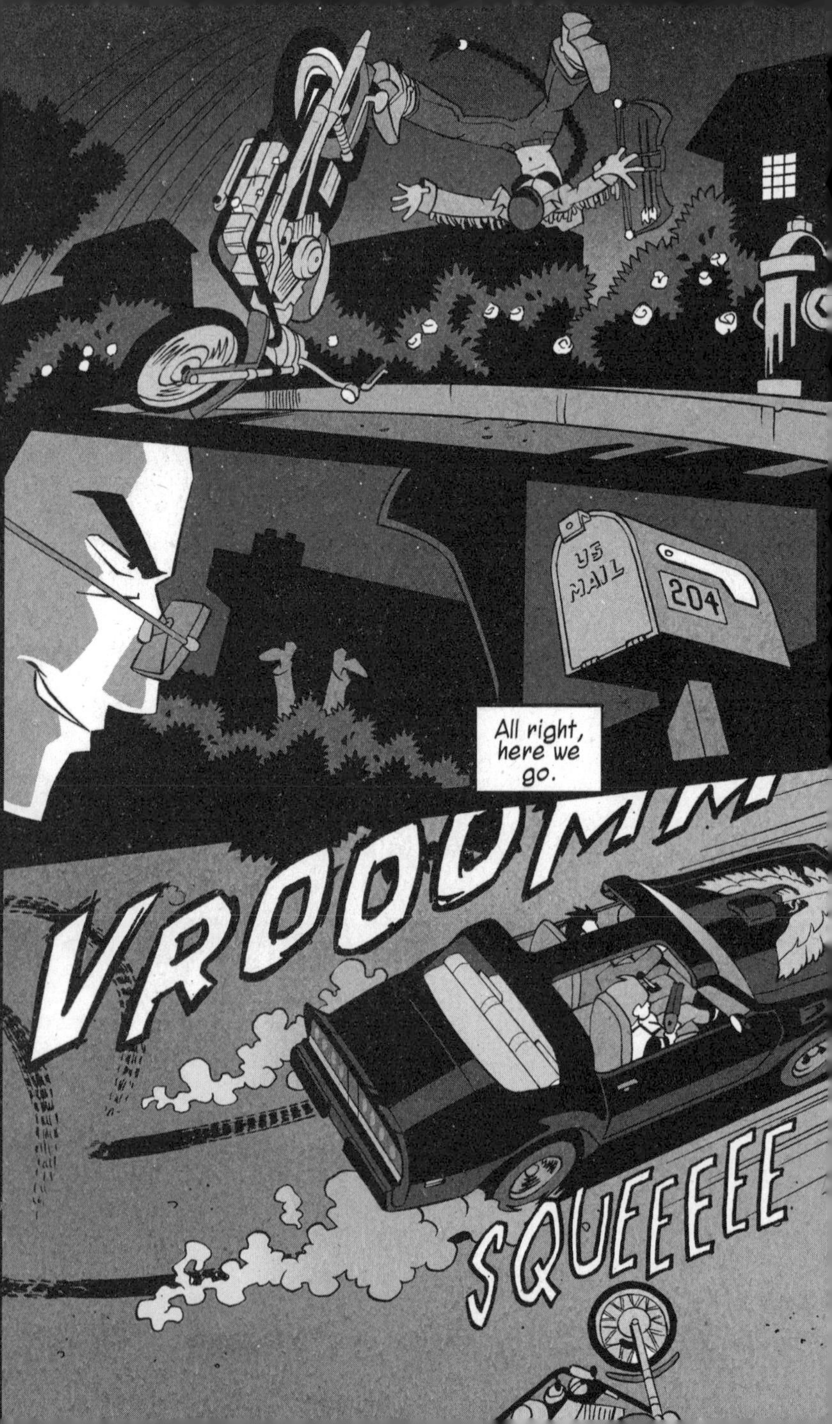
US MAIL
204
All right, here we go.
VROOOMM
SQUEEEEE

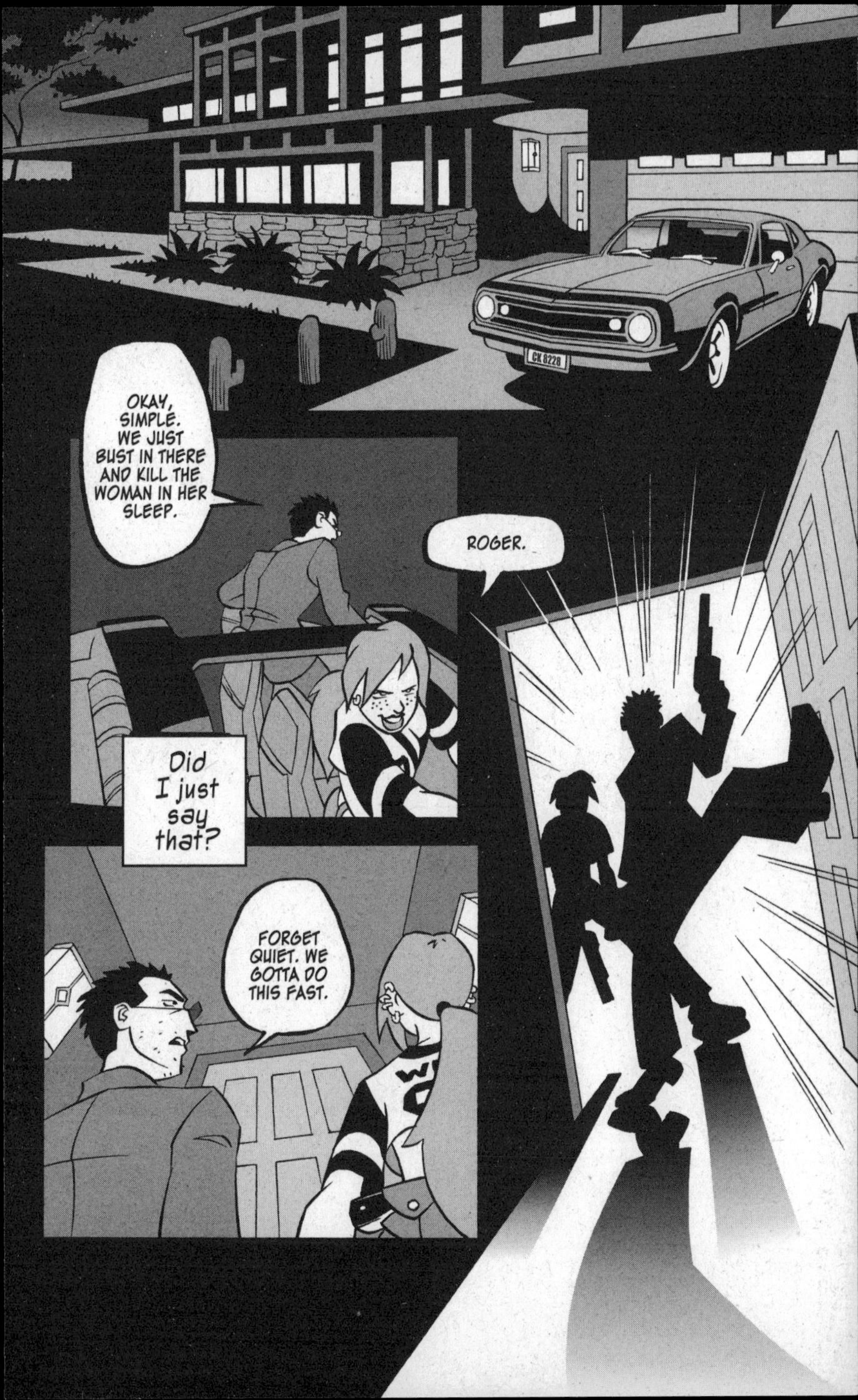
CK 8228
OKAY, SIMPLE. WE JUST BUST IN THERE AND KILL THE WOMAN IN HER SLEEP.
ROGER.
Did I just say that?
FORGET QUIET. WE GOTTA DO THIS FAST.

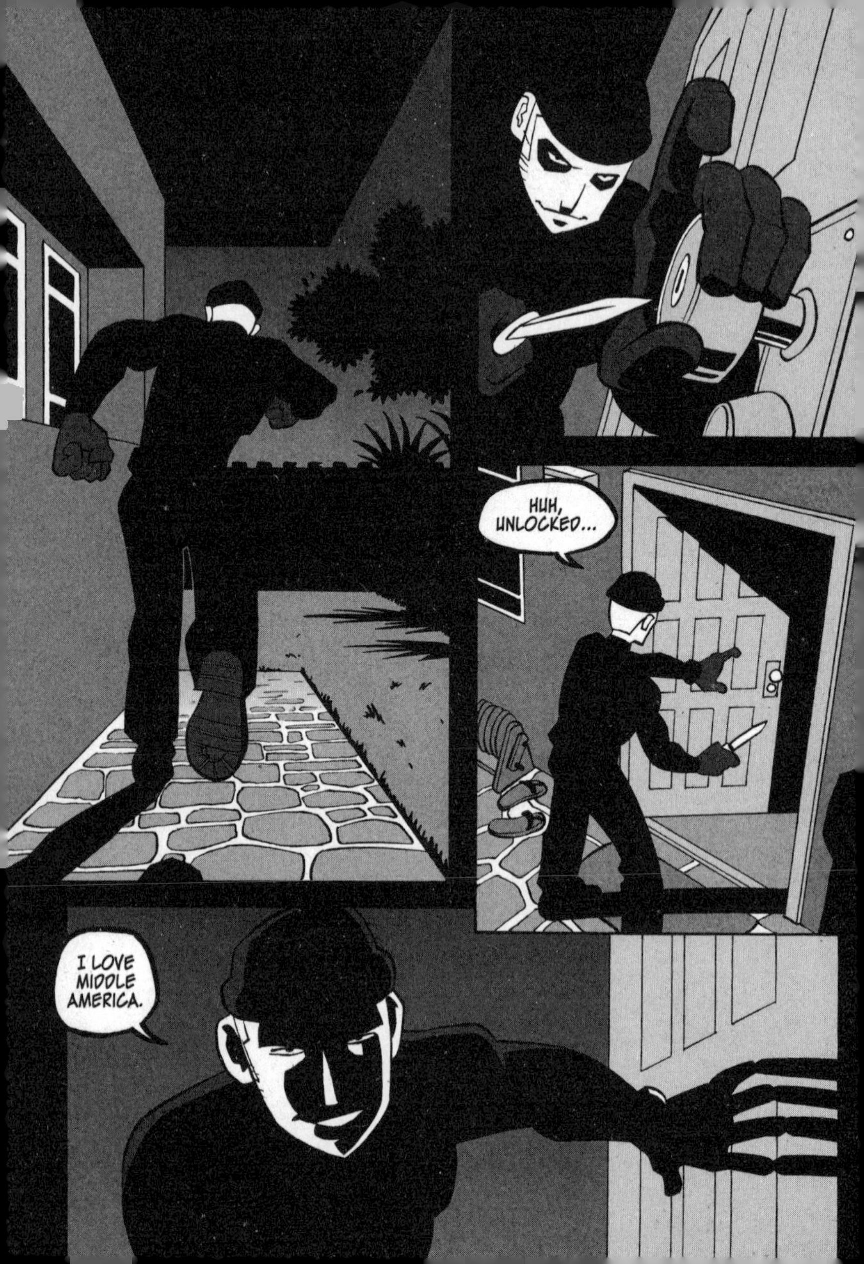
HUH, UNLOCKED...
I LOVE MIDDLE AMERICA.

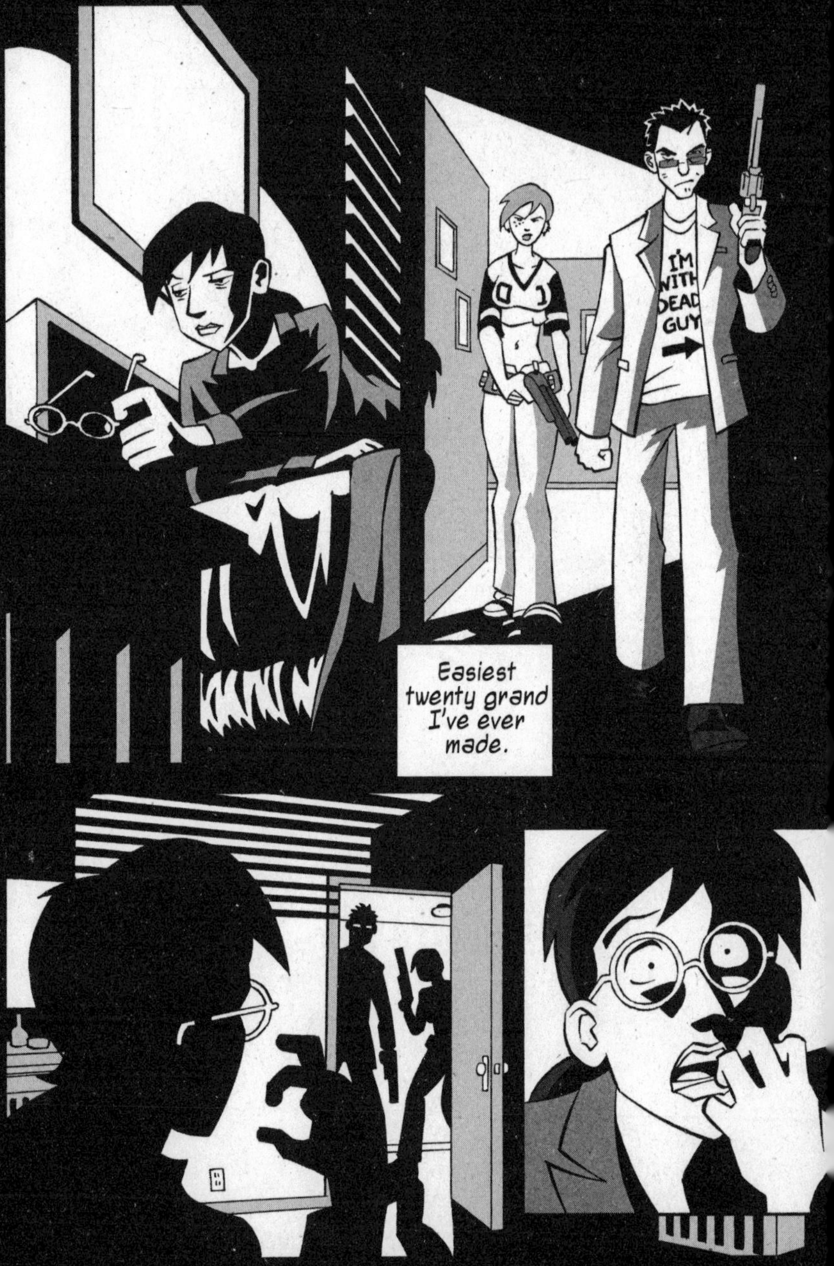
I'M WITH DEAD GUY
Easiest twenty grand I've ever made.

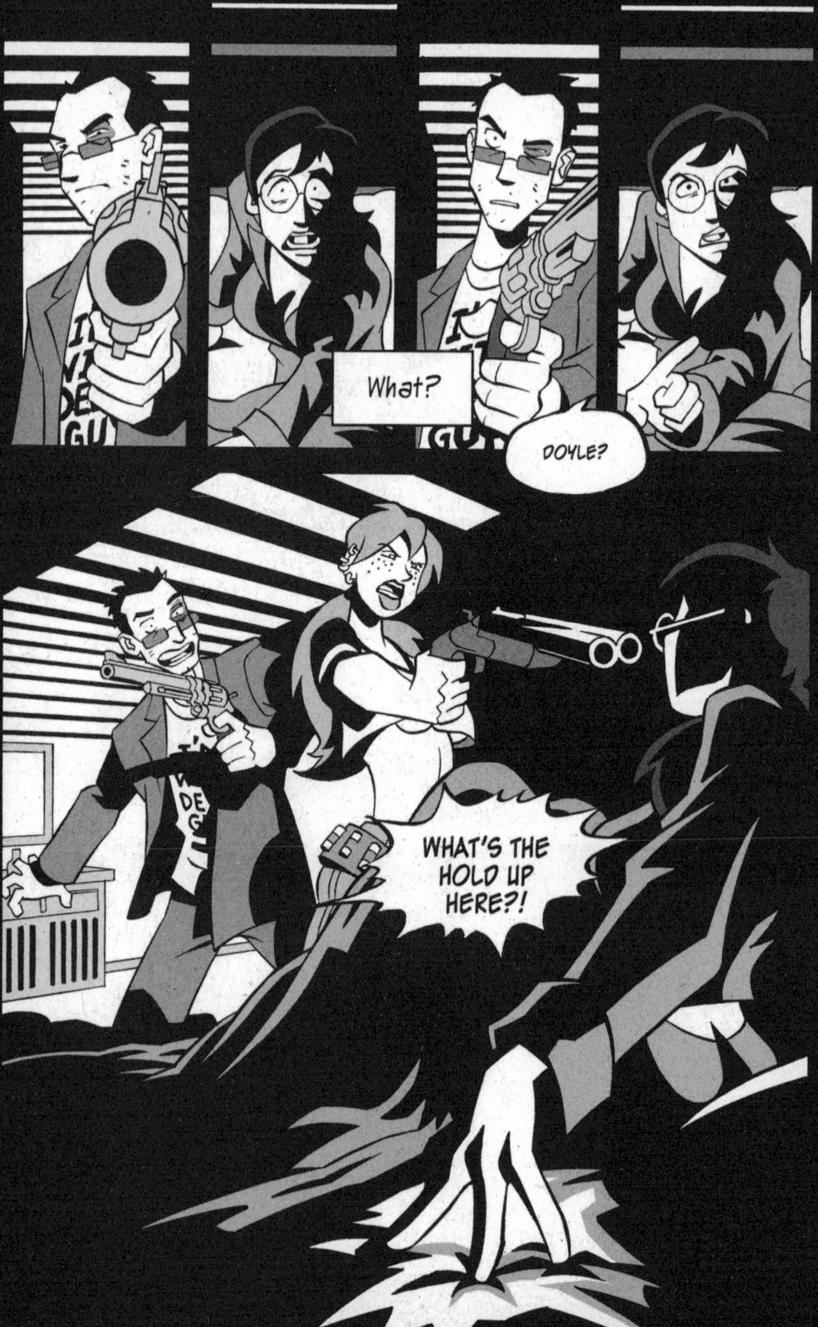
What?
DOYLE?
WHAT'S THE HOLD UP HERE?!

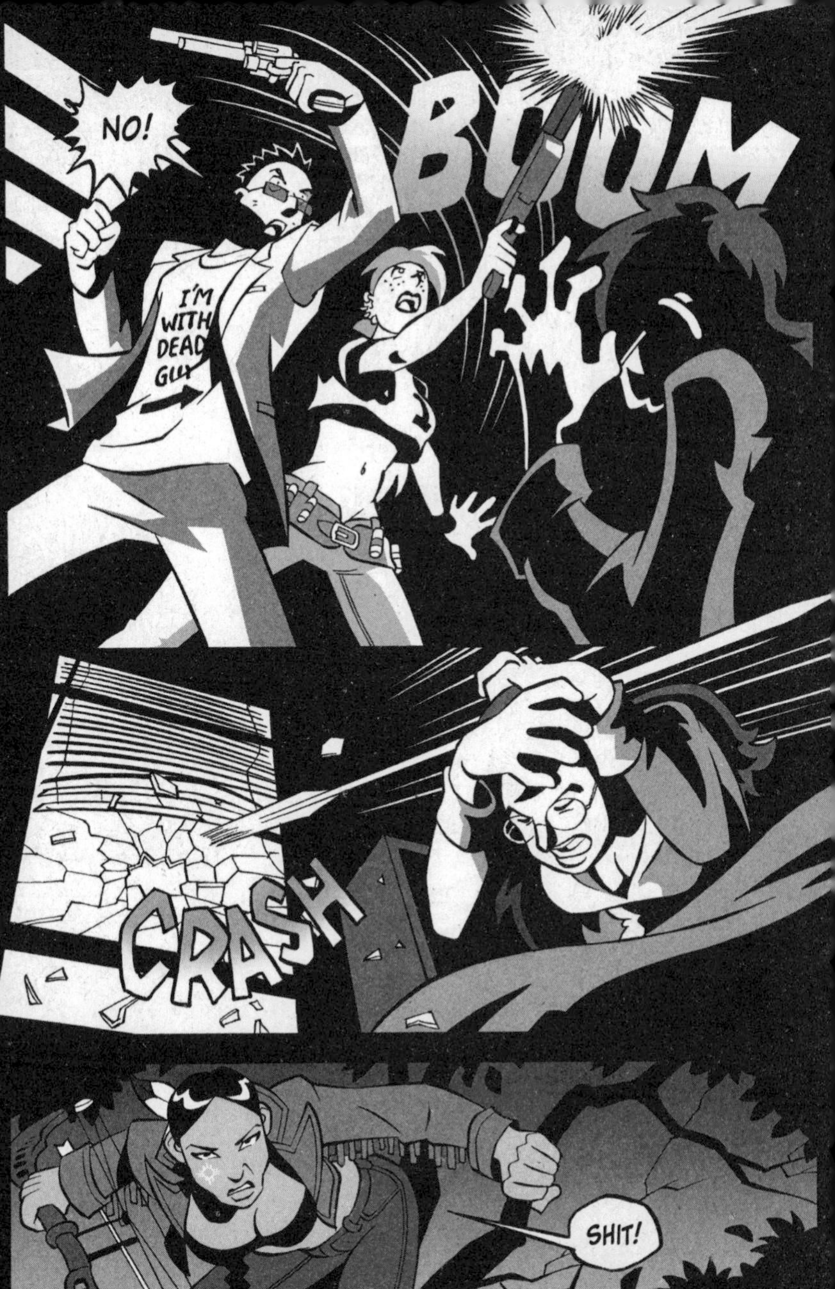
NO!
I'M WITH DEAD GUY
BOOM
CRASH
SHIT!

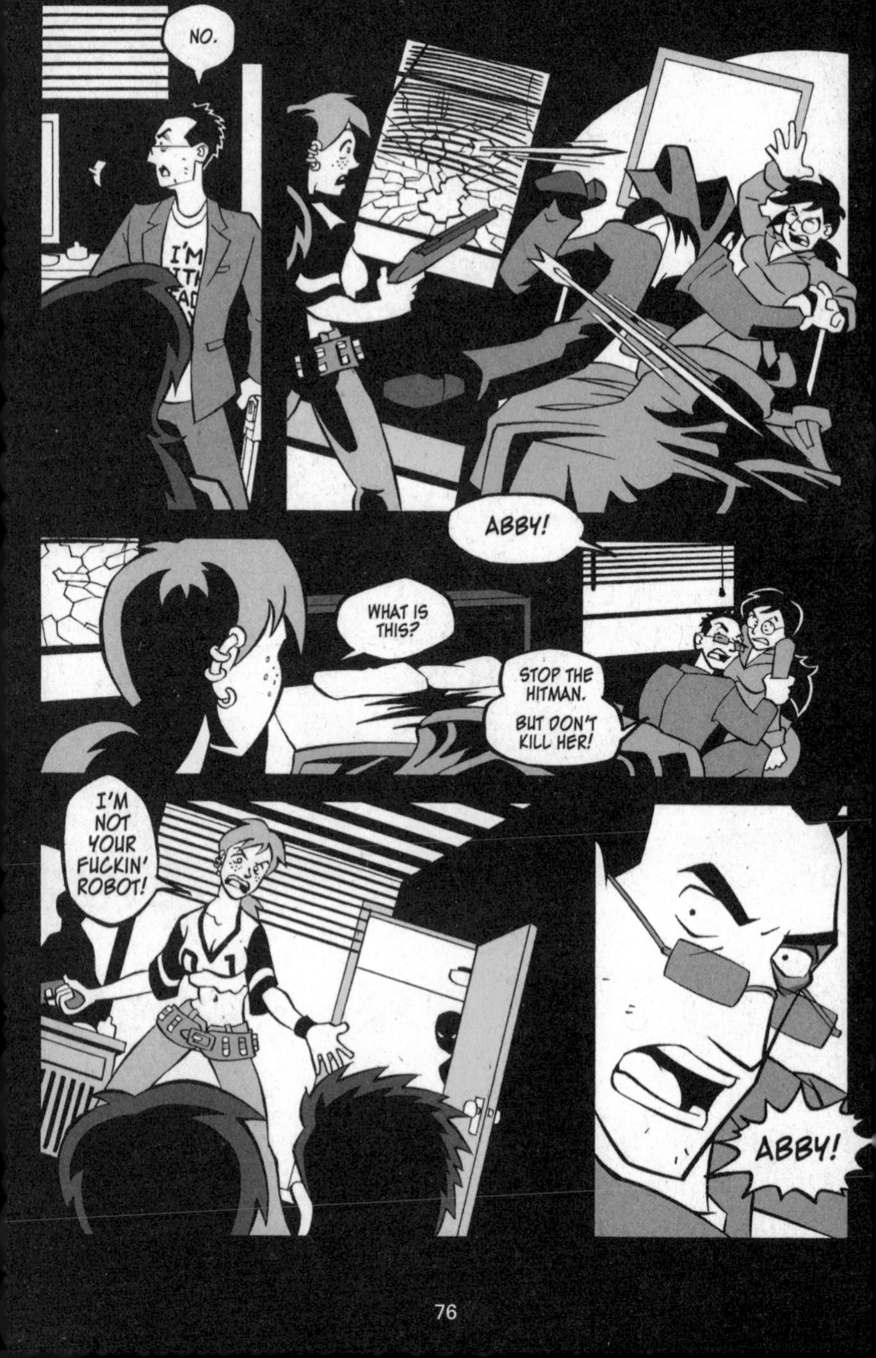
NO.
ABBY!
WHAT IS THIS?
STOP THE HITMAN. BUT DON'T KILL HER!
I'M NOT YOUR FUCKIN' ROBOT!
ABBY!

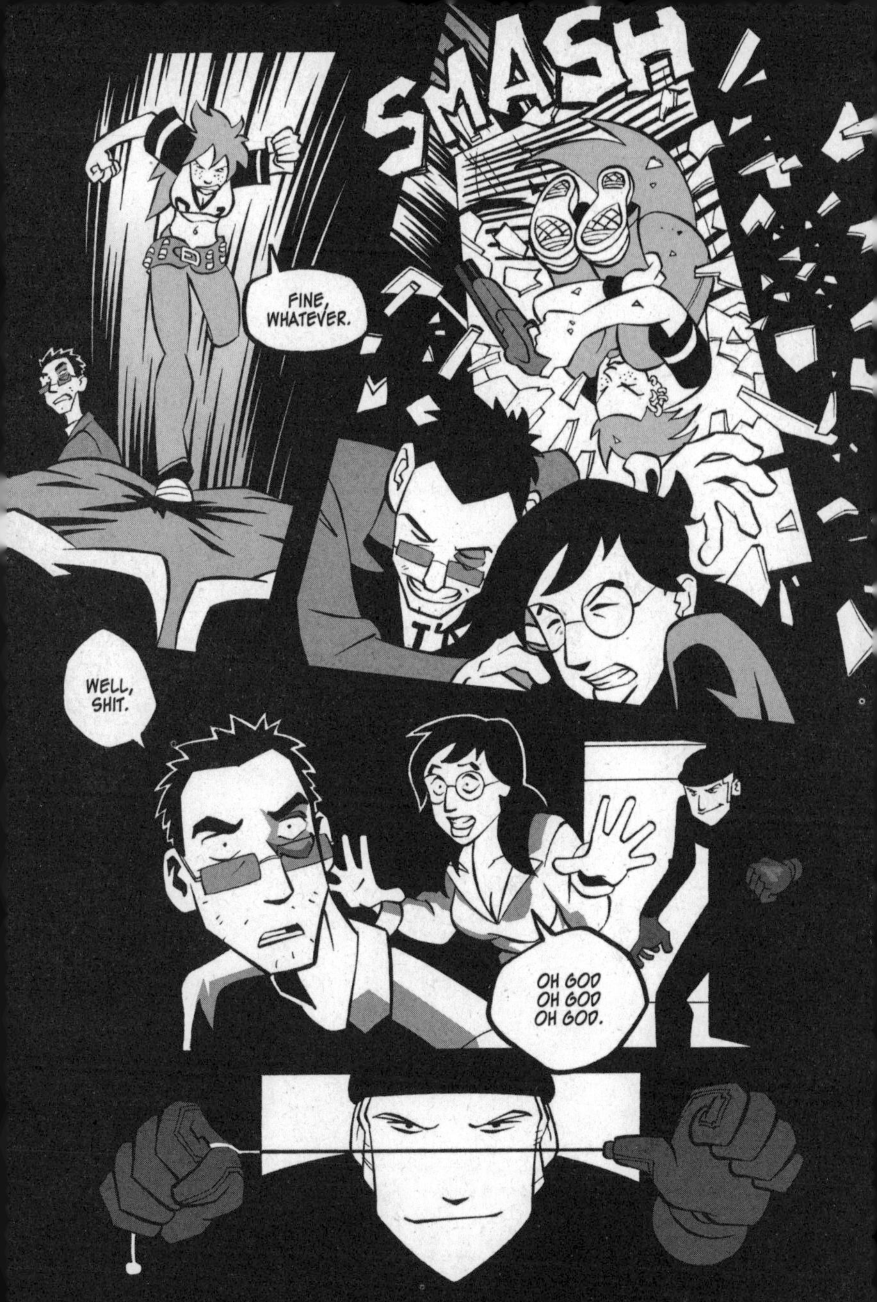
FINE, WHATEVER.
SMASH
WELL, SHIT.
OH GOD OH GOD OH GOD.

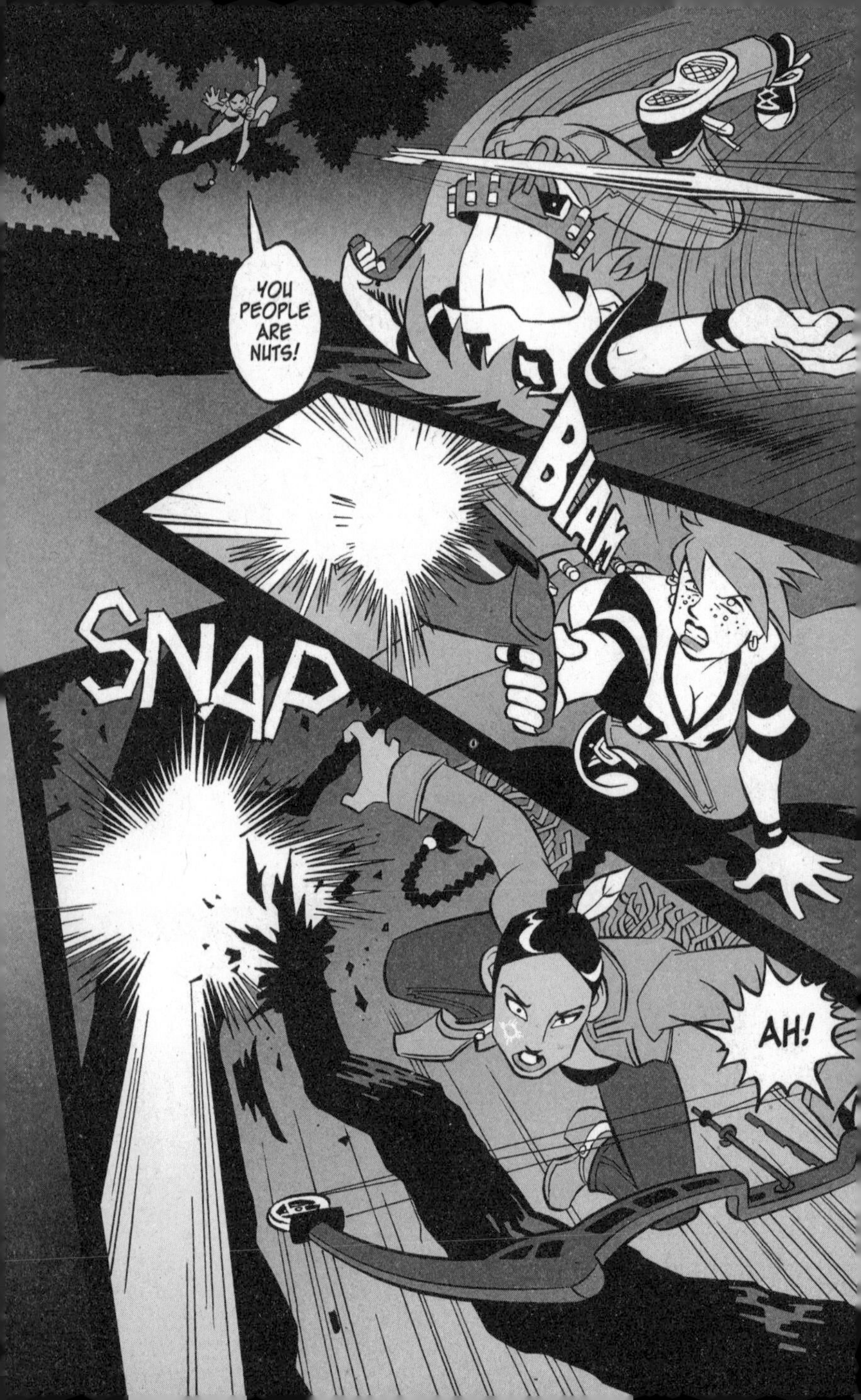
YOU PEOPLE ARE NUTS!
BLAM
SNAP
AH!

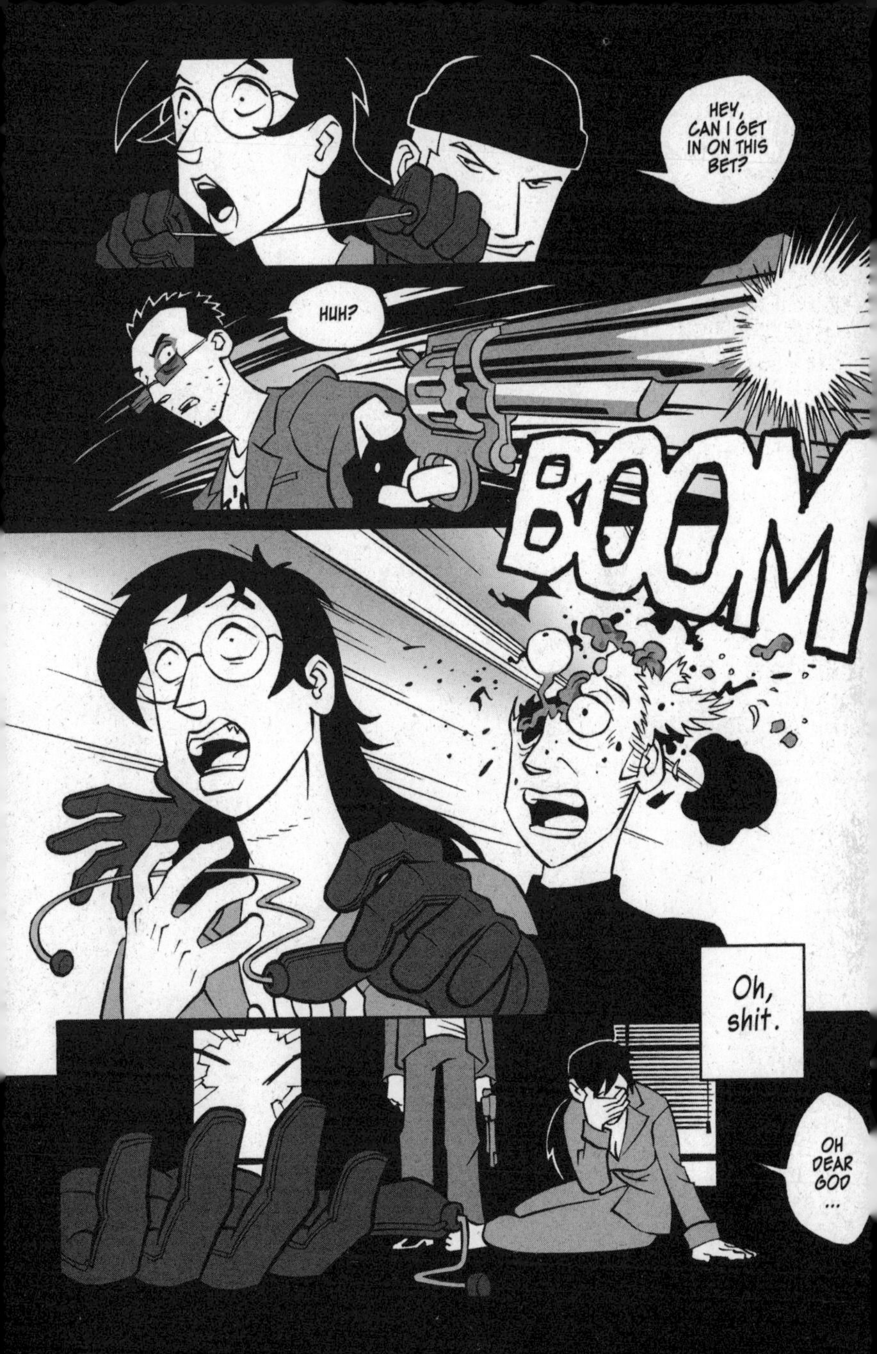
HEY, CAN I GET IN ON THIS BET?
HUH?
BOOM
Oh, shit.
OH DEAR GOD ...

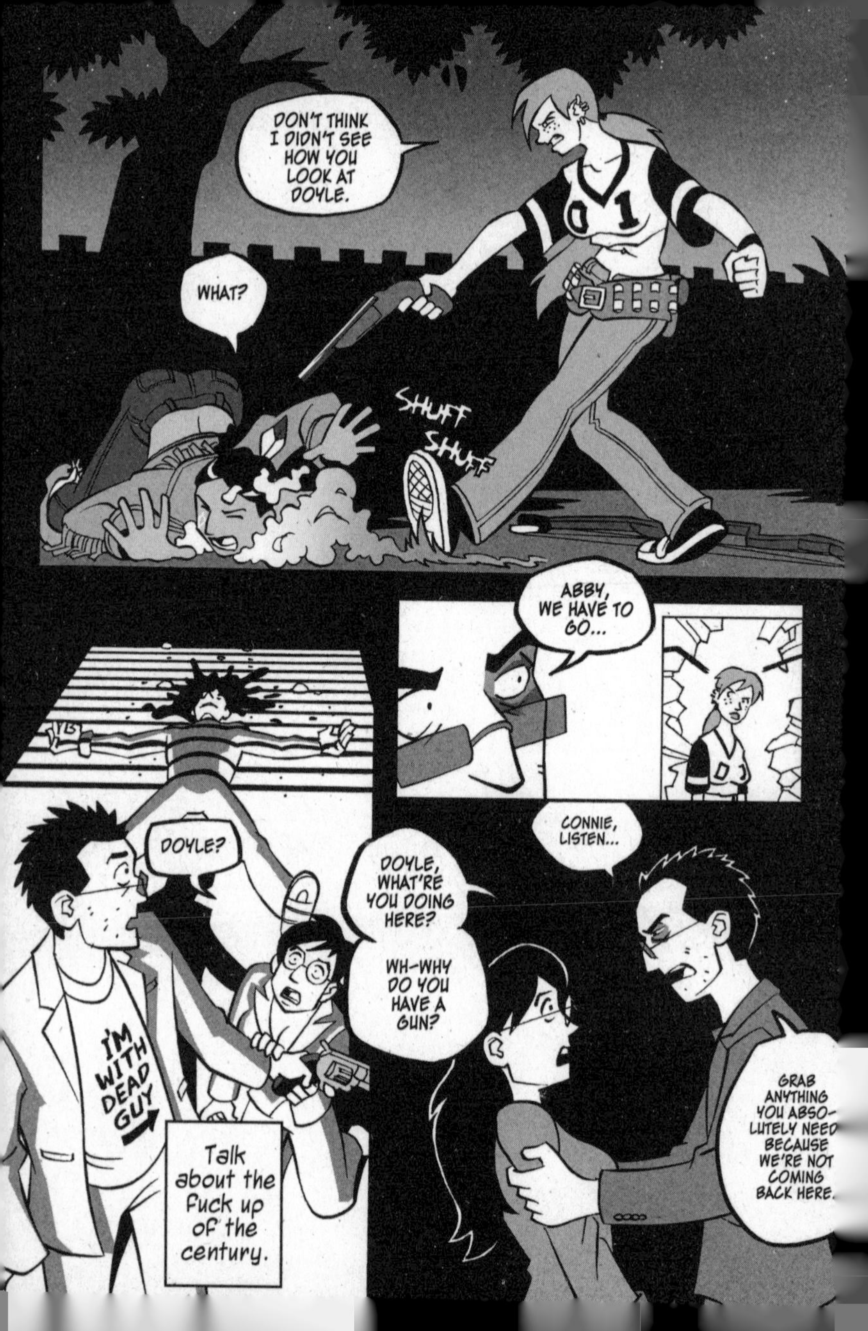
DON'T THINK I DIDN'T SEE HOW YOU LOOK AT DOYLE.
WHAT?
SHUFF SHUFF
ABBY, WE HAVE TO GO...
DOYLE?
I'M WITH DEAD GUY
Talk about the fuck up of the century.
DOYLE, WHAT'RE YOU DOING HERE?
WH-WHY DO YOU HAVE A GUN?
CONNIE, LISTEN...
GRAB ANYTHING YOU ABSOLUTELY NEED BECAUSE WE'RE NOT COMING BACK HERE.

5

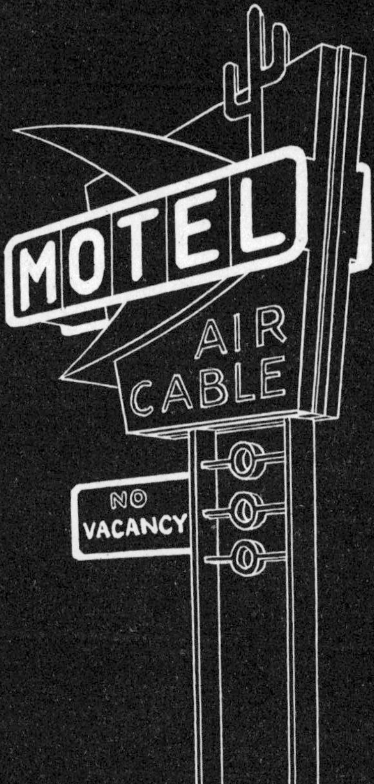
MOTEL
AIR
CABLE
NO
VACANCY

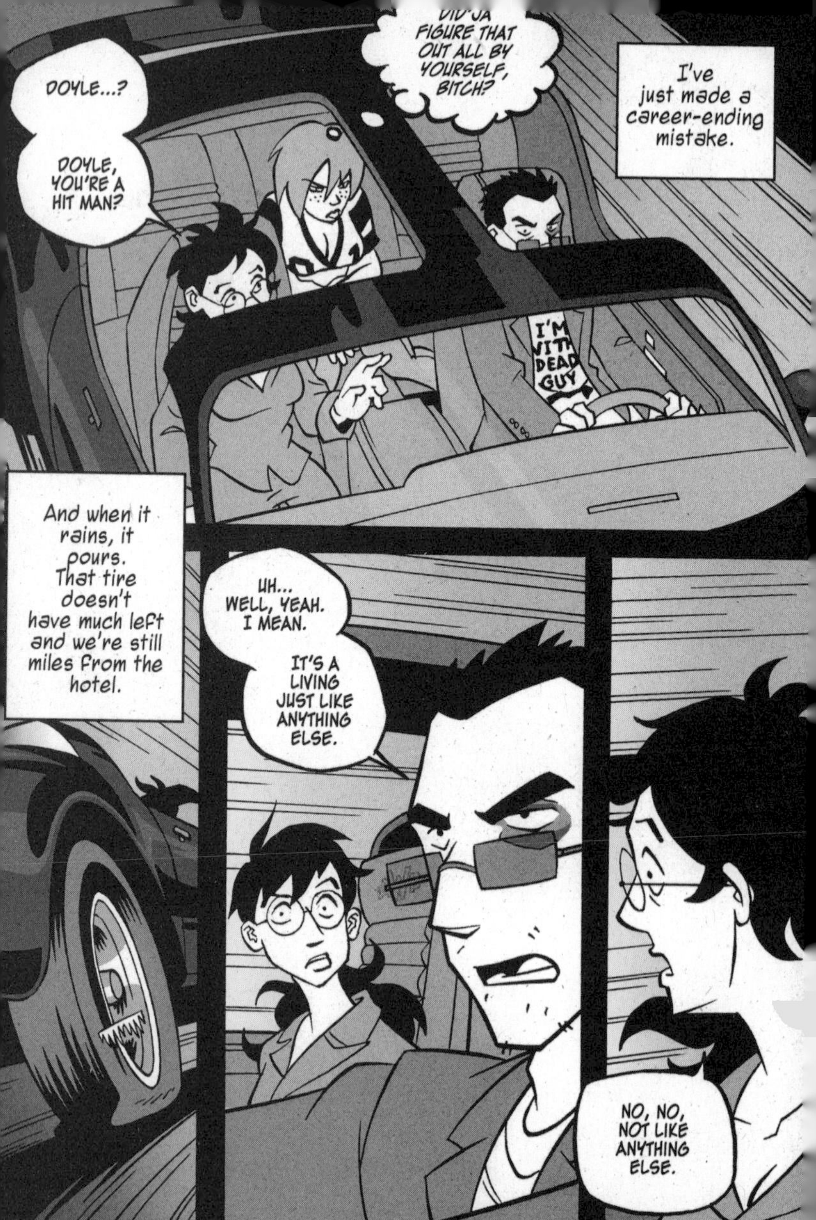
DOYLE...?
DOYLE, YOU'RE A HIT MAN?
DID'JA FIGURE THAT OUT ALL BY YOURSELF, BITCH?
I've just made a career-ending mistake.
I'M WITH DEAD GUY
And when it rains, it pours. That tire doesn't have much left and we're still miles from the hotel.
UH... WELL, YEAH. I MEAN.
IT'S A LIVING JUST LIKE ANYTHING ELSE.
NO, NO, NOT LIKE ANYTHING ELSE.

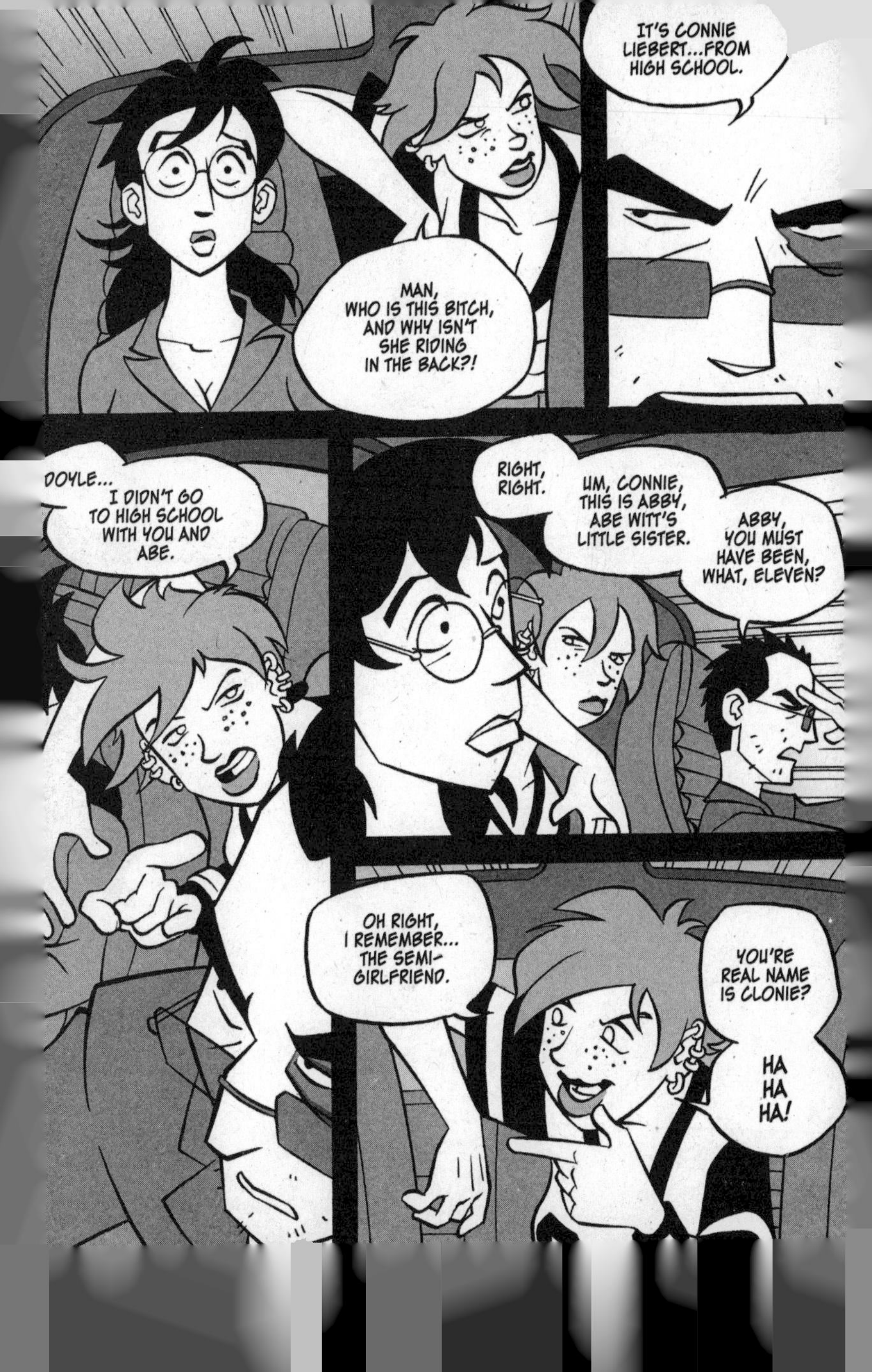
MAN, WHO IS THIS BITCH, AND WHY ISN'T SHE RIDING IN THE BACK?!
IT'S CONNIE LIEBERT...FROM HIGH SCHOOL.
DOYLE... I DIDN'T GO TO HIGH SCHOOL WITH YOU AND ABE.
RIGHT, RIGHT.
UM, CONNIE, THIS IS ABBY, ABE WITT'S LITTLE SISTER.
ABBY, YOU MUST HAVE BEEN, WHAT, ELEVEN?
OH RIGHT, I REMEMBER... THE SEMI-GIRLFRIEND.
YOU'RE REAL NAME IS CLONIE?
HA HA HA!

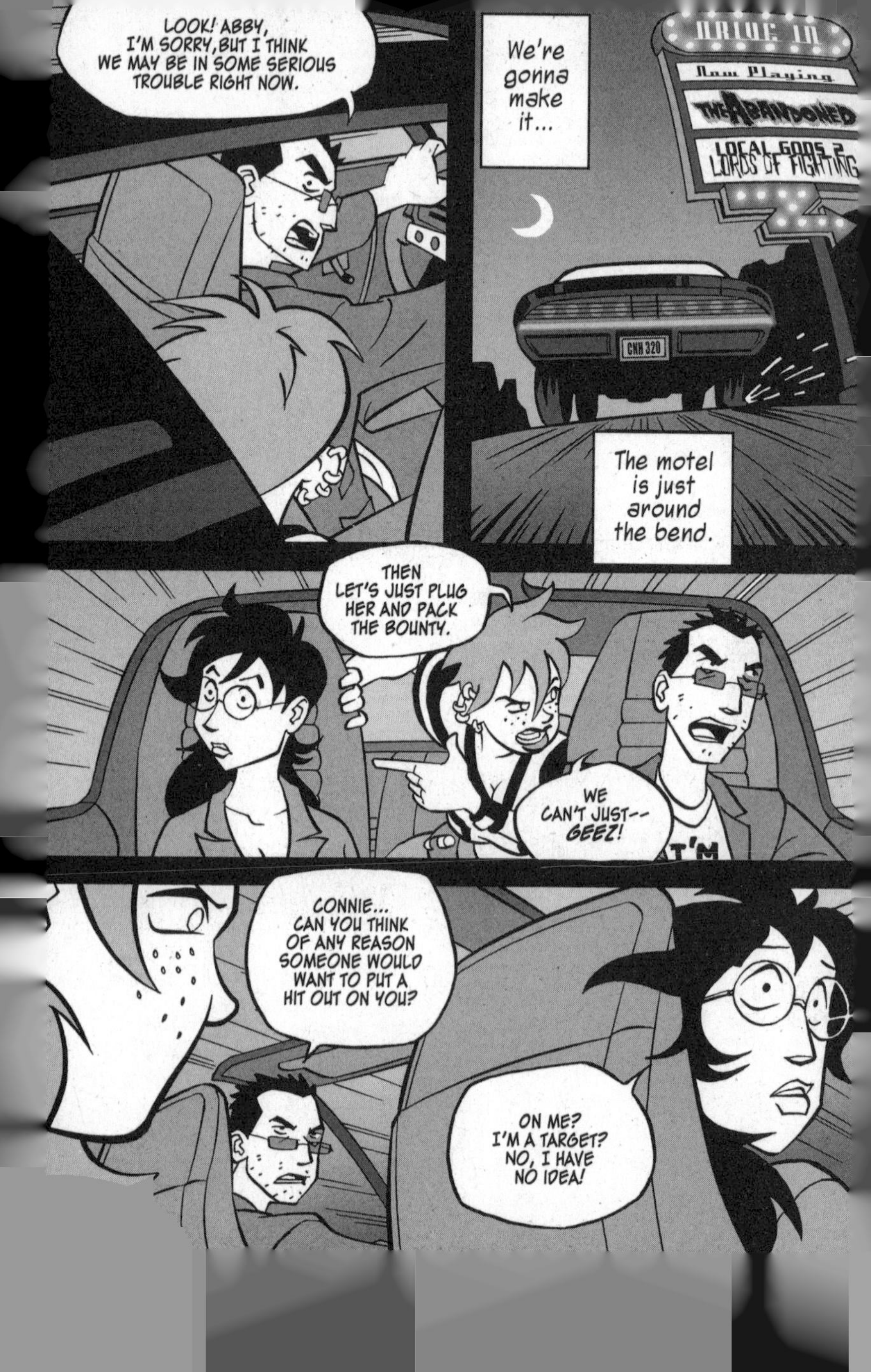
LOOK! ABBY, I'M SORRY, BUT I THINK WE MAY BE IN SOME SERIOUS TROUBLE RIGHT NOW.
We're gonna make it...
DRIVE IN
Now Playing
THE ABANDONED
LOCAL GODS 2
LORDS OF FIGHTING
CNH 320
The motel is just around the bend.
THEN LET'S JUST PLUG HER AND PACK THE BOUNTY.
WE CAN'T JUST-- GEEZ!
CONNIE... CAN YOU THINK OF ANY REASON SOMEONE WOULD WANT TO PUT A HIT OUT ON YOU?
ON ME? I'M A TARGET? NO, I HAVE NO IDEA!

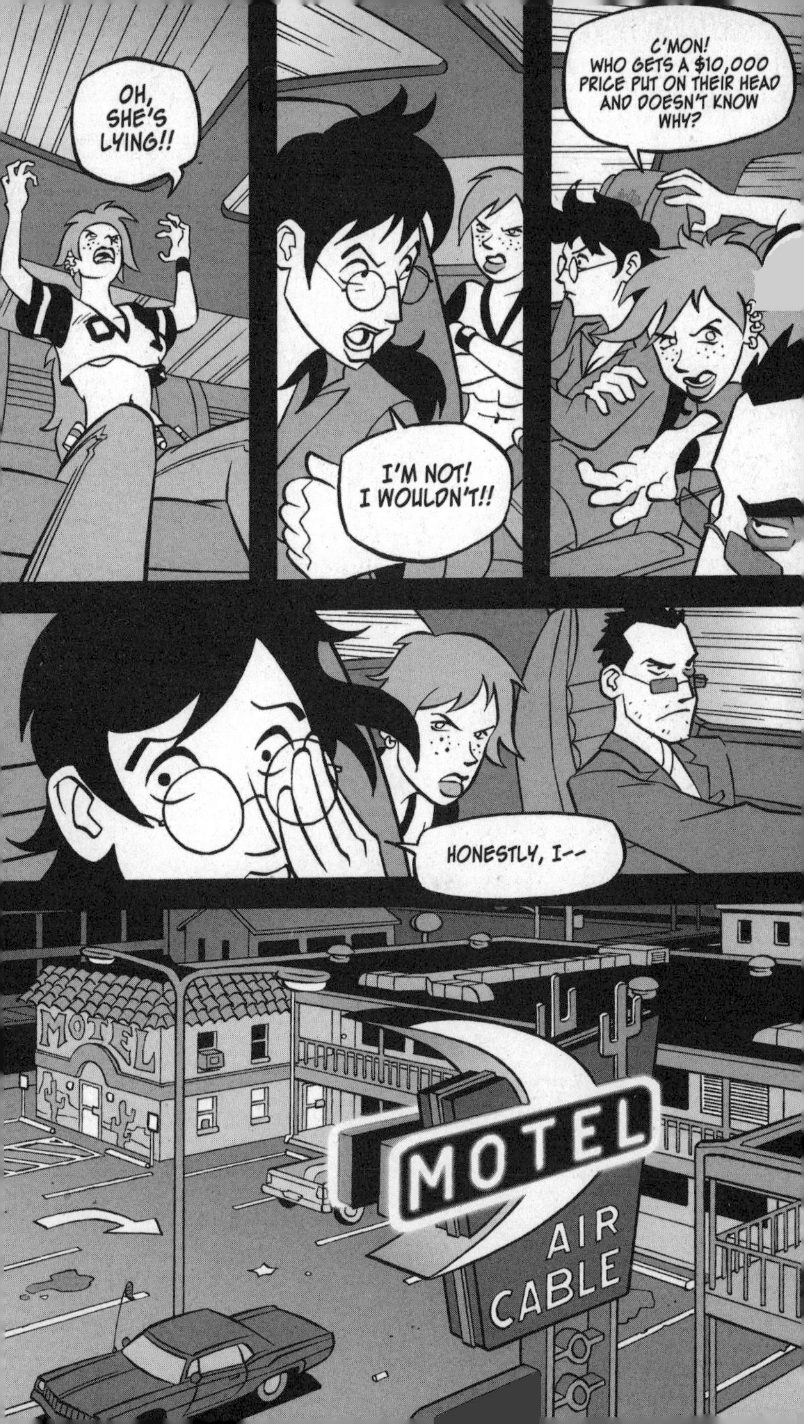
OH, SHE'S LYING!!
I'M NOT! I WOULDN'T!!
C'MON! WHO GETS A $10,000 PRICE PUT ON THEIR HEAD AND DOESN'T KNOW WHY?
HONESTLY, I--
MOTEL
MOTEL
AIR
CABLE

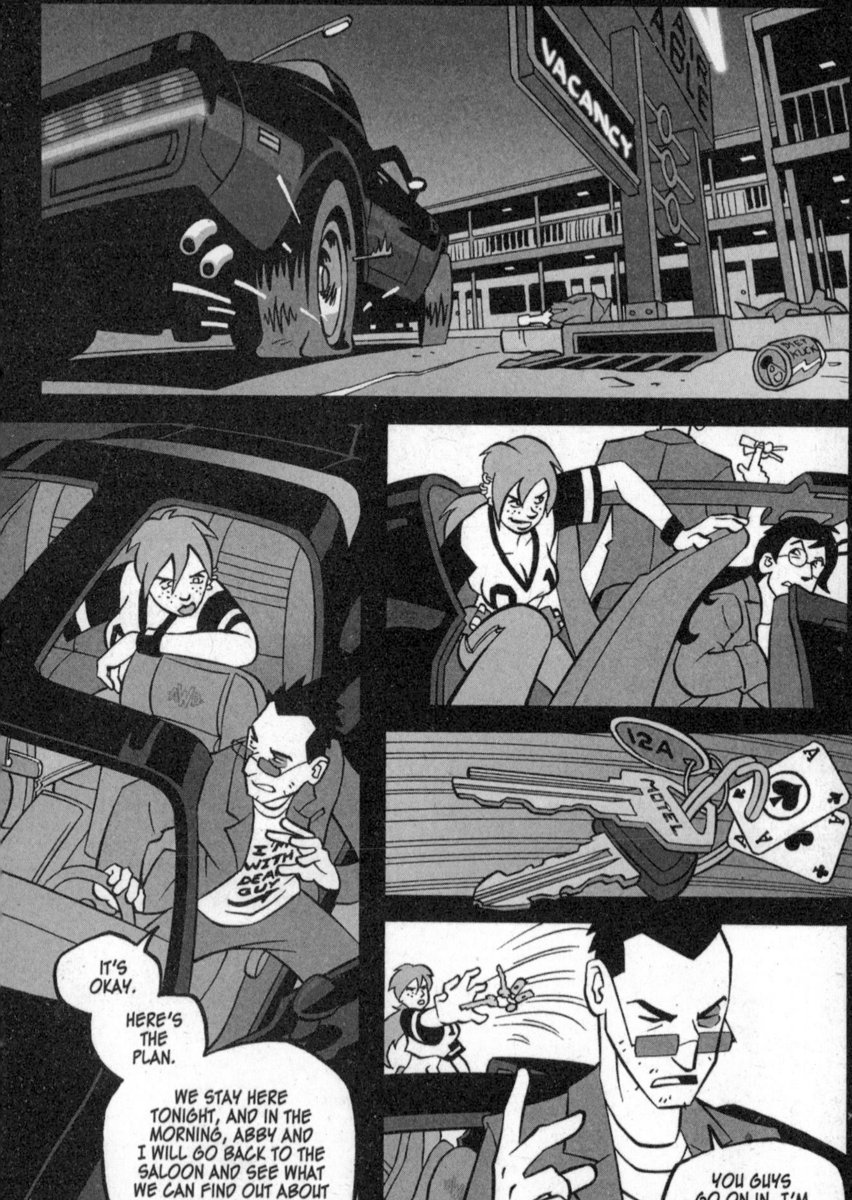
VACANCY
I'M WITH DEAD GUY
12A
MOTEL
IT'S OKAY.
HERE'S THE PLAN.
WE STAY HERE TONIGHT, AND IN THE MORNING, ABBY AND I WILL GO BACK TO THE SALOON AND SEE WHAT WE CAN FIND OUT ABOUT THE HIT ON YOU.
YOU GUYS GO ON IN. I'M GONNA FIX THIS TIRE.

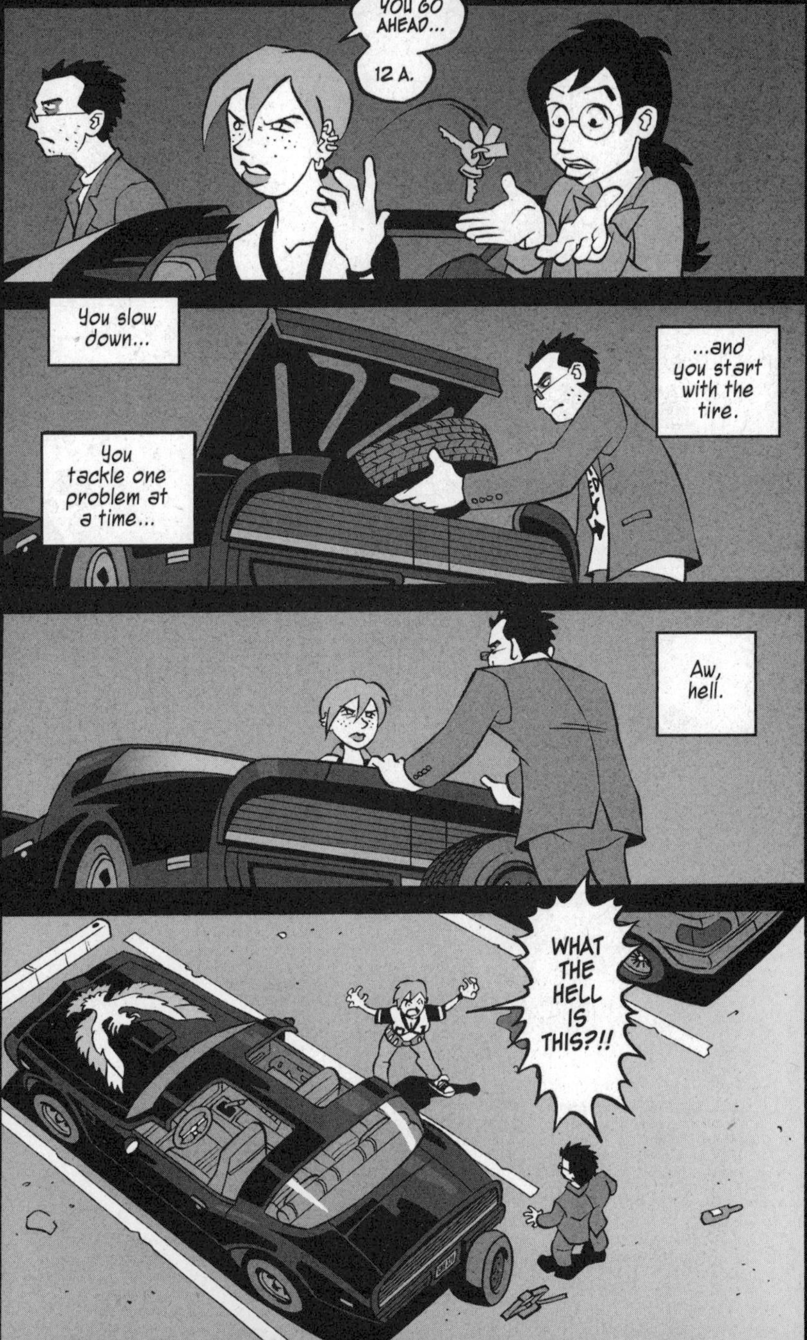
YOU GO AHEAD...
12 A.
You slow down...
You tackle one problem at a time...
...and you start with the tire.
Aw, hell.
WHAT THE HELL IS THIS?!!

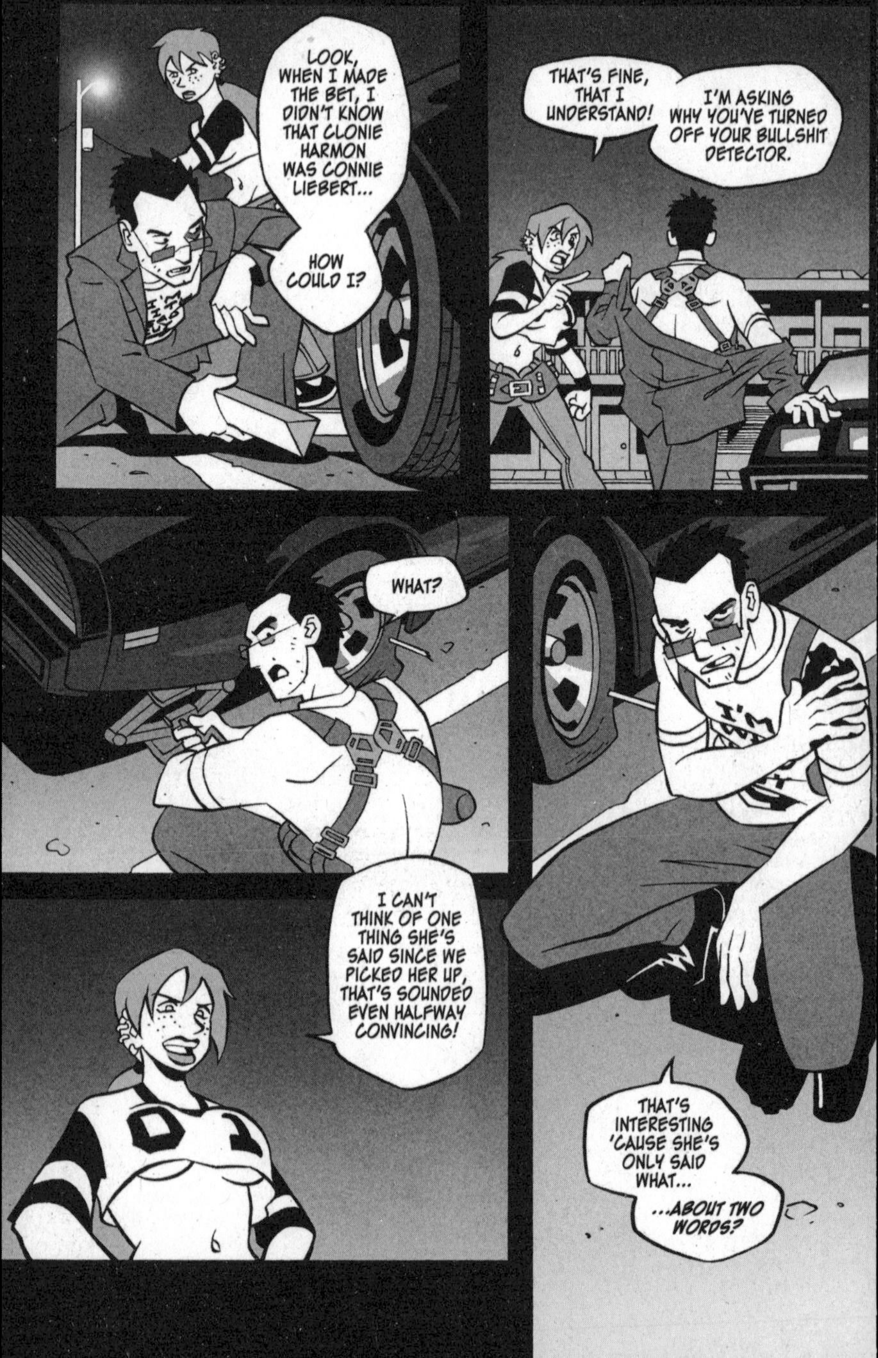
LOOK, WHEN I MADE THE BET, I DIDN'T KNOW THAT CLONIE HARMON WAS CONNIE LIEBERT...
HOW COULD I?
THAT'S FINE, THAT I UNDERSTAND!
I'M ASKING WHY YOU'VE TURNED OFF YOUR BULLSHIT DETECTOR.
WHAT?
I CAN'T THINK OF ONE THING SHE'S SAID SINCE WE PICKED HER UP, THAT'S SOUNDED EVEN HALFWAY CONVINCING!
THAT'S INTERESTING 'CAUSE SHE'S ONLY SAID WHAT...
...ABOUT TWO WORDS?

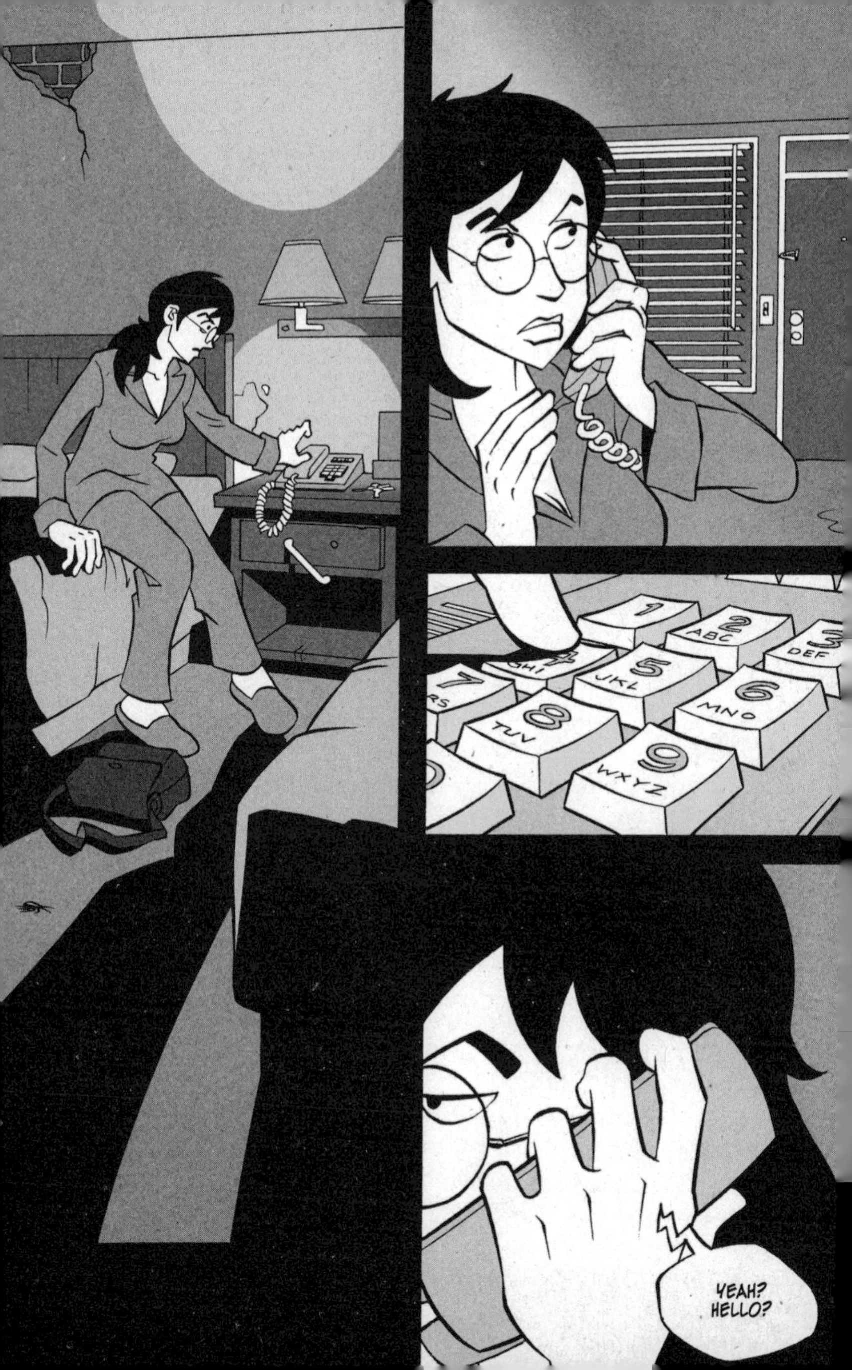
YEAH?
HELLO?

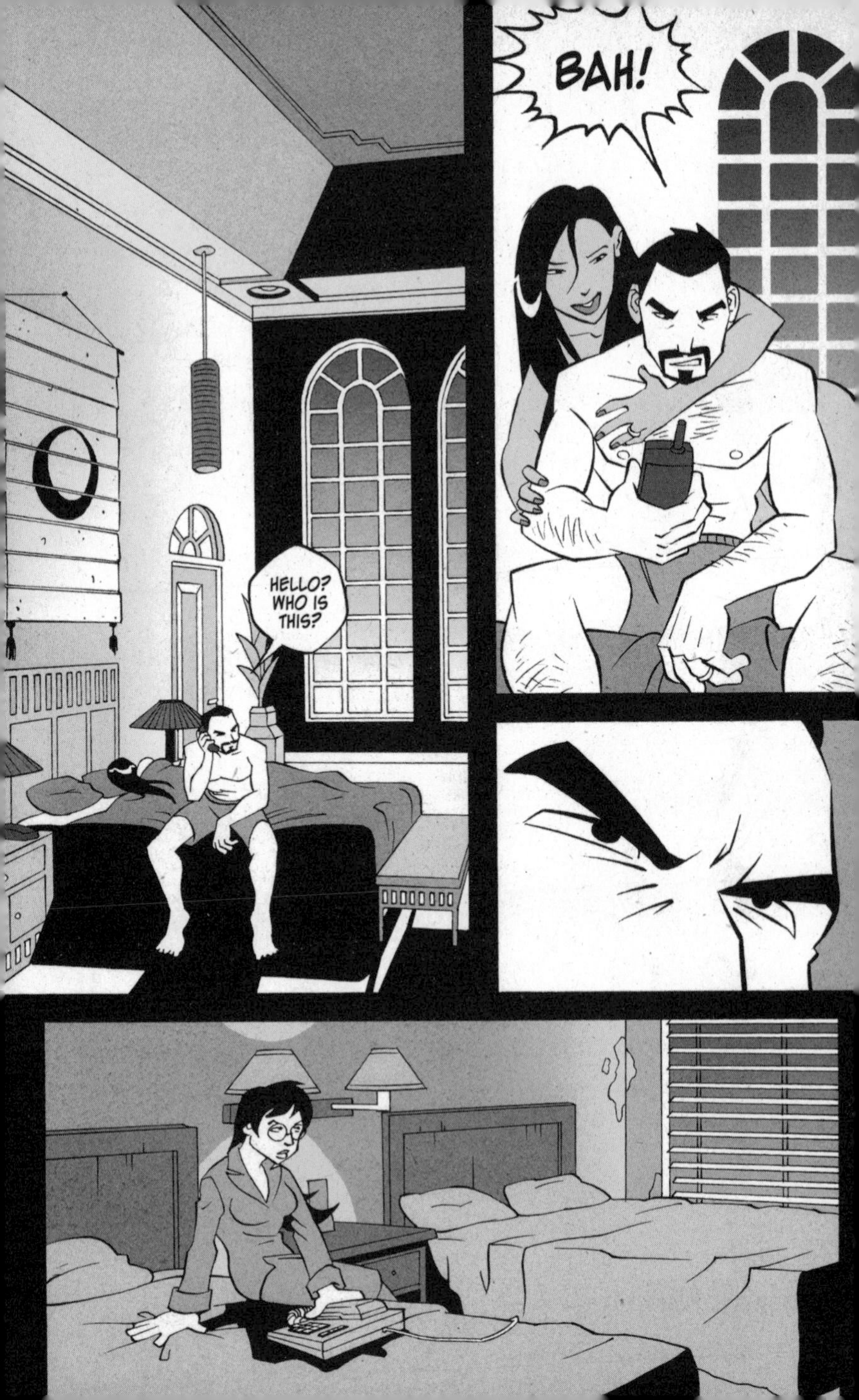
HELLO? WHO IS THIS?
BAH!

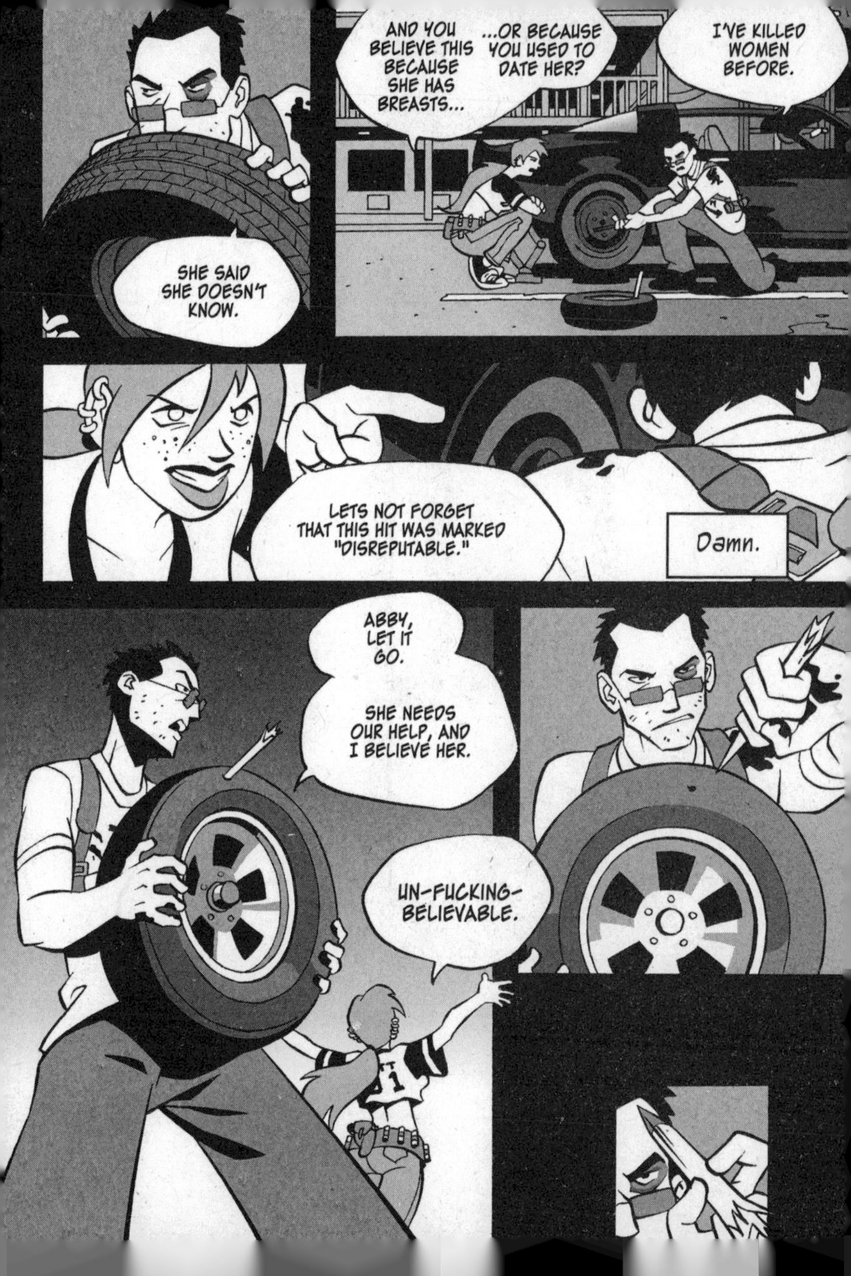
SHE SAID SHE DOESN'T KNOW.
AND YOU BELIEVE THIS BECAUSE SHE HAS BREASTS...
...OR BECAUSE YOU USED TO DATE HER?
I'VE KILLED WOMEN BEFORE.
LETS NOT FORGET THAT THIS HIT WAS MARKED "DISREPUTABLE."
Damn.
ABBY, LET IT GO.
SHE NEEDS OUR HELP, AND I BELIEVE HER.
UN-FUCKING-BELIEVABLE.

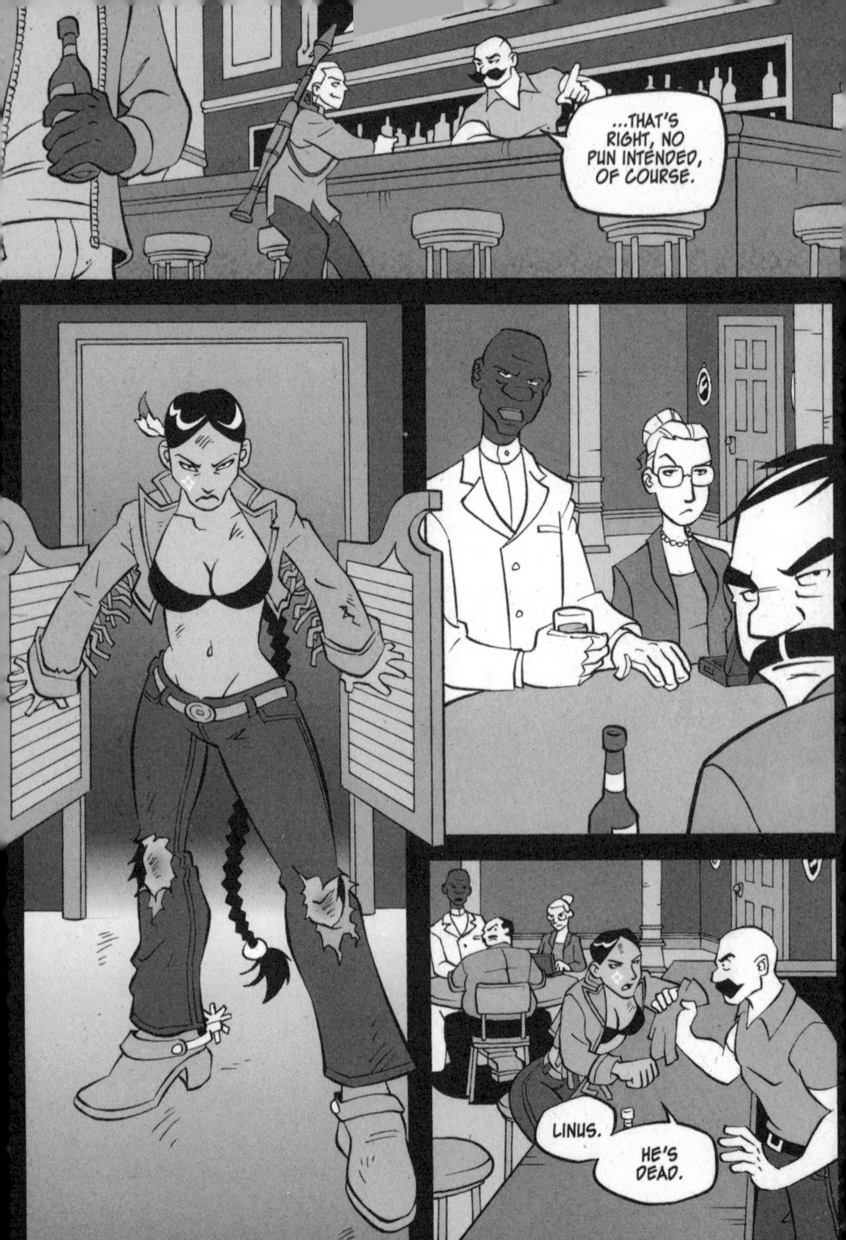
...THAT'S RIGHT, NO PUN INTENDED, OF COURSE.
LINUS.
HE'S DEAD.

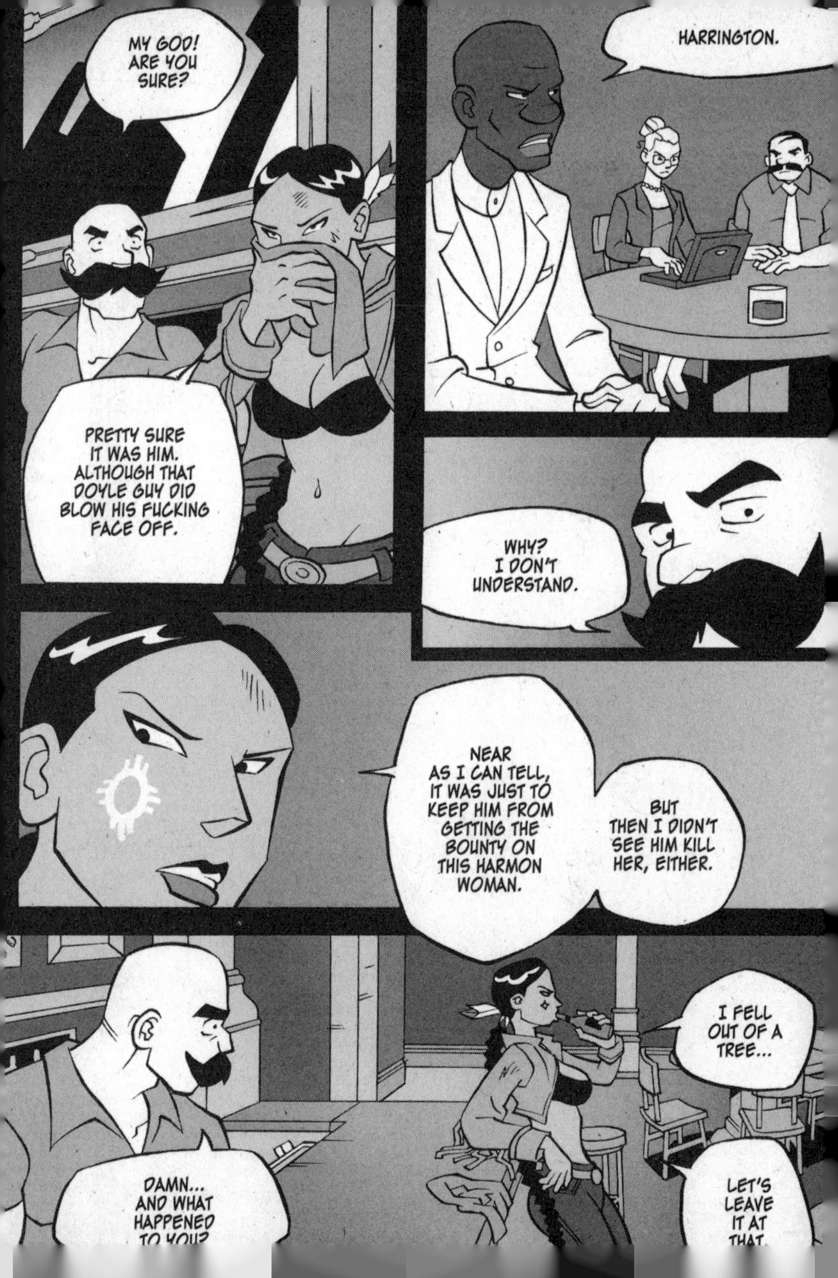
MY GOD! ARE YOU SURE?
PRETTY SURE IT WAS HIM. ALTHOUGH THAT DOYLE GUY DID BLOW HIS FUCKING FACE OFF.
HARRINGTON.
WHY? I DON'T UNDERSTAND.
NEAR AS I CAN TELL, IT WAS JUST TO KEEP HIM FROM GETTING THE BOUNTY ON THIS HARMON WOMAN.
BUT THEN I DIDN'T SEE HIM KILL HER, EITHER.
DAMN... AND WHAT HAPPENED TO YOU?
I FELL OUT OF A TREE...
LET'S LEAVE IT AT THAT.

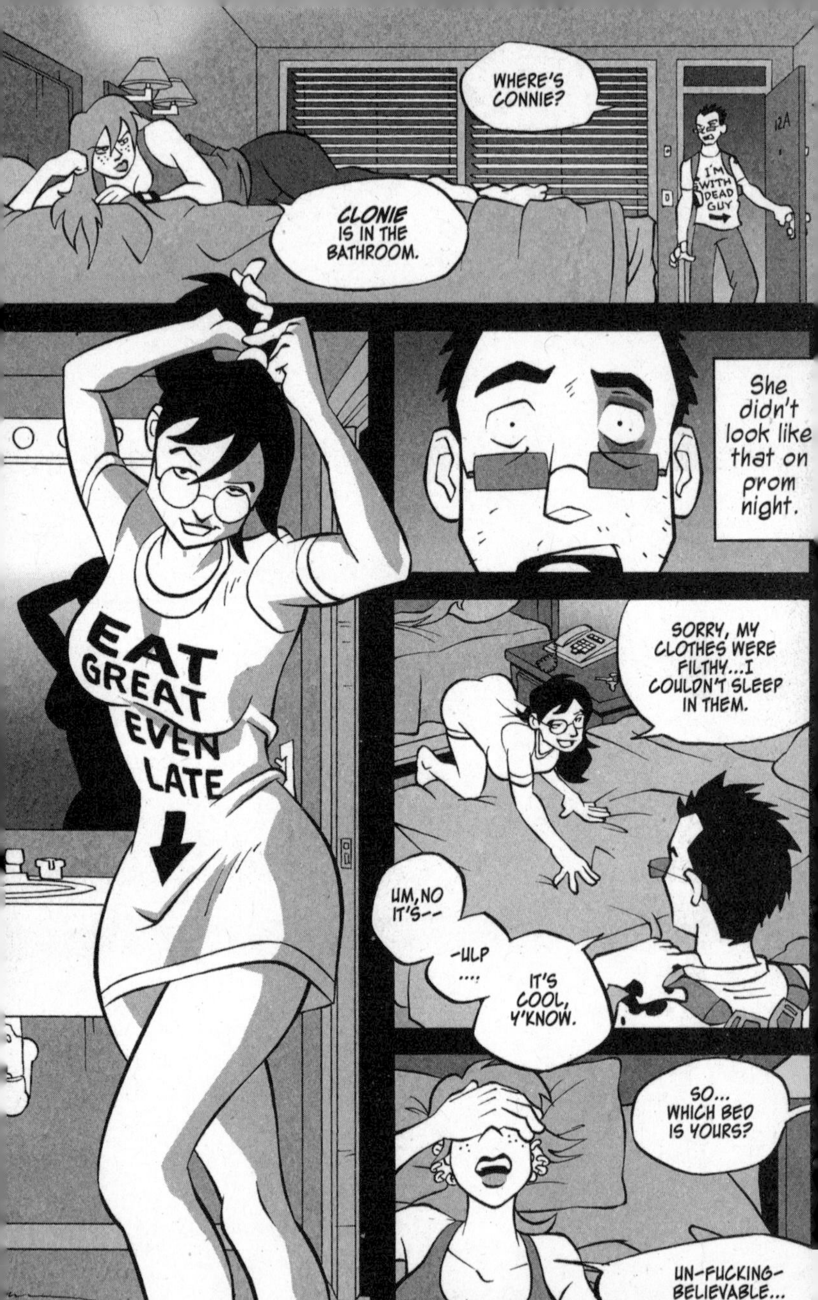
WHERE'S CONNIE?
12A
I'M WITH DEAD GUY
CLONIE IS IN THE BATHROOM.
EAT GREAT EVEN LATE
She didn't look like that on prom night.
SORRY, MY CLOTHES WERE FILTHY...I COULDN'T SLEEP IN THEM.
UM, NO IT'S--
-ULP ....
IT'S COOL, Y'KNOW.
SO... WHICH BED IS YOURS?
UN-FUCKING-BELIEVABLE...

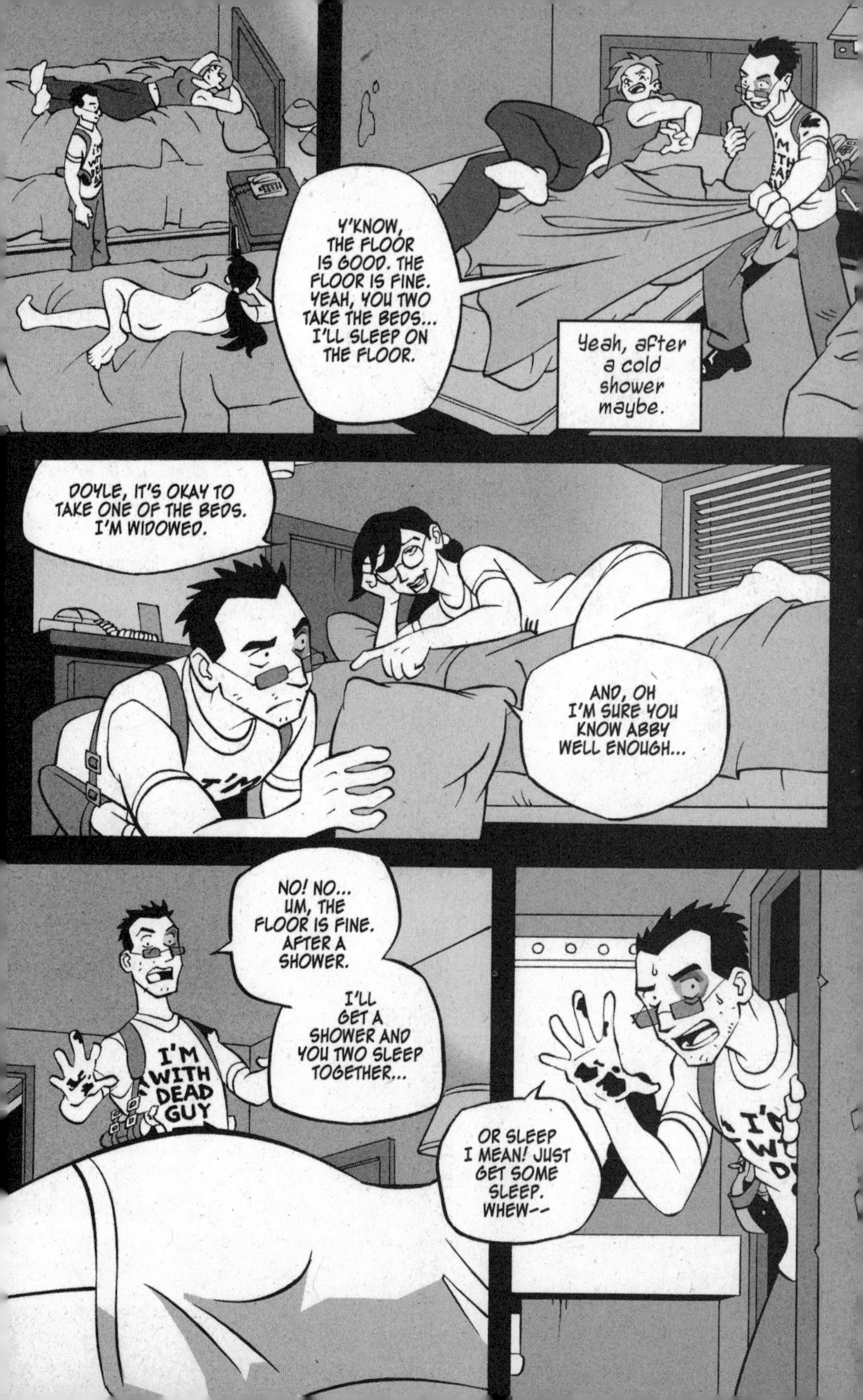
Y'KNOW, THE FLOOR IS GOOD. THE FLOOR IS FINE. YEAH, YOU TWO TAKE THE BEDS... I'LL SLEEP ON THE FLOOR.
Yeah, after a cold shower maybe.
DOYLE, IT'S OKAY TO TAKE ONE OF THE BEDS. I'M WIDOWED.
AND, OH I'M SURE YOU KNOW ABBY WELL ENOUGH...
NO! NO... UM, THE FLOOR IS FINE. AFTER A SHOWER.
I'LL GET A SHOWER AND YOU TWO SLEEP TOGETHER...
I'M WITH DEAD GUY
OR SLEEP I MEAN! JUST GET SOME SLEEP. WHEW--

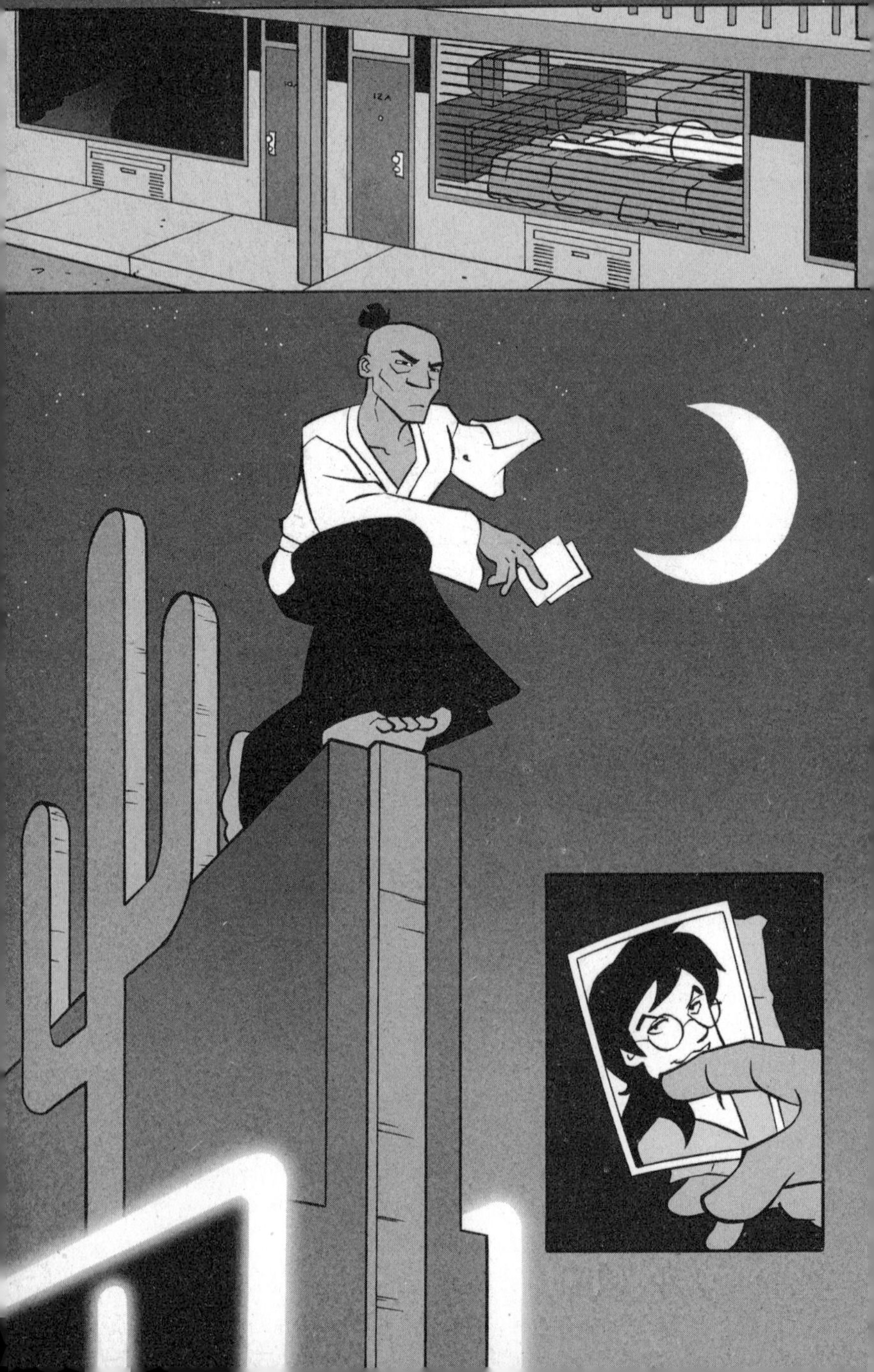

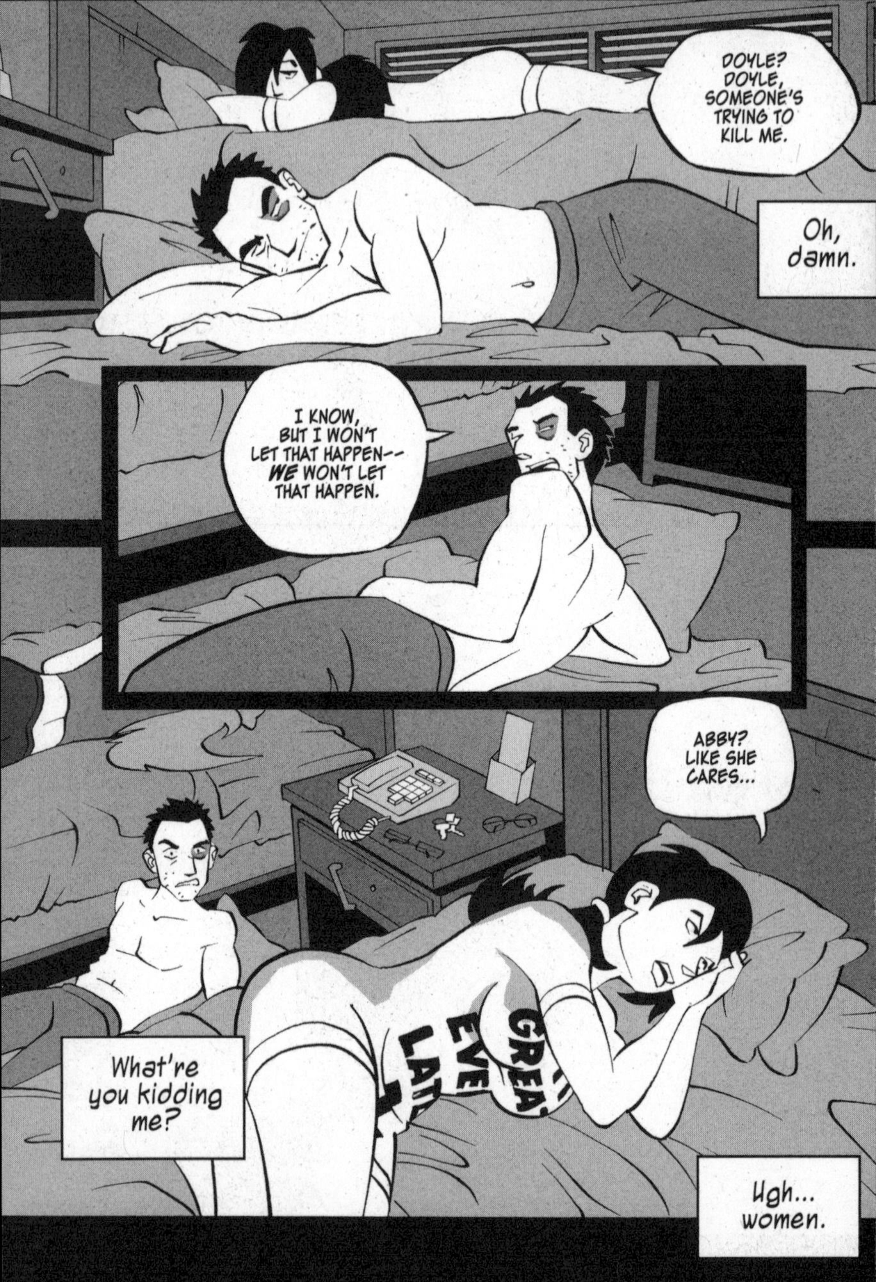
DOYLE? DOYLE, SOMEONE'S TRYING TO KILL ME.
Oh, damn.
I KNOW, BUT I WON'T LET THAT HAPPEN-- WE WON'T LET THAT HAPPEN.
ABBY? LIKE SHE CARES...
What're you kidding me?
Ugh... women.

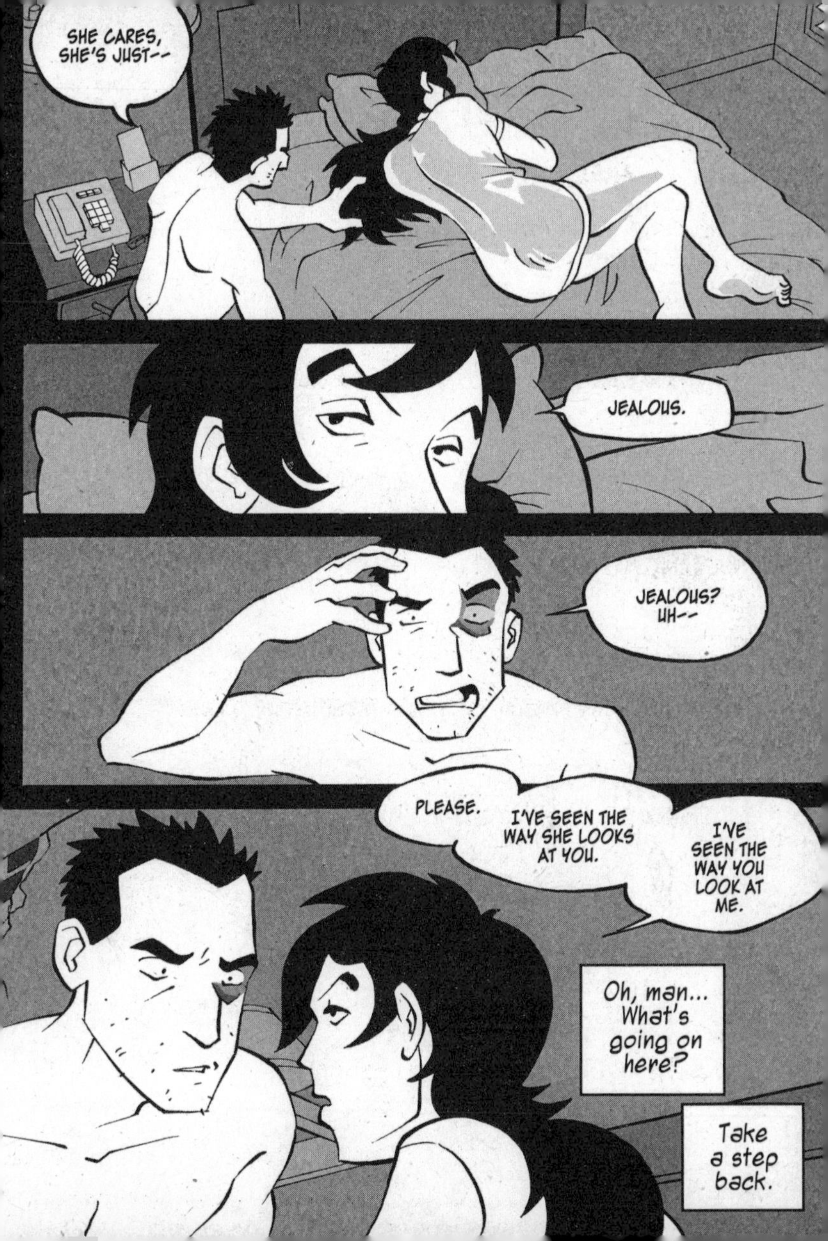
SHE CARES, SHE'S JUST--
JEALOUS.
JEALOUS? UH--
PLEASE. I'VE SEEN THE WAY SHE LOOKS AT YOU. I'VE SEEN THE WAY YOU LOOK AT ME.
Oh, man... What's going on here?
Take a step back.

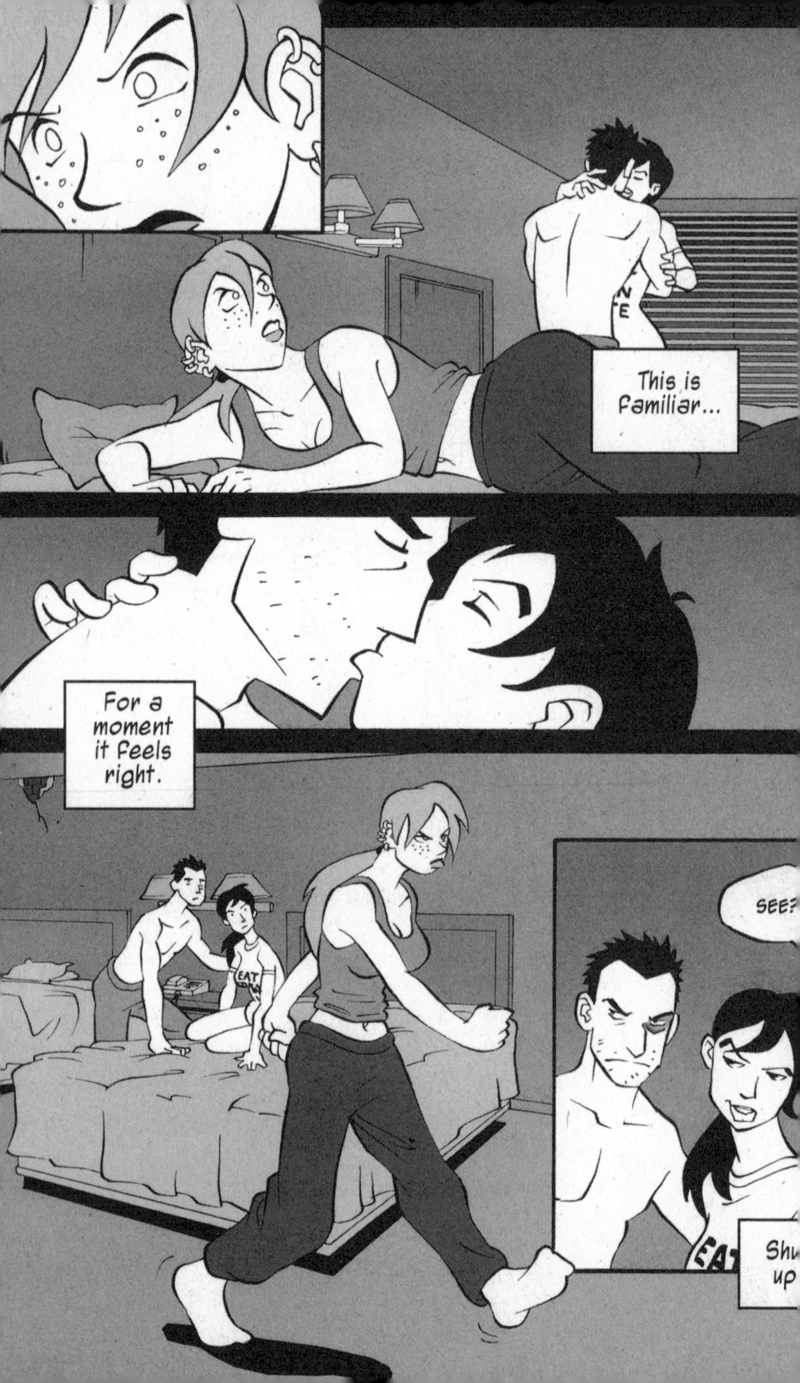
This is familiar...
For a moment it feels right.
SEE?

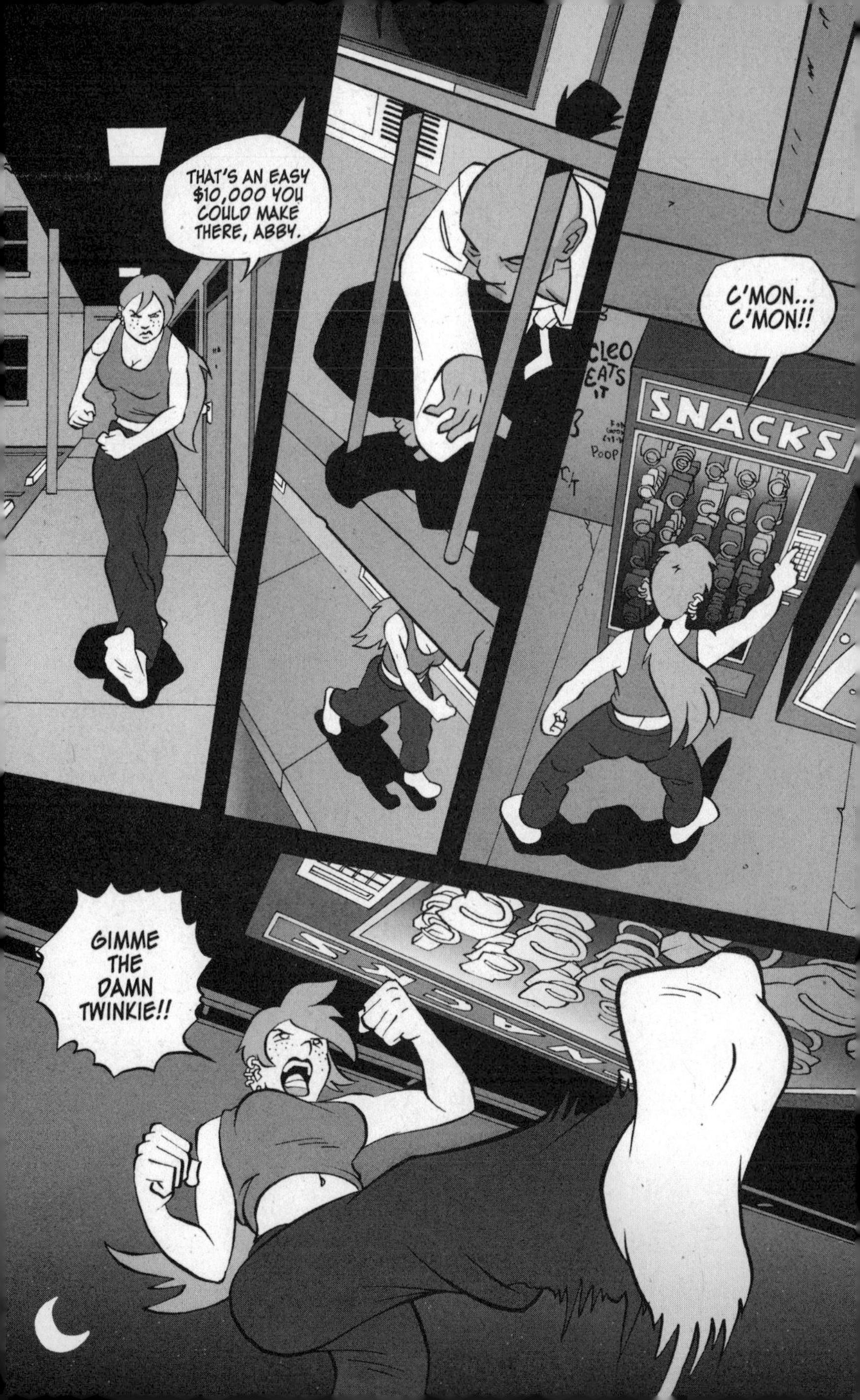
THAT'S AN EASY $10,000 YOU COULD MAKE THERE, ABBY.
CLEO EATS IT
POOP
SNACKS
C'MON... C'MON!!
GIMME THE DAMN TWINKIE!!

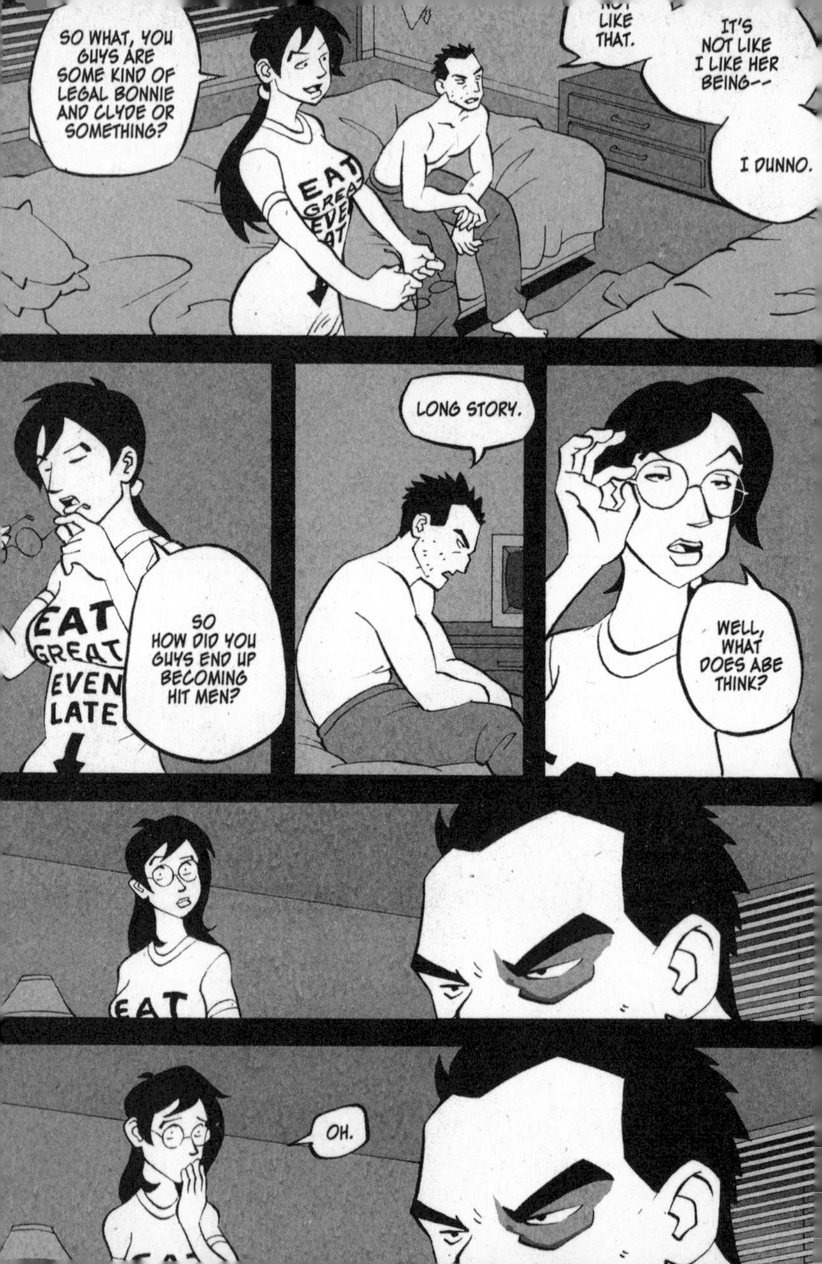
SO WHAT, YOU GUYS ARE SOME KIND OF LEGAL BONNIE AND CLYDE OR SOMETHING?
LIKE THAT.
IT'S NOT LIKE I LIKE HER BEING--
I DUNNO.
EAT GREAT EVEN LATE
SO HOW DID YOU GUYS END UP BECOMING HIT MEN?
LONG STORY.
WELL, WHAT DOES ABE THINK?
OH.

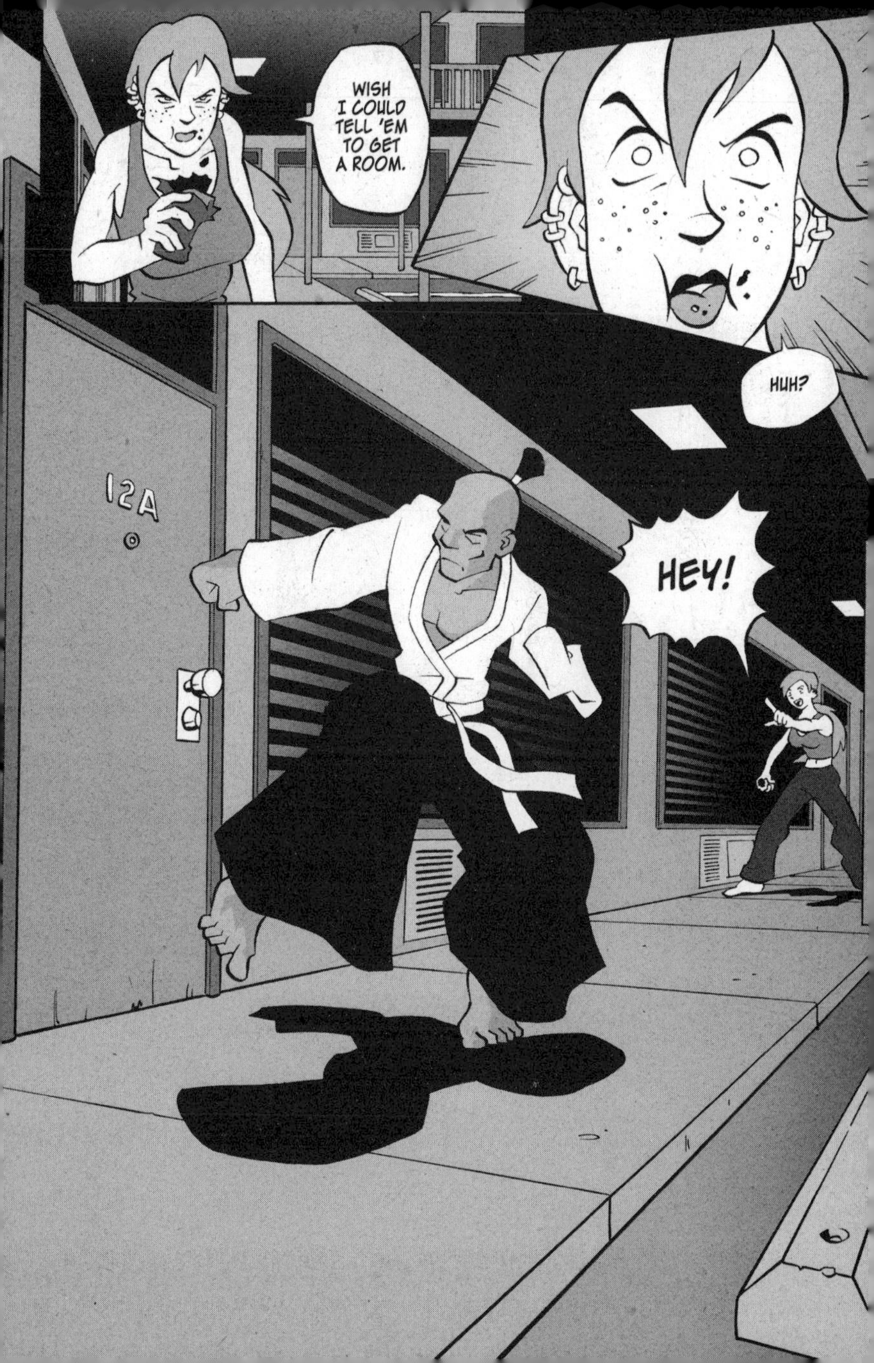
WISH I COULD TELL 'EM TO GET A ROOM.
HUH?
12A
HEY!

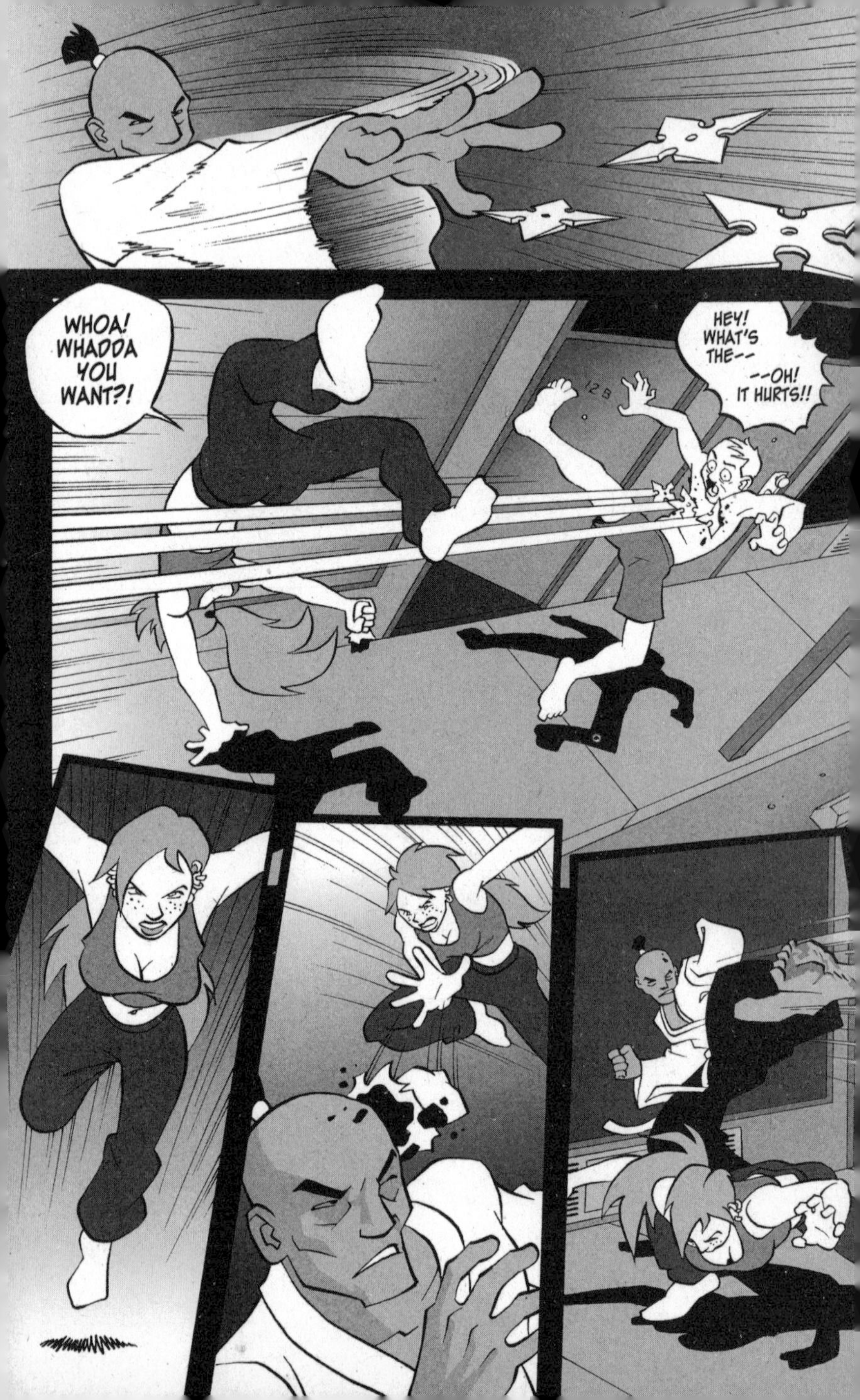
WHOA! WHADDA YOU WANT?!
HEY! WHAT'S THE--
--OH! IT HURTS!!

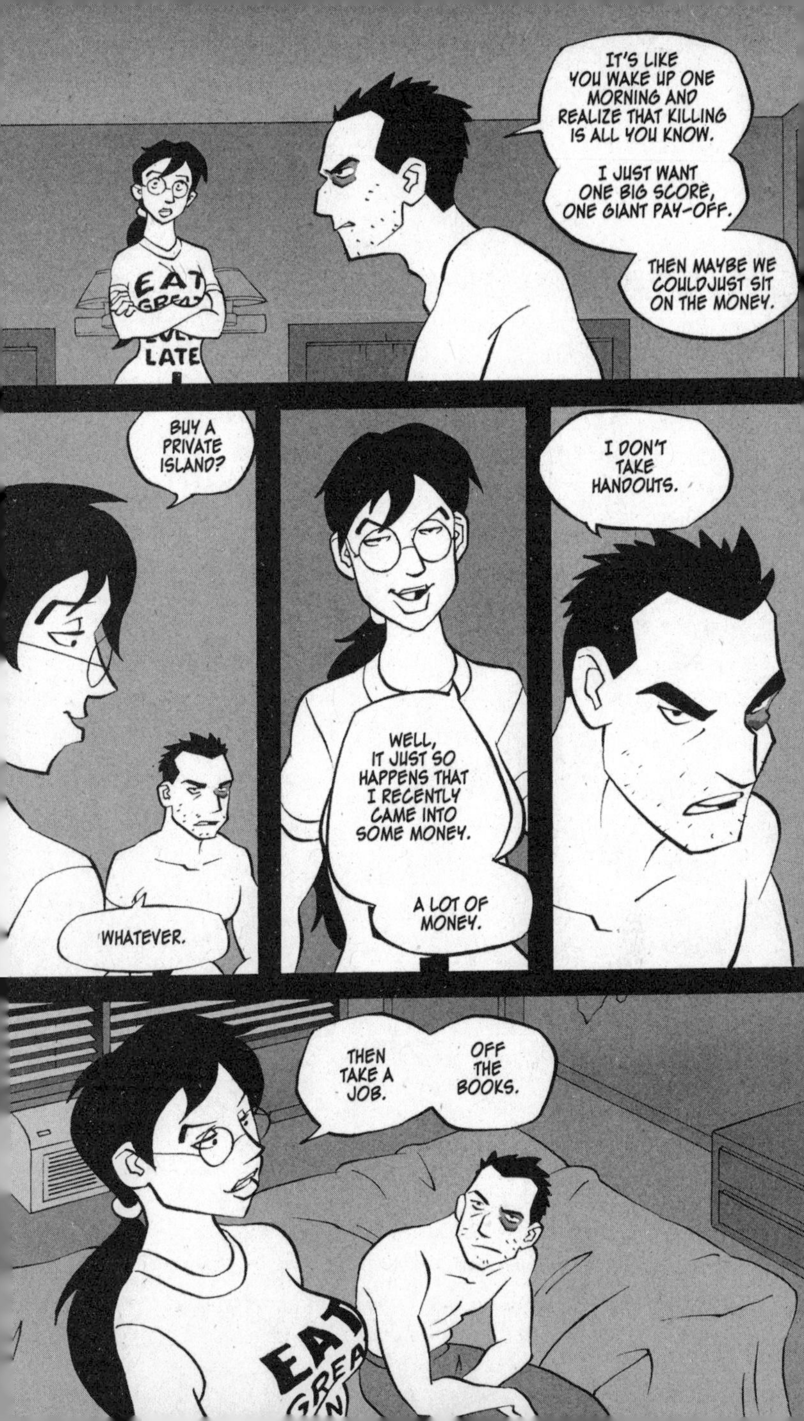
IT'S LIKE YOU WAKE UP ONE MORNING AND REALIZE THAT KILLING IS ALL YOU KNOW.
I JUST WANT ONE BIG SCORE, ONE GIANT PAY-OFF.
THEN MAYBE WE COULDJUST SIT ON THE MONEY.
EAT GREAT EVEN LATE
BUY A PRIVATE ISLAND?
WHATEVER.
WELL, IT JUST SO HAPPENS THAT I RECENTLY CAME INTO SOME MONEY.
A LOT OF MONEY.
I DON'T TAKE HANDOUTS.
THEN TAKE A JOB.
OFF THE BOOKS.

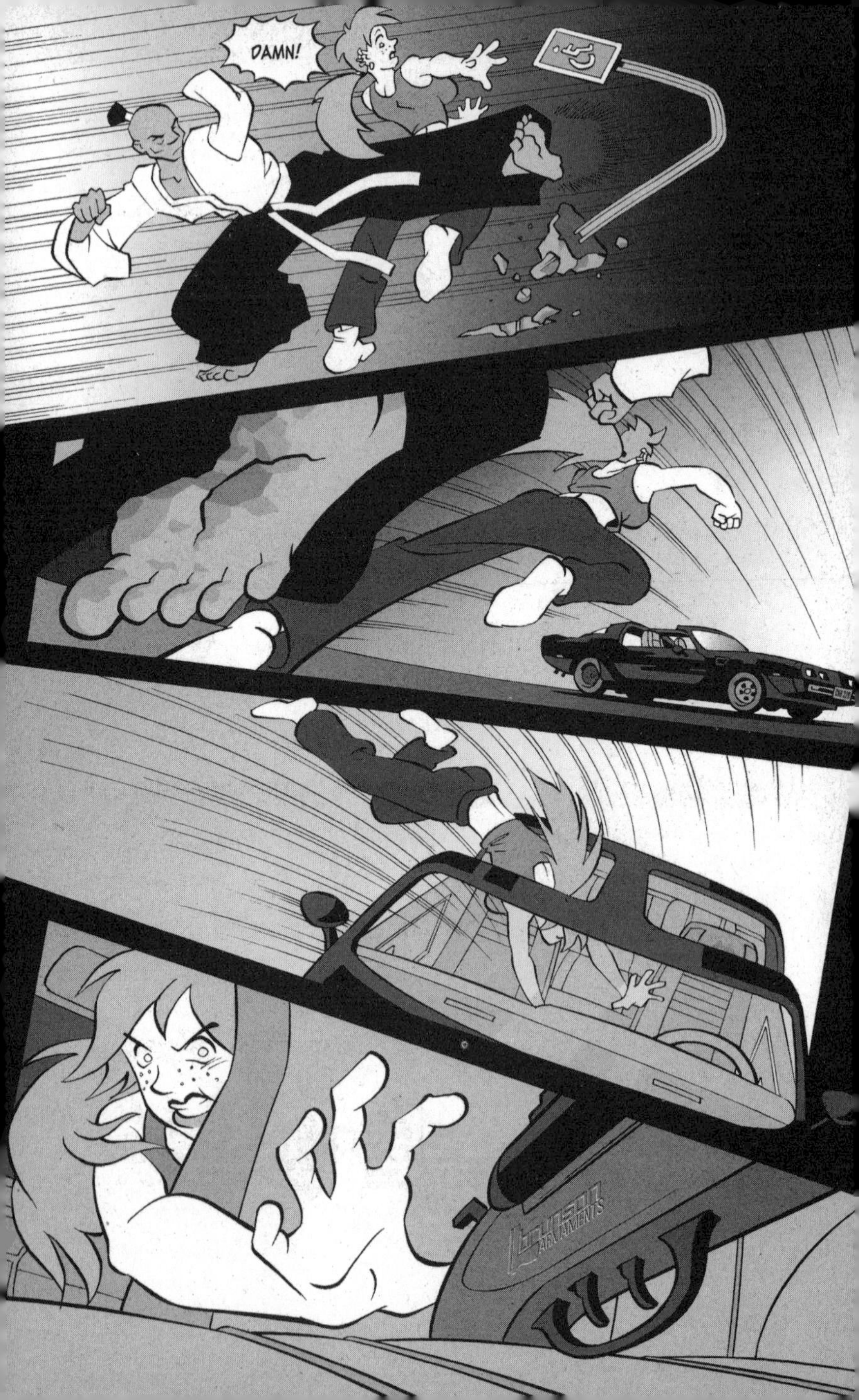
DAMN!

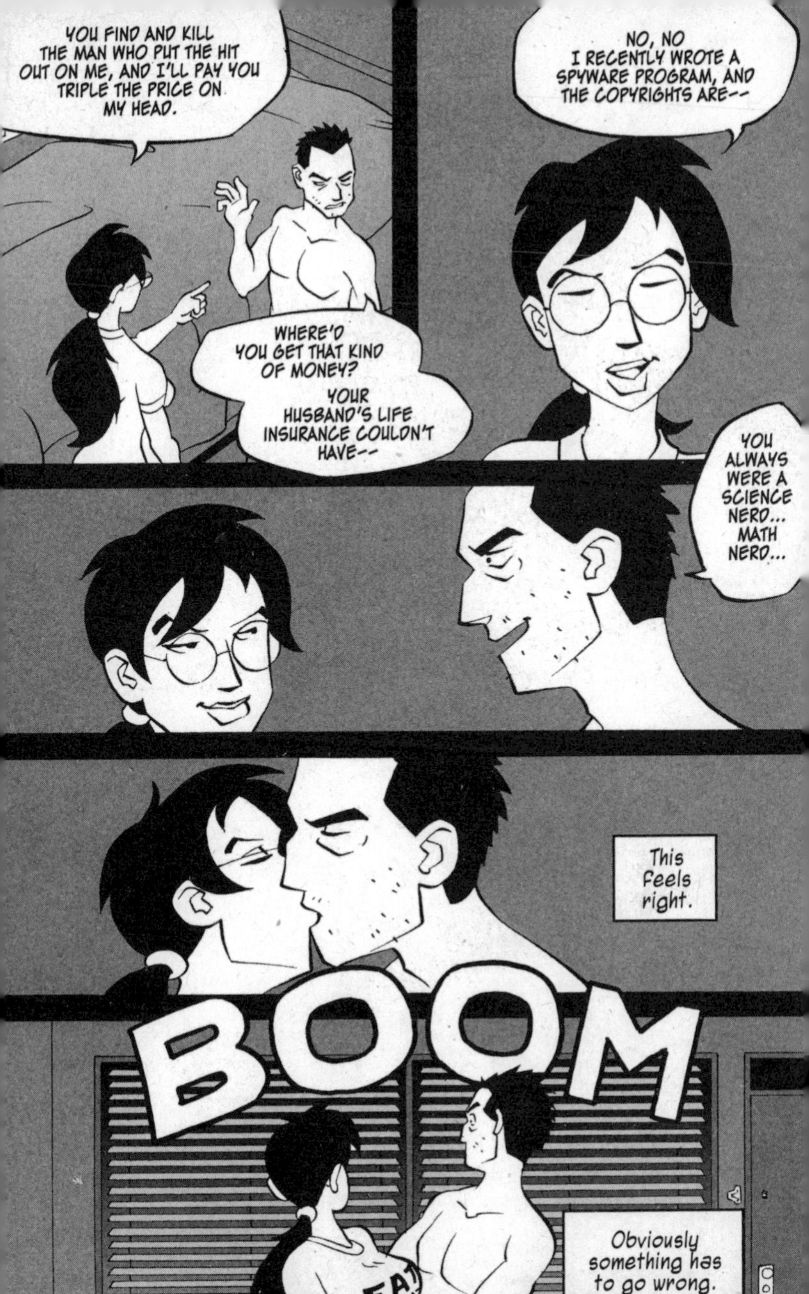
YOU FIND AND KILL THE MAN WHO PUT THE HIT OUT ON ME, AND I'LL PAY YOU TRIPLE THE PRICE ON MY HEAD.
WHERE'D YOU GET THAT KIND OF MONEY?
YOUR HUSBAND'S LIFE INSURANCE COULDN'T HAVE--
NO, NO I RECENTLY WROTE A SPYWARE PROGRAM, AND THE COPYRIGHTS ARE--
YOU ALWAYS WERE A SCIENCE NERD... MATH NERD...
This feels right.
BOOM
Obviously something has to go wrong.

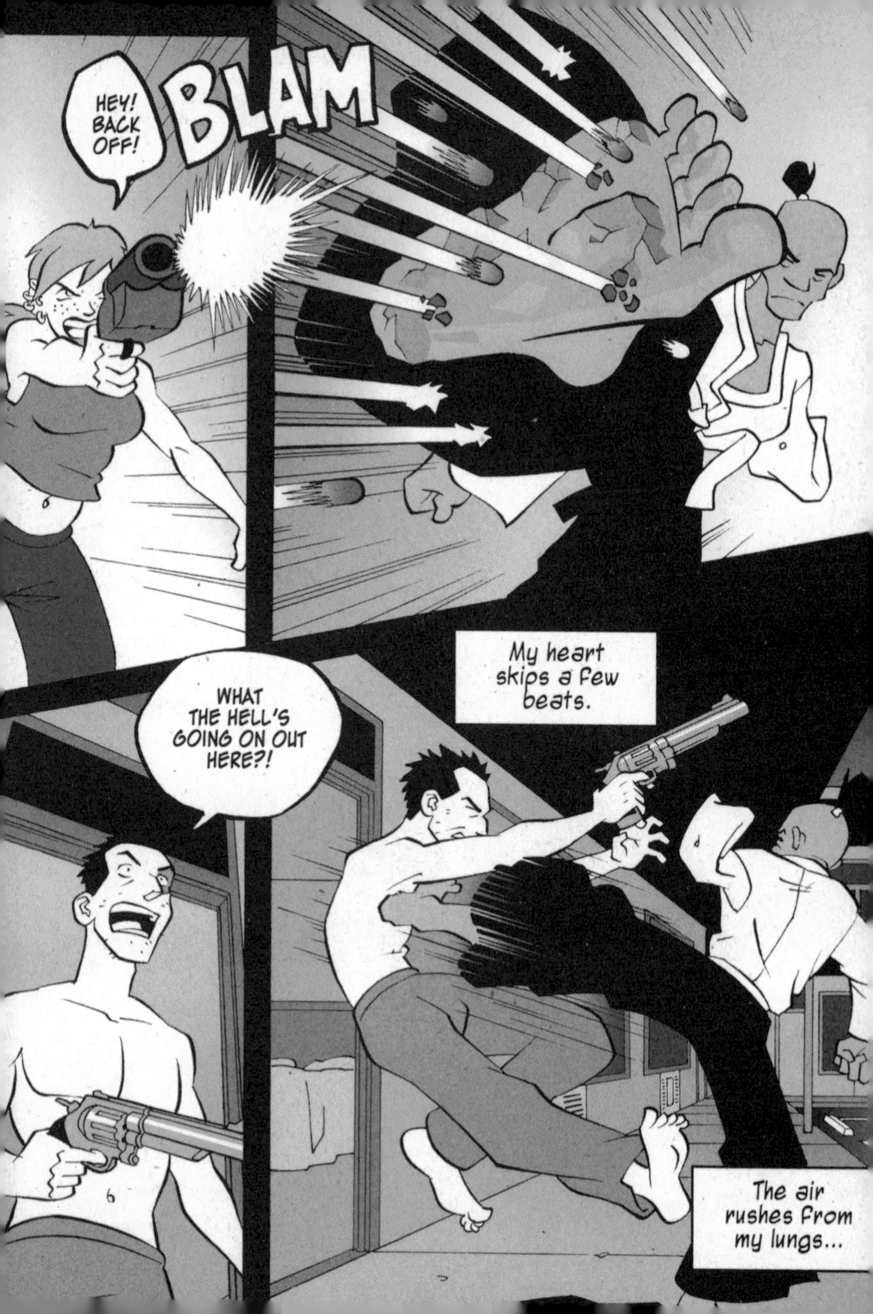
HEY! BACK OFF!
BLAM
WHAT THE HELL'S GOING ON OUT HERE?!
My heart skips a few beats.
The air rushes from my lungs...

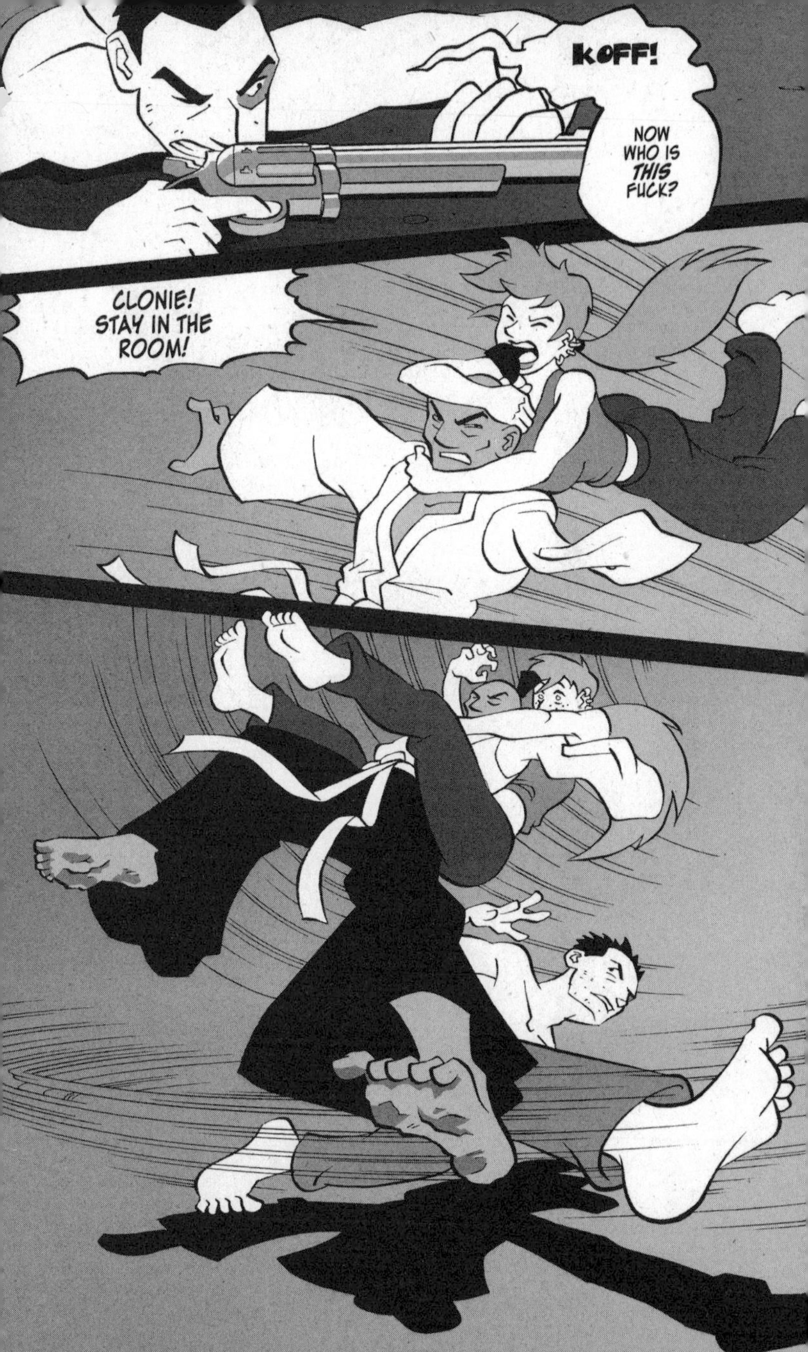
KOFF!
NOW WHO IS THIS FUCK?
CLONIE! STAY IN THE ROOM!

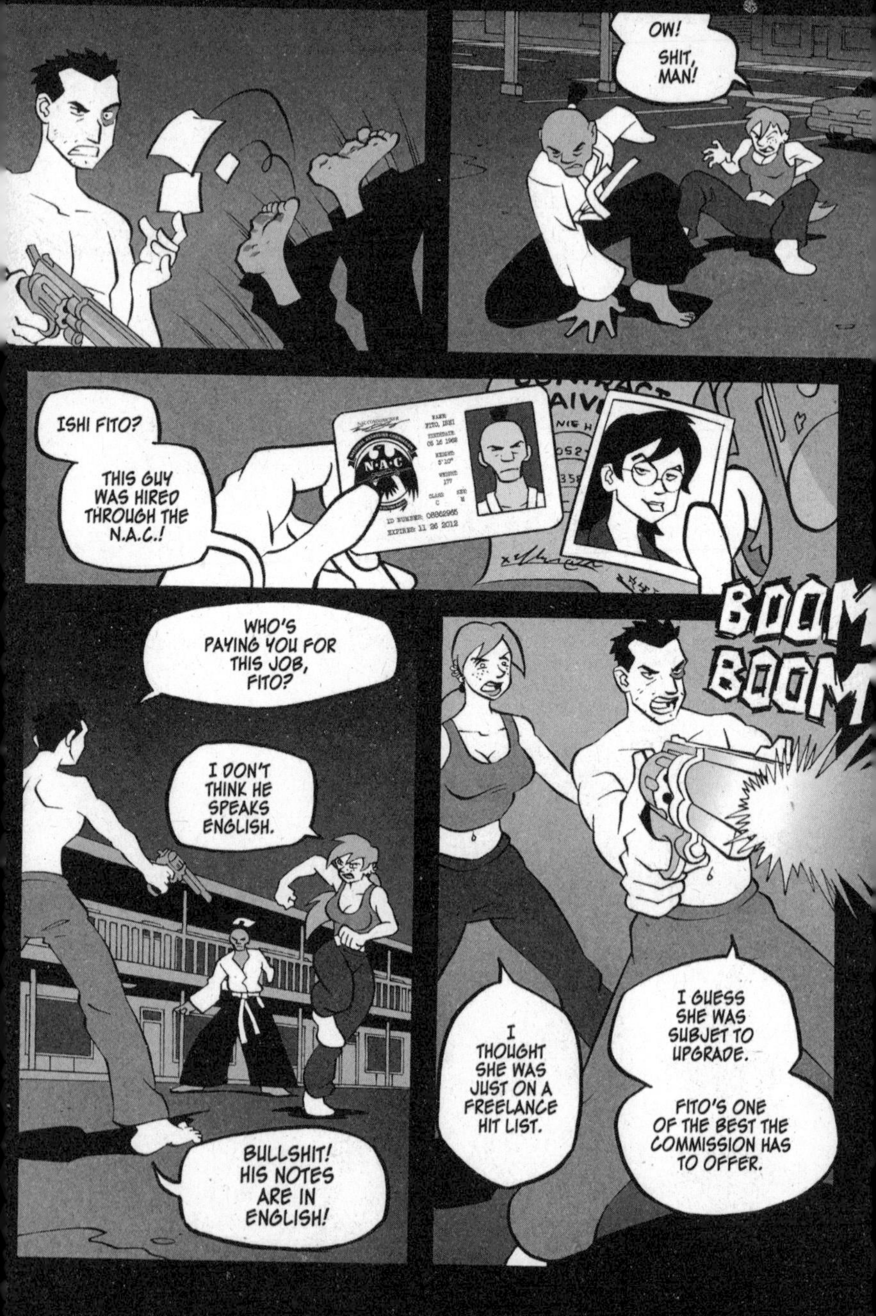
OW!
SHIT, MAN!
ISHI FITO?
THIS GUY WAS HIRED THROUGH THE N.A.C.!
WHO'S PAYING YOU FOR THIS JOB, FITO?
I DON'T THINK HE SPEAKS ENGLISH.
BULLSHIT! HIS NOTES ARE IN ENGLISH!
BOOM BOOM
I THOUGHT SHE WAS JUST ON A FREELANCE HIT LIST.
I GUESS SHE WAS SUBJET TO UPGRADE.
FITO'S ONE OF THE BEST THE COMMISSION HAS TO OFFER.

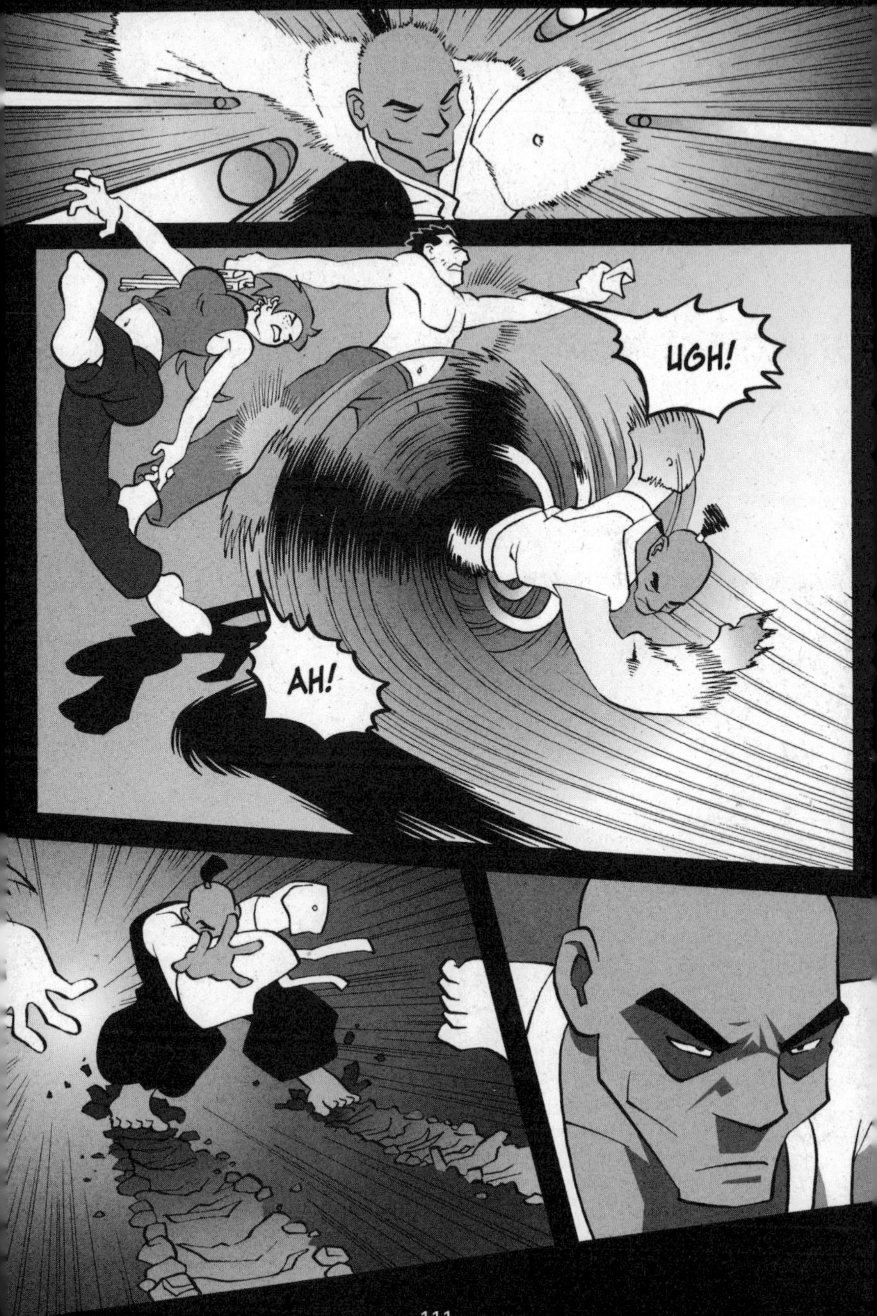
UGH!
AH!

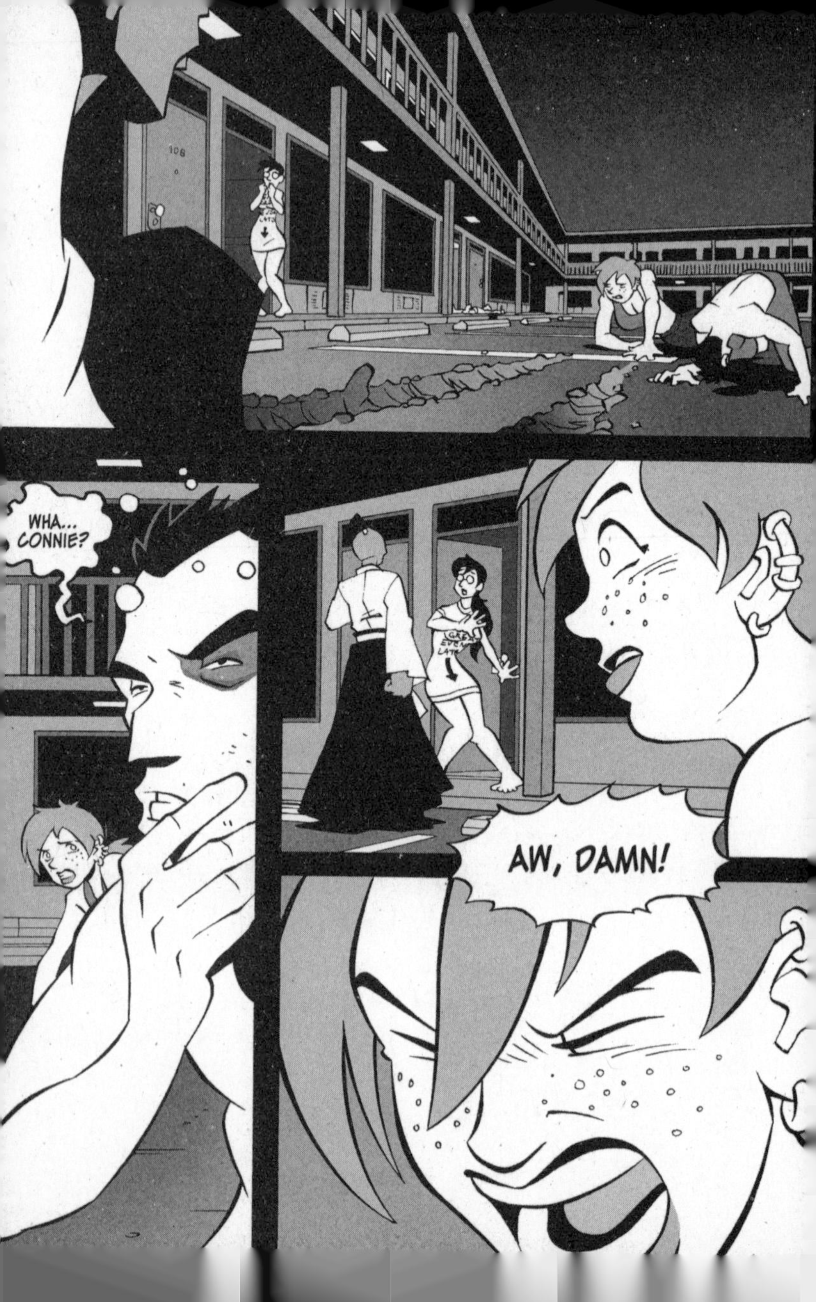
WHA... CONNIE?
AW, DAMN!

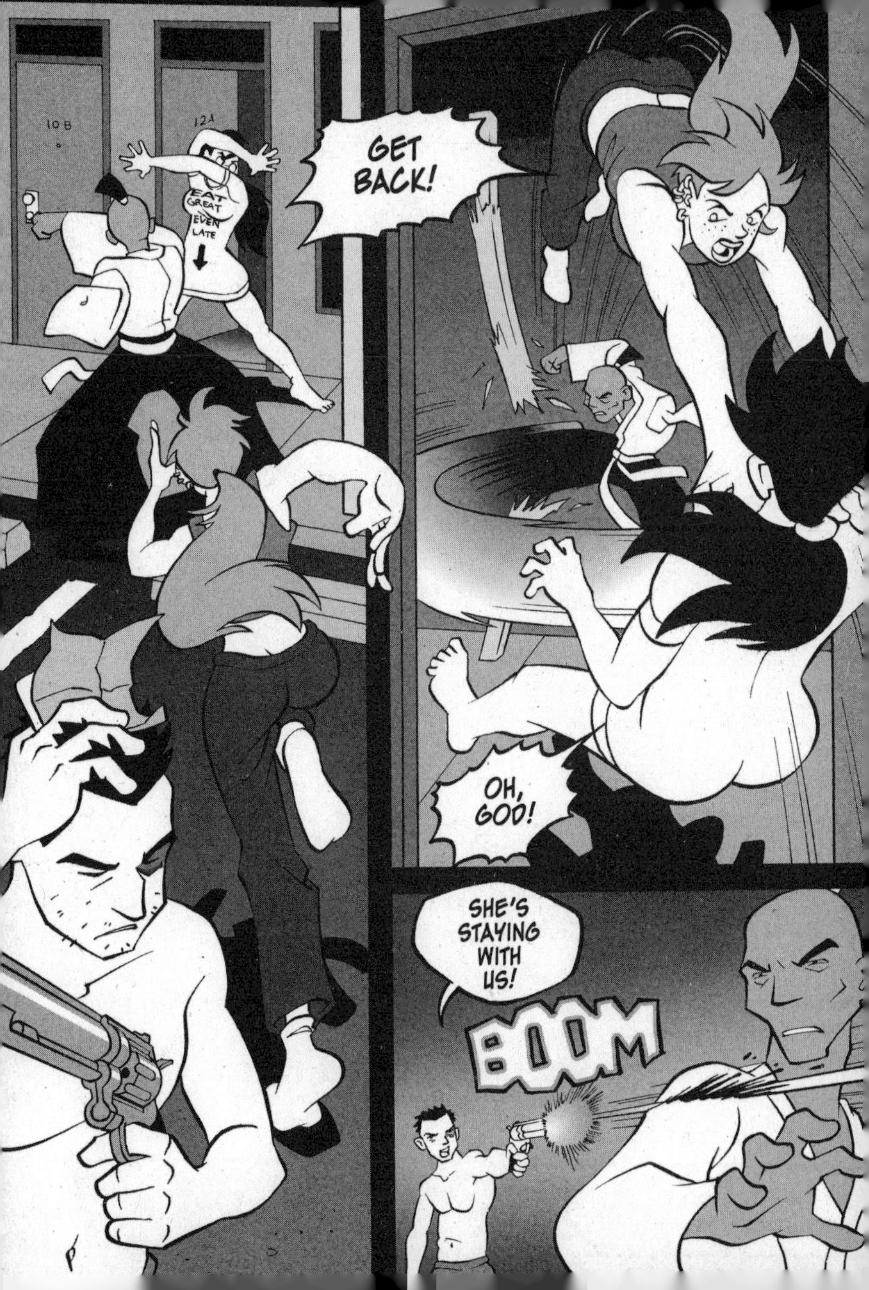
10B
12A
NY
EAT GREAT EVEN LATE
GET BACK!
OH, GOD!
SHE'S STAYING WITH US!
BOOM

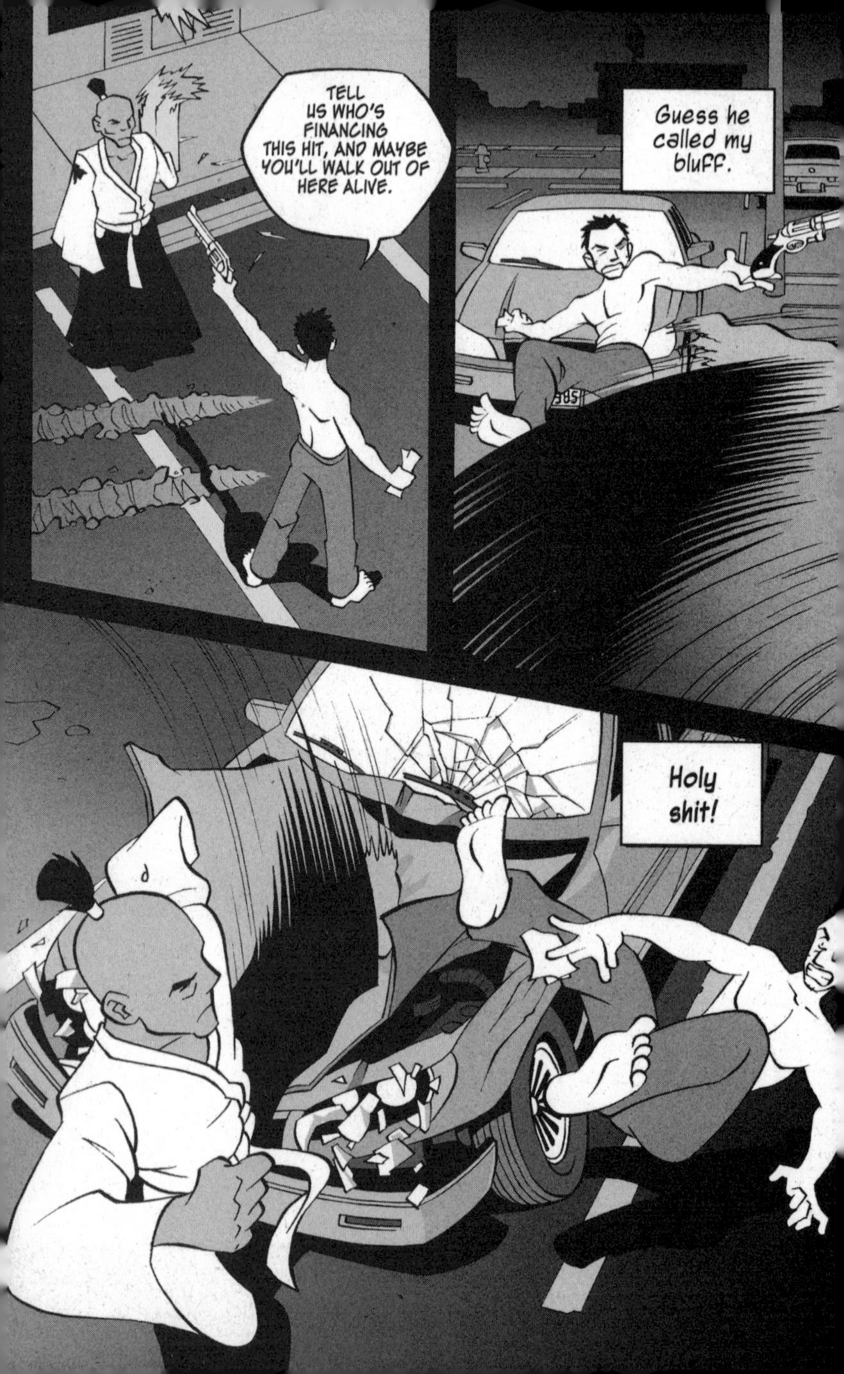
TELL US WHO'S FINANCING THIS HIT, AND MAYBE YOU'LL WALK OUT OF HERE ALIVE.
Guess he called my bluff.
Holy shit!

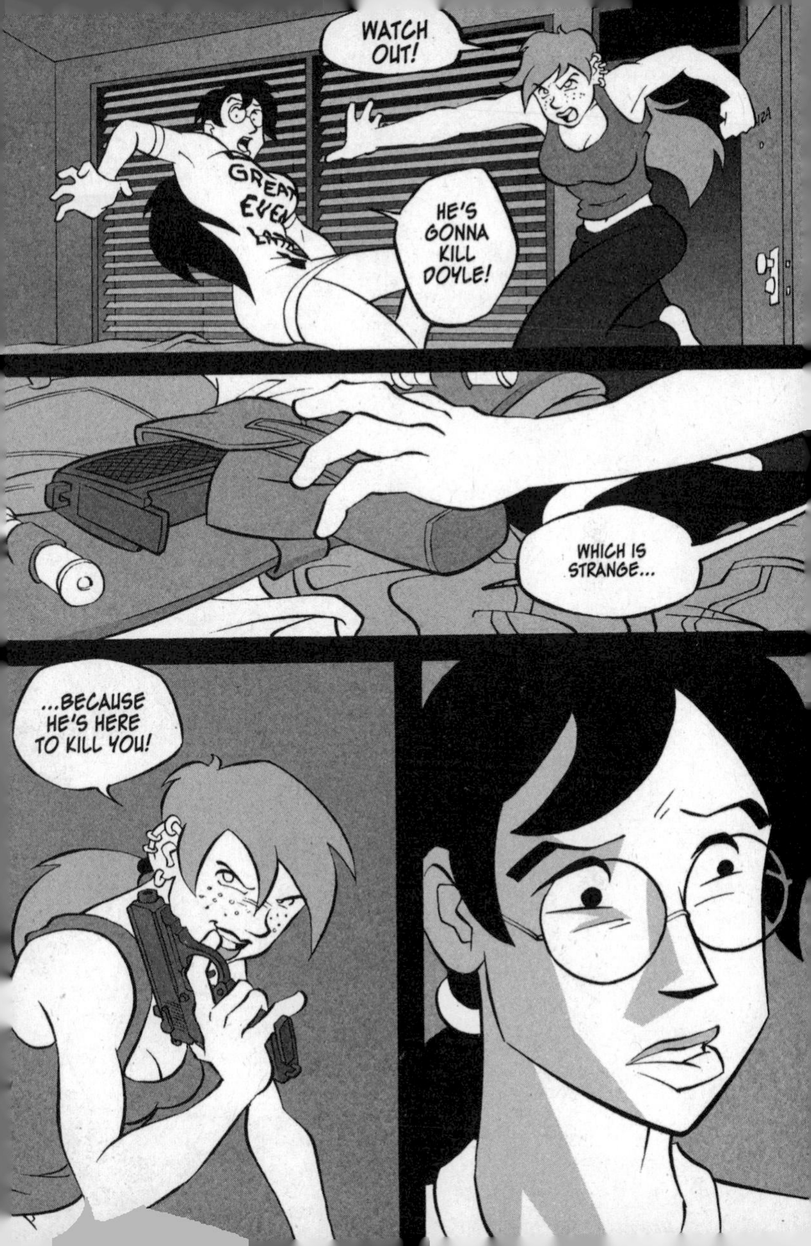
WATCH OUT!
HE'S GONNA KILL DOYLE!
WHICH IS STRANGE...
...BECAUSE HE'S HERE TO KILL YOU!

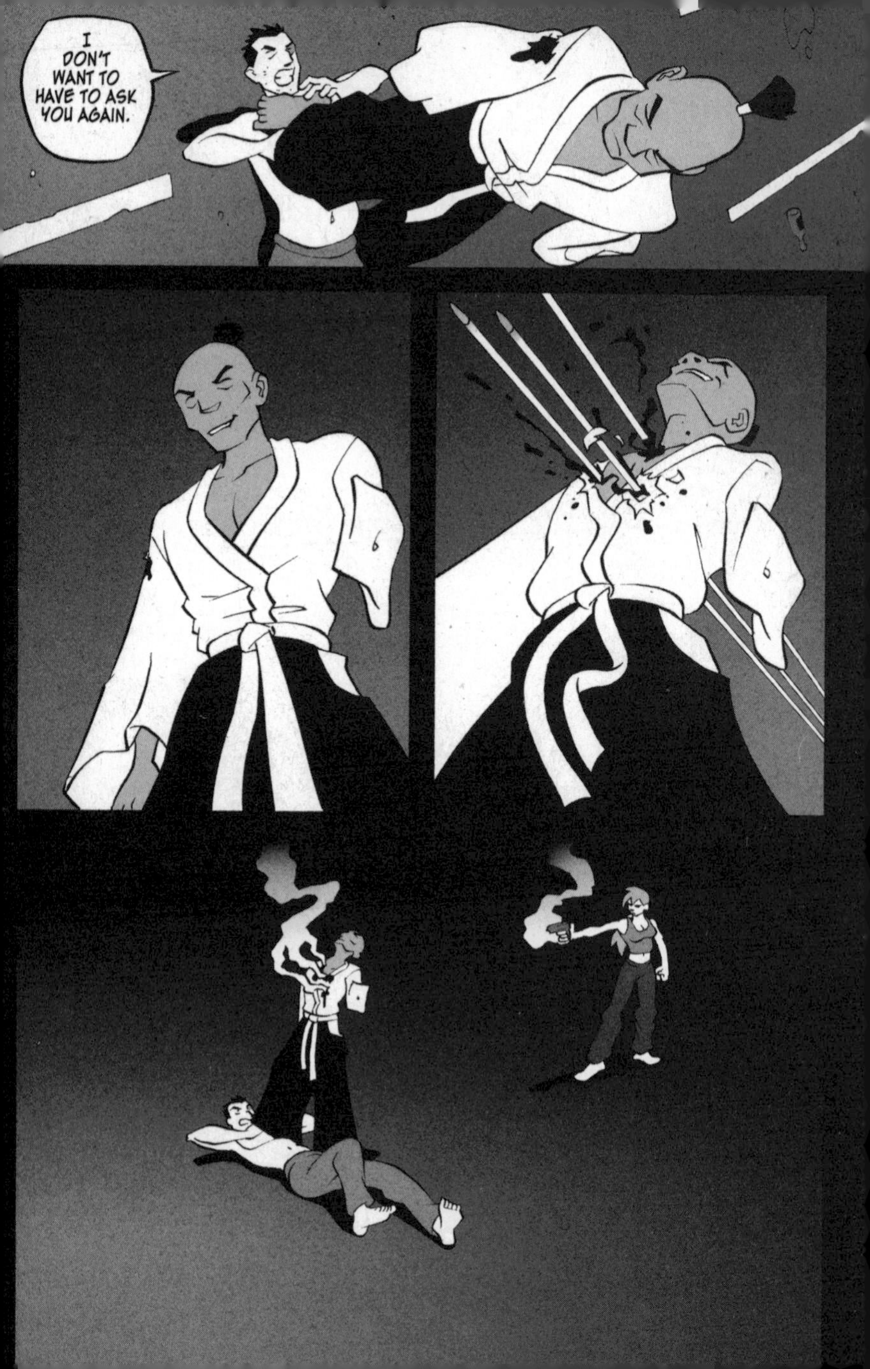
I DON'T WANT TO HAVE TO ASK YOU AGAIN.

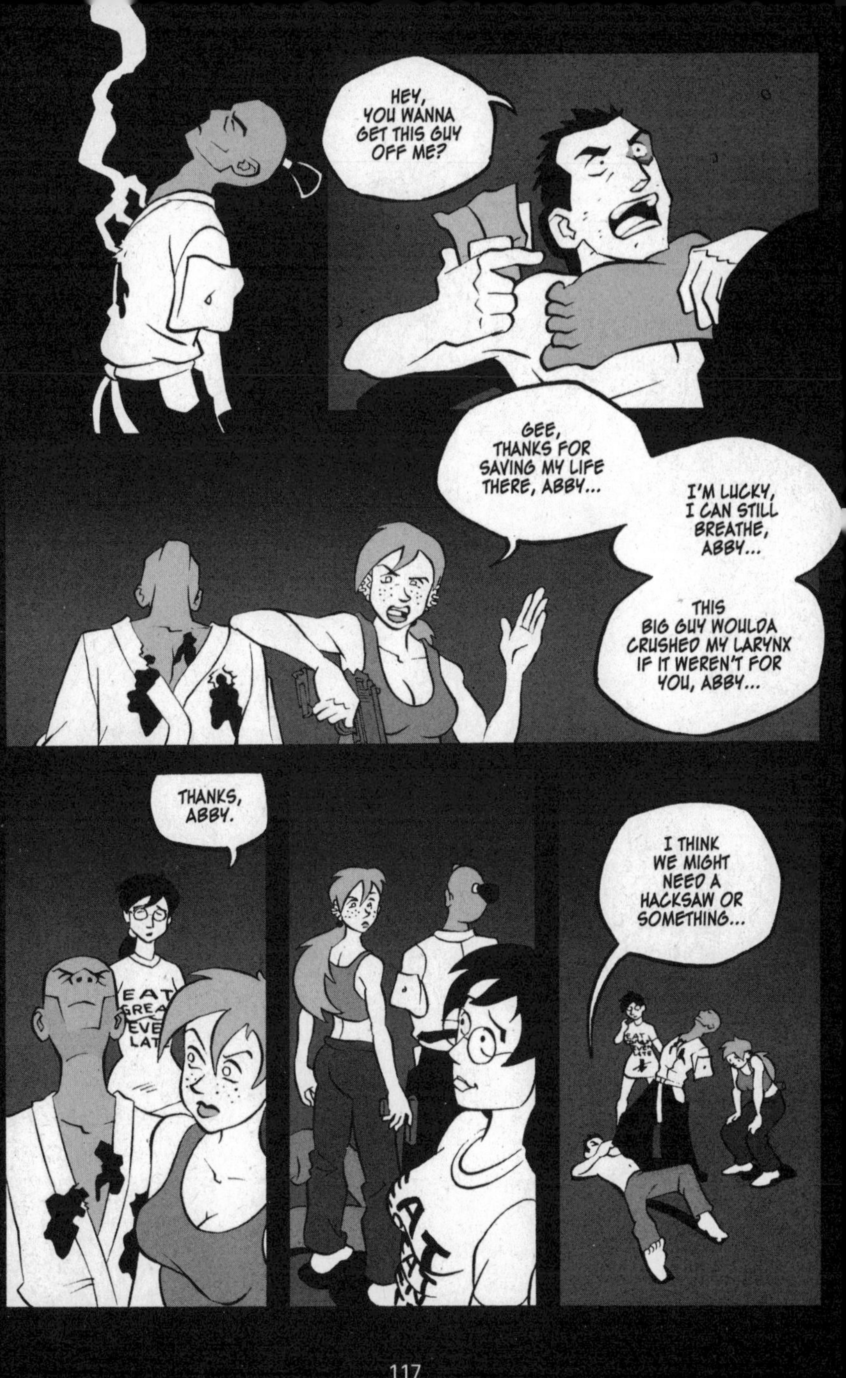
HEY, YOU WANNA GET THIS GUY OFF ME?
GEE, THANKS FOR SAVING MY LIFE THERE, ABBY...
I'M LUCKY, I CAN STILL BREATHE, ABBY...
THIS BIG GUY WOULDA CRUSHED MY LARYNX IF IT WEREN'T FOR YOU, ABBY...
THANKS, ABBY.
I THINK WE MIGHT NEED A HACKSAW OR SOMETHING...

7

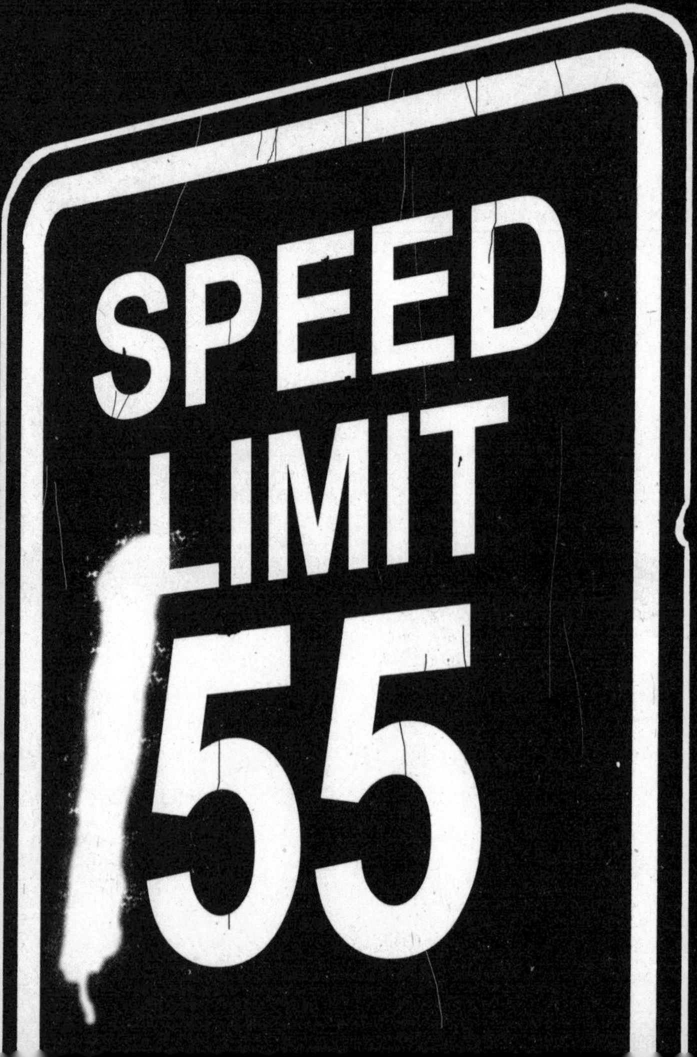

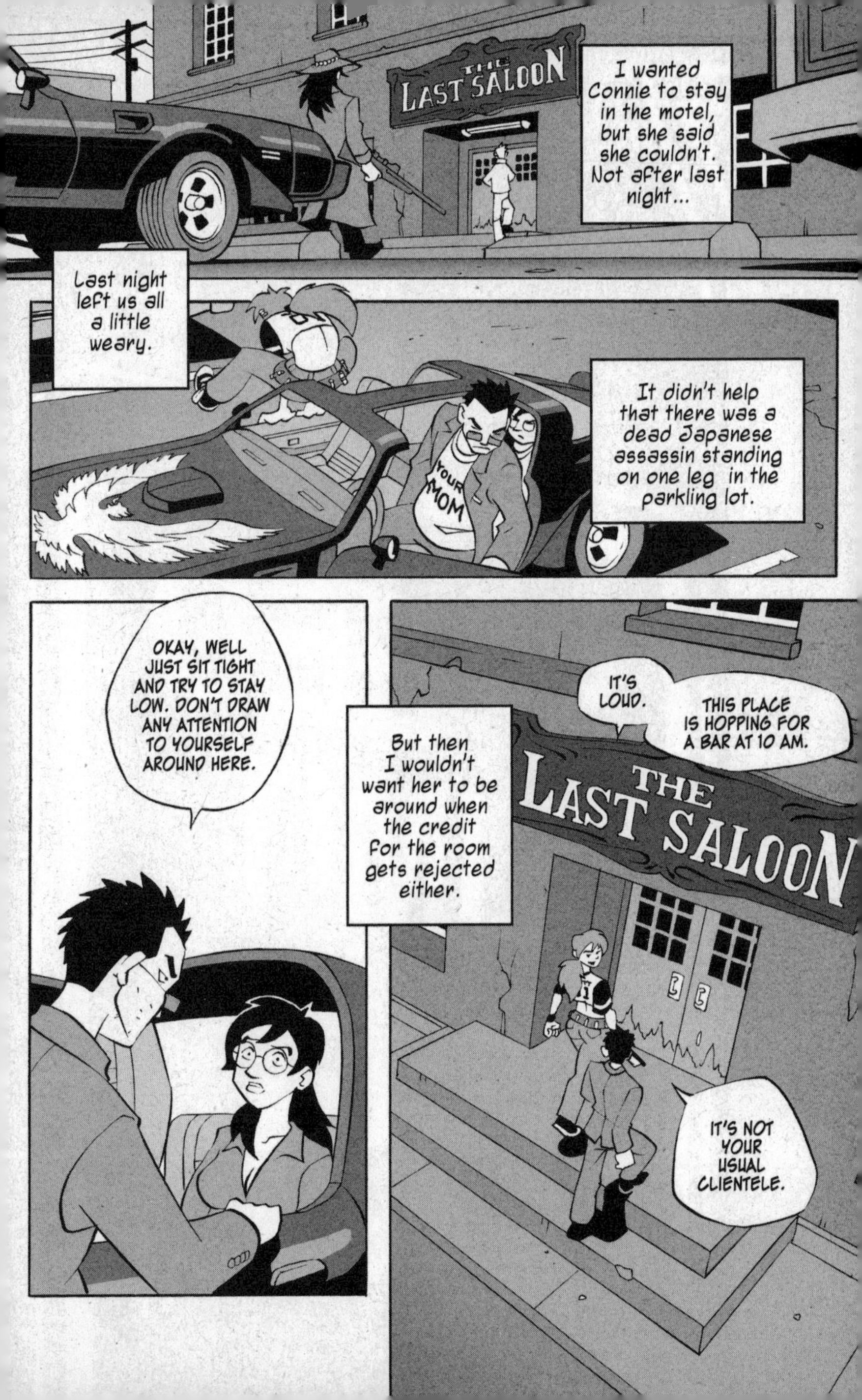
THE LAST SALOON
I wanted Connie to stay in the motel, but she said she couldn't. Not after last night...
Last night left us all a little weary.
YOUR MOM
It didn't help that there was a dead Japanese assassin standing on one leg in the parkling lot.
OKAY, WELL JUST SIT TIGHT AND TRY TO STAY LOW. DON'T DRAW ANY ATTENTION TO YOURSELF AROUND HERE.
But then I wouldn't want her to be around when the credit for the room gets rejected either.
IT'S LOUD.
THIS PLACE IS HOPPING FOR A BAR AT 10 AM.
THE LAST SALOON
IT'S NOT YOUR USUAL CLIENTELE.

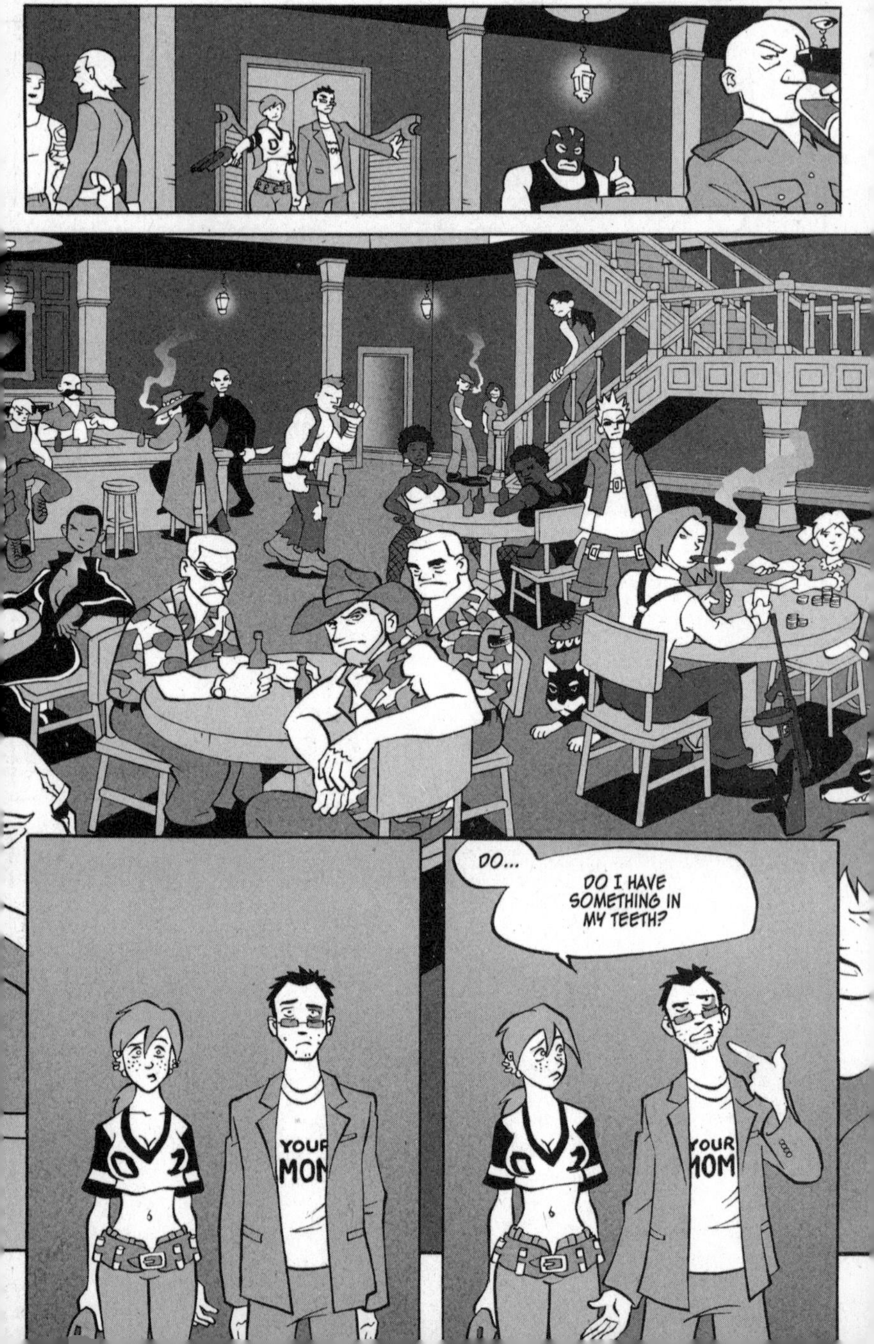
DO...
DO I HAVE SOMETHING IN MY TEETH?

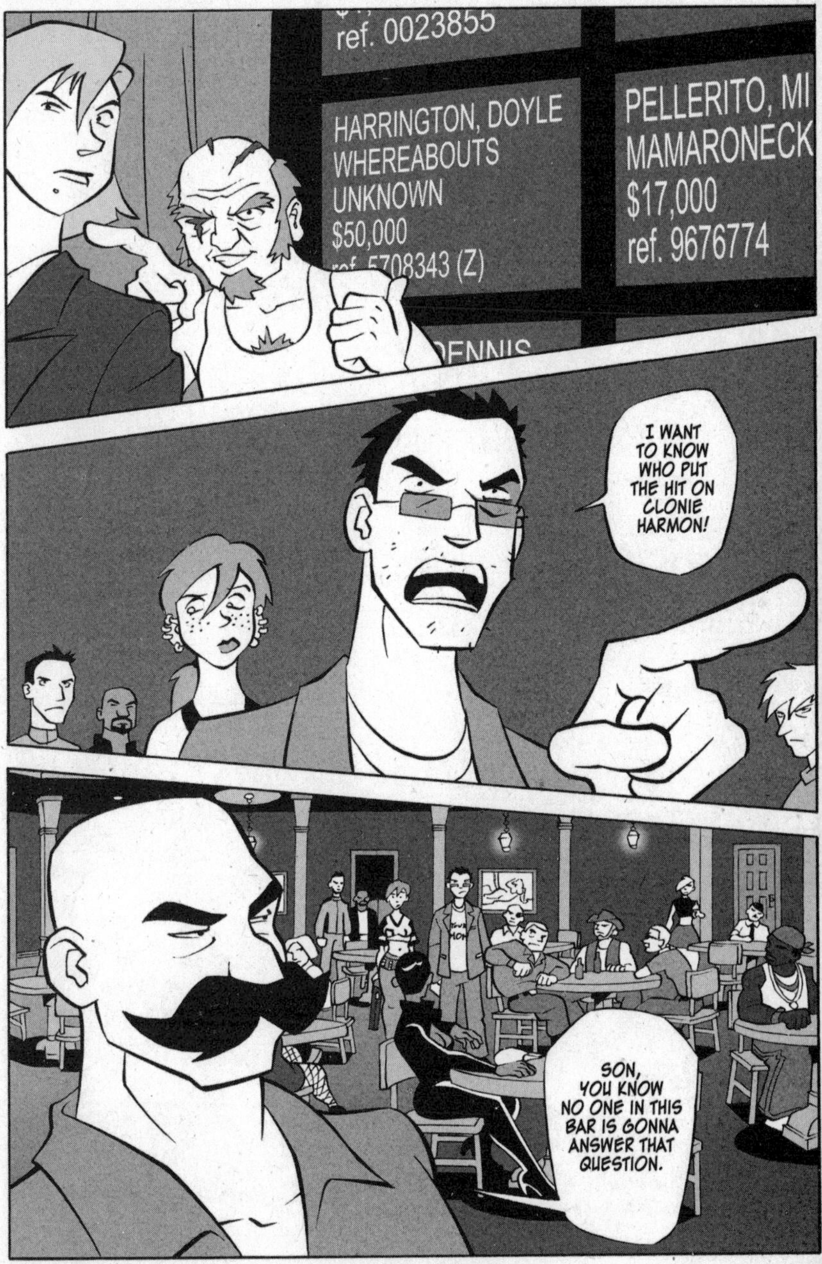
ref. 0023855
HARRINGTON, DOYLE
WHEREABOUTS
UNKNOWN
$50,000
PELLERITO, MI
MAMARONECK
$17,000
ref. 9676774
I WANT TO KNOW WHO PUT THE HIT ON CLONIE HARMON!
SON, YOU KNOW NO ONE IN THIS BAR IS GONNA ANSWER THAT QUESTION.

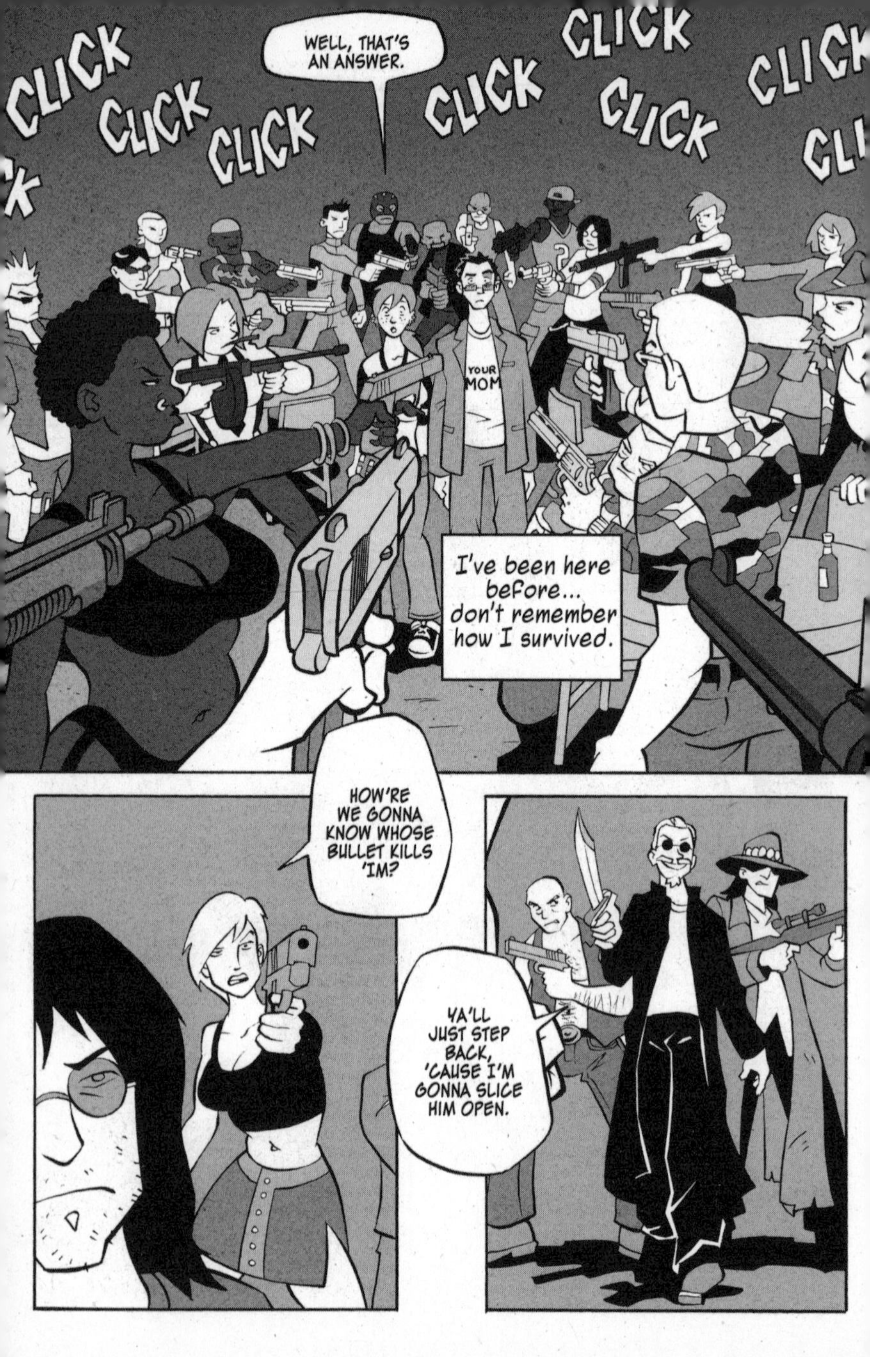
CLICK CLICK CLICK
WELL, THAT'S AN ANSWER.
CLICK CLICK CLICK CLICK
I've been here before... don't remember how I survived.
HOW'RE WE GONNA KNOW WHOSE BULLET KILLS 'IM?
YA'LL JUST STEP BACK, 'CAUSE I'M GONNA SLICE HIM OPEN.

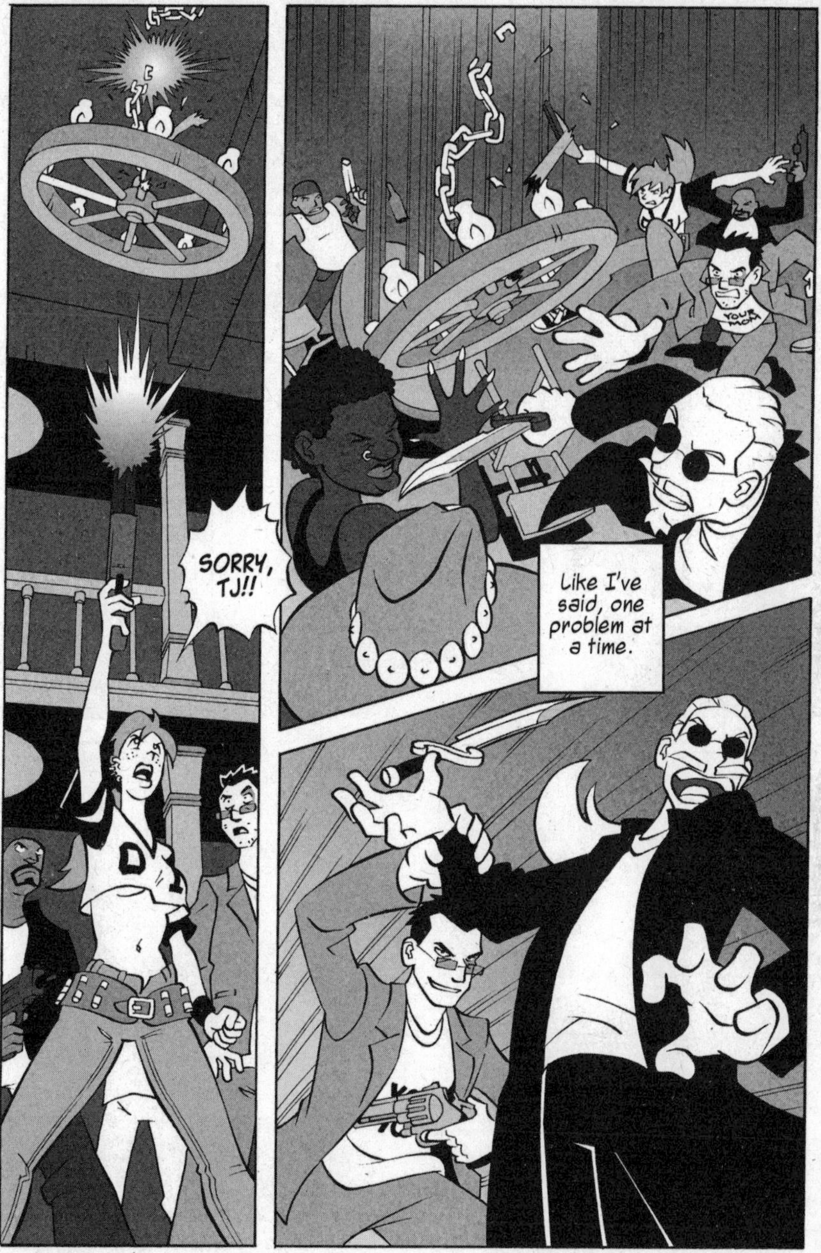
SORRY, TJ!!
YOUR MOM
Like I've said, one problem at a time.

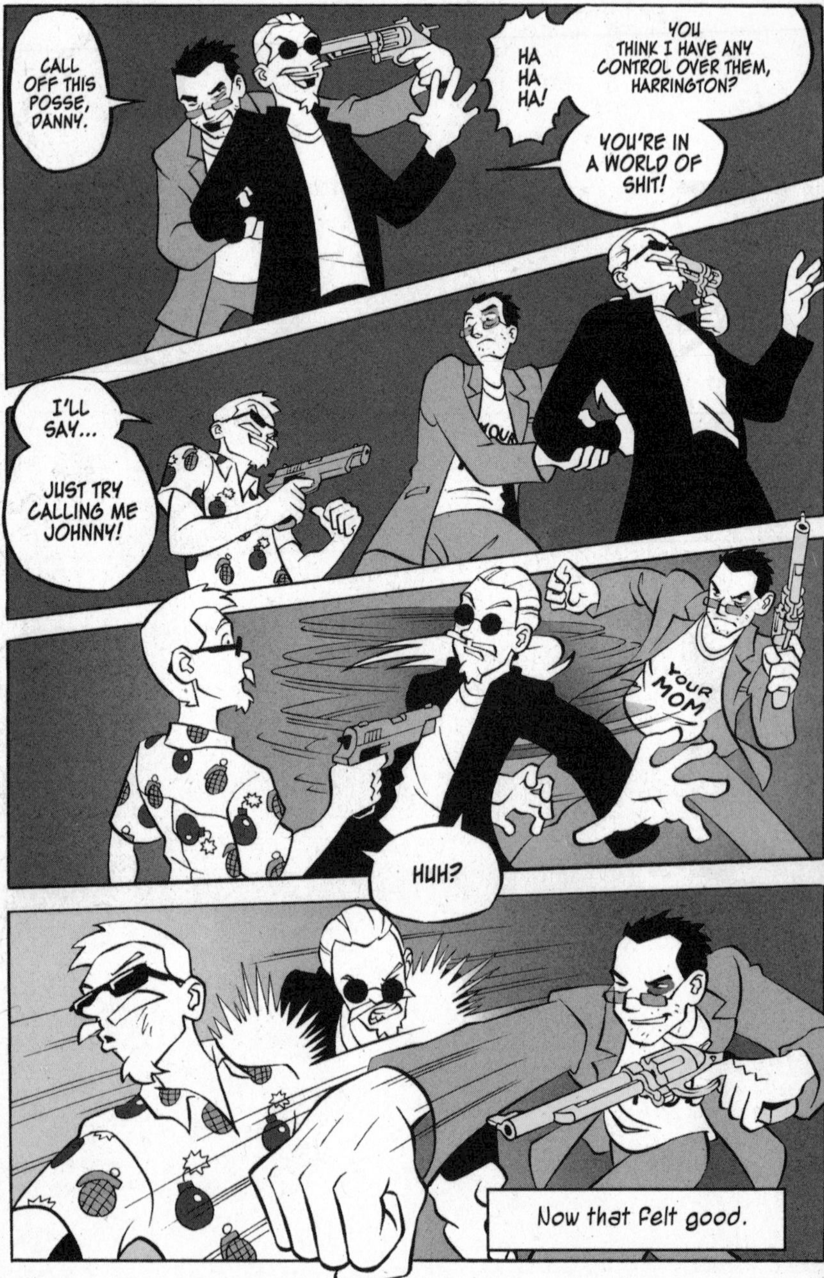
CALL OFF THIS POSSE, DANNY.
HA HA HA!
YOU THINK I HAVE ANY CONTROL OVER THEM, HARRINGTON?
YOU'RE IN A WORLD OF SHIT!
I'LL SAY...
JUST TRY CALLING ME JOHNNY!
YOUR MOM
HUH?
Now that felt good.

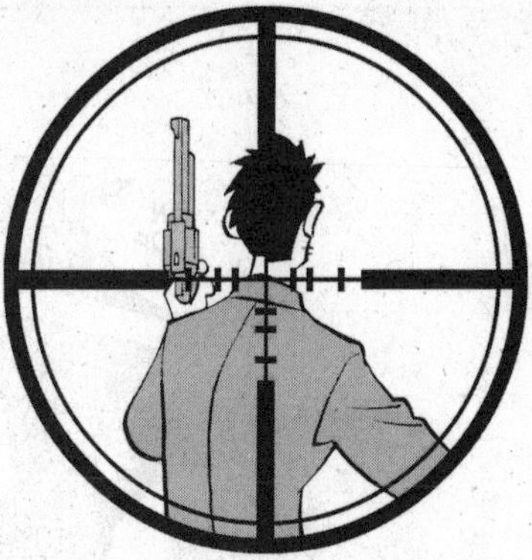

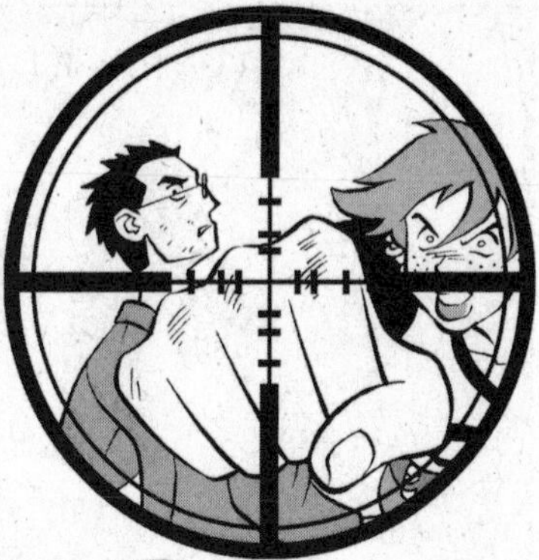

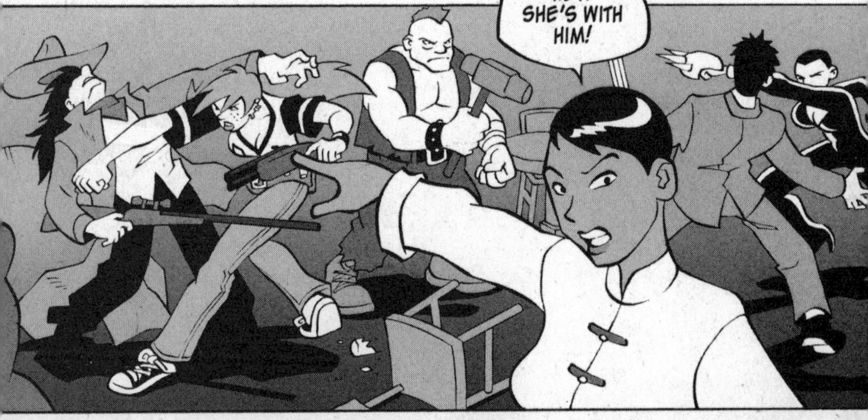
HEY! SHE'S WITH HIM!

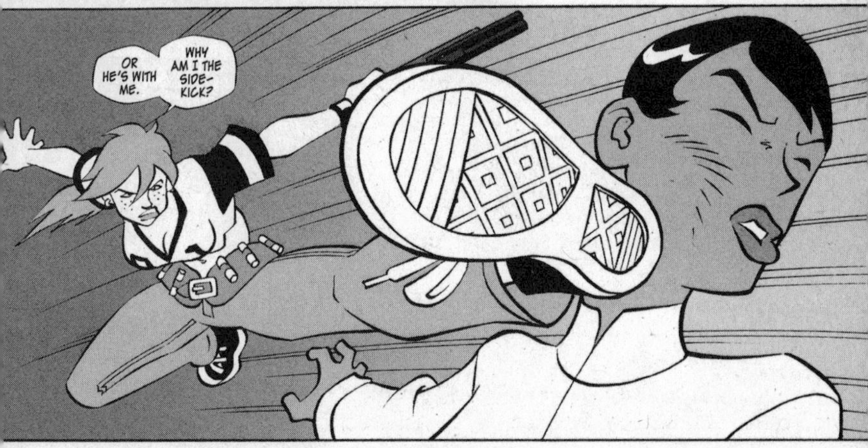
OR HE'S WITH ME.
WHY AM I THE SIDE-KICK?

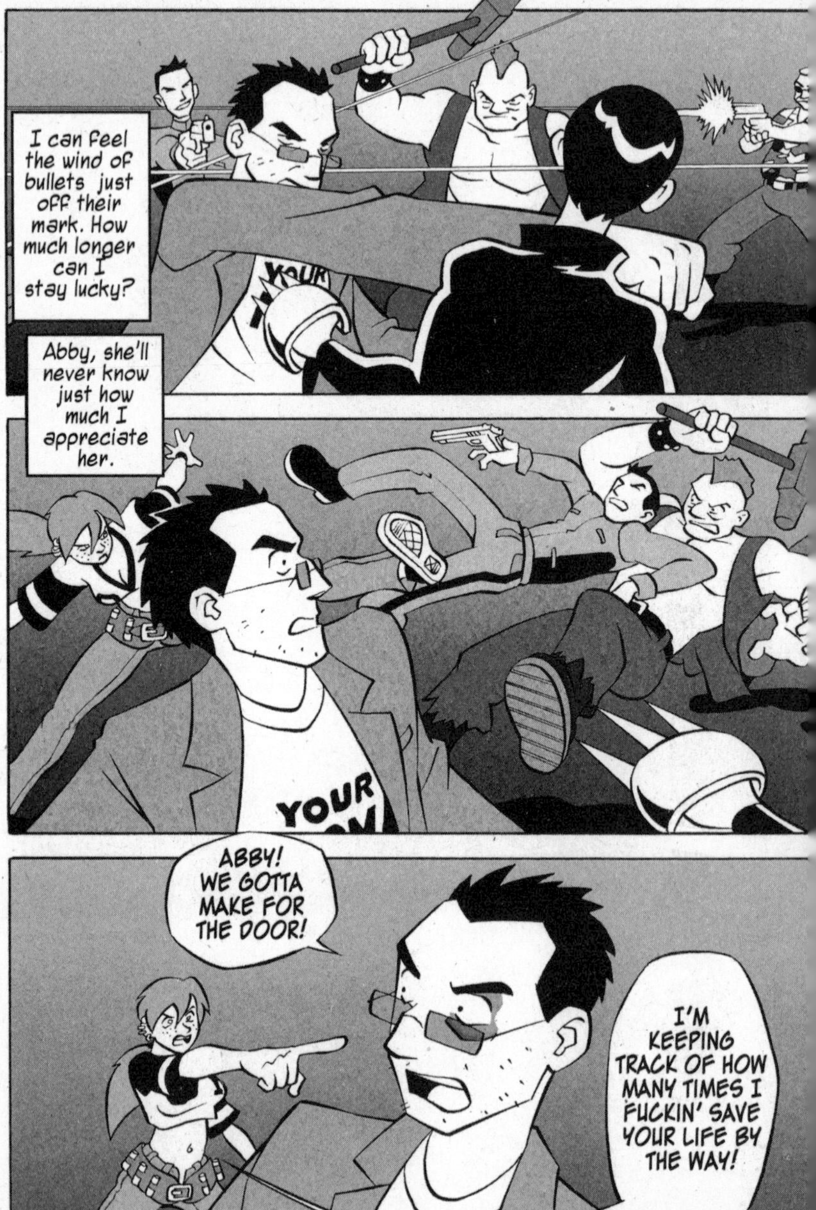
I can feel the wind of bullets just off their mark. How much longer can I stay lucky?
Abby, she'll never know just how much I appreciate her.
YOUR
ABBY! WE GOTTA MAKE FOR THE DOOR!
I'M KEEPING TRACK OF HOW MANY TIMES I FUCKIN' SAVE YOUR LIFE BY THE WAY!

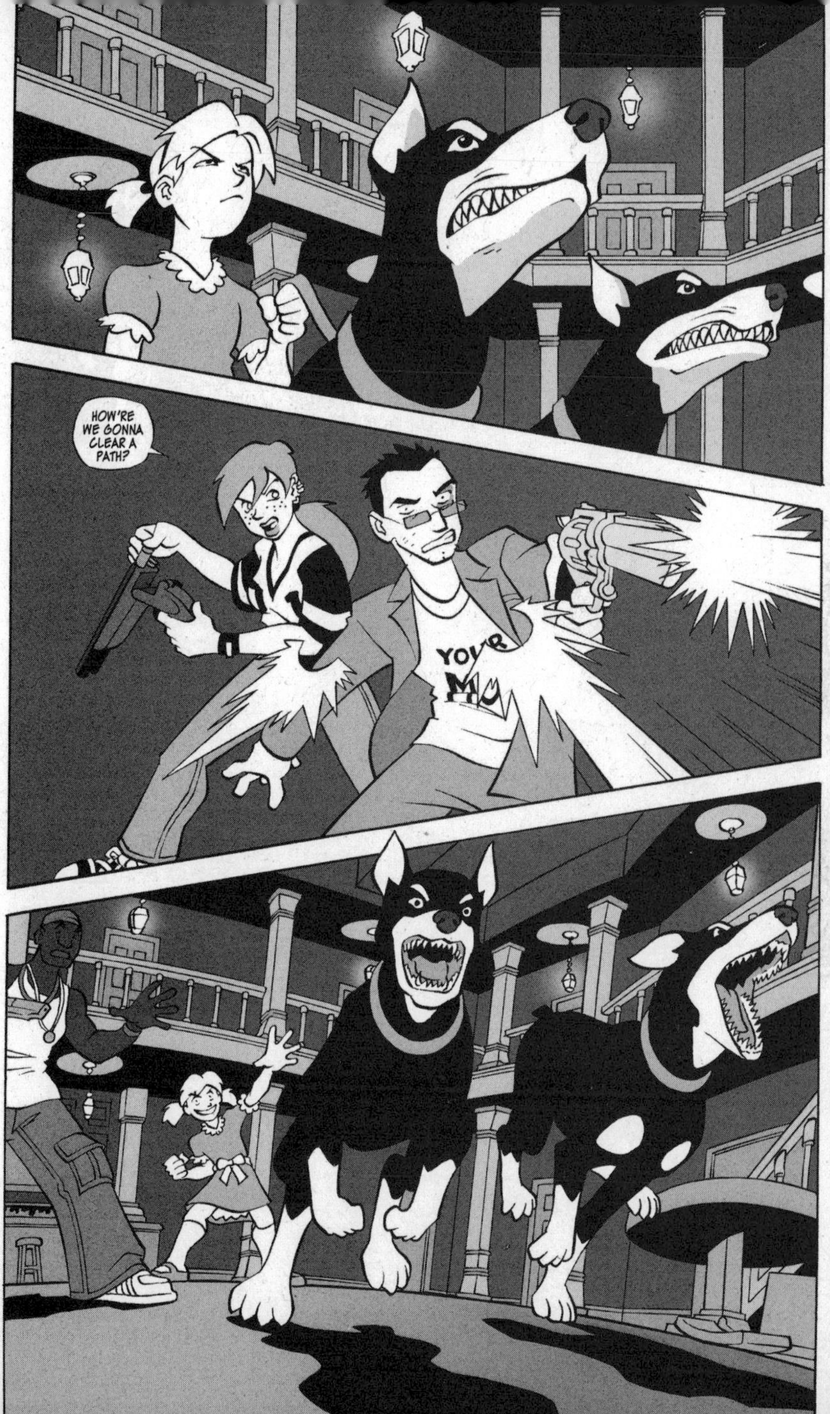
HOW'RE WE GONNA CLEAR A PATH?

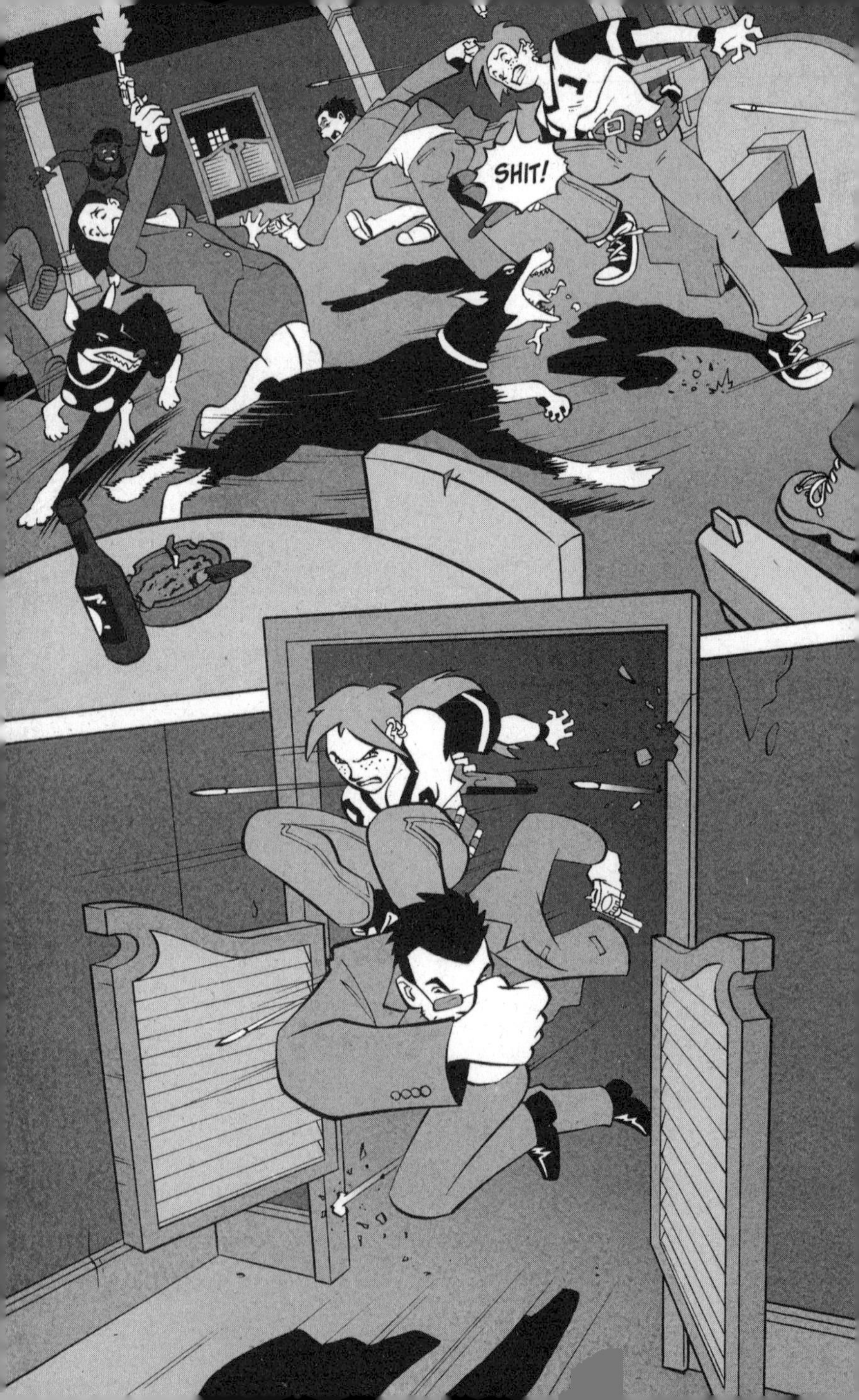
SHIT!

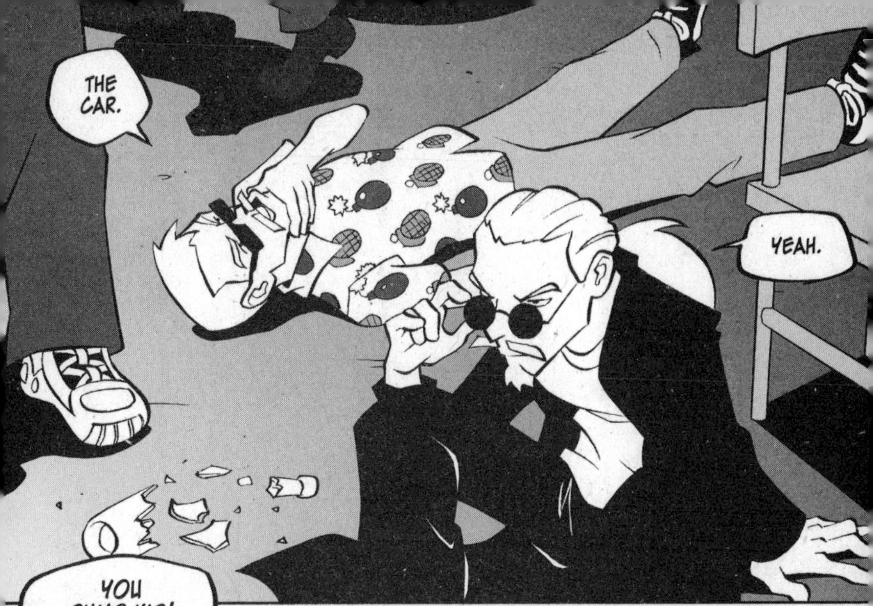
THE CAR.
YEAH.

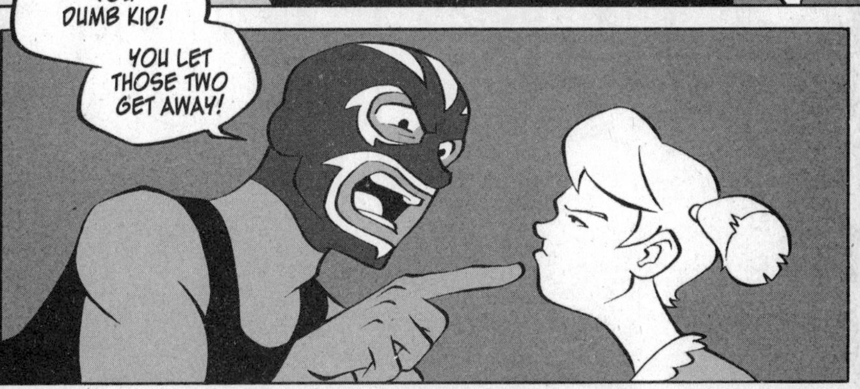
YOU DUMB KID!
YOU LET THOSE TWO GET AWAY!

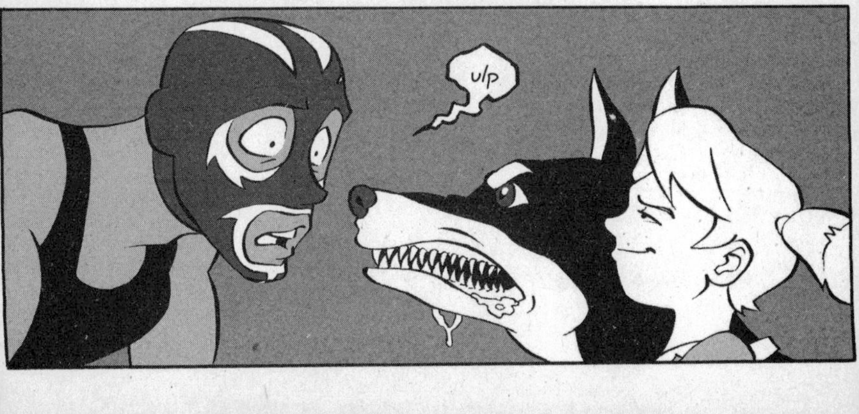
ulp

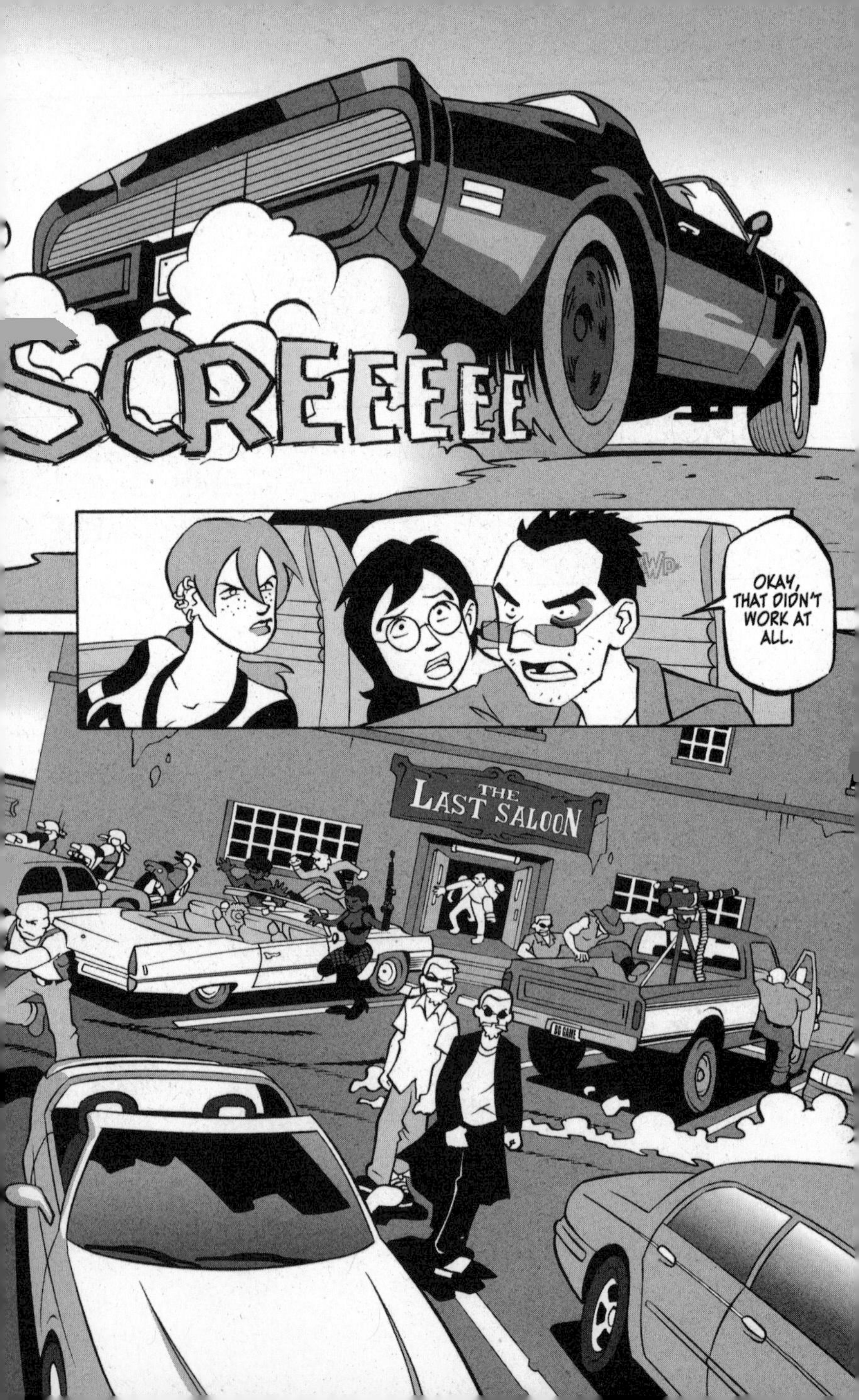
SCREEEEEE
OKAY, THAT DIDN'T WORK AT ALL.
THE LAST SALOON
BG GAME

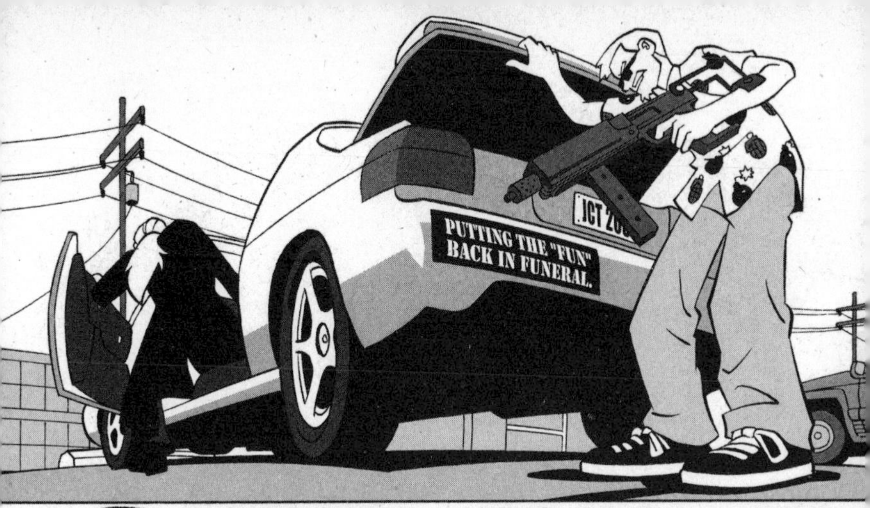
PUTTING THE "FUN" BACK IN FUNERAL.

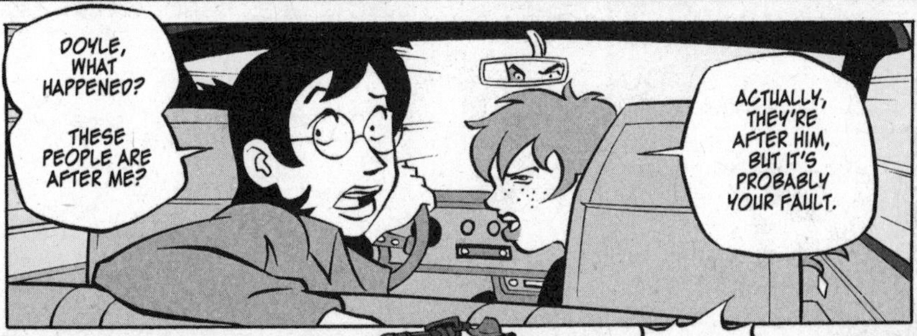
DOYLE, WHAT HAPPENED?
THESE PEOPLE ARE AFTER ME?
ACTUALLY, THEY'RE AFTER HIM, BUT IT'S PROBABLY YOUR FAULT.

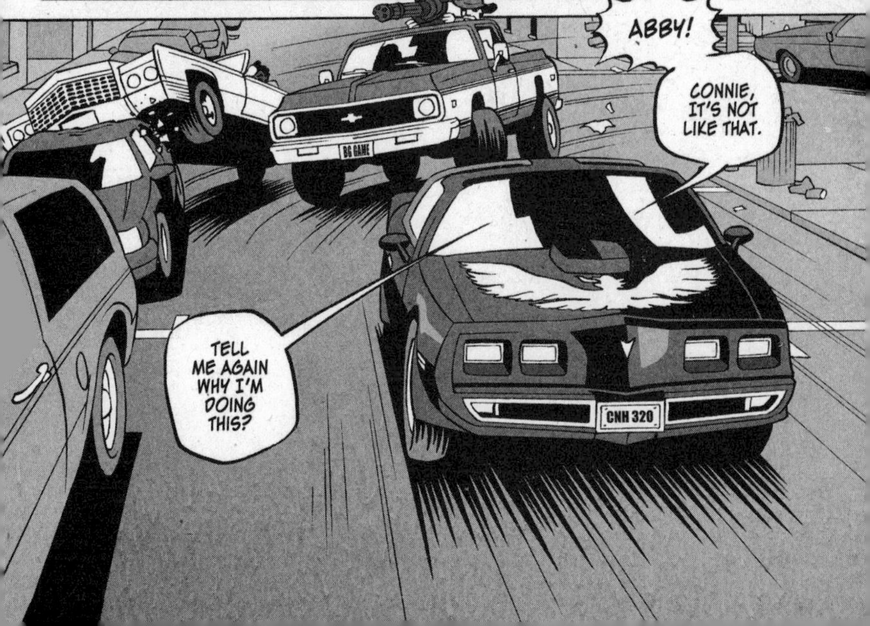
ABBY!
BG GAME
CONNIE, IT'S NOT LIKE THAT.
TELL ME AGAIN WHY I'M DOING THIS?
CNH 320

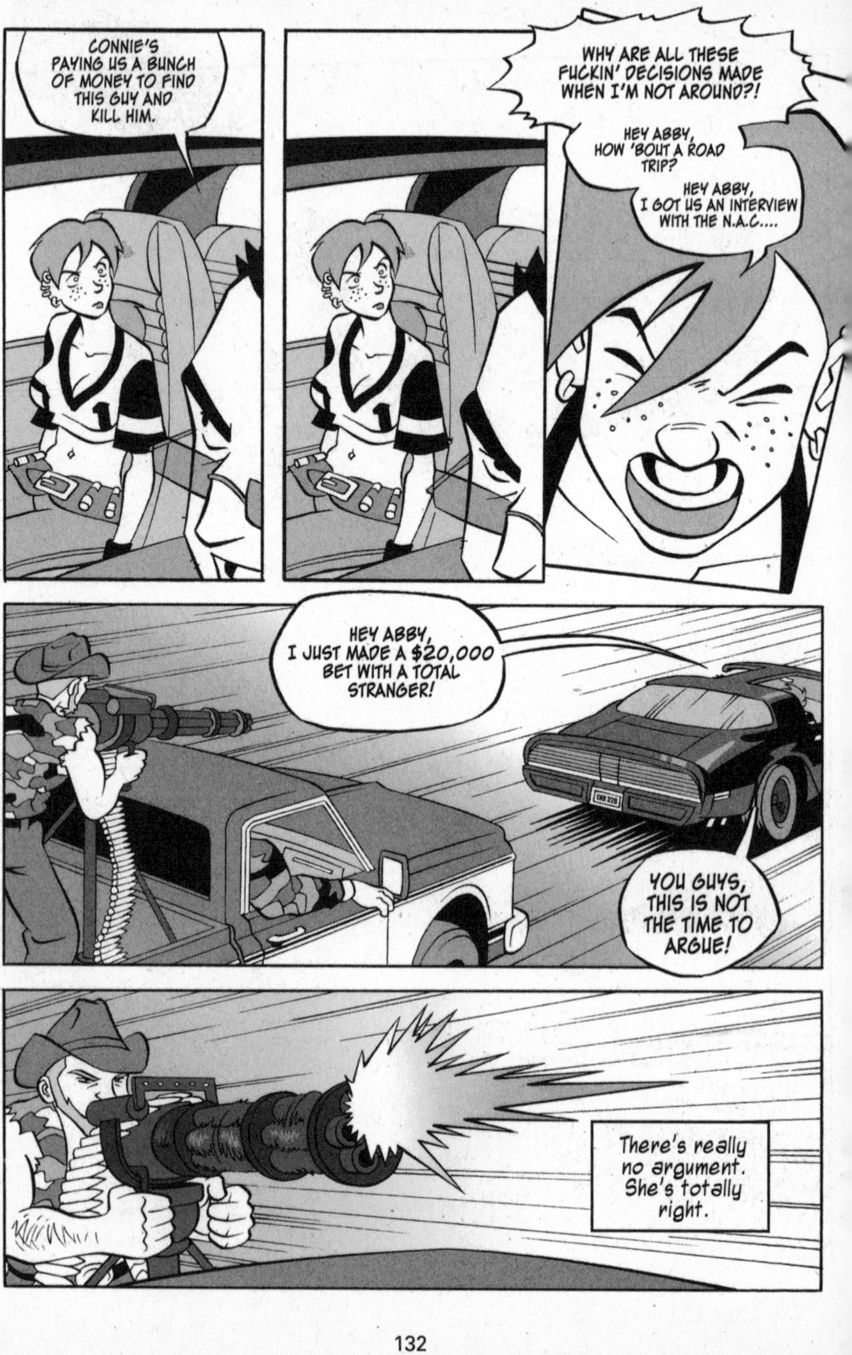
CONNIE'S PAYING US A BUNCH OF MONEY TO FIND THIS GUY AND KILL HIM.
WHY ARE ALL THESE FUCKIN' DECISIONS MADE WHEN I'M NOT AROUND?!
HEY ABBY, HOW 'BOUT A ROAD TRIP?
HEY ABBY, I GOT US AN INTERVIEW WITH THE N.A.C....
HEY ABBY, I JUST MADE A $20,000 BET WITH A TOTAL STRANGER!
YOU GUYS, THIS IS NOT THE TIME TO ARGUE!
There's really no argument. She's totally right.

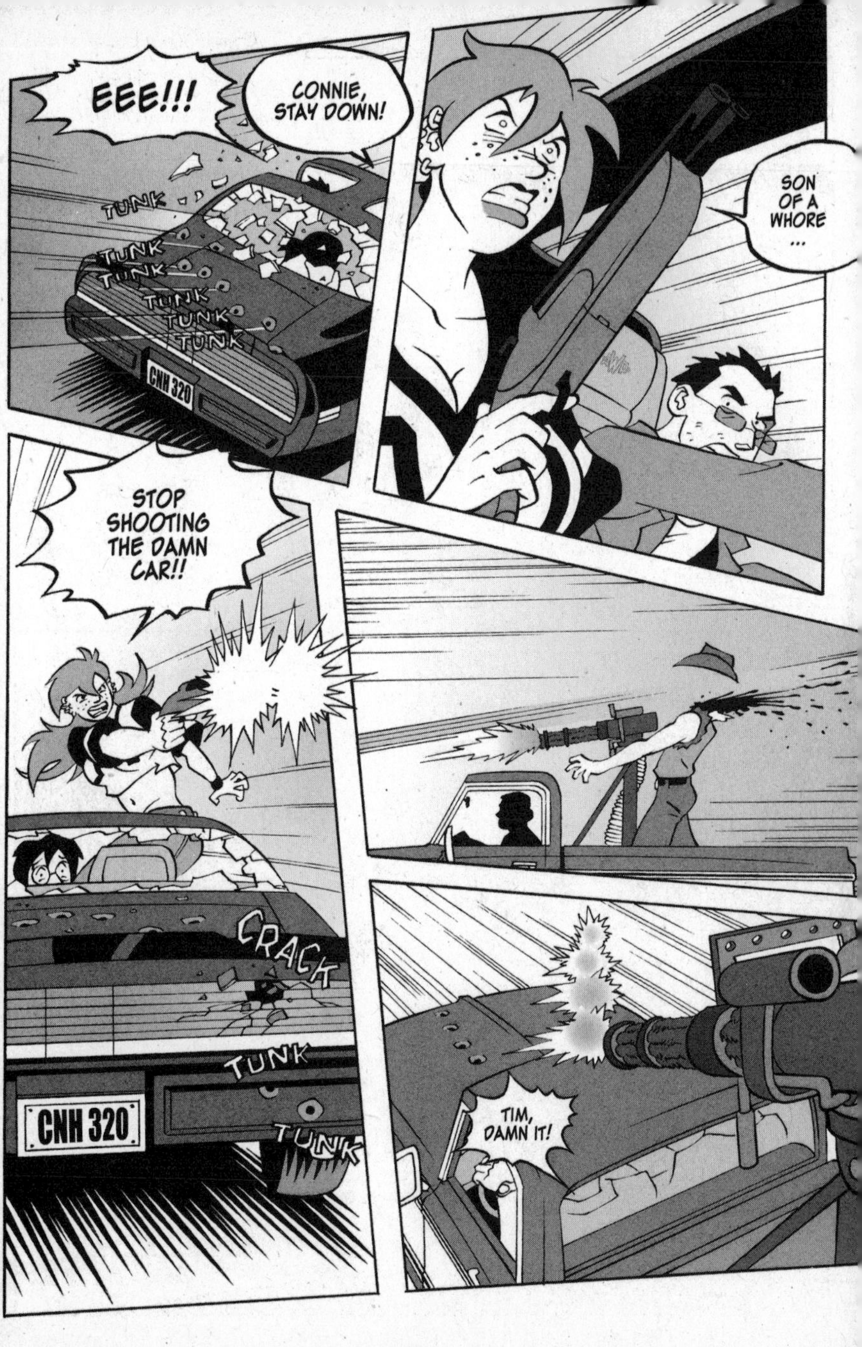
EEE!!!
CONNIE, STAY DOWN!
TUNK
TUNK
TUNK
TUNK
TUNK
TUNK
CNH 320
SON OF A WHORE ...
STOP SHOOTING THE DAMN CAR!!
CRACK
TUNK
TUNK
CNH 320
TIM, DAMN IT!

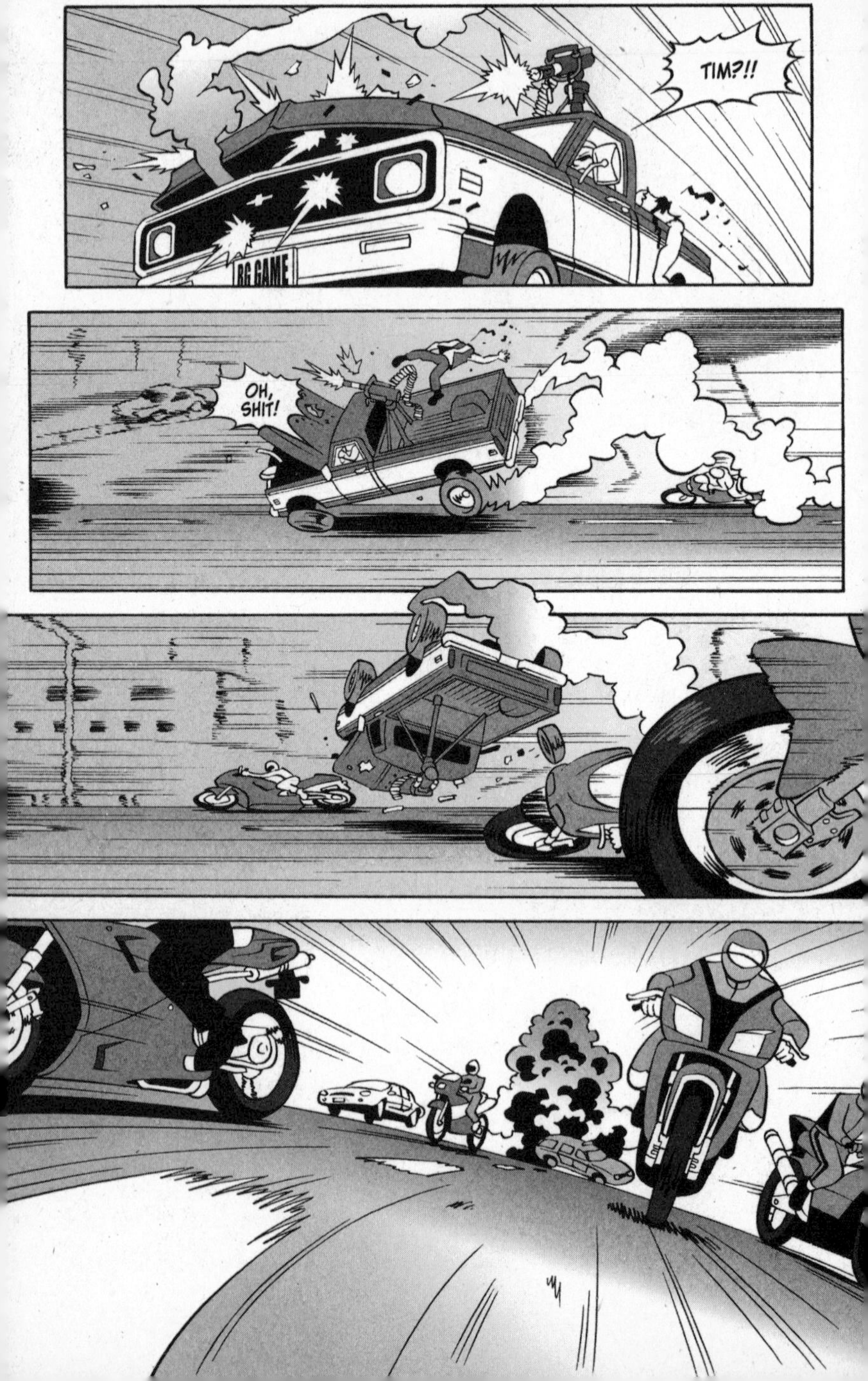
TIM?!!
OH, SHIT!

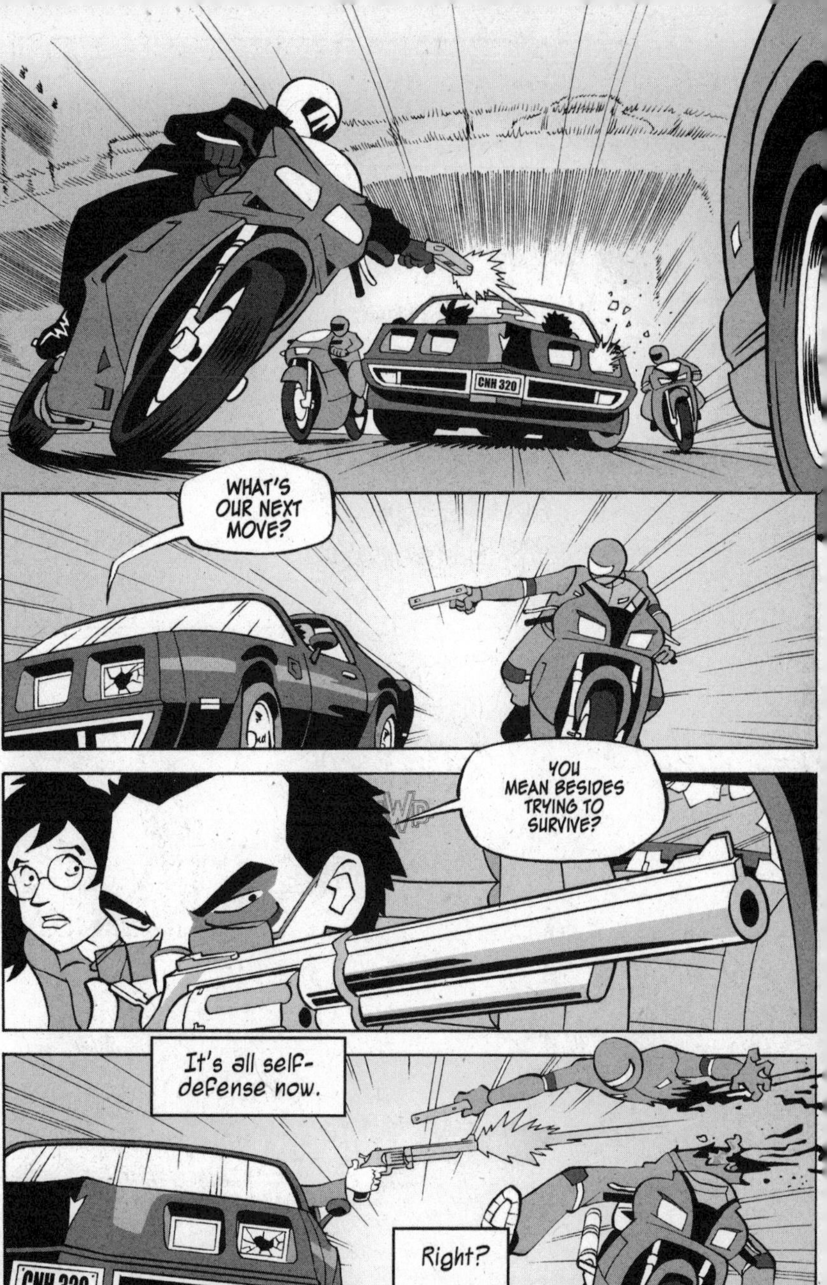
CNH 320
WHAT'S OUR NEXT MOVE?
YOU MEAN BESIDES TRYING TO SURVIVE?
It's all self-defense now.
Right?
CNH 320

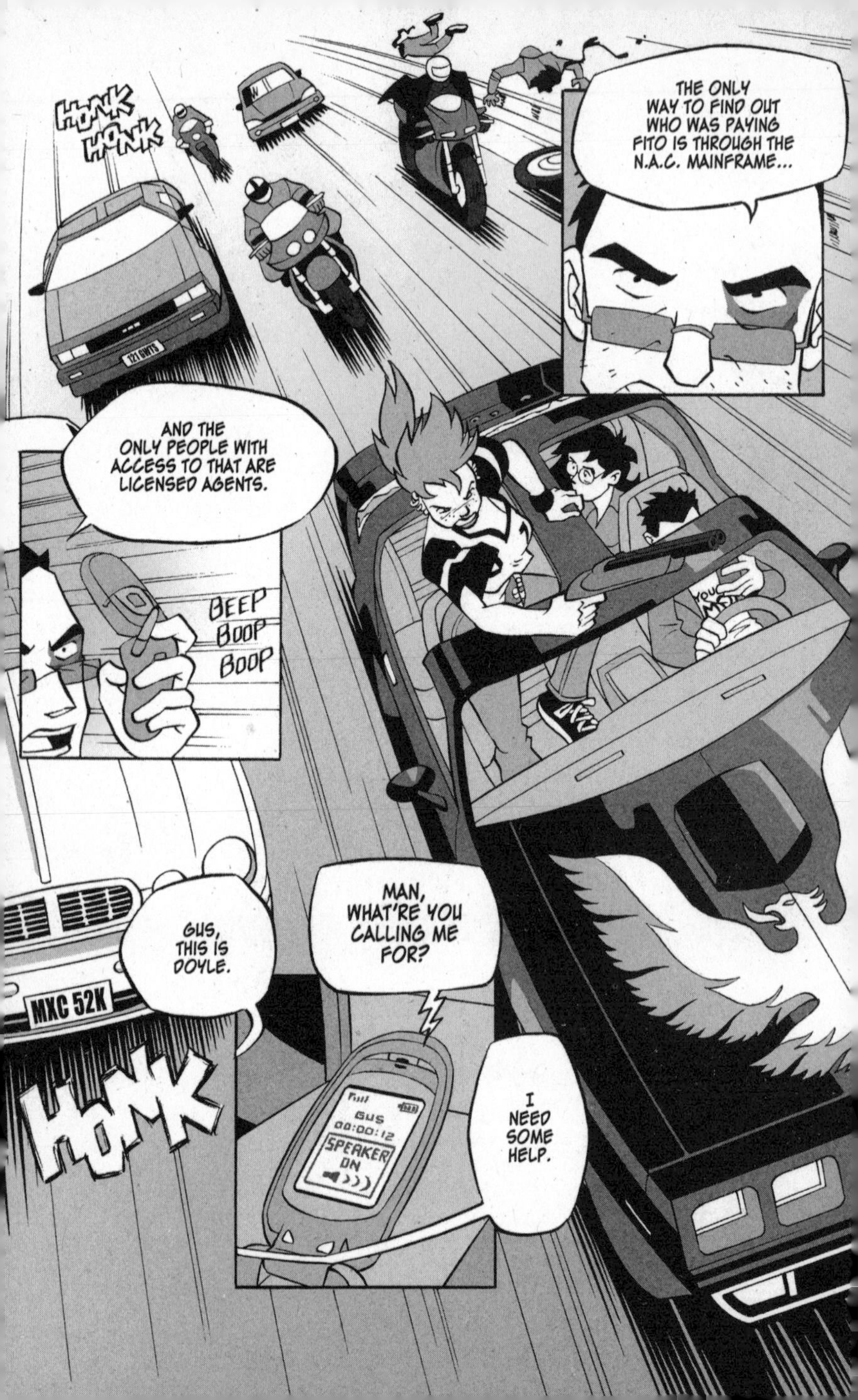
HONK
HONK
THE ONLY WAY TO FIND OUT WHO WAS PAYING FITO IS THROUGH THE N.A.C. MAINFRAME...
AND THE ONLY PEOPLE WITH ACCESS TO THAT ARE LICENSED AGENTS.
BEEP
BOOP
BOOP
MXC 52K
GUS, THIS IS DOYLE.
MAN, WHAT'RE YOU CALLING ME FOR?
GUS
00:00:12
SPEAKER ON
I NEED SOME HELP.
HONK

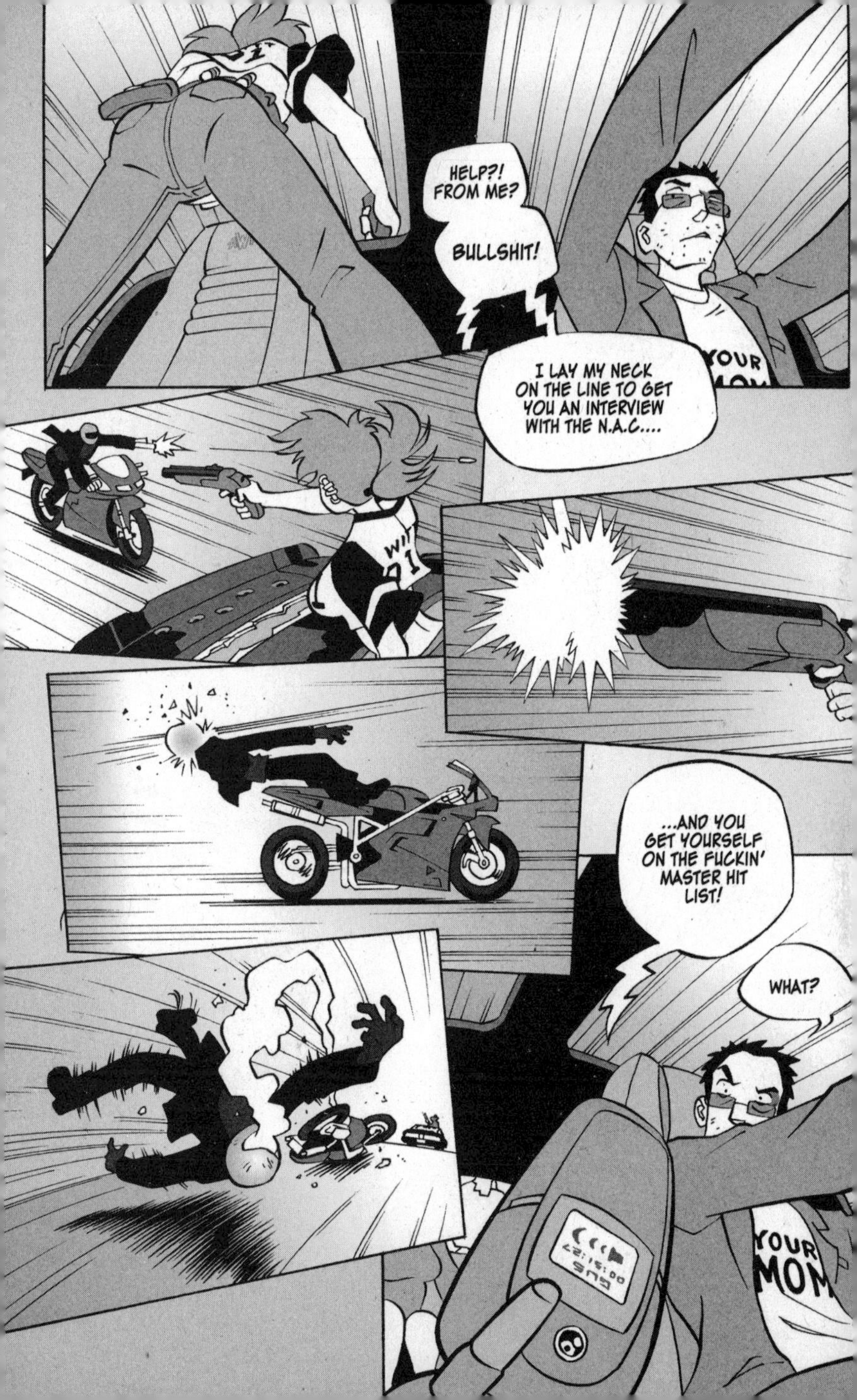
HELP?! FROM ME?
BULLSHIT!
I LAY MY NECK ON THE LINE TO GET YOU AN INTERVIEW WITH THE N.A.C....
...AND YOU GET YOURSELF ON THE FUCKIN' MASTER HIT LIST!
WHAT?
YOUR MOM

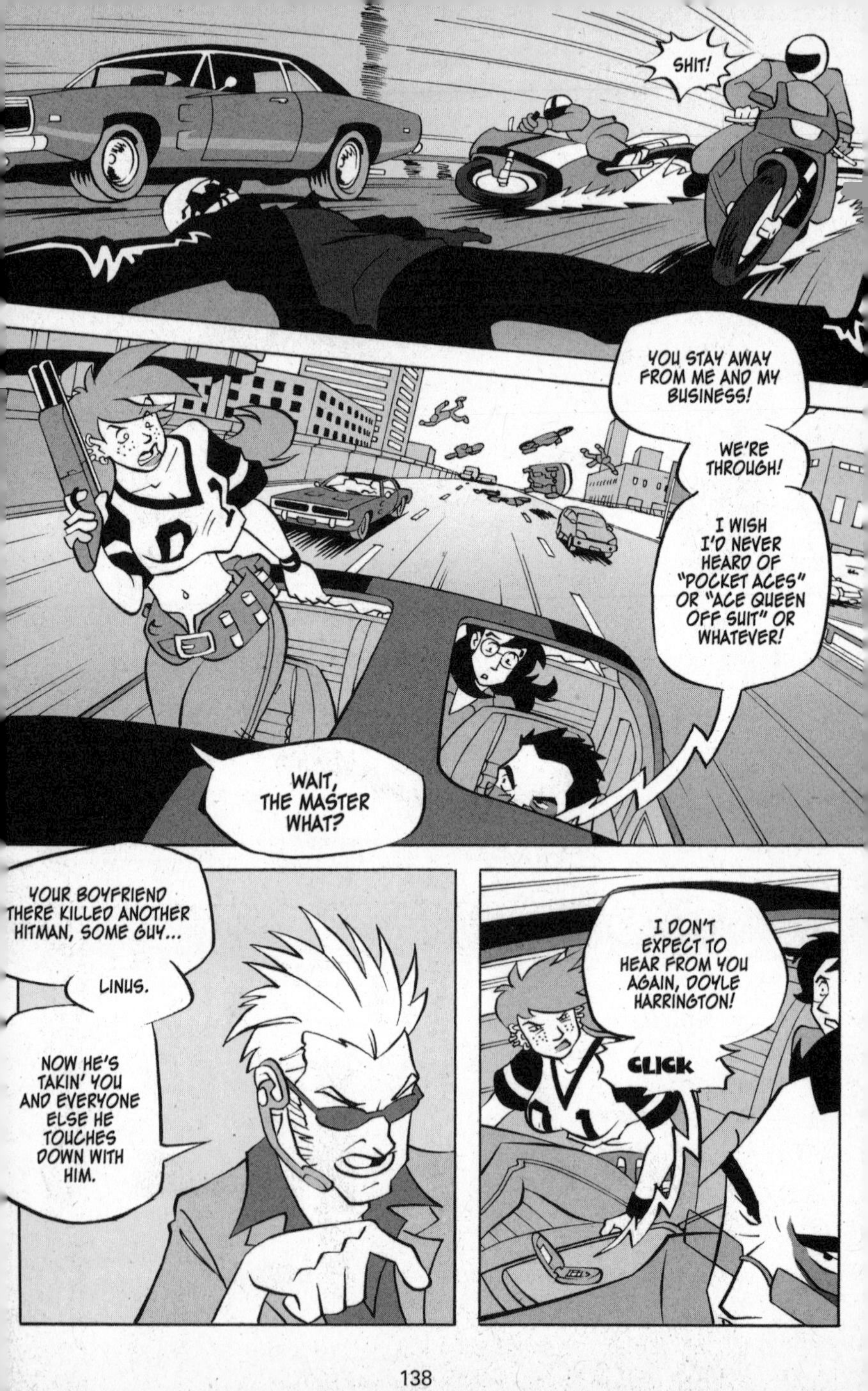
SHIT!
YOU STAY AWAY FROM ME AND MY BUSINESS!
WE'RE THROUGH!
I WISH I'D NEVER HEARD OF "POCKET ACES" OR "ACE QUEEN OFF SUIT" OR WHATEVER!
WAIT, THE MASTER WHAT?
YOUR BOYFRIEND THERE KILLED ANOTHER HITMAN, SOME GUY...
LINUS.
NOW HE'S TAKIN' YOU AND EVERYONE ELSE HE TOUCHES DOWN WITH HIM.
I DON'T EXPECT TO HEAR FROM YOU AGAIN, DOYLE HARRINGTON!
CLICK

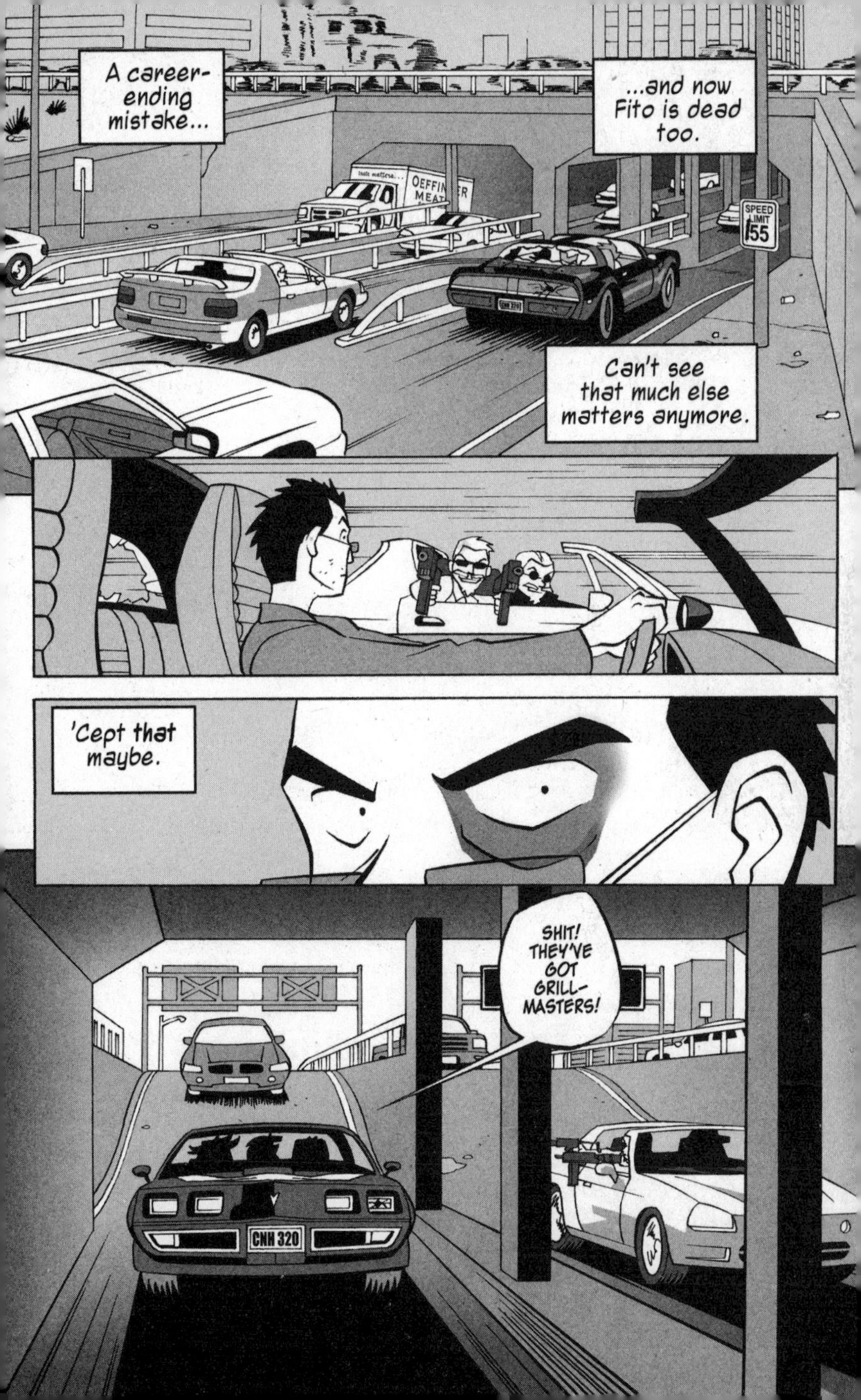
A career-ending mistake...
...and now Fito is dead too.
SPEED LIMIT 55
Can't see that much else matters anymore.
'Cept that maybe.
SHIT! THEY'VE GOT GRILL-MASTERS!
CNH 320

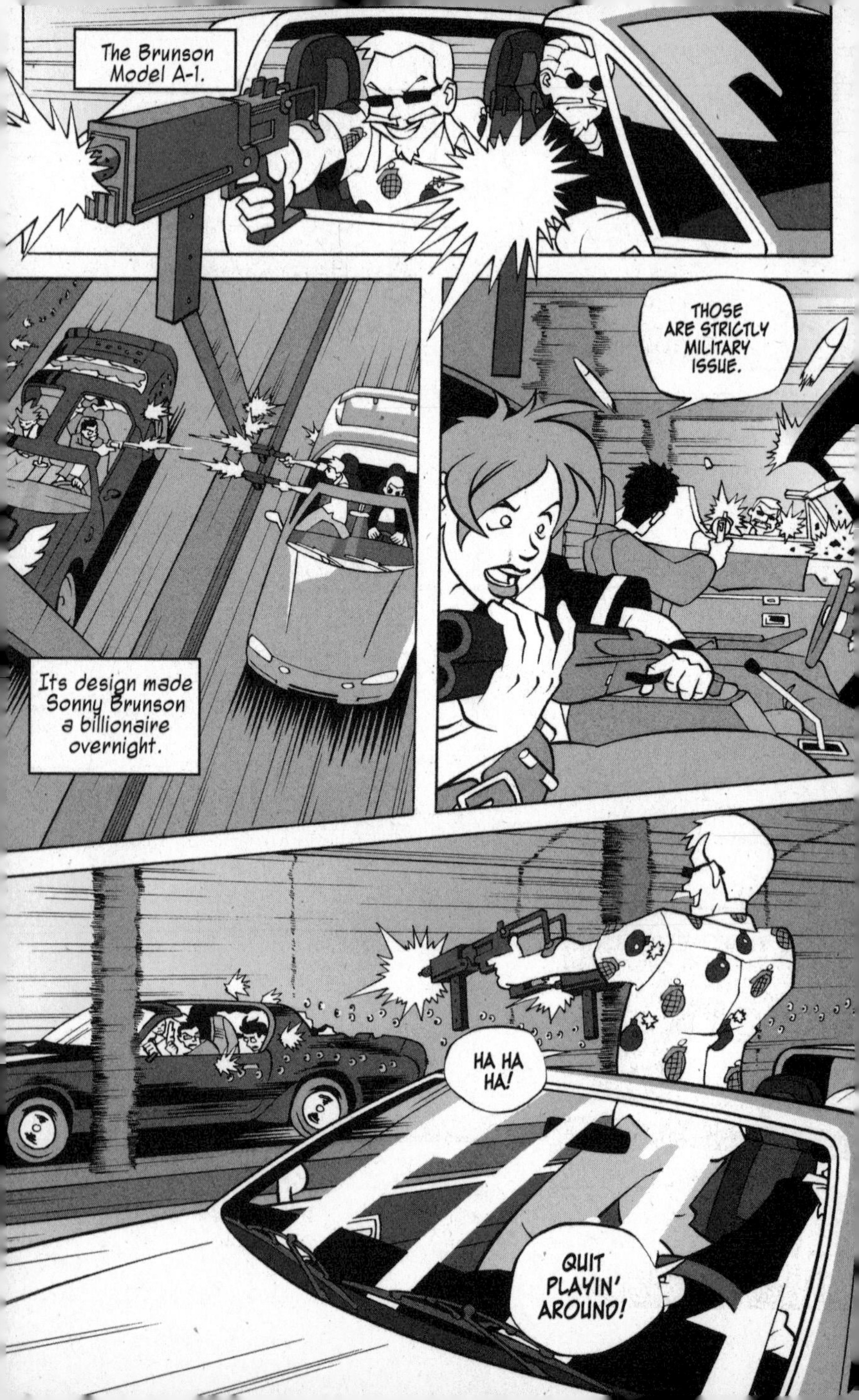
The Brunson Model A-1.
Its design made Sonny Brunson a billionaire overnight.
THOSE ARE STRICTLY MILITARY ISSUE.
HA HA HA!
QUIT PLAYIN' AROUND!

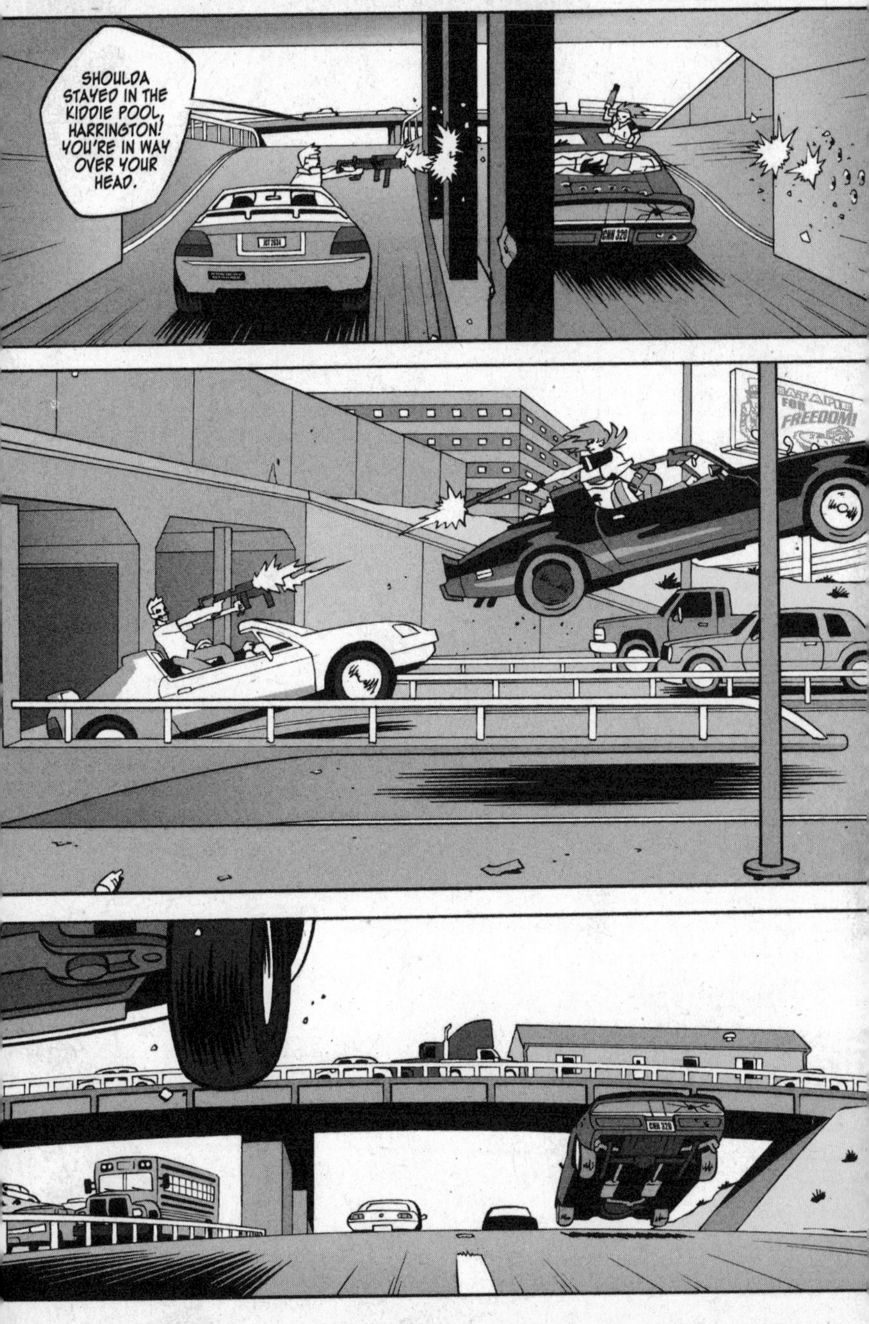
SHOULDA STAYED IN THE KIDDIE POOL, HARRINGTON! YOU'RE IN WAY OVER YOUR HEAD.
CNH 320
FOR
FREEDOM!

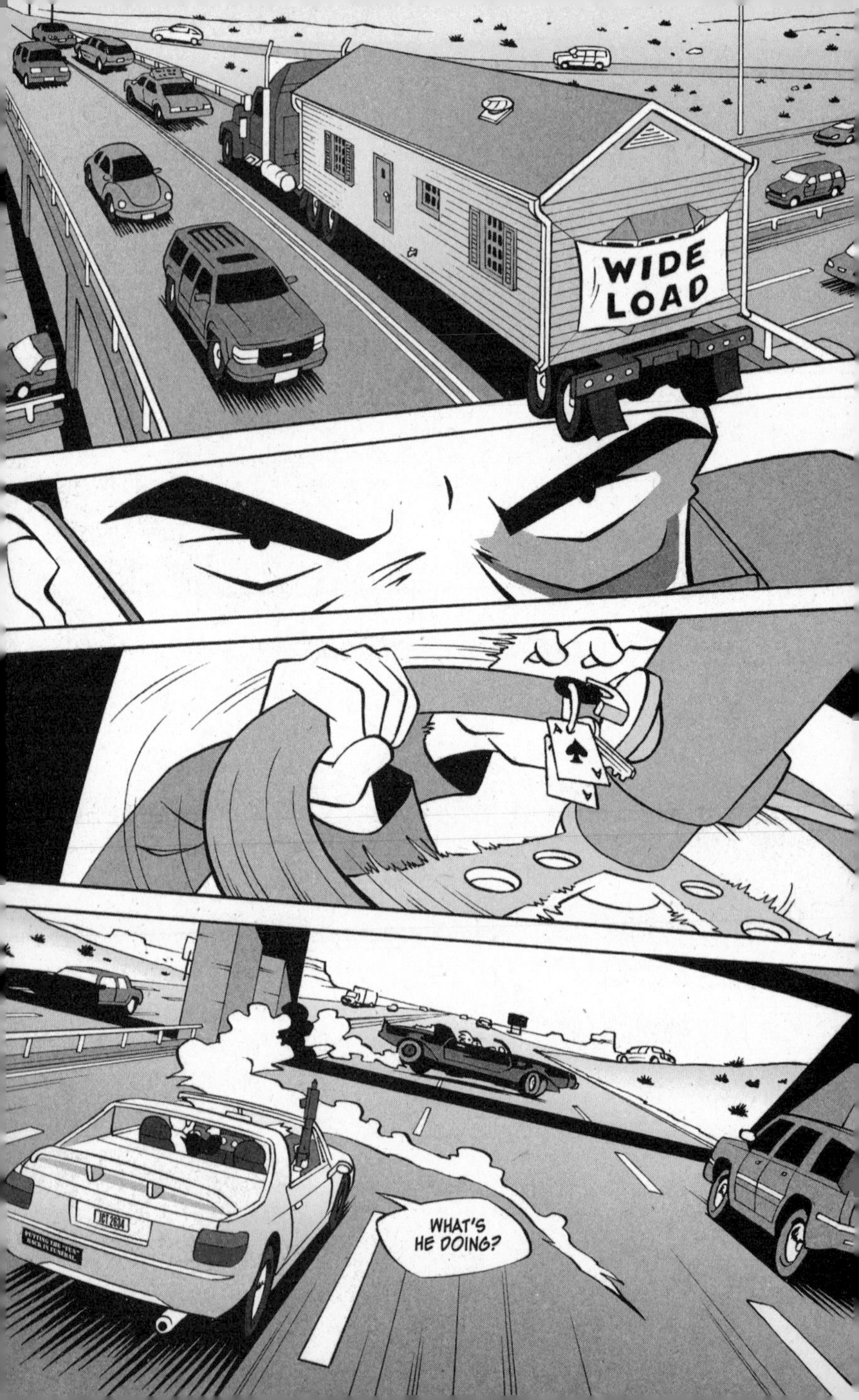
WIDE LOAD
JCT 2634
PUTTING THE "FUN" BACK IN FUNERAL
WHAT'S HE DOING?

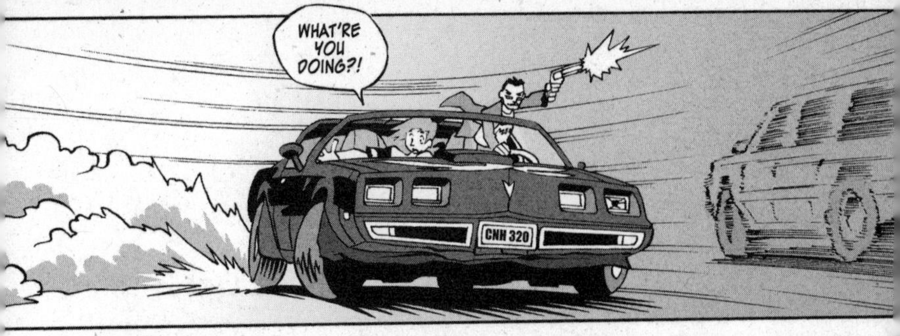
WHAT'RE YOU DOING?!
CNH 320

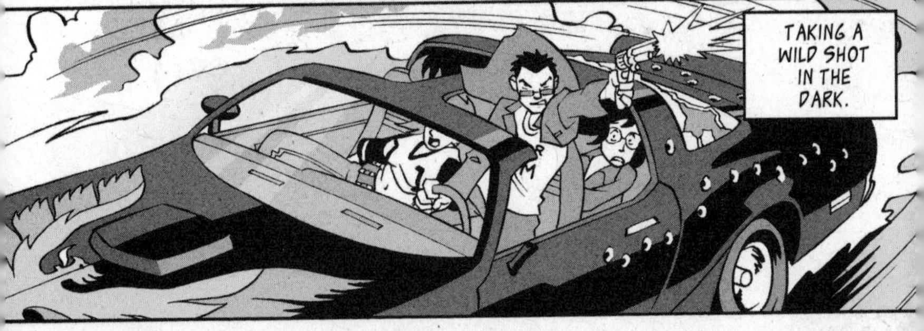
TAKING A WILD SHOT IN THE DARK.

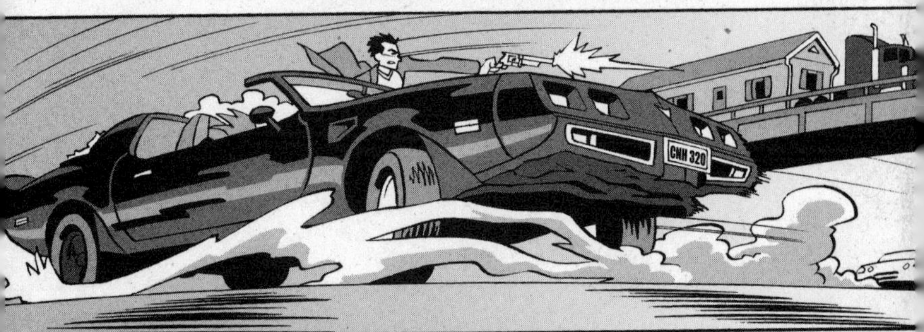
CNH 320

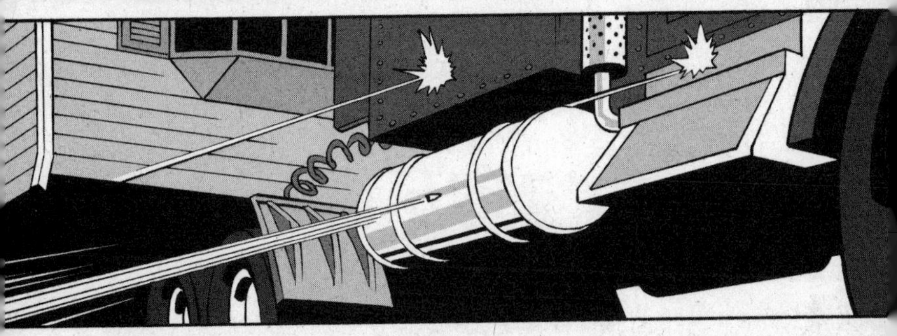

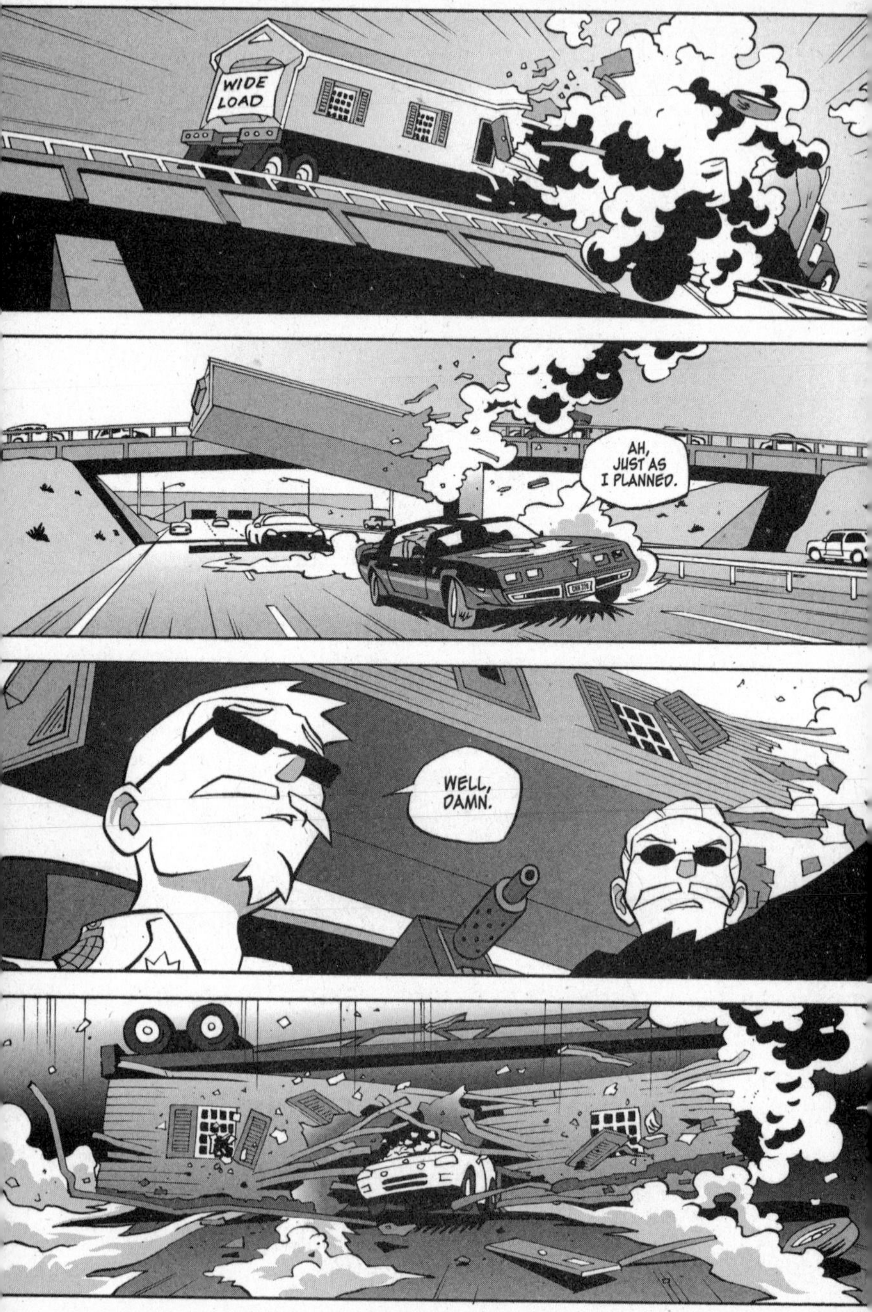
WIDE LOAD
AH, JUST AS I PLANNED.
WELL, DAMN.

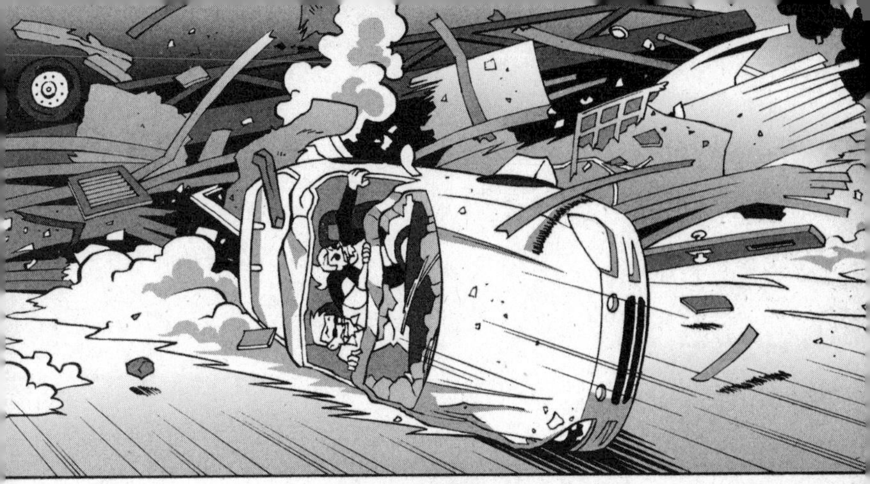

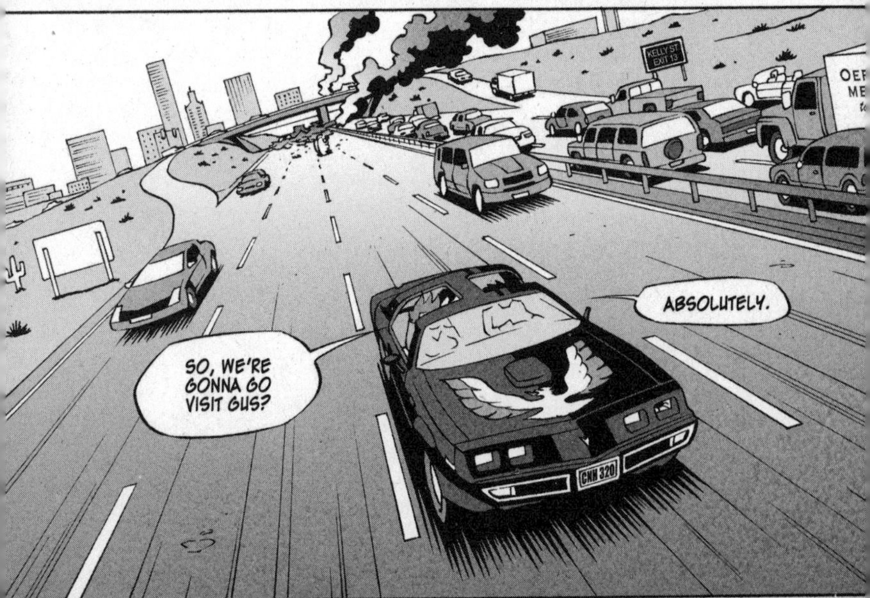
KELLY ST
EXIT 13
CNH 320
SO, WE'RE GONNA GO VISIT GUS?
ABSOLUTELY.

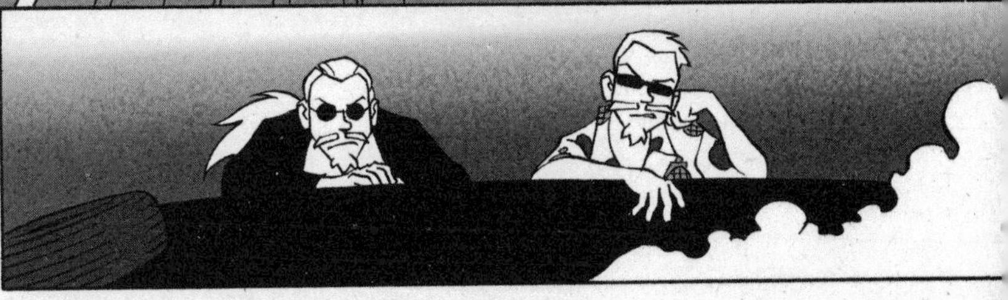

8

GASC

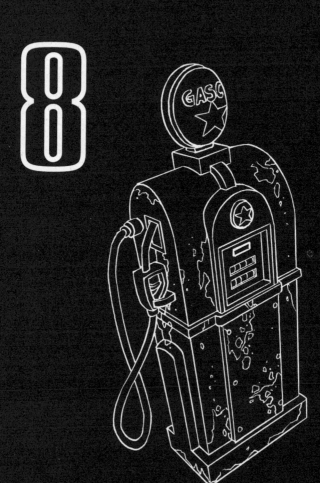

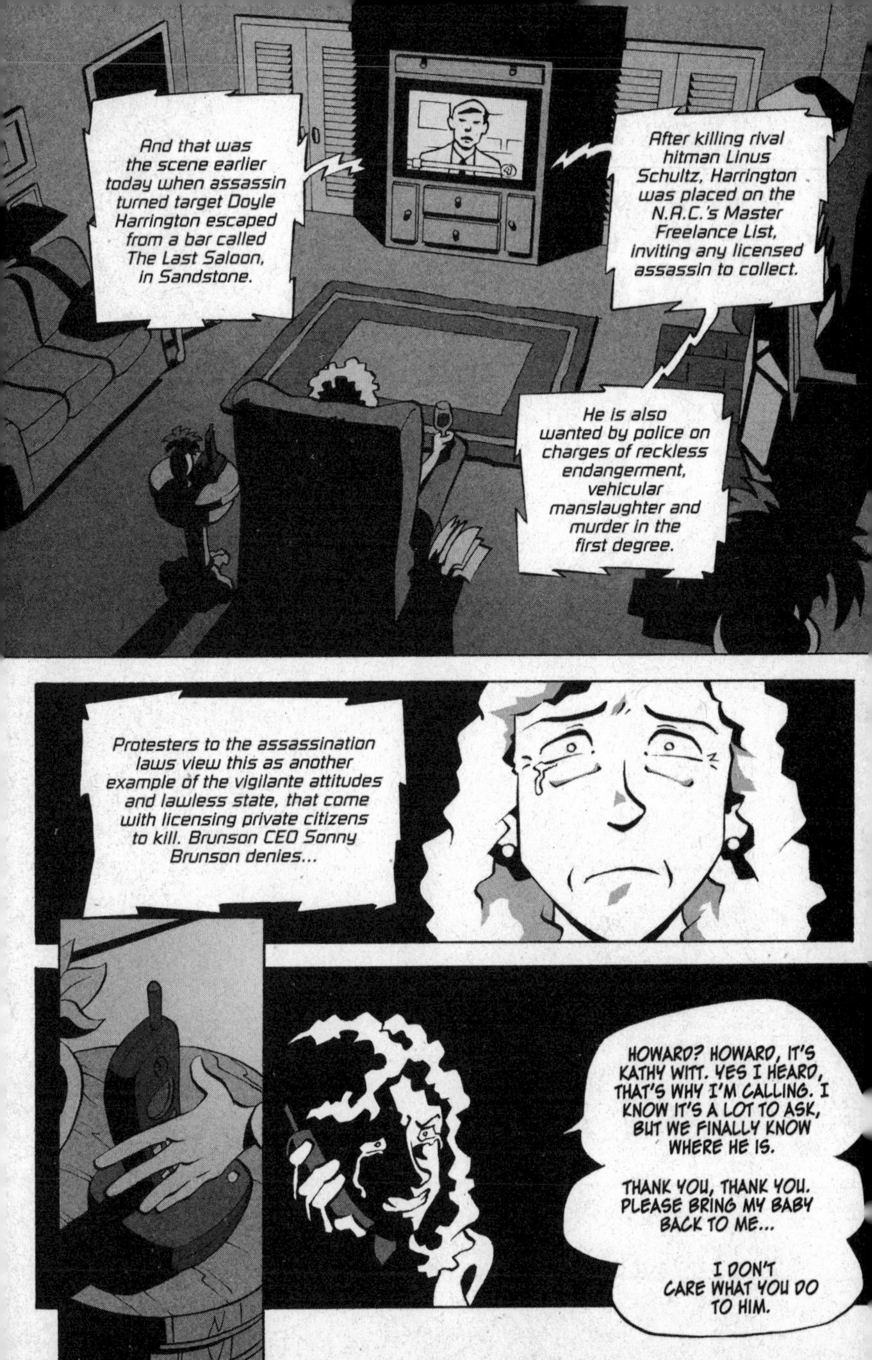
And that was the scene earlier today when assassin turned target Doyle Harrington escaped from a bar called The Last Saloon, in Sandstone.
After killing rival hitman Linus Schultz, Harrington was placed on the N.A.C.'s Master Freelance List, inviting any licensed assassin to collect.
He is also wanted by police on charges of reckless endangerment, vehicular manslaughter and murder in the first degree.
Protesters to the assassination laws view this as another example of the vigilante attitudes and lawless state, that come with licensing private citizens to kill. Brunson CEO Sonny Brunson denies...
HOWARD? HOWARD, IT'S KATHY WITT. YES I HEARD, THAT'S WHY I'M CALLING. I KNOW IT'S A LOT TO ASK, BUT WE FINALLY KNOW WHERE HE IS.
THANK YOU, THANK YOU. PLEASE BRING MY BABY BACK TO ME...
I DON'T CARE WHAT YOU DO TO HIM.

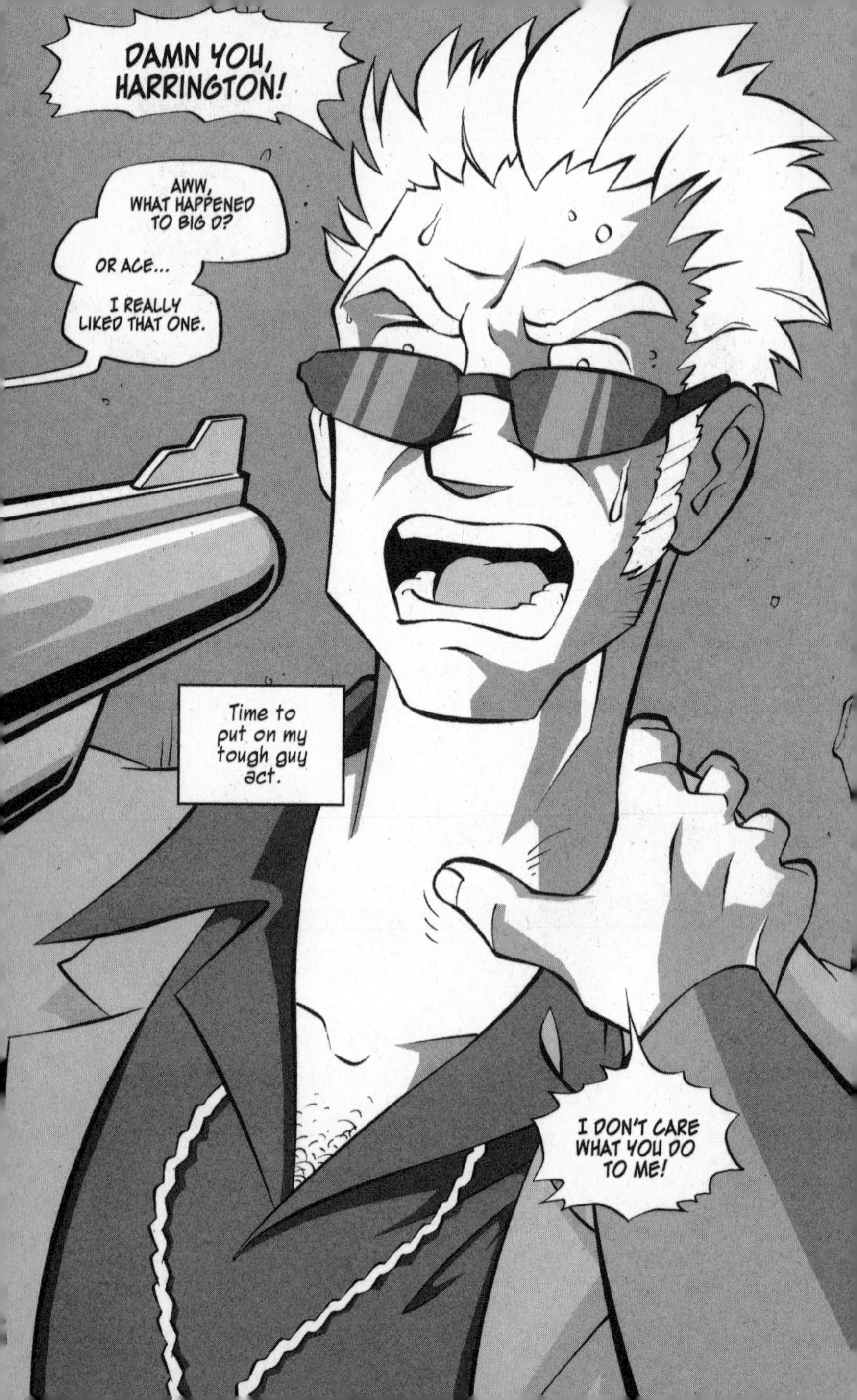
DAMN YOU, HARRINGTON!
AWW, WHAT HAPPENED TO BIG D?
OR ACE...
I REALLY LIKED THAT ONE.
Time to put on my tough guy act.
I DON'T CARE WHAT YOU DO TO ME!

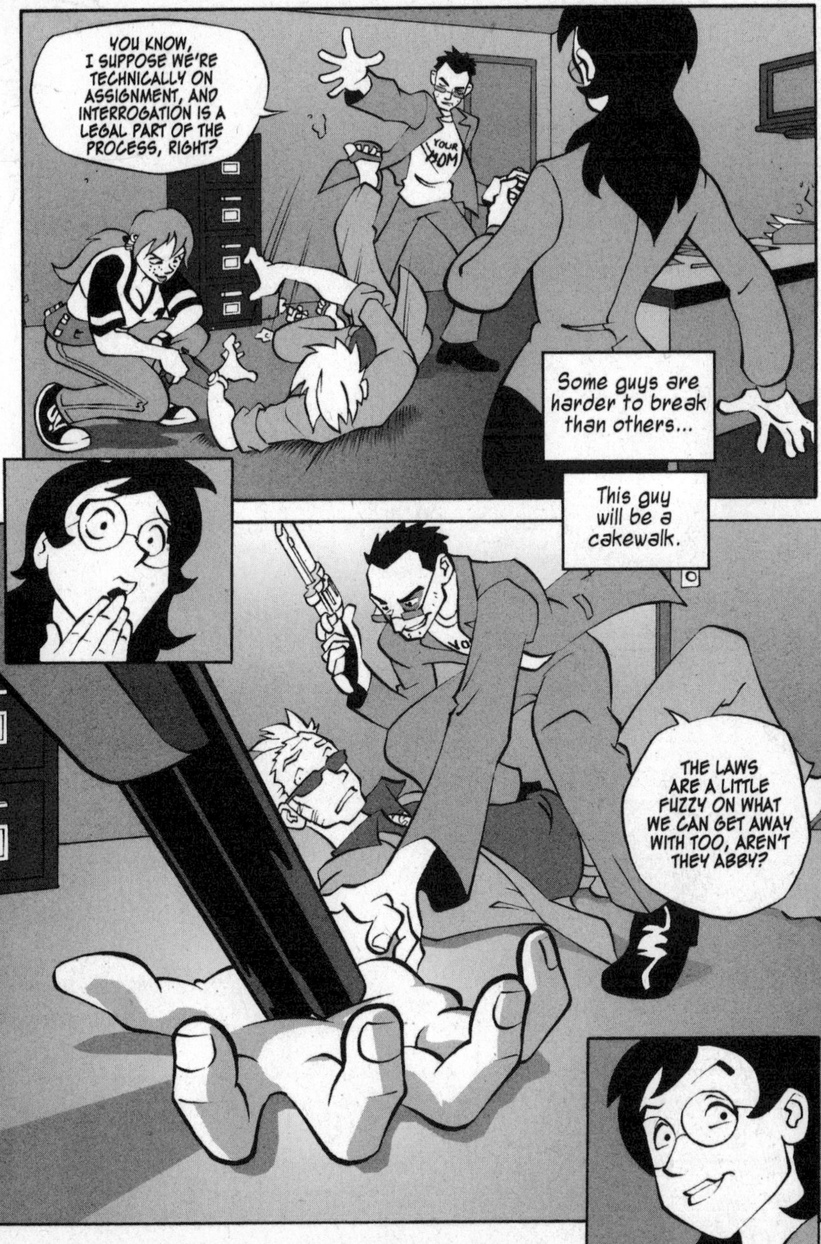
YOU KNOW, I SUPPOSE WE'RE TECHNICALLY ON ASSIGNMENT, AND INTERROGATION IS A LEGAL PART OF THE PROCESS, RIGHT?
YOUR MOM
Some guys are harder to break than others...
This guy will be a cakewalk.
THE LAWS ARE A LITTLE FUZZY ON WHAT WE CAN GET AWAY WITH TOO, AREN'T THEY ABBY?

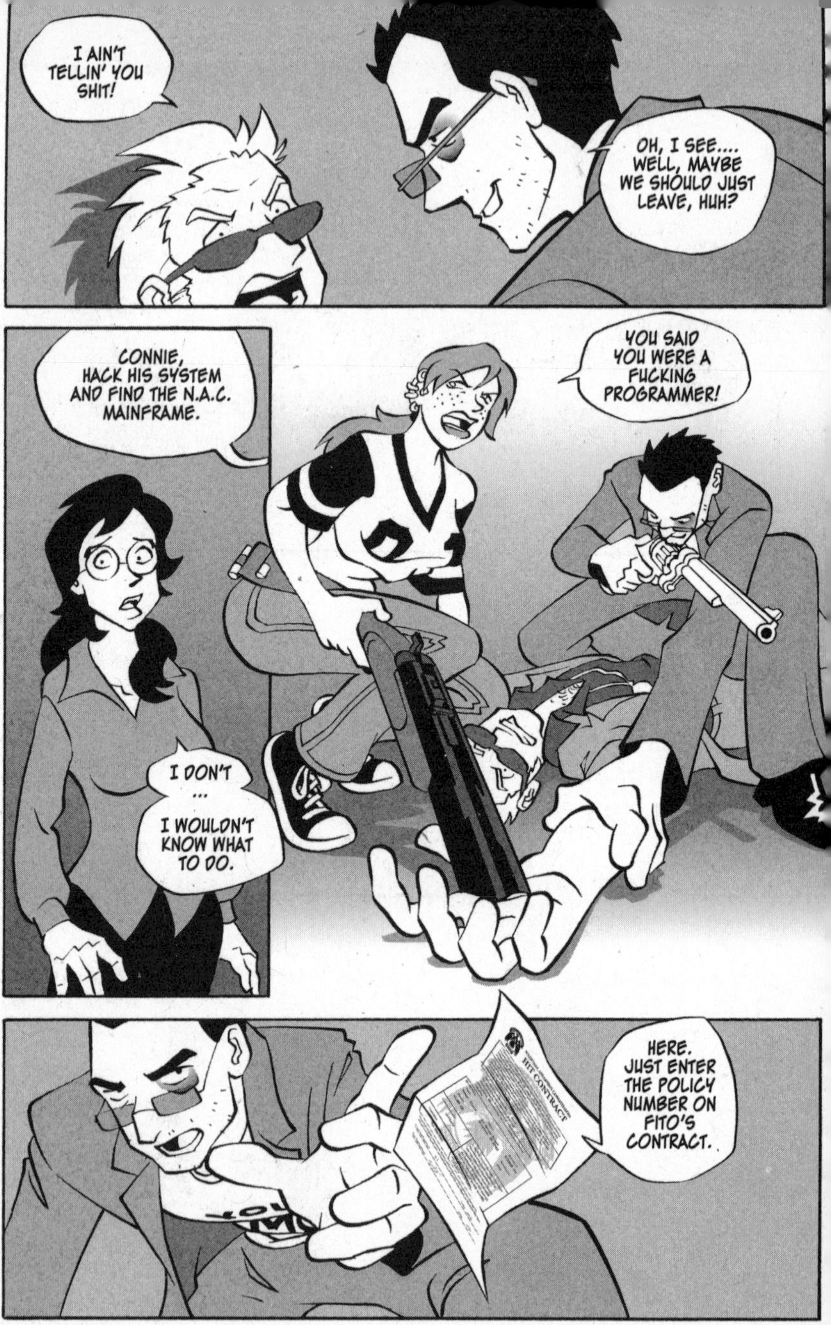
I AIN'T TELLIN' YOU SHIT!
OH, I SEE.... WELL, MAYBE WE SHOULD JUST LEAVE, HUH?
CONNIE, HACK HIS SYSTEM AND FIND THE N.A.C. MAINFRAME.
I DON'T ...
I WOULDN'T KNOW WHAT TO DO.
YOU SAID YOU WERE A FUCKING PROGRAMMER!
HIT CONTRACT
HERE. JUST ENTER THE POLICY NUMBER ON FITO'S CONTRACT.

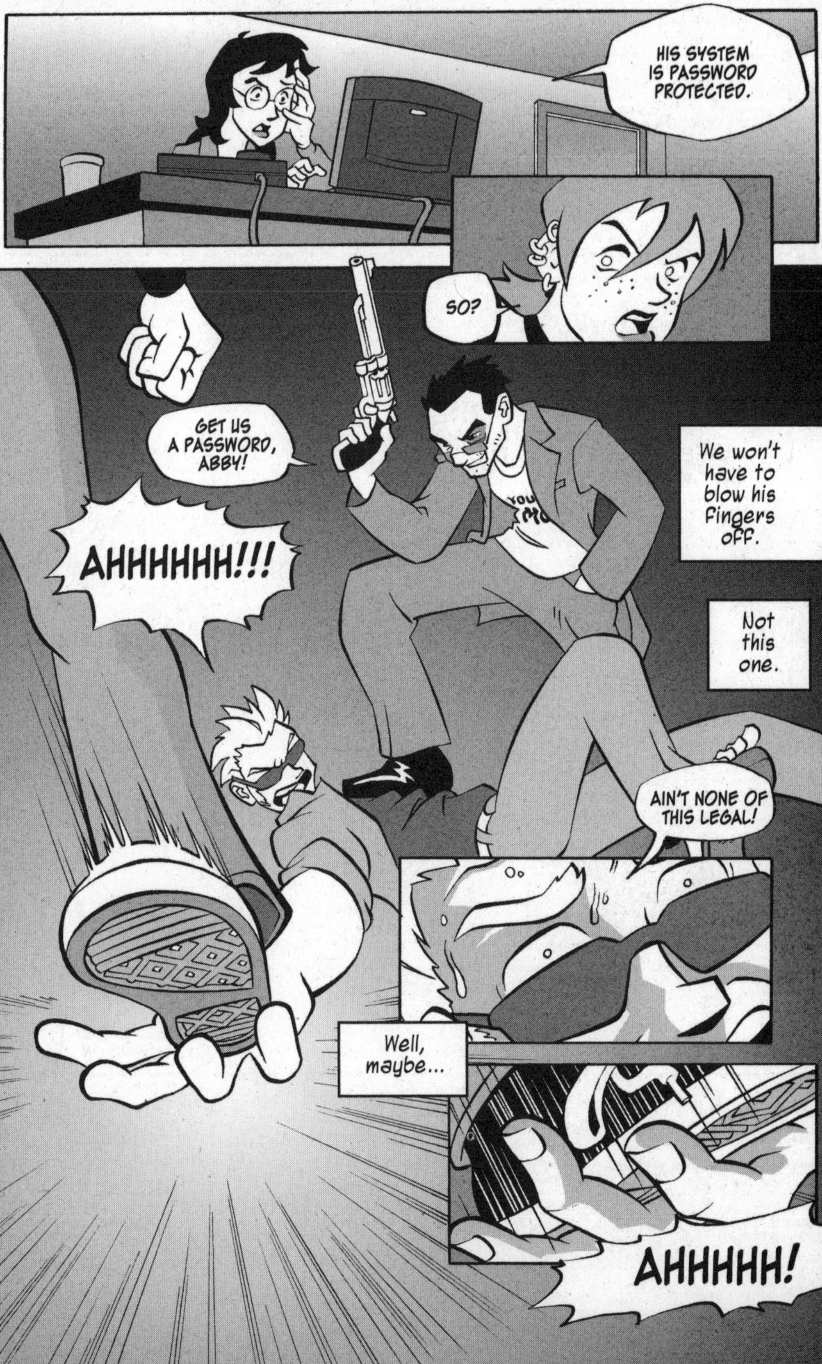
HIS SYSTEM IS PASSWORD PROTECTED.
SO?
GET US A PASSWORD, ABBY!
AHHHHHH!!!
We won't have to blow his fingers off.
Not this one.
AIN'T NONE OF THIS LEGAL!
Well, maybe...
AHHHHH!

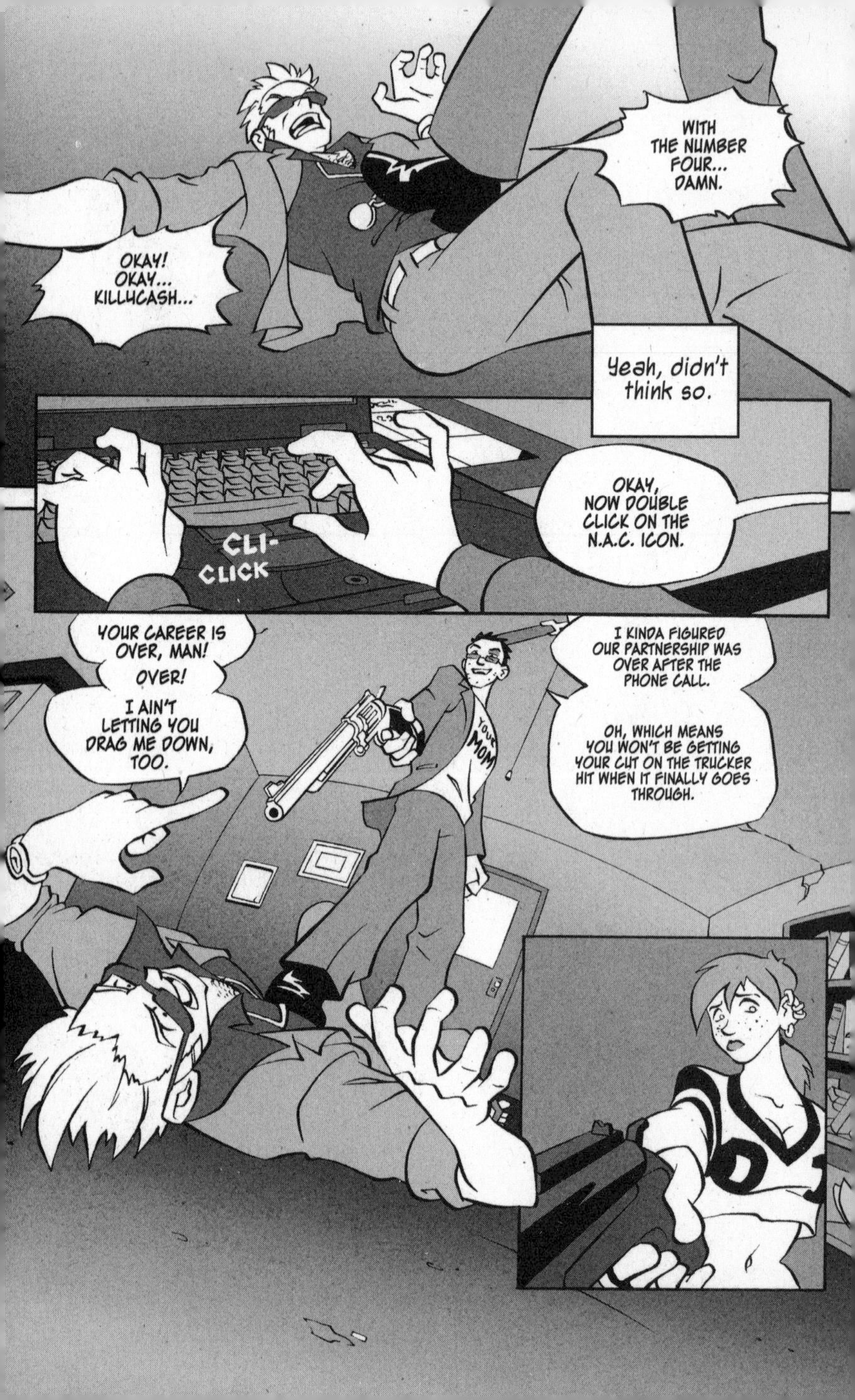
OKAY! OKAY... KILLUCASH...
WITH THE NUMBER FOUR... DAMN.
Yeah, didn't think so.
CLI- CLICK
OKAY, NOW DOUBLE CLICK ON THE N.A.C. ICON.
YOUR CAREER IS OVER, MAN!
OVER!
I AIN'T LETTING YOU DRAG ME DOWN, TOO.
YOUR MOM
I KINDA FIGURED OUR PARTNERSHIP WAS OVER AFTER THE PHONE CALL.
OH, WHICH MEANS YOU WON'T BE GETTING YOUR CUT ON THE TRUCKER HIT WHEN IT FINALLY GOES THROUGH.

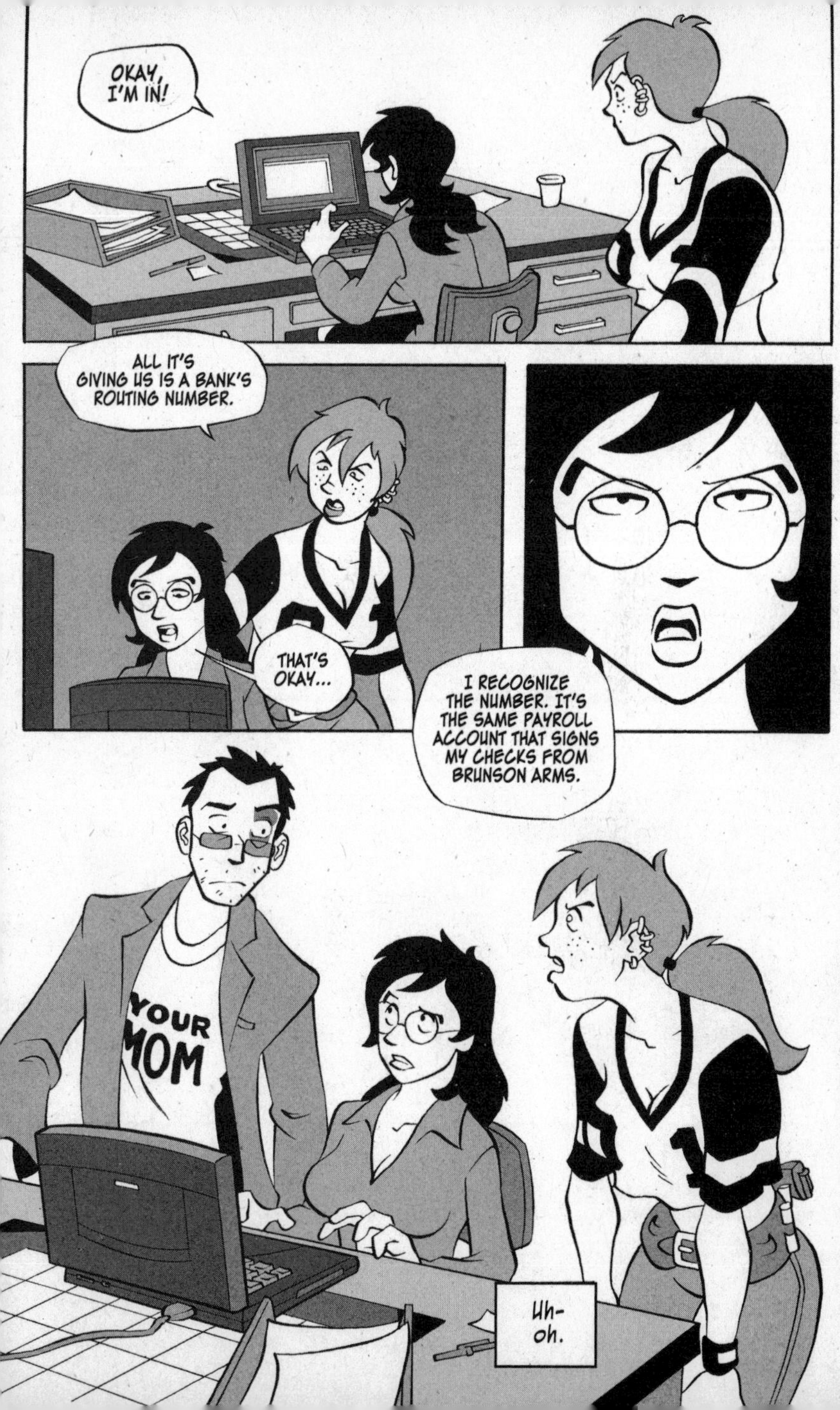
OKAY, I'M IN!
ALL IT'S GIVING US IS A BANK'S ROUTING NUMBER.
THAT'S OKAY...
I RECOGNIZE THE NUMBER. IT'S THE SAME PAYROLL ACCOUNT THAT SIGNS MY CHECKS FROM BRUNSON ARMS.
YOUR MOM
Uh-oh.

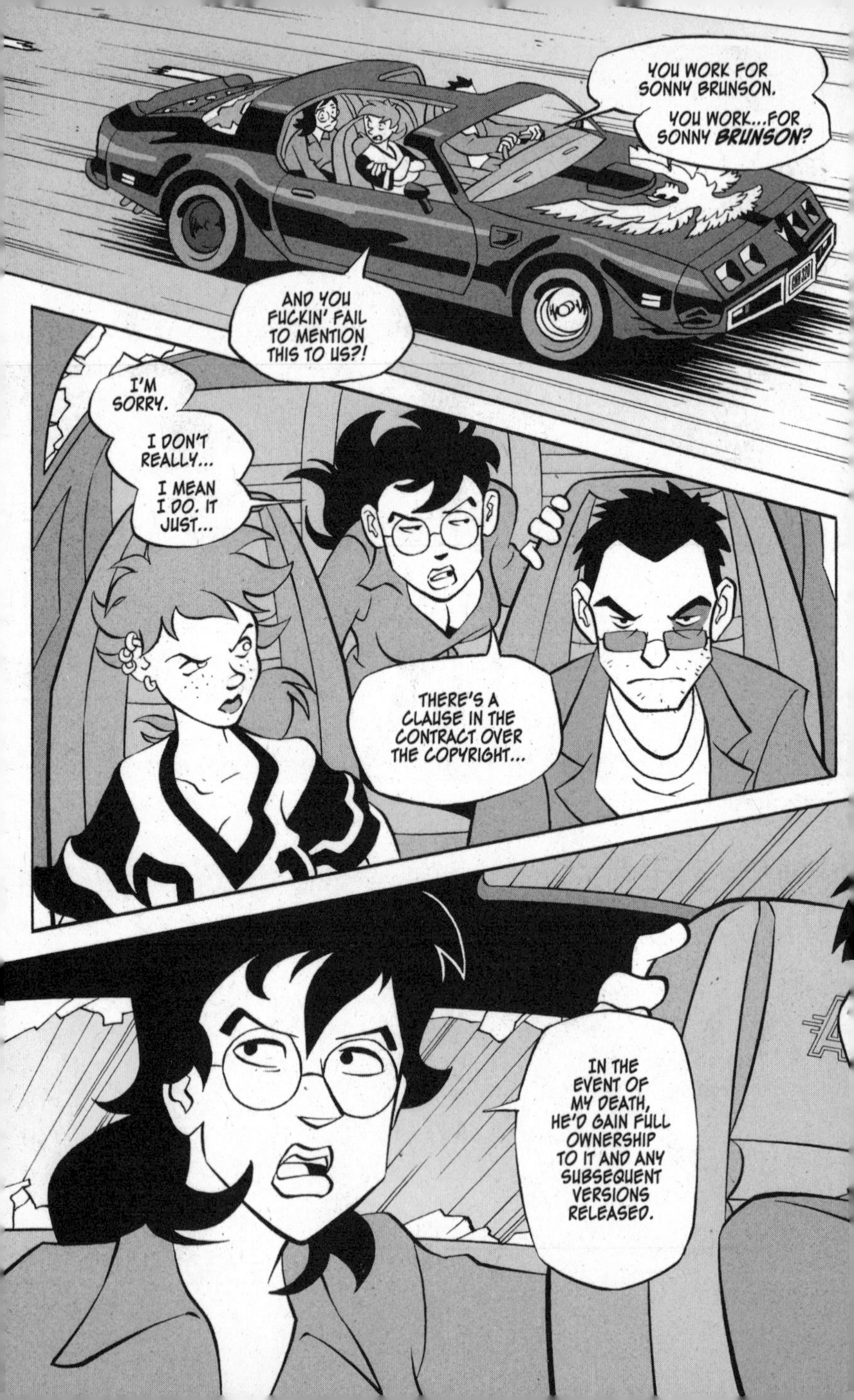
YOU WORK FOR SONNY BRUNSON.
YOU WORK...FOR SONNY BRUNSON?
AND YOU FUCKIN' FAIL TO MENTION THIS TO US?!
I'M SORRY.
I DON'T REALLY...
I MEAN I DO. IT JUST...
THERE'S A CLAUSE IN THE CONTRACT OVER THE COPYRIGHT...
IN THE EVENT OF MY DEATH, HE'D GAIN FULL OWNERSHIP TO IT AND ANY SUBSEQUENT VERSIONS RELEASED.

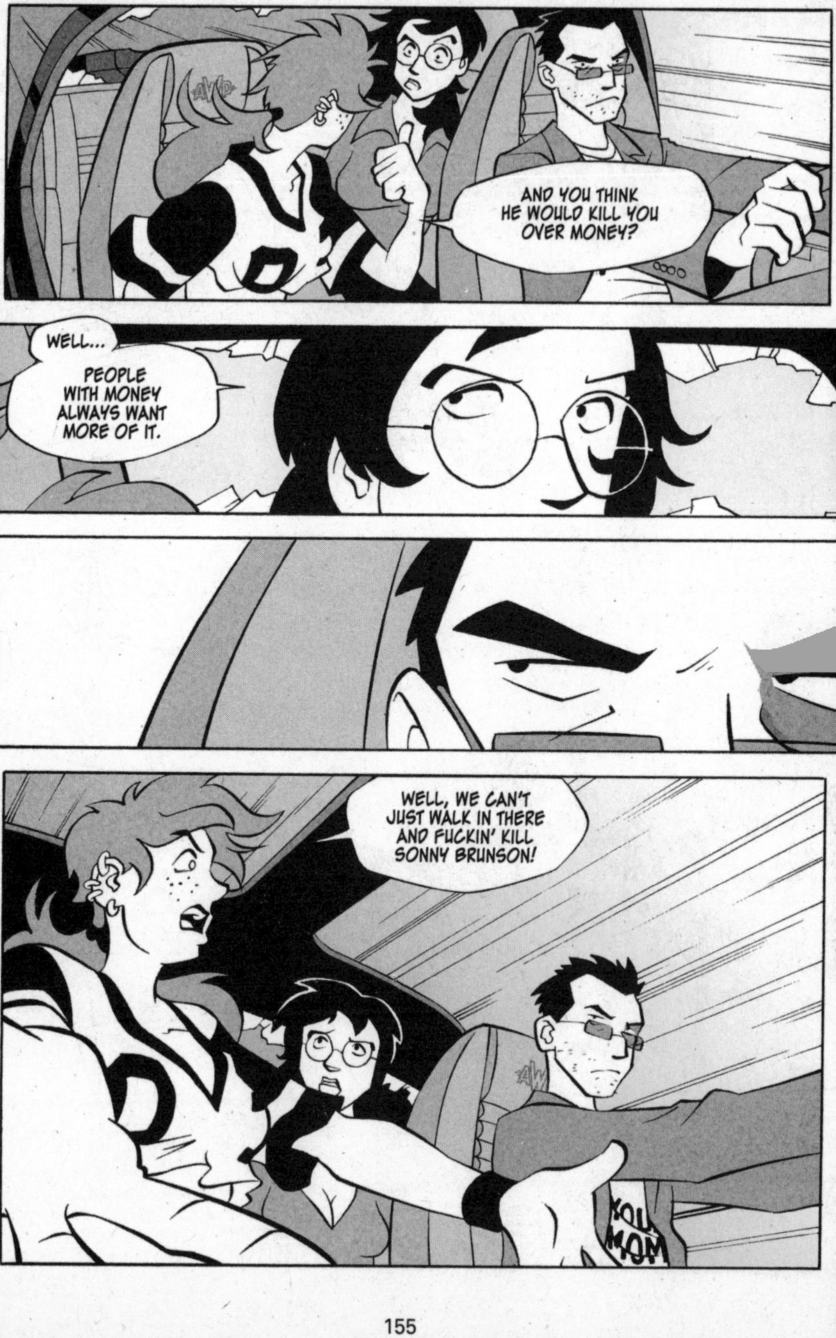
AND YOU THINK HE WOULD KILL YOU OVER MONEY?
WELL...
PEOPLE WITH MONEY ALWAYS WANT MORE OF IT.
WELL, WE CAN'T JUST WALK IN THERE AND FUCKIN' KILL SONNY BRUNSON!

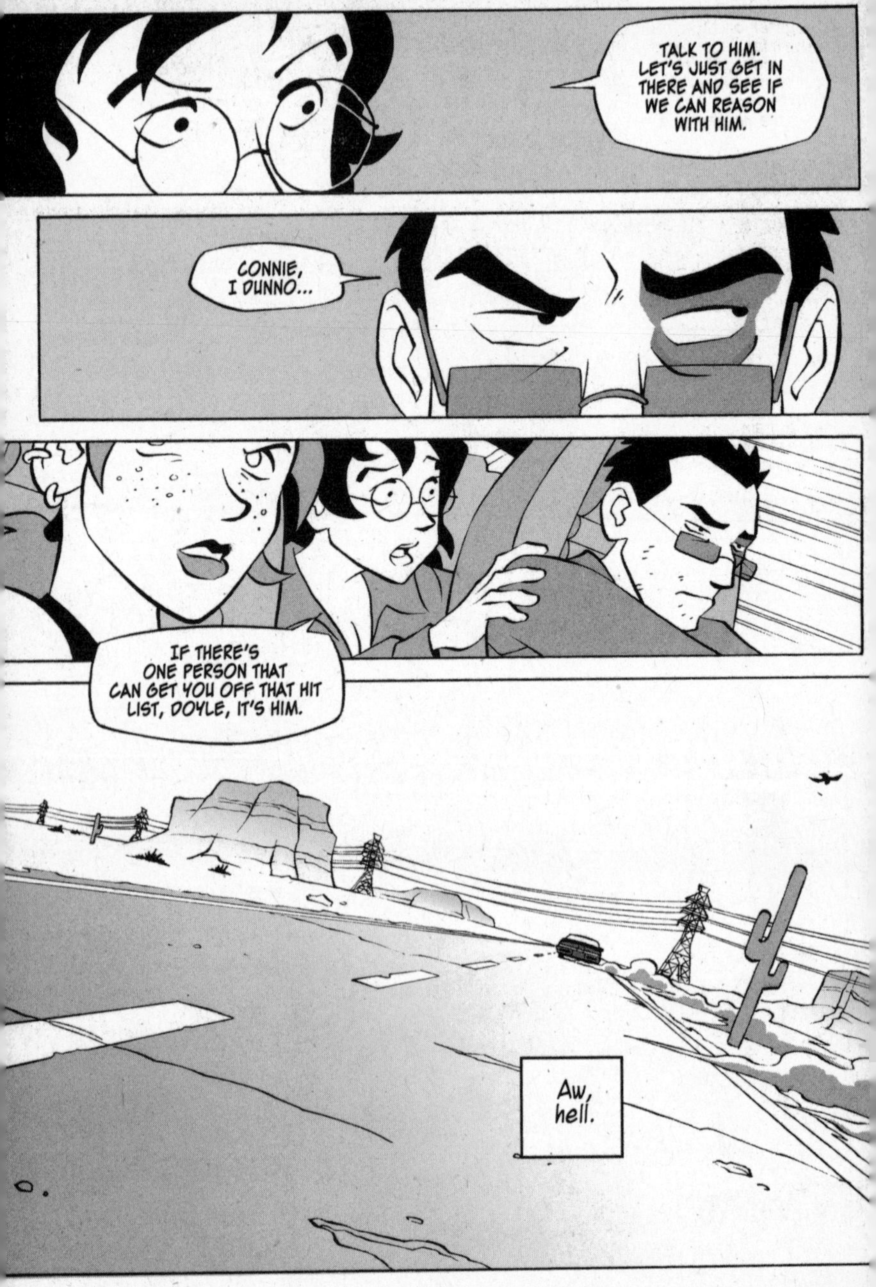
TALK TO HIM. LET'S JUST GET IN THERE AND SEE IF WE CAN REASON WITH HIM.
CONNIE, I DUNNO...
IF THERE'S ONE PERSON THAT CAN GET YOU OFF THAT HIT LIST, DOYLE, IT'S HIM.
Aw, hell.

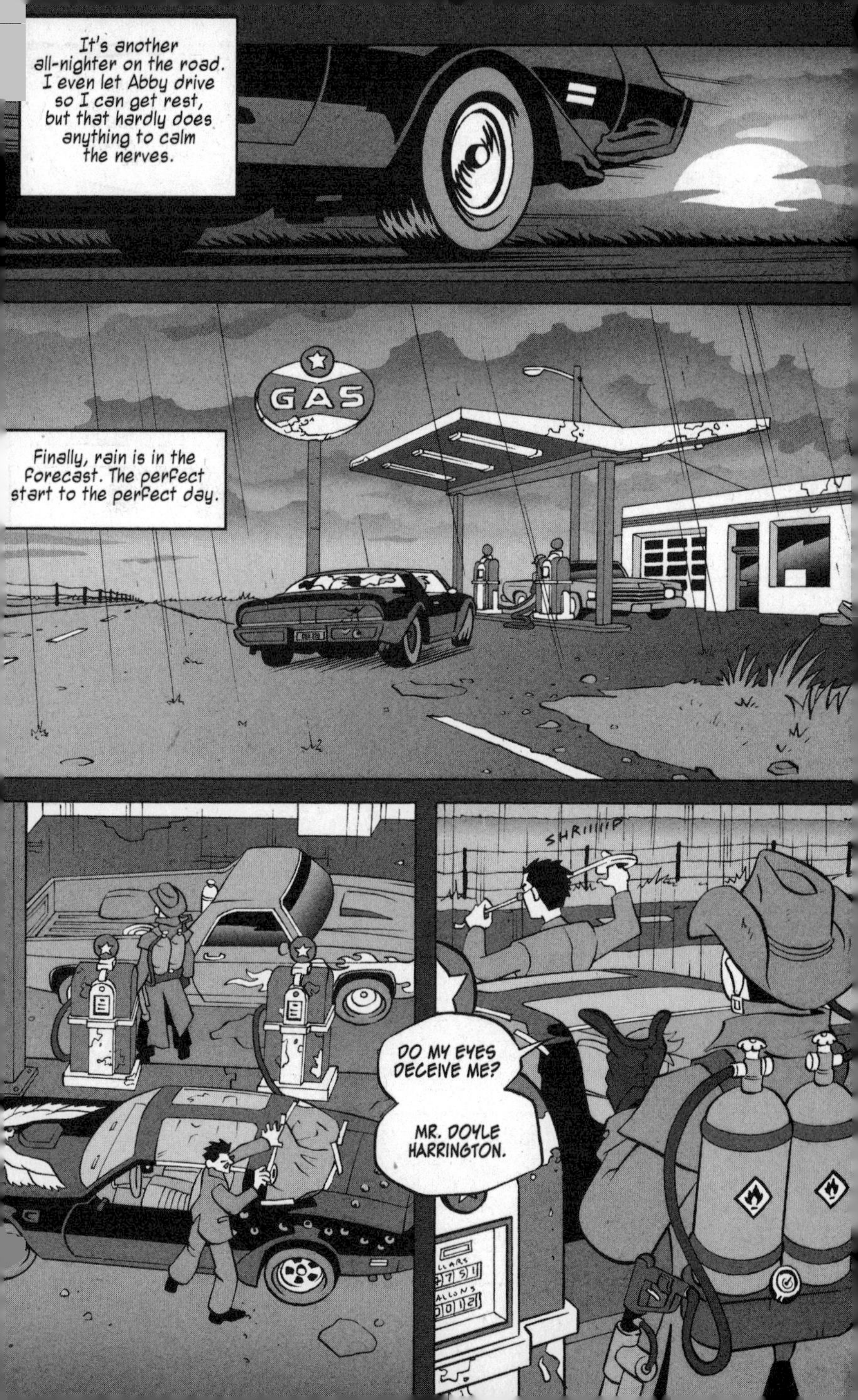
It's another all-nighter on the road. I even let Abby drive so I can get rest, but that hardly does anything to calm the nerves.
GAS
Finally, rain is in the forecast. The perfect start to the perfect day.
SHRIIIIP
DO MY EYES DECEIVE ME?
MR. DOYLE HARRINGTON.

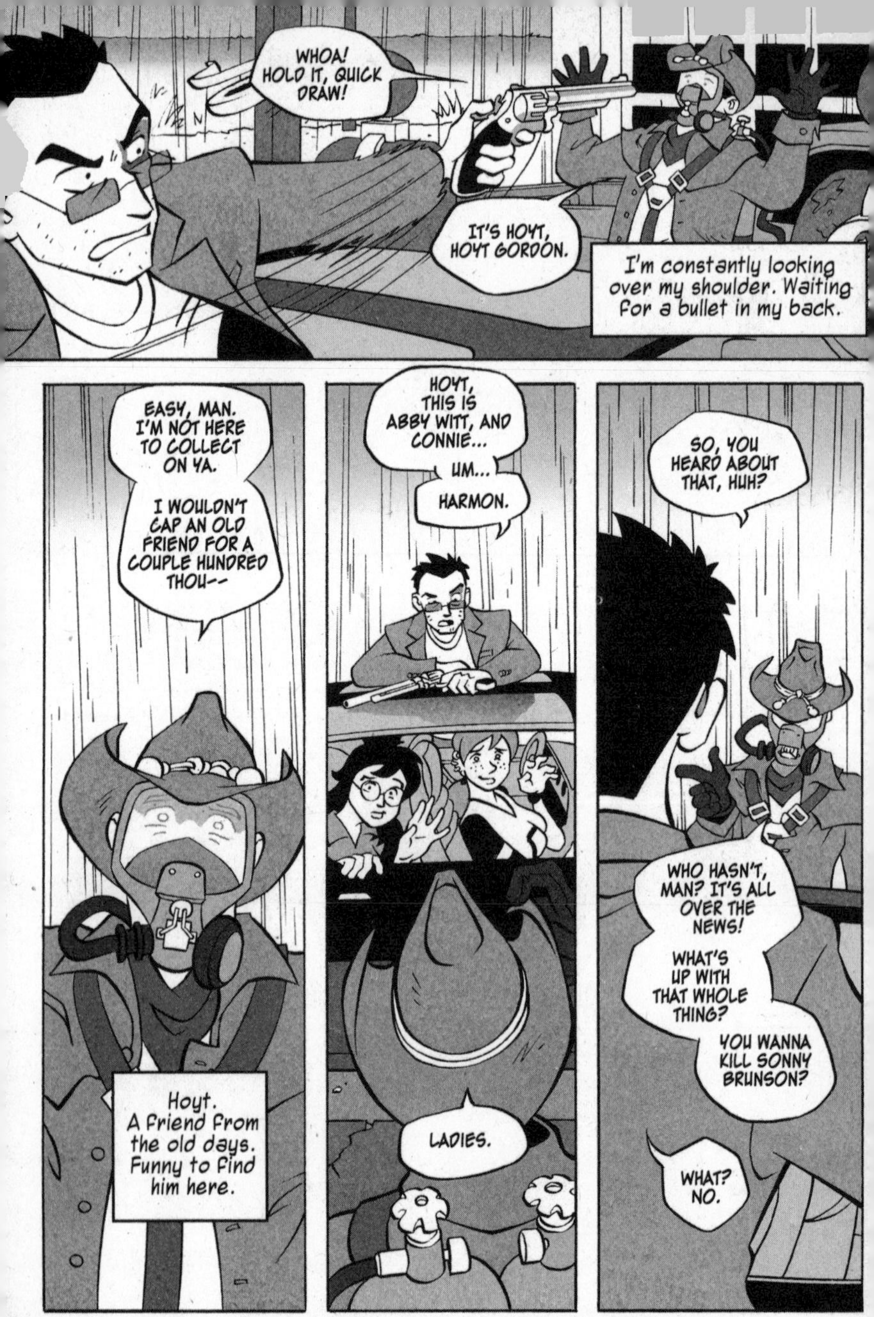
WHOA! HOLD IT, QUICK DRAW!
IT'S HOYT, HOYT GORDON.
I'm constantly looking over my shoulder. Waiting for a bullet in my back.
EASY, MAN. I'M NOT HERE TO COLLECT ON YA.
I WOULDN'T CAP AN OLD FRIEND FOR A COUPLE HUNDRED THOU--
Hoyt. A friend from the old days. Funny to find him here.
HOYT, THIS IS ABBY WITT, AND CONNIE...
UM...
HARMON.
LADIES.
SO, YOU HEARD ABOUT THAT, HUH?
WHO HASN'T, MAN? IT'S ALL OVER THE NEWS!
WHAT'S UP WITH THAT WHOLE THING?
YOU WANNA KILL SONNY BRUNSON?
WHAT? NO.

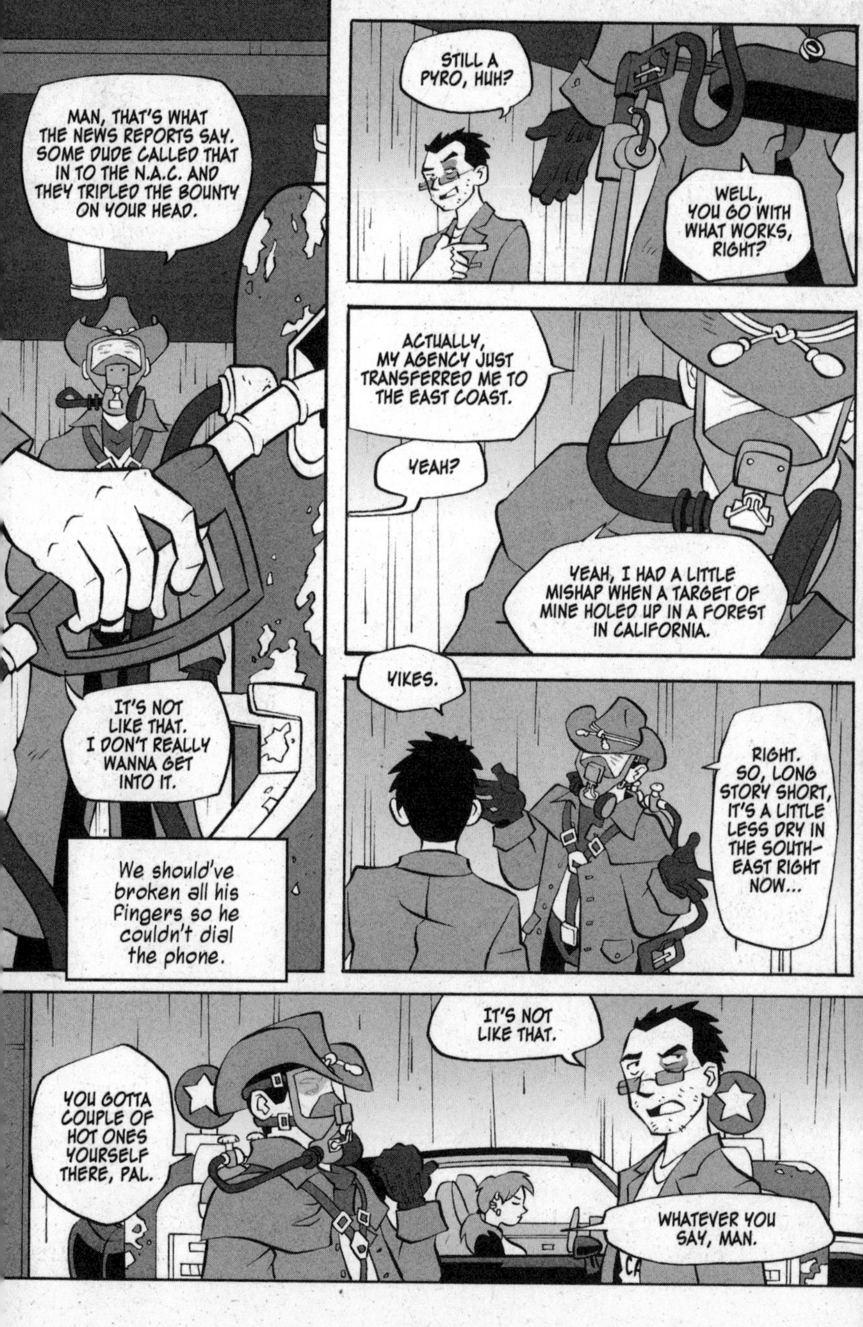
MAN, THAT'S WHAT THE NEWS REPORTS SAY. SOME DUDE CALLED THAT IN TO THE N.A.C. AND THEY TRIPLED THE BOUNTY ON YOUR HEAD.
IT'S NOT LIKE THAT. I DON'T REALLY WANNA GET INTO IT.
We should've broken all his fingers so he couldn't dial the phone.
STILL A PYRO, HUH?
WELL, YOU GO WITH WHAT WORKS, RIGHT?
ACTUALLY, MY AGENCY JUST TRANSFERRED ME TO THE EAST COAST.
YEAH?
YEAH, I HAD A LITTLE MISHAP WHEN A TARGET OF MINE HOLED UP IN A FOREST IN CALIFORNIA.
YIKES.
RIGHT. SO, LONG STORY SHORT, IT'S A LITTLE LESS DRY IN THE SOUTH-EAST RIGHT NOW...
YOU GOTTA COUPLE OF HOT ONES YOURSELF THERE, PAL.
IT'S NOT LIKE THAT.
WHATEVER YOU SAY, MAN.

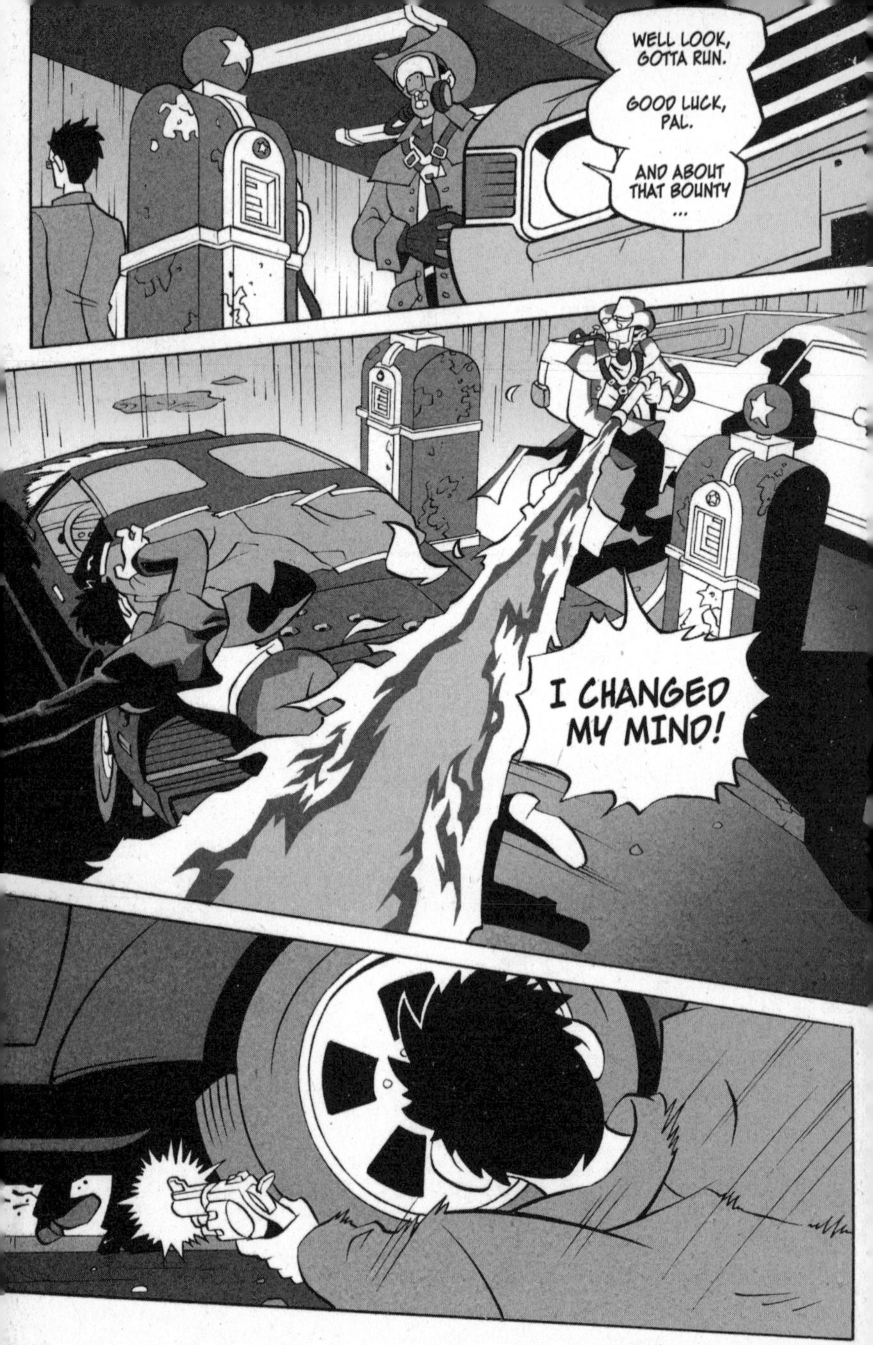
WELL LOOK, GOTTA RUN.
GOOD LUCK, PAL.
AND ABOUT THAT BOUNTY ...
I CHANGED MY MIND!

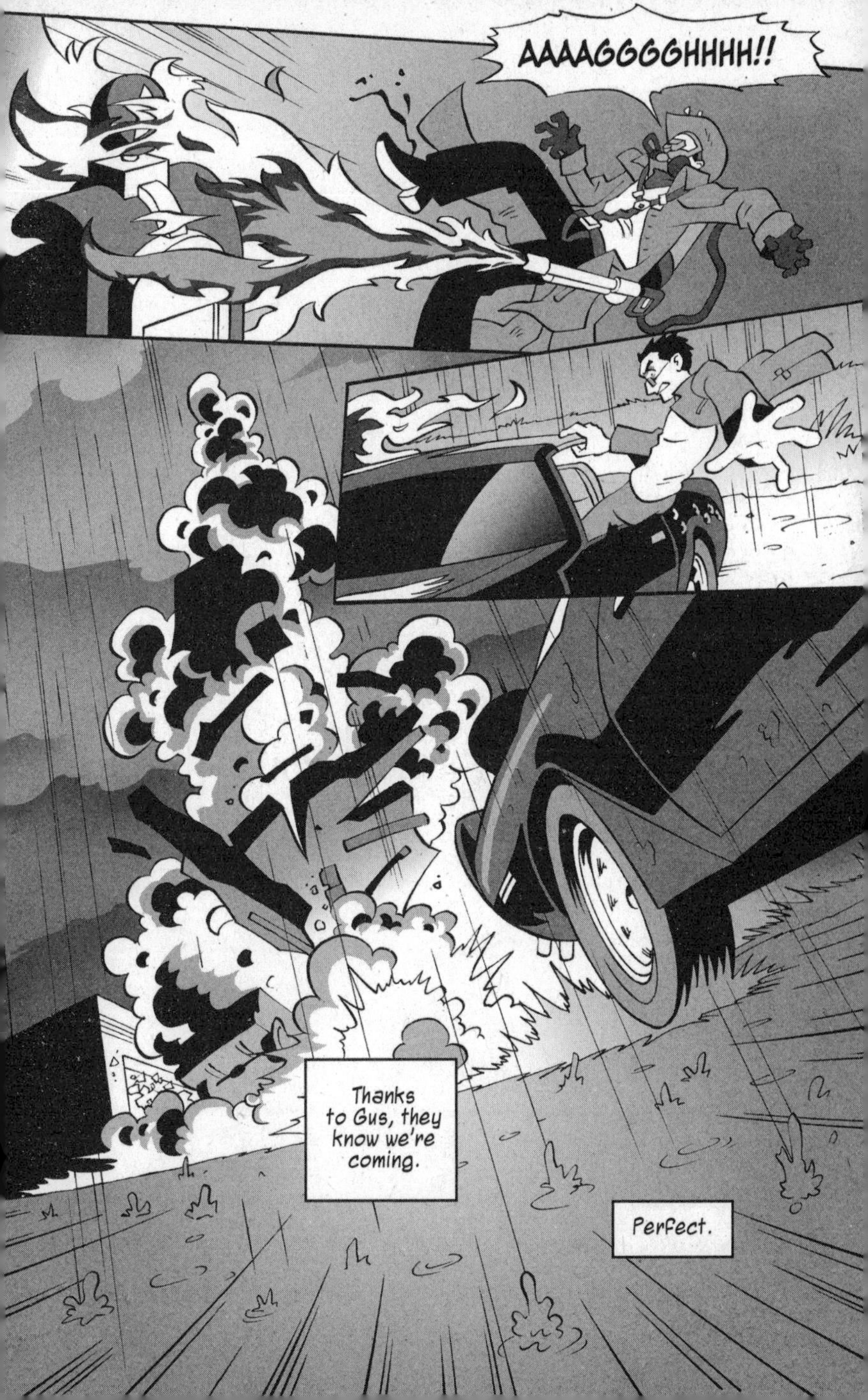
AAAAGGGGHHHH!!
Thanks to Gus, they know we're coming.
Perfect.

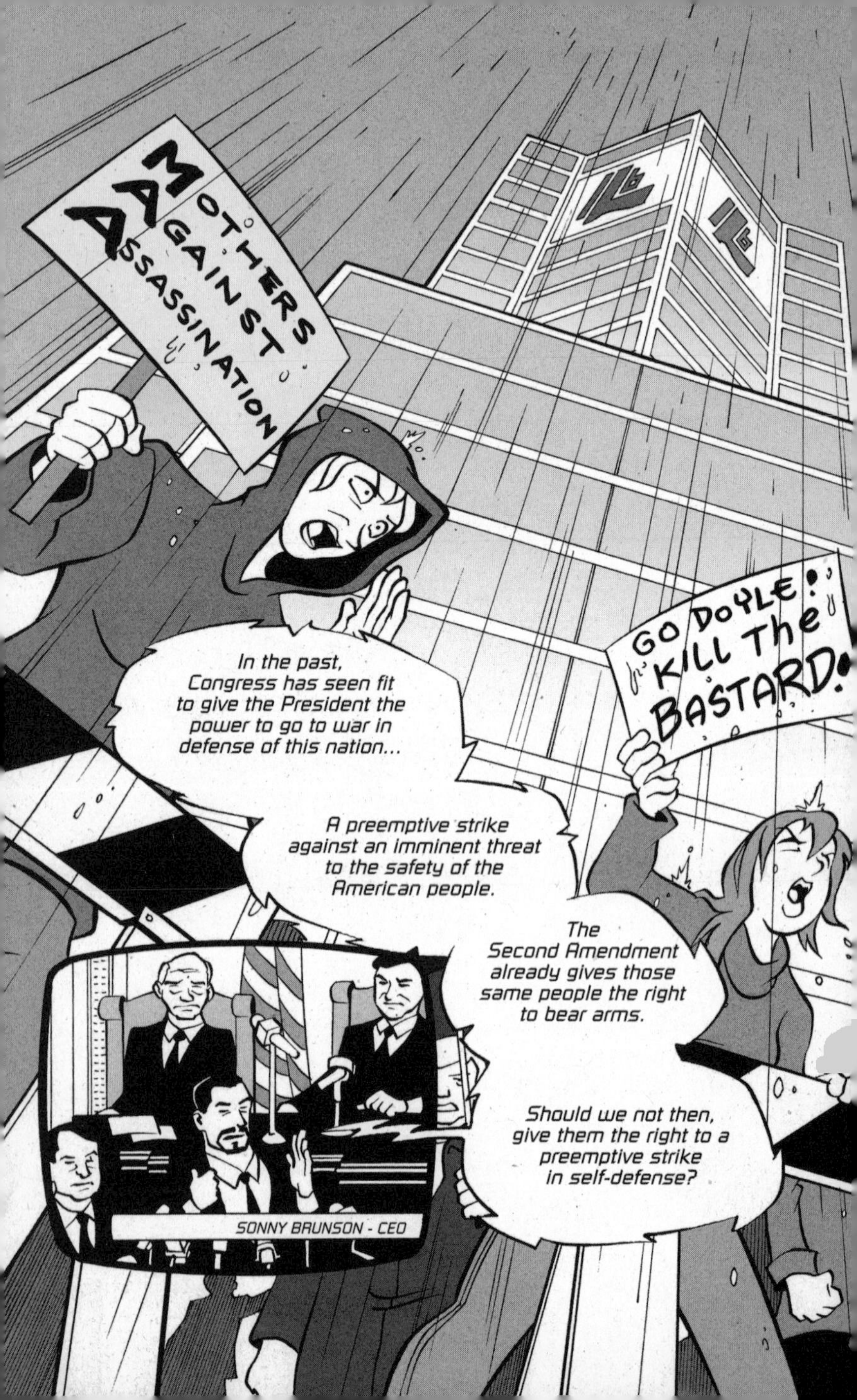
MOTHERS AGAINST ASSASSINATION
GO DOYLE! KILL THE BASTARD!
In the past, Congress has seen fit to give the President the power to go to war in defense of this nation...
A preemptive strike against an imminent threat to the safety of the American people.
The Second Amendment already gives those same people the right to bear arms.
Should we not then, give them the right to a preemptive strike in self-defense?
SONNY BRUNSON - CEO

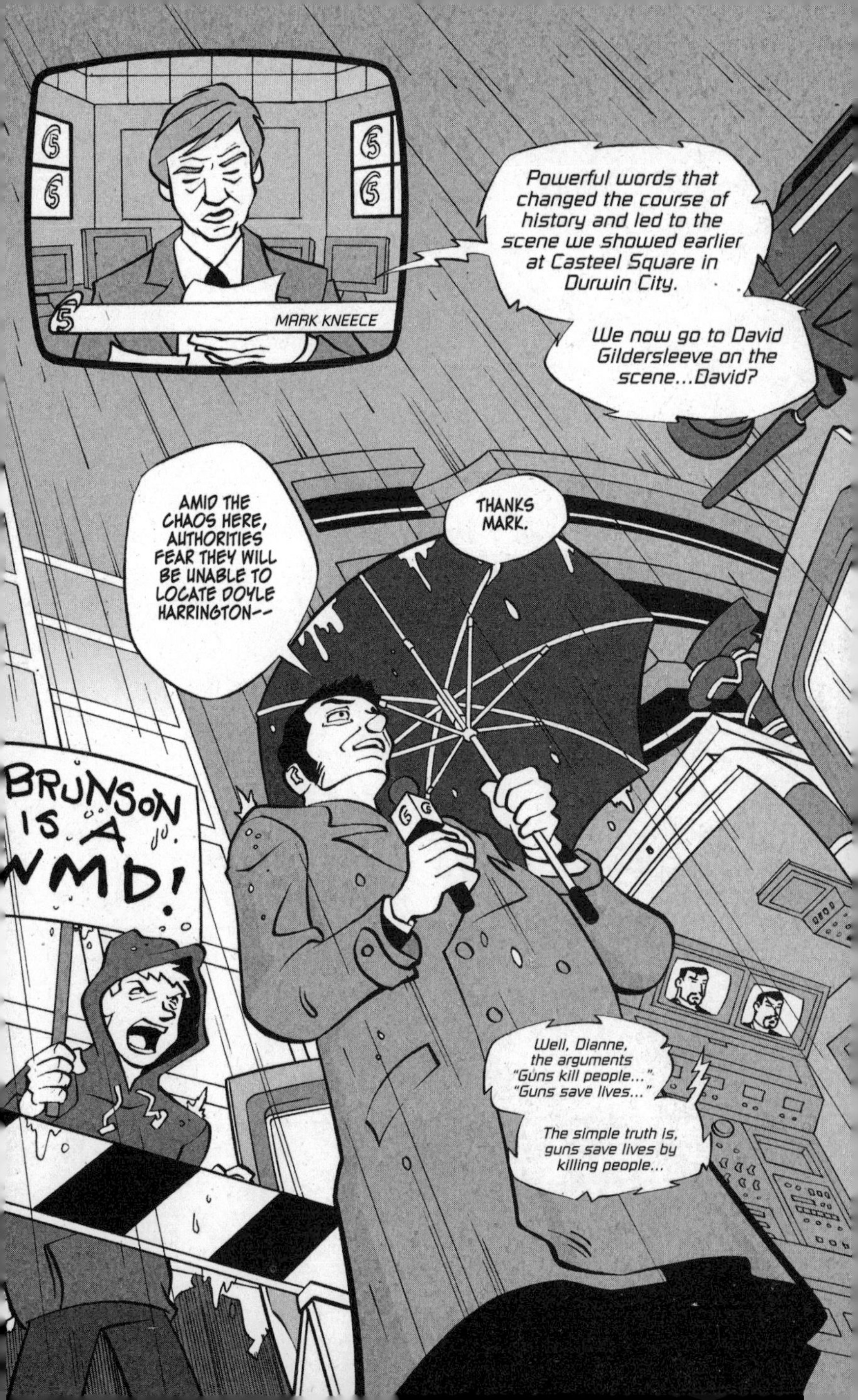
MARK KNEECE
Powerful words that changed the course of history and led to the scene we showed earlier at Casteel Square in Durwin City.
We now go to David Gildersleeve on the scene...David?
THANKS MARK.
AMID THE CHAOS HERE, AUTHORITIES FEAR THEY WILL BE UNABLE TO LOCATE DOYLE HARRINGTON--
BRUNSON IS A WMD!
Well, Dianne, the arguments "Guns kill people...". "Guns save lives..."
The simple truth is, guns save lives by killing people...

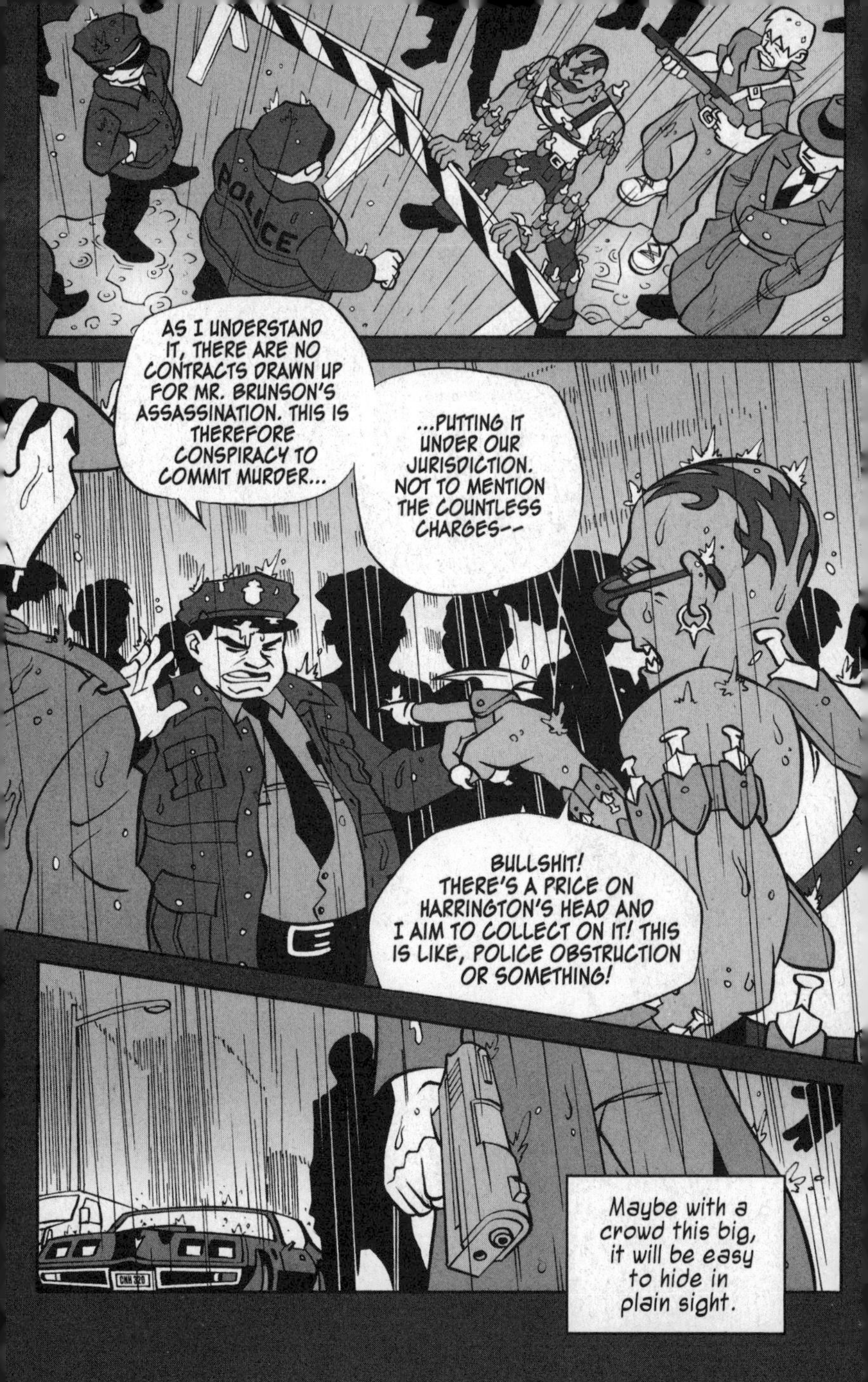
AS I UNDERSTAND IT, THERE ARE NO CONTRACTS DRAWN UP FOR MR. BRUNSON'S ASSASSINATION. THIS IS THEREFORE CONSPIRACY TO COMMIT MURDER...
...PUTTING IT UNDER OUR JURISDICTION. NOT TO MENTION THE COUNTLESS CHARGES--
BULLSHIT! THERE'S A PRICE ON HARRINGTON'S HEAD AND I AIM TO COLLECT ON IT! THIS IS LIKE, POLICE OBSTRUCTION OR SOMETHING!
POLICE
Maybe with a crowd this big, it will be easy to hide in plain sight.

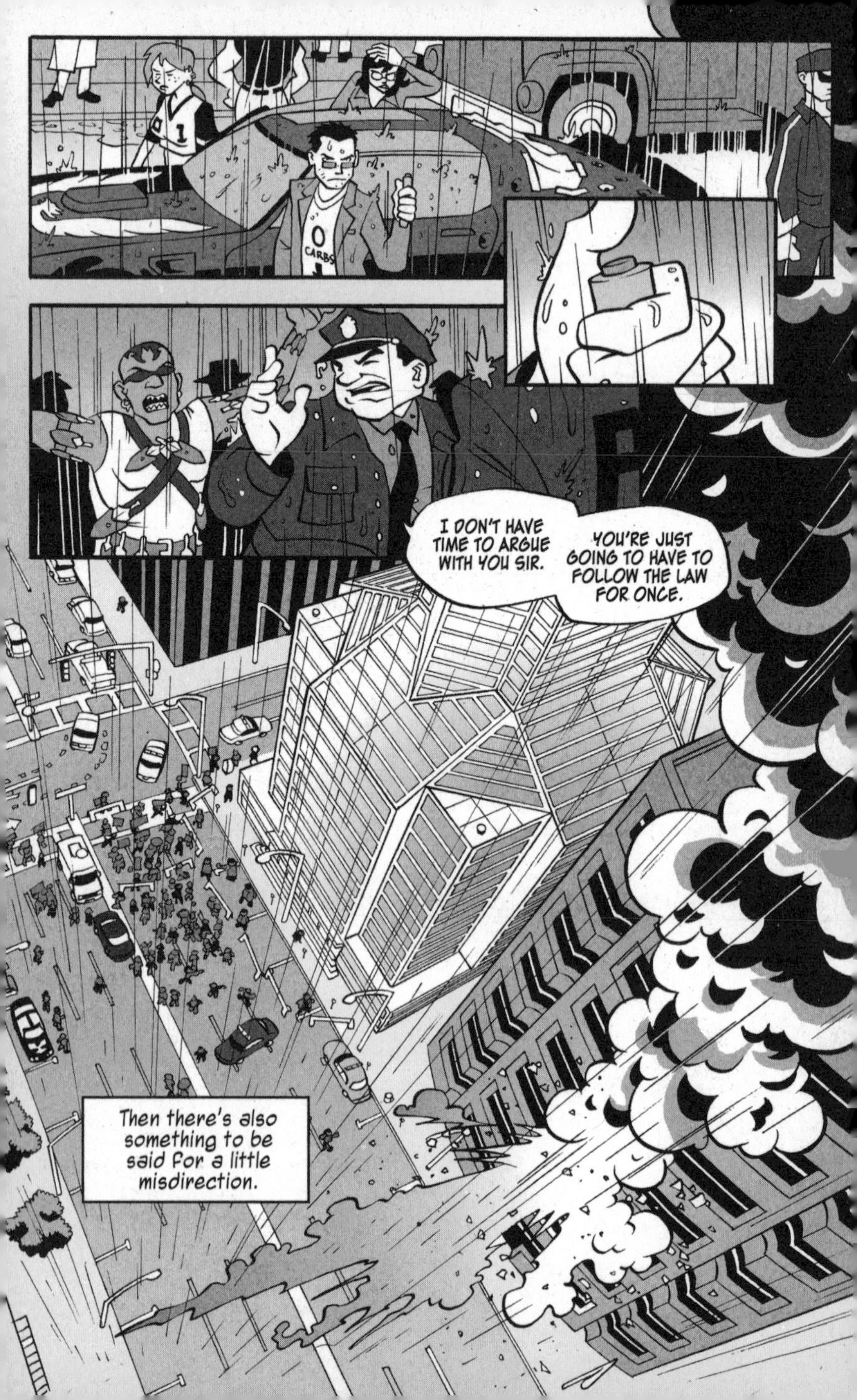
I DON'T HAVE TIME TO ARGUE WITH YOU SIR.
YOU'RE JUST GOING TO HAVE TO FOLLOW THE LAW FOR ONCE.
Then there's also something to be said for a little misdirection.

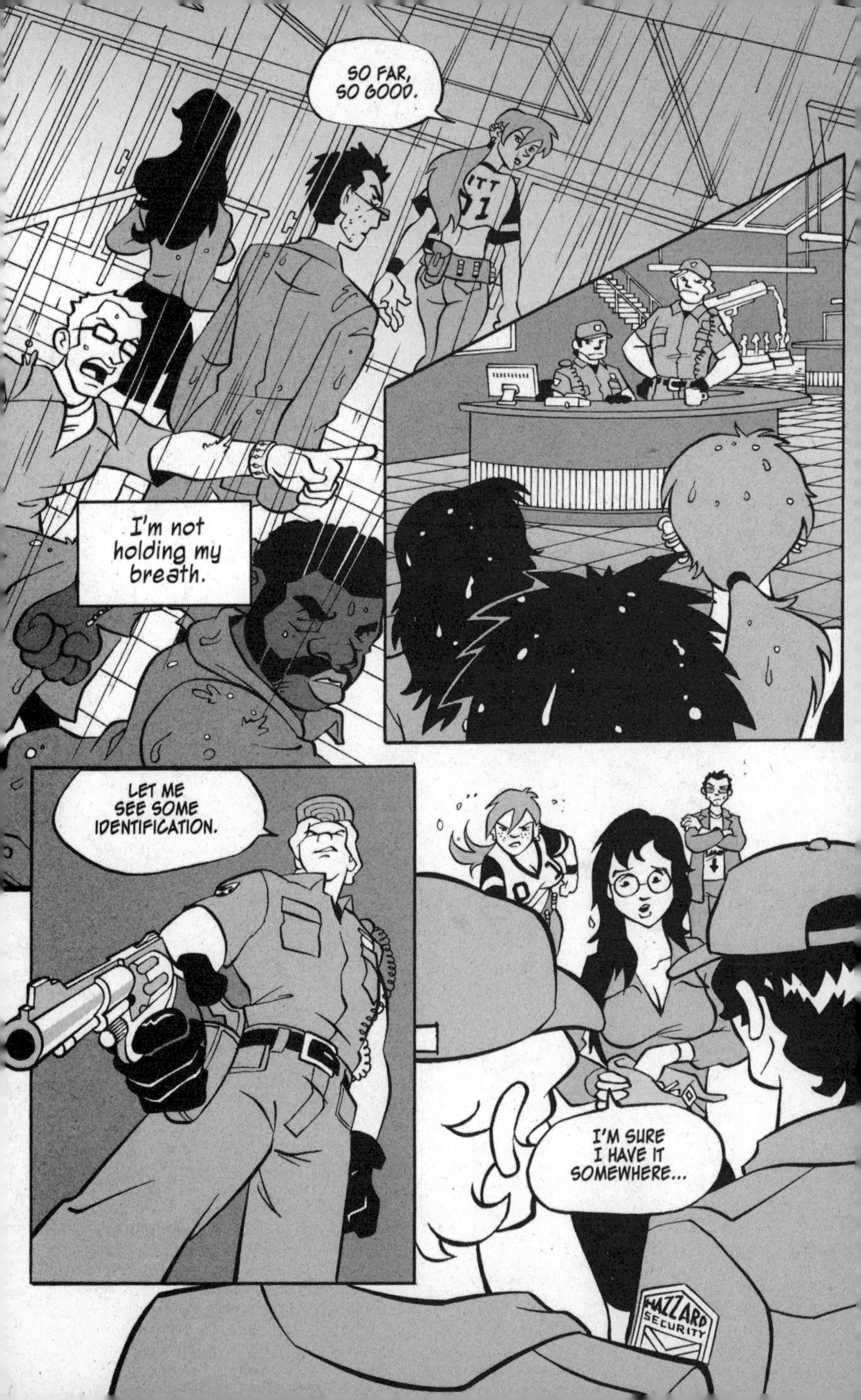
SO FAR, SO GOOD.
I'm not holding my breath.
LET ME SEE SOME IDENTIFICATION.
I'M SURE I HAVE IT SOMEWHERE...

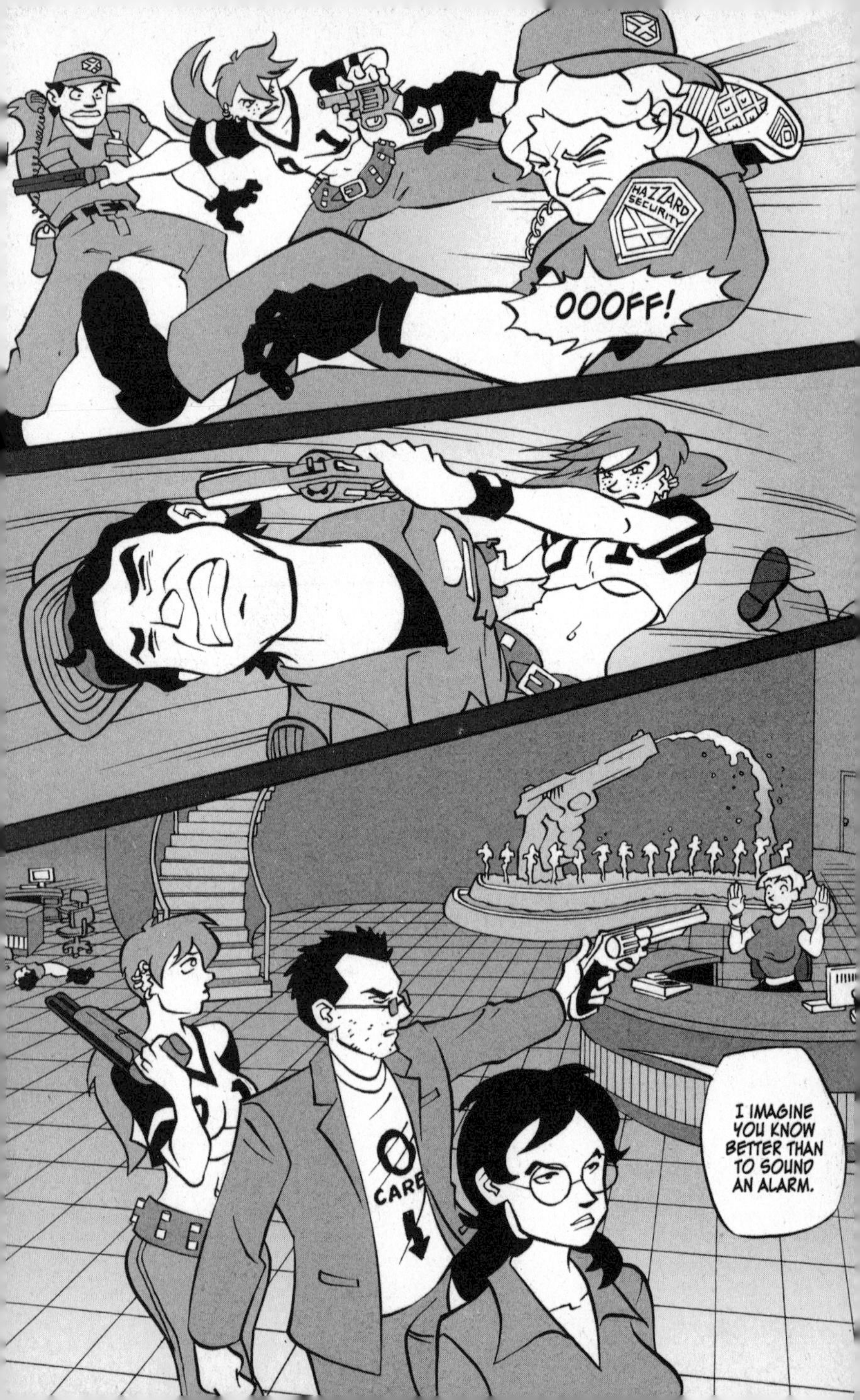
HAZZARD SECURITY
OOOFF!
CARE
I IMAGINE YOU KNOW BETTER THAN TO SOUND AN ALARM.

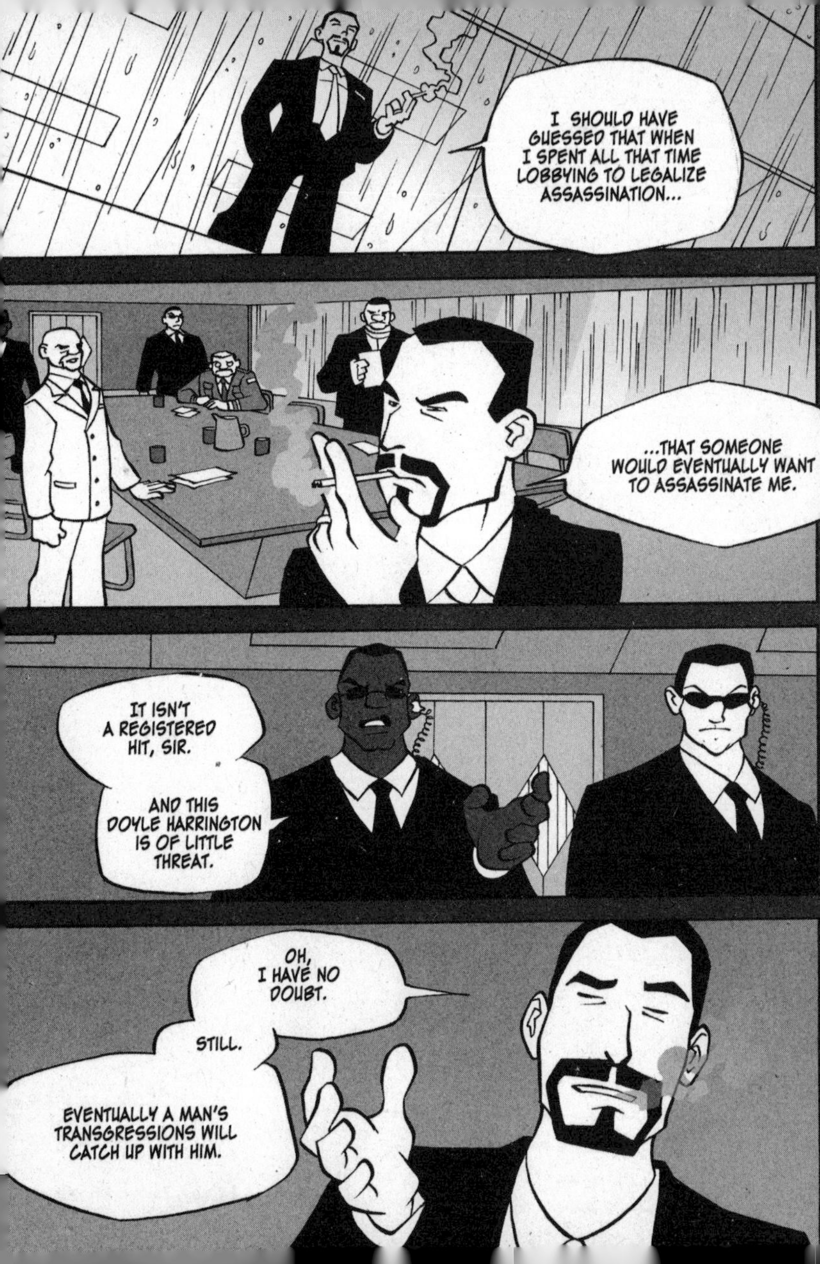
I SHOULD HAVE GUESSED THAT WHEN I SPENT ALL THAT TIME LOBBYING TO LEGALIZE ASSASSINATION...
...THAT SOMEONE WOULD EVENTUALLY WANT TO ASSASSINATE ME.
IT ISN'T A REGISTERED HIT, SIR.
AND THIS DOYLE HARRINGTON IS OF LITTLE THREAT.
OH, I HAVE NO DOUBT.
STILL.
EVENTUALLY A MAN'S TRANSGRESSIONS WILL CATCH UP WITH HIM.

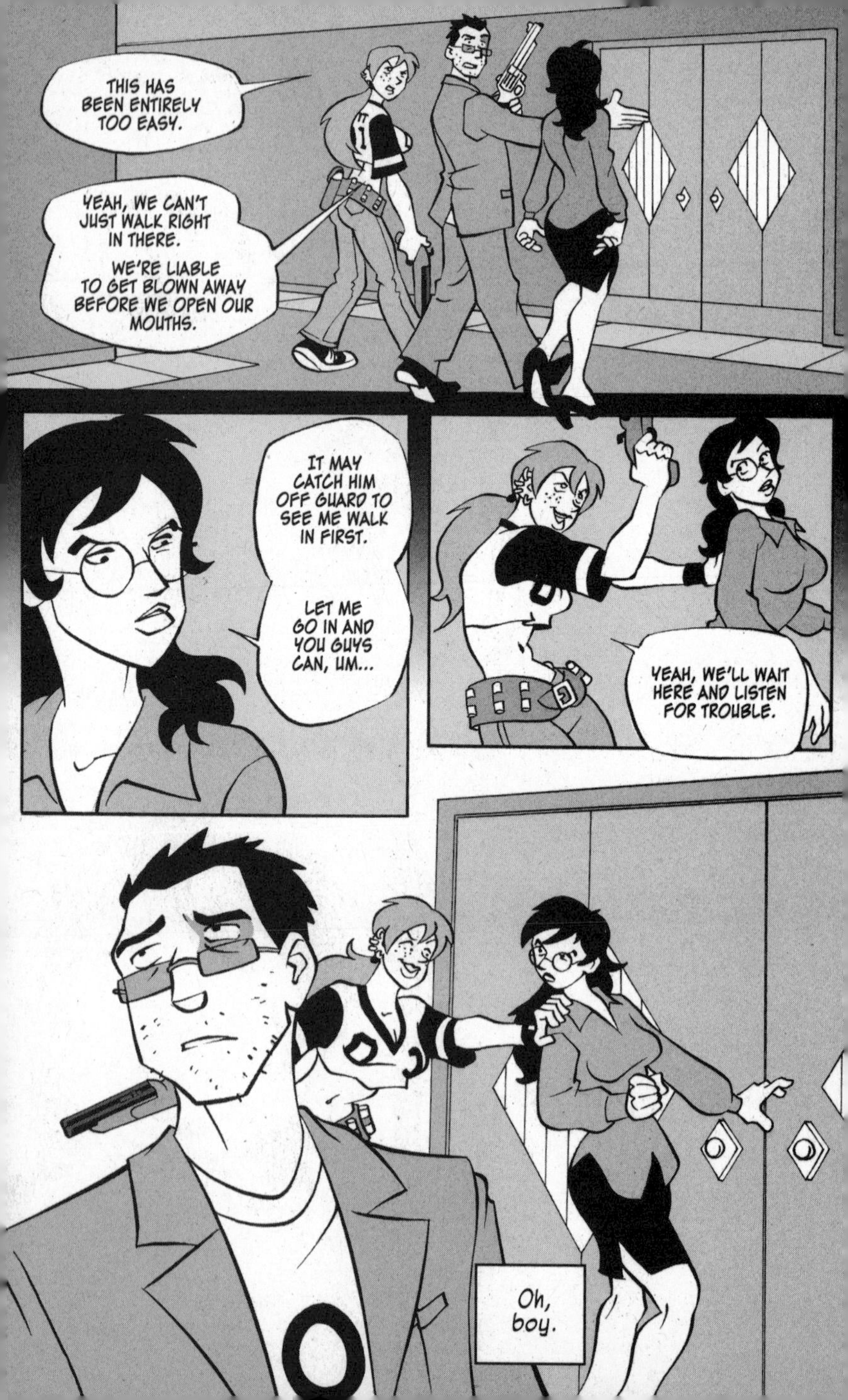
THIS HAS BEEN ENTIRELY TOO EASY.
YEAH, WE CAN'T JUST WALK RIGHT IN THERE.
WE'RE LIABLE TO GET BLOWN AWAY BEFORE WE OPEN OUR MOUTHS.
IT MAY CATCH HIM OFF GUARD TO SEE ME WALK IN FIRST.
LET ME GO IN AND YOU GUYS CAN, UM...
YEAH, WE'LL WAIT HERE AND LISTEN FOR TROUBLE.
Oh, boy.

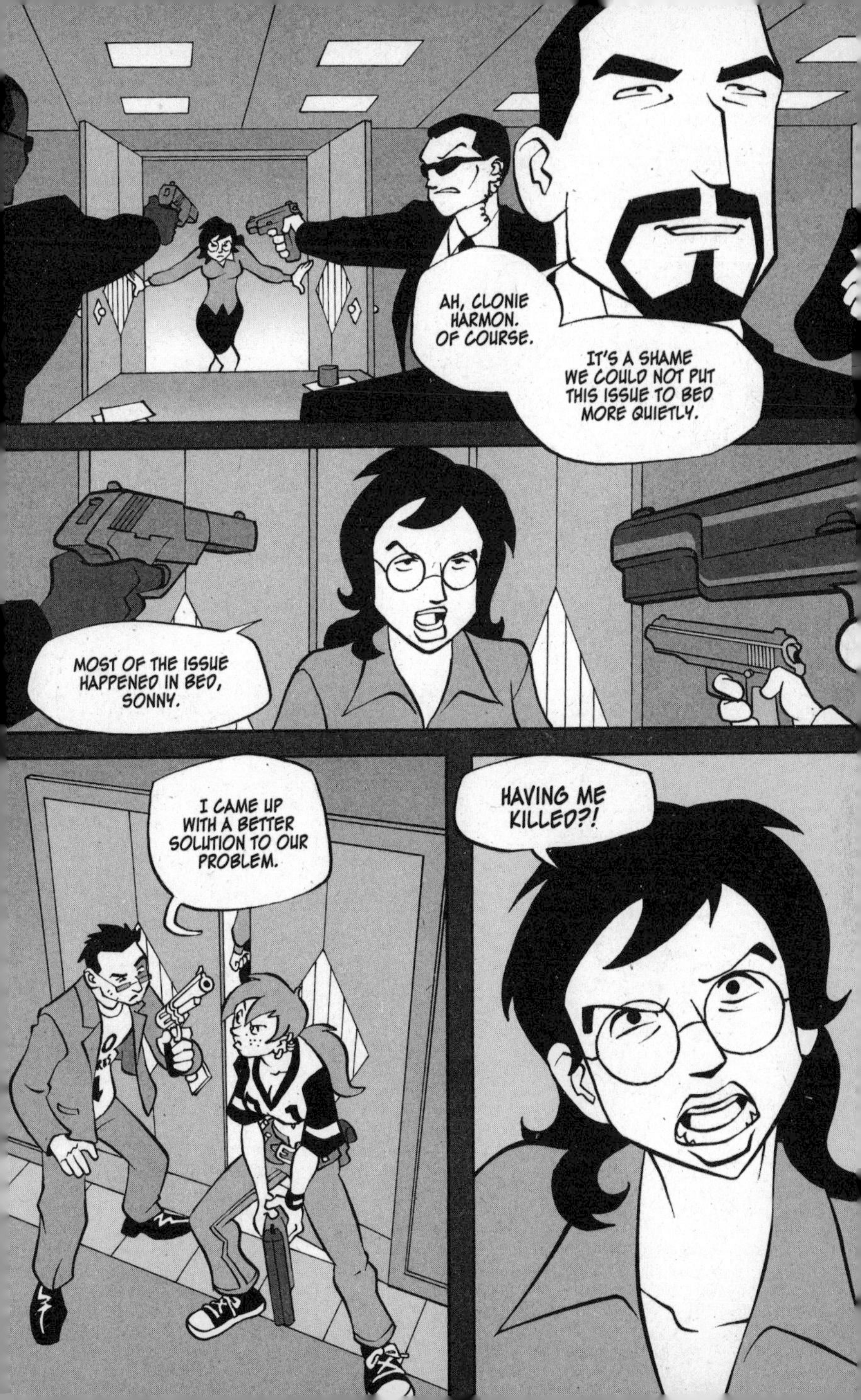
AH, CLONIE HARMON. OF COURSE.
IT'S A SHAME WE COULD NOT PUT THIS ISSUE TO BED MORE QUIETLY.
MOST OF THE ISSUE HAPPENED IN BED, SONNY.
I CAME UP WITH A BETTER SOLUTION TO OUR PROBLEM.
HAVING ME KILLED?!

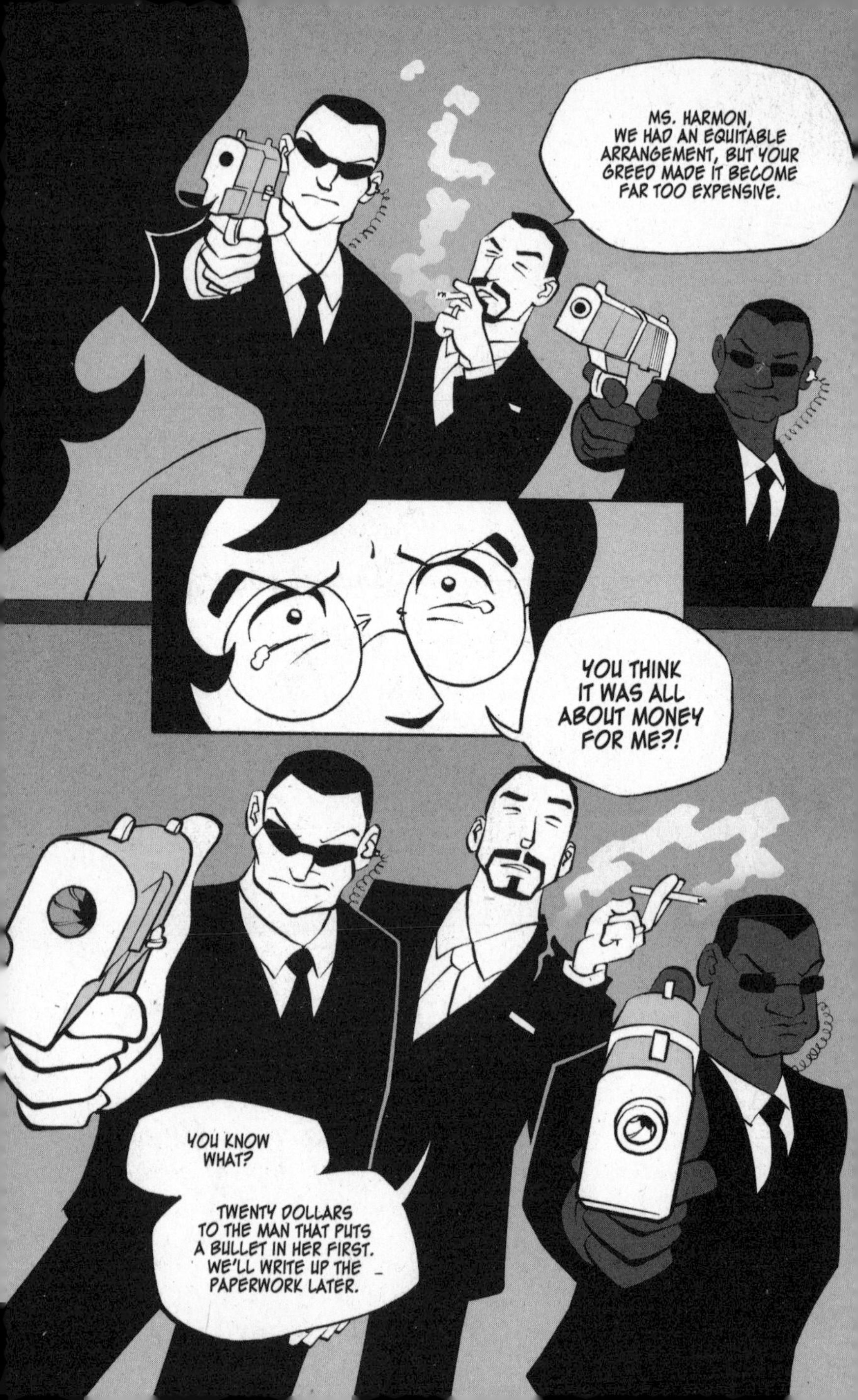
MS. HARMON, WE HAD AN EQUITABLE ARRANGEMENT, BUT YOUR GREED MADE IT BECOME FAR TOO EXPENSIVE.
YOU THINK IT WAS ALL ABOUT MONEY FOR ME?!
YOU KNOW WHAT?
TWENTY DOLLARS TO THE MAN THAT PUTS A BULLET IN HER FIRST. WE'LL WRITE UP THE PAPERWORK LATER.

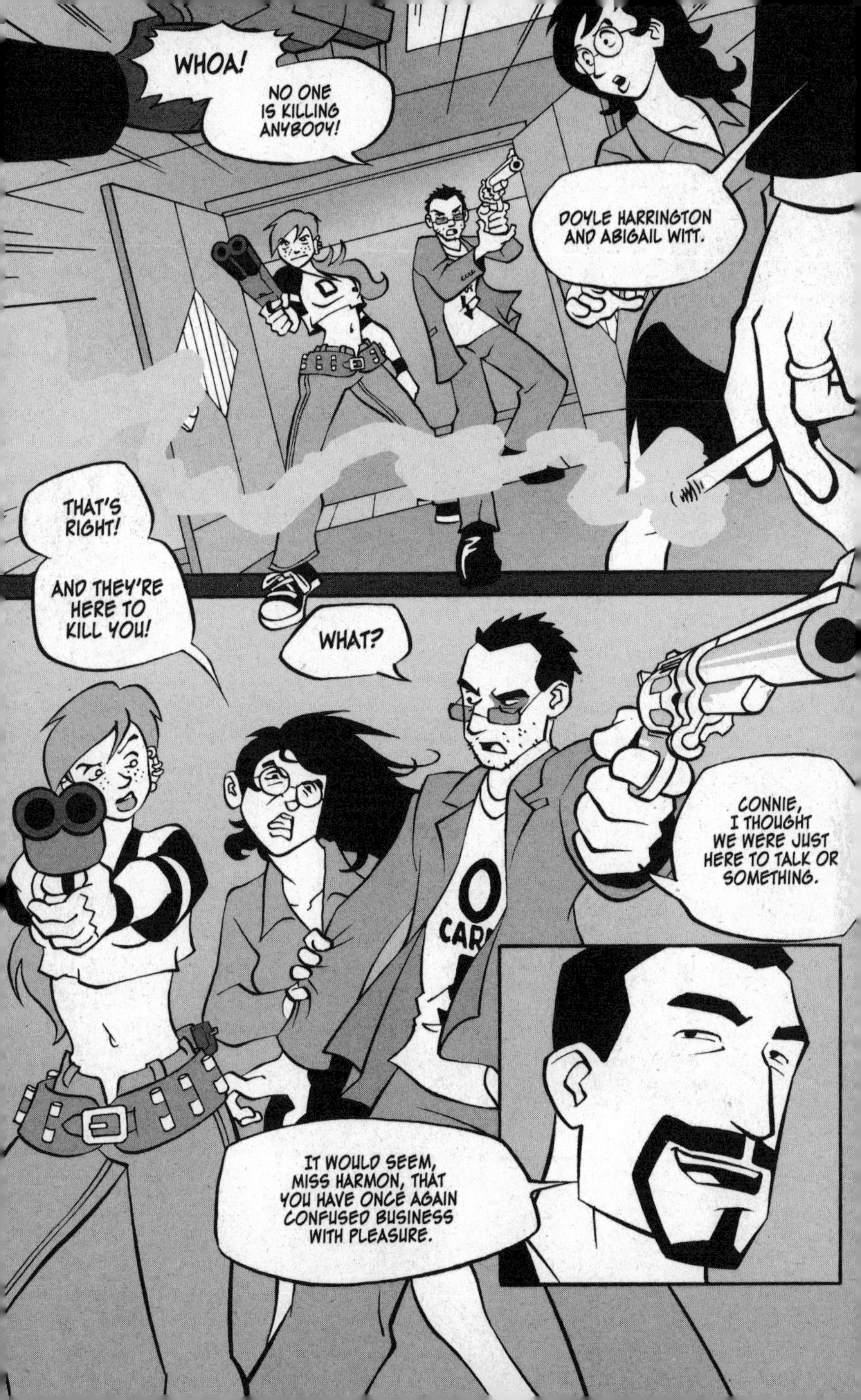
WHOA!
NO ONE IS KILLING ANYBODY!
DOYLE HARRINGTON AND ABIGAIL WITT.
THAT'S RIGHT!
AND THEY'RE HERE TO KILL YOU!
WHAT?
CONNIE, I THOUGHT WE WERE JUST HERE TO TALK OR SOMETHING.
IT WOULD SEEM, MISS HARMON, THAT YOU HAVE ONCE AGAIN CONFUSED BUSINESS WITH PLEASURE.

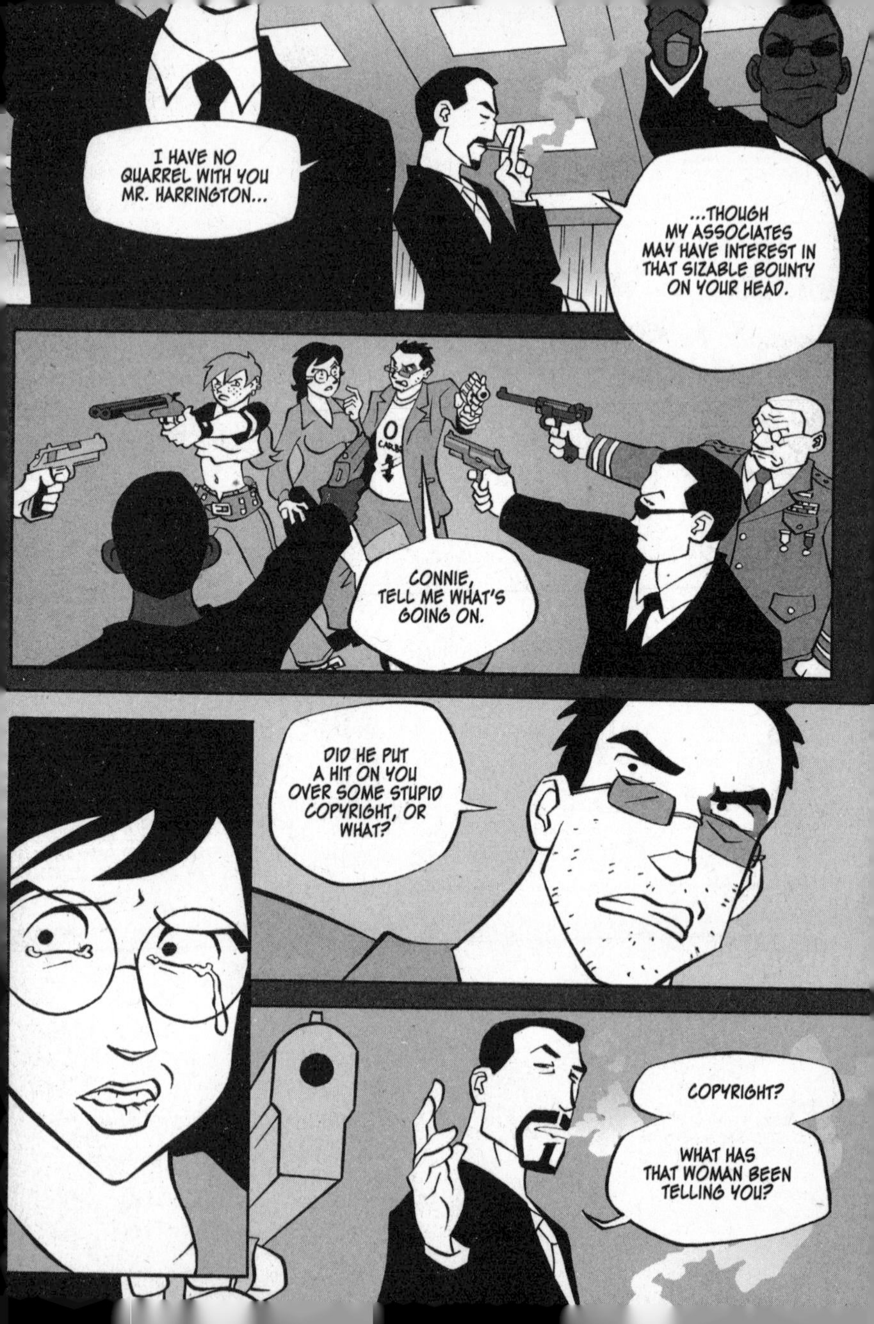
I HAVE NO QUARREL WITH YOU MR. HARRINGTON...
...THOUGH MY ASSOCIATES MAY HAVE INTEREST IN THAT SIZABLE BOUNTY ON YOUR HEAD.
CONNIE, TELL ME WHAT'S GOING ON.
DID HE PUT A HIT ON YOU OVER SOME STUPID COPYRIGHT, OR WHAT?
COPYRIGHT?
WHAT HAS THAT WOMAN BEEN TELLING YOU?

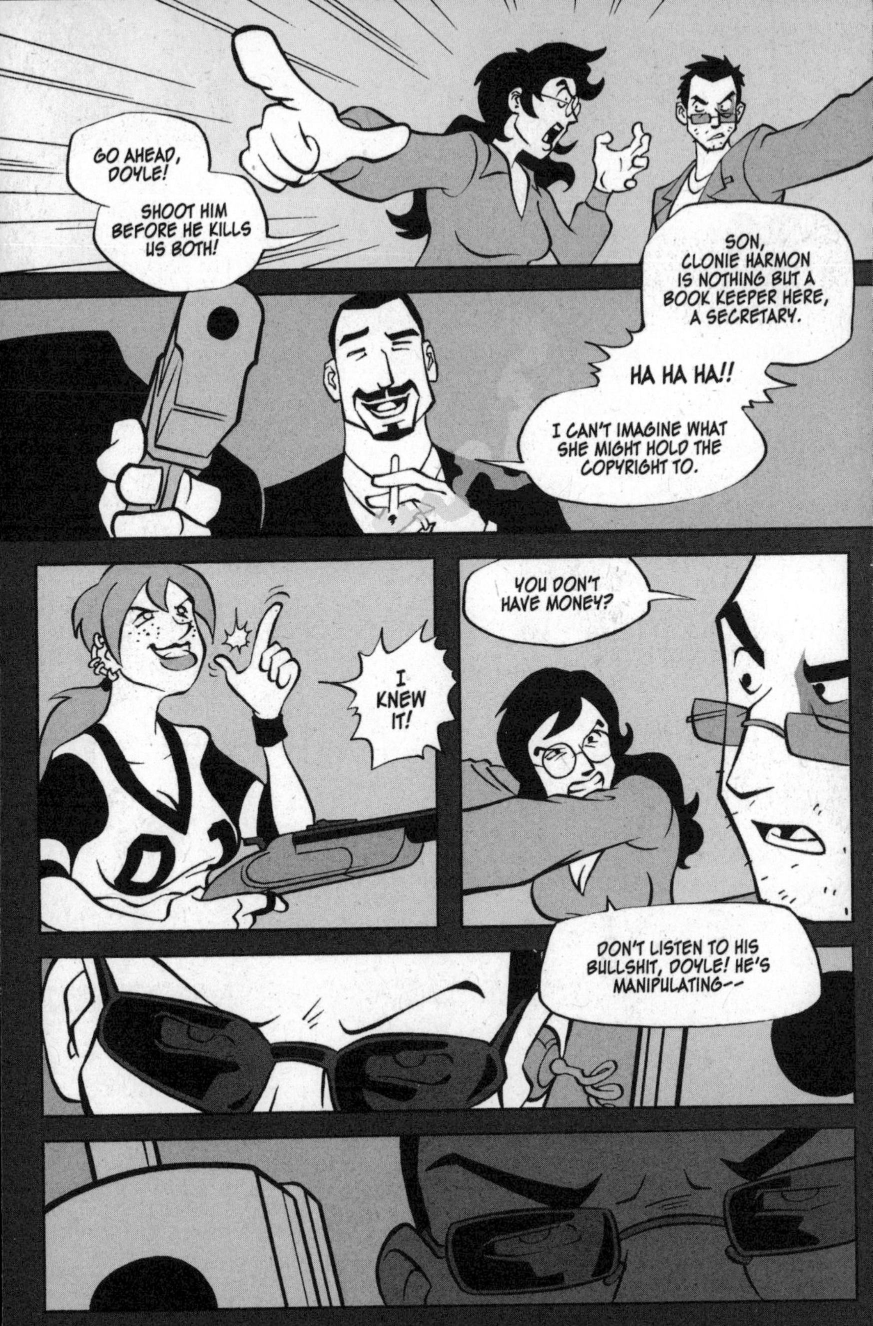
GO AHEAD, DOYLE!
SHOOT HIM BEFORE HE KILLS US BOTH!
SON, CLONIE HARMON IS NOTHING BUT A BOOK KEEPER HERE, A SECRETARY.
HA HA HA!!
I CAN'T IMAGINE WHAT SHE MIGHT HOLD THE COPYRIGHT TO.
I KNEW IT!
YOU DON'T HAVE MONEY?
DON'T LISTEN TO HIS BULLSHIT, DOYLE! HE'S MANIPULATING--

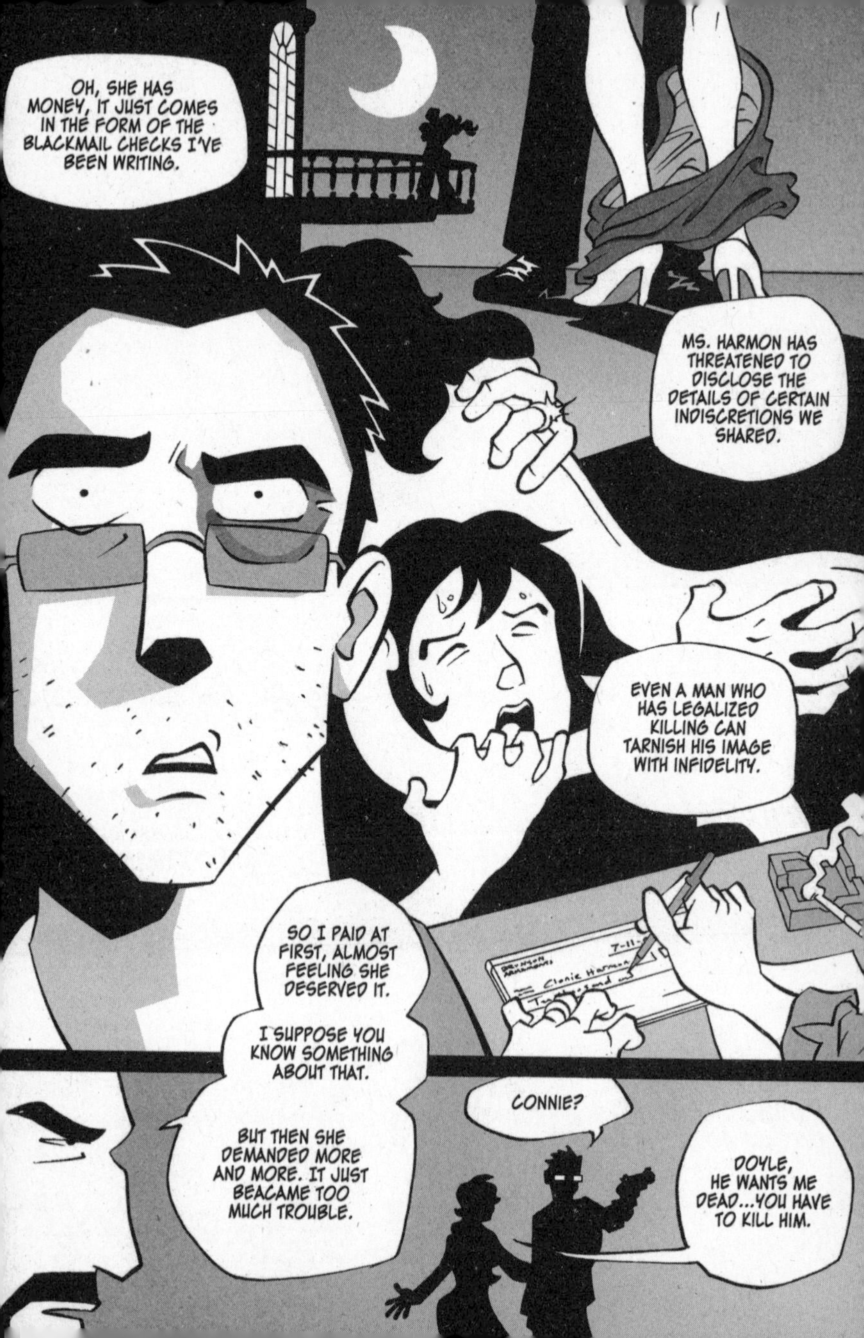
OH, SHE HAS MONEY, IT JUST COMES IN THE FORM OF THE BLACKMAIL CHECKS I'VE BEEN WRITING.
MS. HARMON HAS THREATENED TO DISCLOSE THE DETAILS OF CERTAIN INDISCRETIONS WE SHARED.
EVEN A MAN WHO HAS LEGALIZED KILLING CAN TARNISH HIS IMAGE WITH INFIDELITY.
SO I PAID AT FIRST, ALMOST FEELING SHE DESERVED IT.
I SUPPOSE YOU KNOW SOMETHING ABOUT THAT.
BUT THEN SHE DEMANDED MORE AND MORE. IT JUST BEACAME TOO MUCH TROUBLE.
CONNIE?
DOYLE, HE WANTS ME DEAD...YOU HAVE TO KILL HIM.

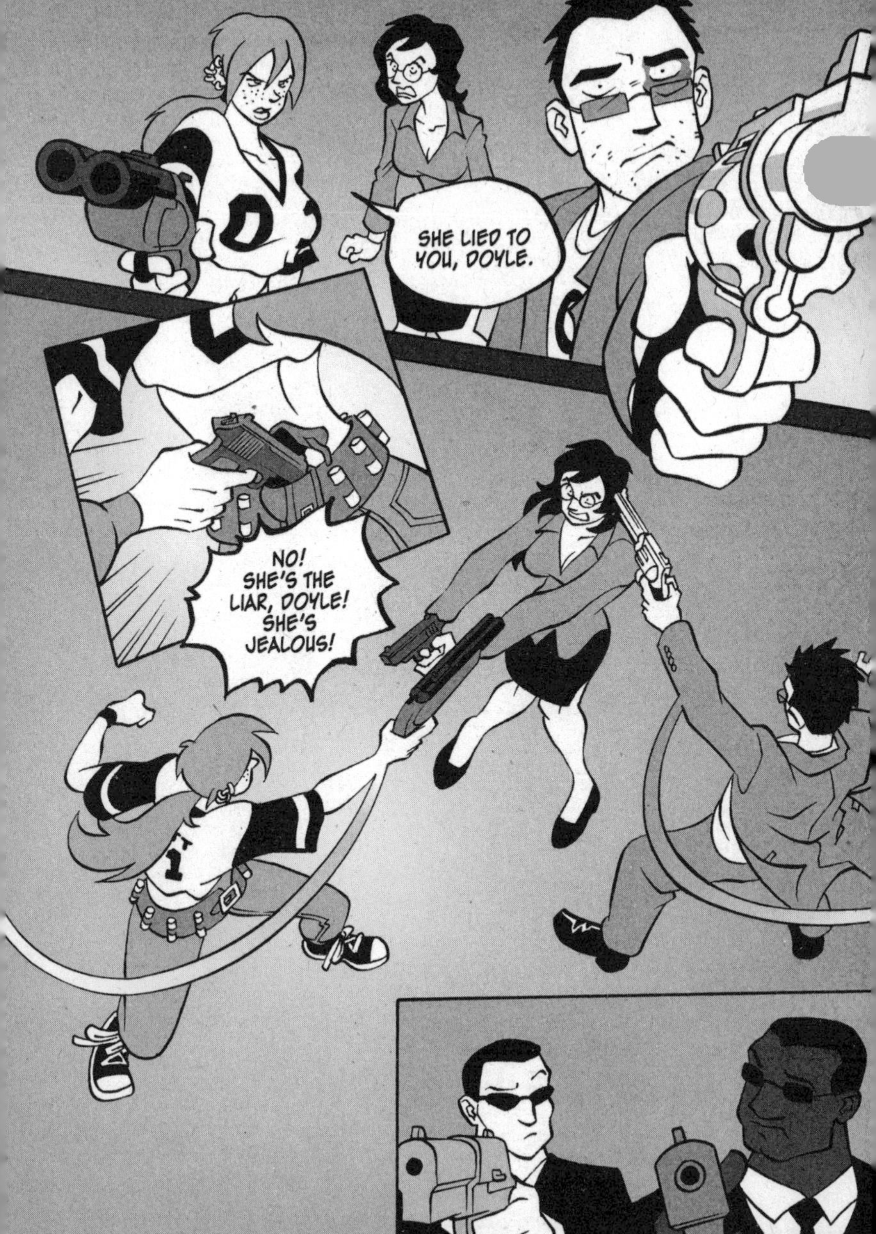
SHE LIED TO YOU, DOYLE.
NO! SHE'S THE LIAR, DOYLE! SHE'S JEALOUS!

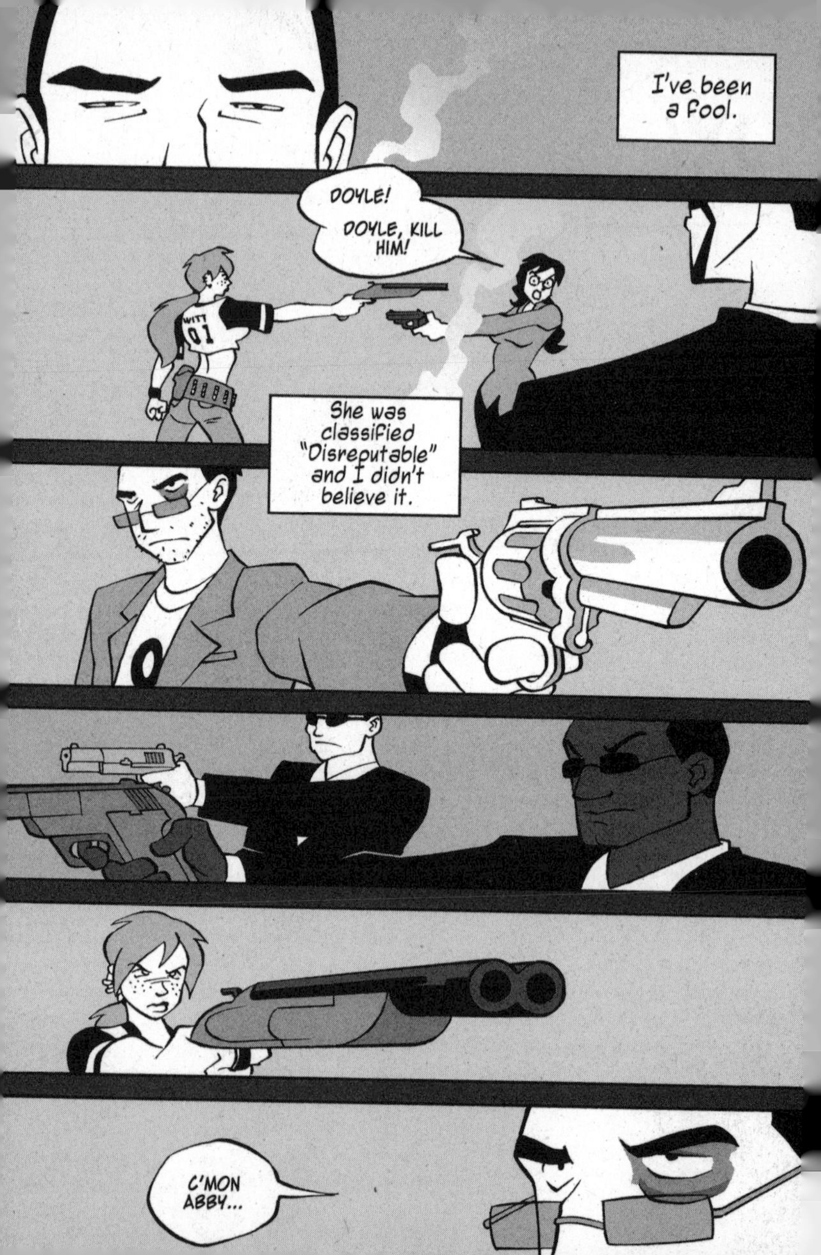
I've been a fool.
DOYLE! DOYLE, KILL HIM!
WITT 01
She was classified "Disreputable" and I didn't believe it.
C'MON ABBY...

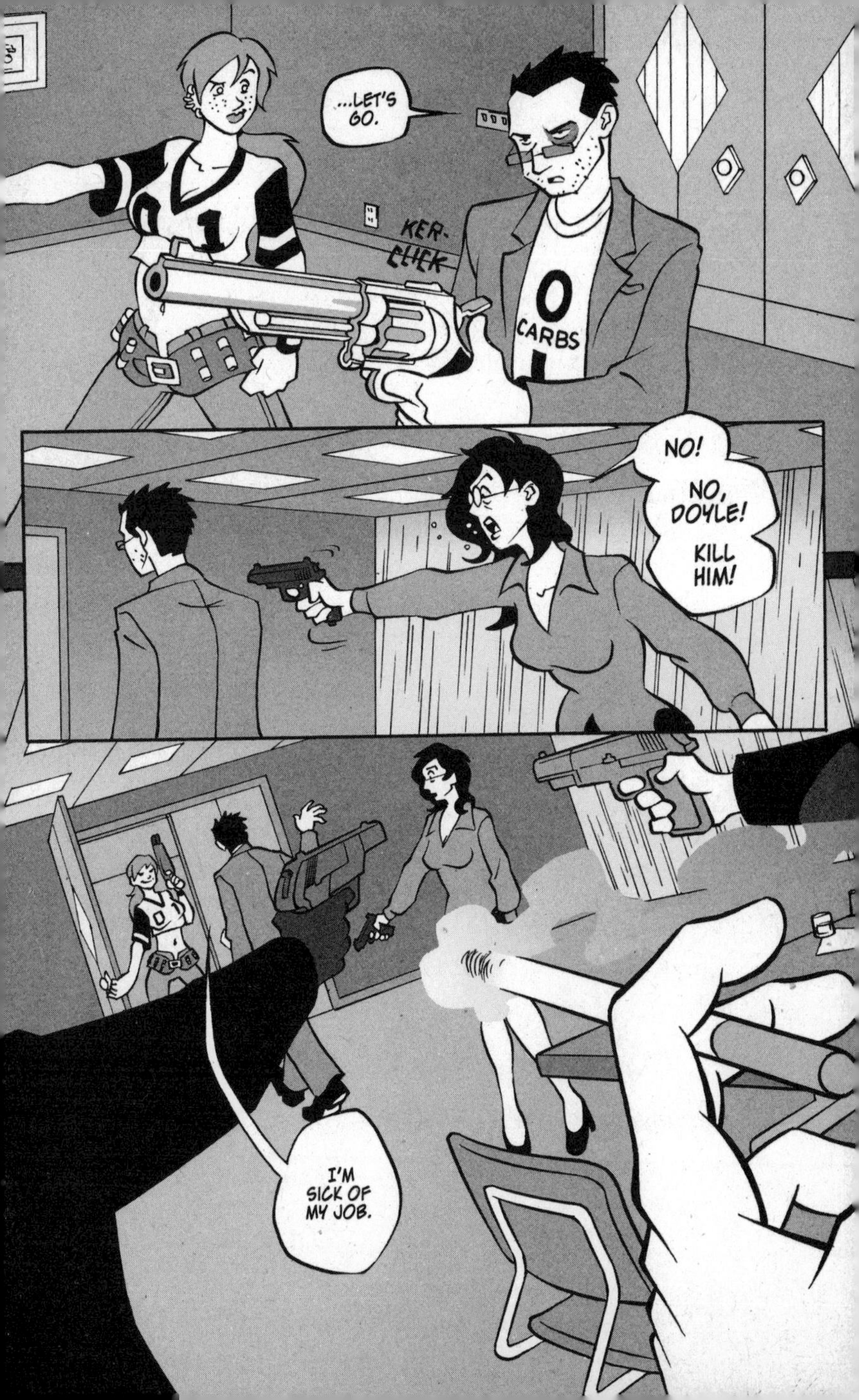
...LET'S GO.
KER-CLICK
NO! NO, DOYLE! KILL HIM!
I'M SICK OF MY JOB.

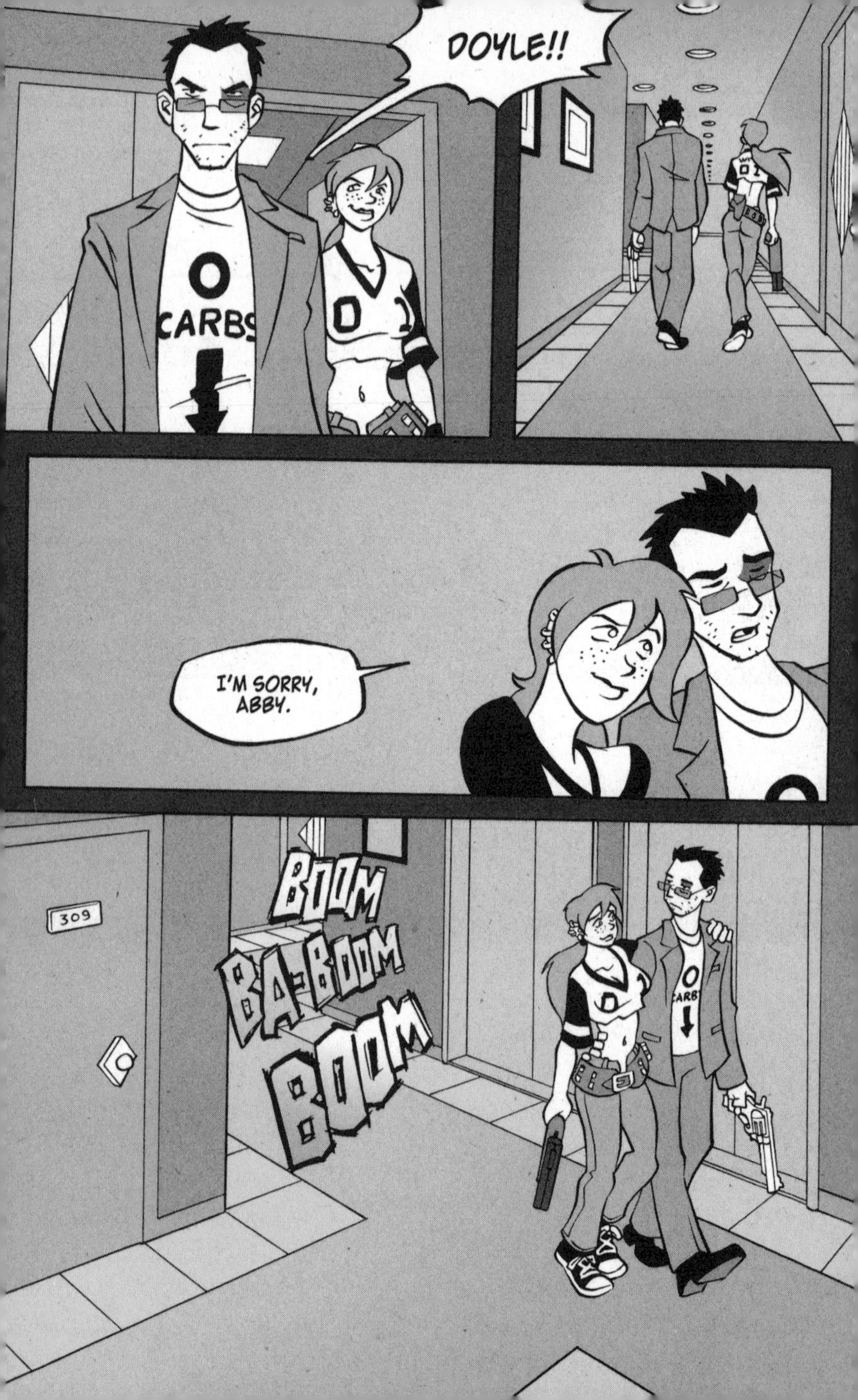
DOYLE!!
I'M SORRY, ABBY.
309
BOOM
BA-BOOM
BOOM

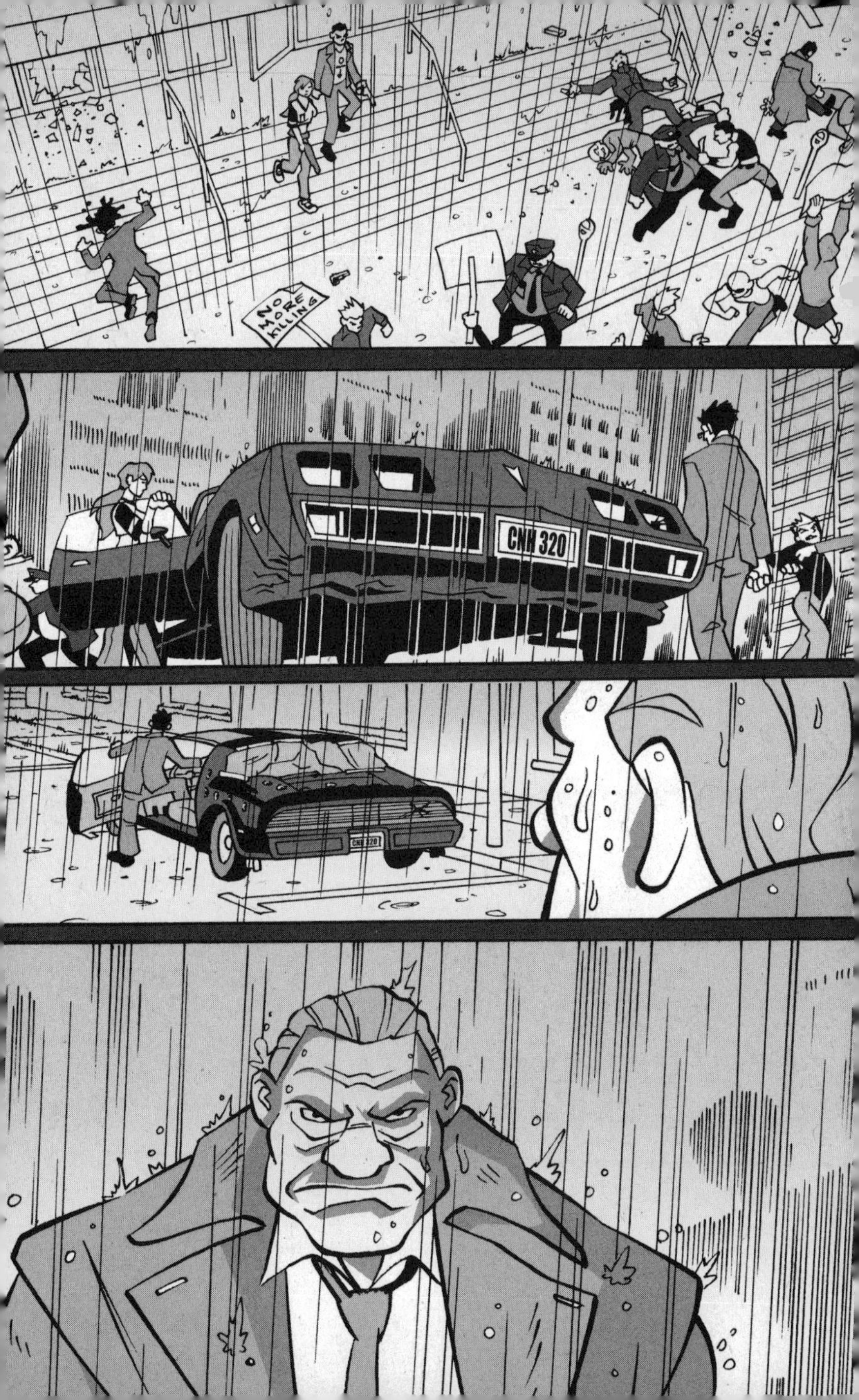
NO MORE KILLING
CNH 320

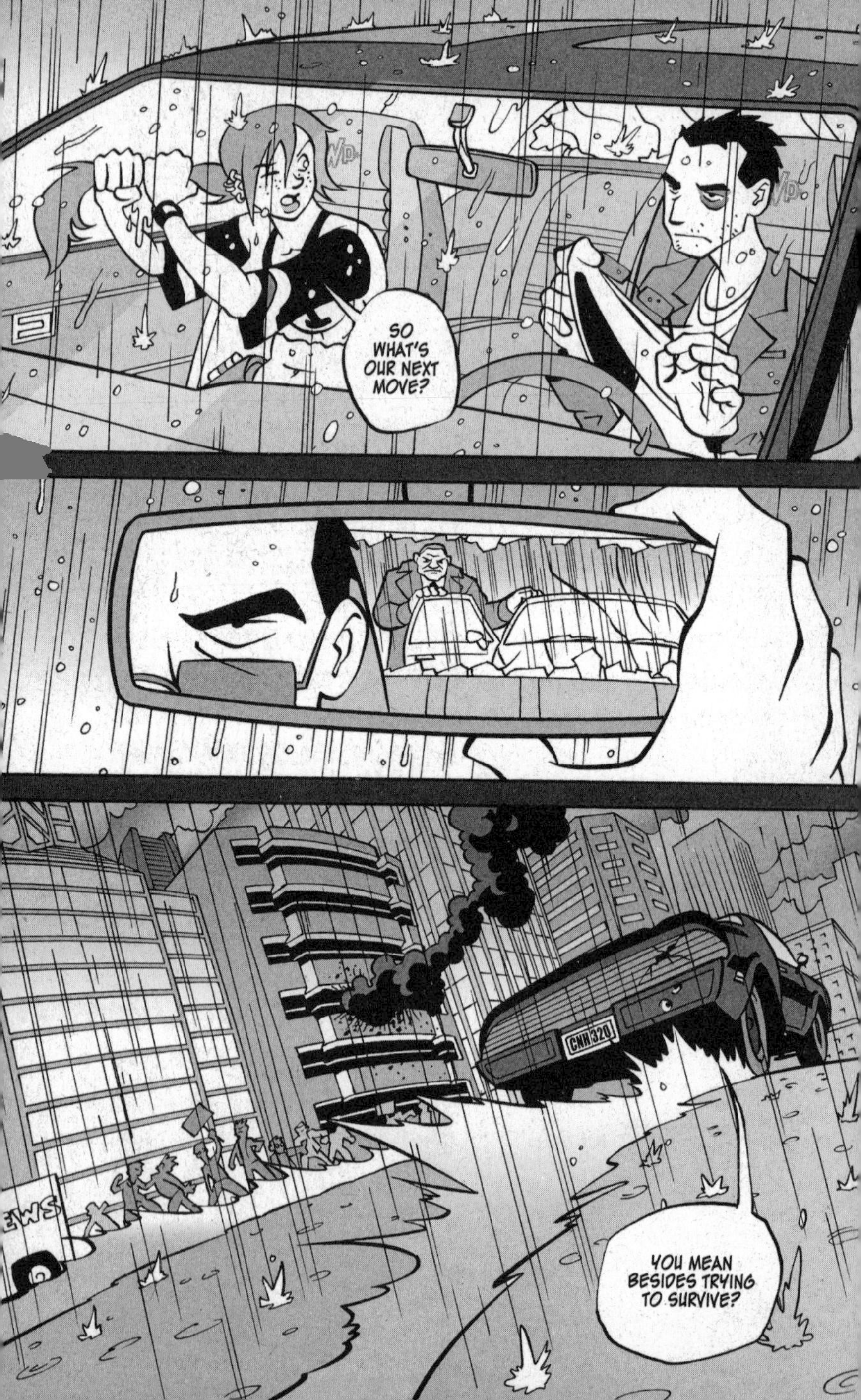
SO WHAT'S OUR NEXT MOVE?
CNH 320
YOU MEAN BESIDES TRYING TO SURVIVE?

In the next volume

Doyle and Abby are pursued by Howard Raymer—an old enemy with a secret to keep. Raymer is the source of some painful memories the two may not be ready to face, but the way things are going, history may be the least of their worries! Doyle has risen to number one on the N.A.C.'s hit list, and he refuses to allow Abby, despite her protests, to remain at his side.

With warrants out for their arrest, and bounties on their heads, Doyle takes Abby home to the only haven she might have. But this presents him with his greatest adversary yet... Abby's mother!

ACKNOWLEDGEMENTS

Thanks to

BOB PENDARVIS, DURWIN TALON, MARK KNEECE, JAMES STURM, PAUL HUDSON, DAVID GILDERSLEEVE AND JOHN LOWE.
OUR MUTUAL FRIENDS: MELISSA CONSTANDSE, AMANDA JOSEPH, CARLA LOPEZ DE AZUA, LEE OAKS, DANIEL OEFFINGER, BRANDON PAGE, SCOTT REINHARD, PJ TAMAYO, STEVEN WEITZ AND ELIZABETH YOUNG.
THE STAFF AT TOKYOPOP, LUIS REYES AND JODI BRYSON.

from Nate

THANK YOU MOM AND DAD FOR NOT ONLY SUPPORTING BUT ENCOURAGING MY INTEREST IN WRITING AND DRAWING FUNNY BOOKS.
I NEED YOUR AID AND GUIDENCE. I COULDN'T HAVE DONE IT ALONE.
MY SISTER NATASHA AND THE REST OF MY NUMEROUS FRIENDS!
DURWIN TALON, MY PERSONAL MENTOR, OPENED MY EYES TO OPTIONS BEYOND DRAWING A MONTHLY COMIC.
AND OF COURSE, TRACY YARDLEY, WITHOUT WHOM I WOULD NEVER HAVE GOTTEN OFF THE GROUND.
(FRANK MILLER, THE DUKES OF HAZZARD, WILD WEST TECH AND MY SHOWER....)

from Tracy!

THANKS TO MY MOM, DAD AND BROTHERS FOR ALL THEIR SUPPORT. THANKS TO ALL MY FRIENDS. THANKS TO MIKE PELLERITO, IAN FLYNN, JIM AMASH, LEE LOUGHRIDGE, JASON LOSS, KEN BREWER, KARYN THOMAS, AARON DANKER AND THE MCKAY FAMILY. THANKS SO MUCH TO MY BELOVED MEGAN FOR HER PATIENCE, LOVE AND SUPPORT WHILE I WORKED ON THE BOOK, AND THANKS MOST OF ALL TO THE LORD WHO GAVE ME THE SKILL AND THE WILL TO BRING THIS BOOK TO LIFE.

SPECIAL THANKS TO

ROSS CAMPBELL
(NO ROSS, NO RIDING SHOTGUN)

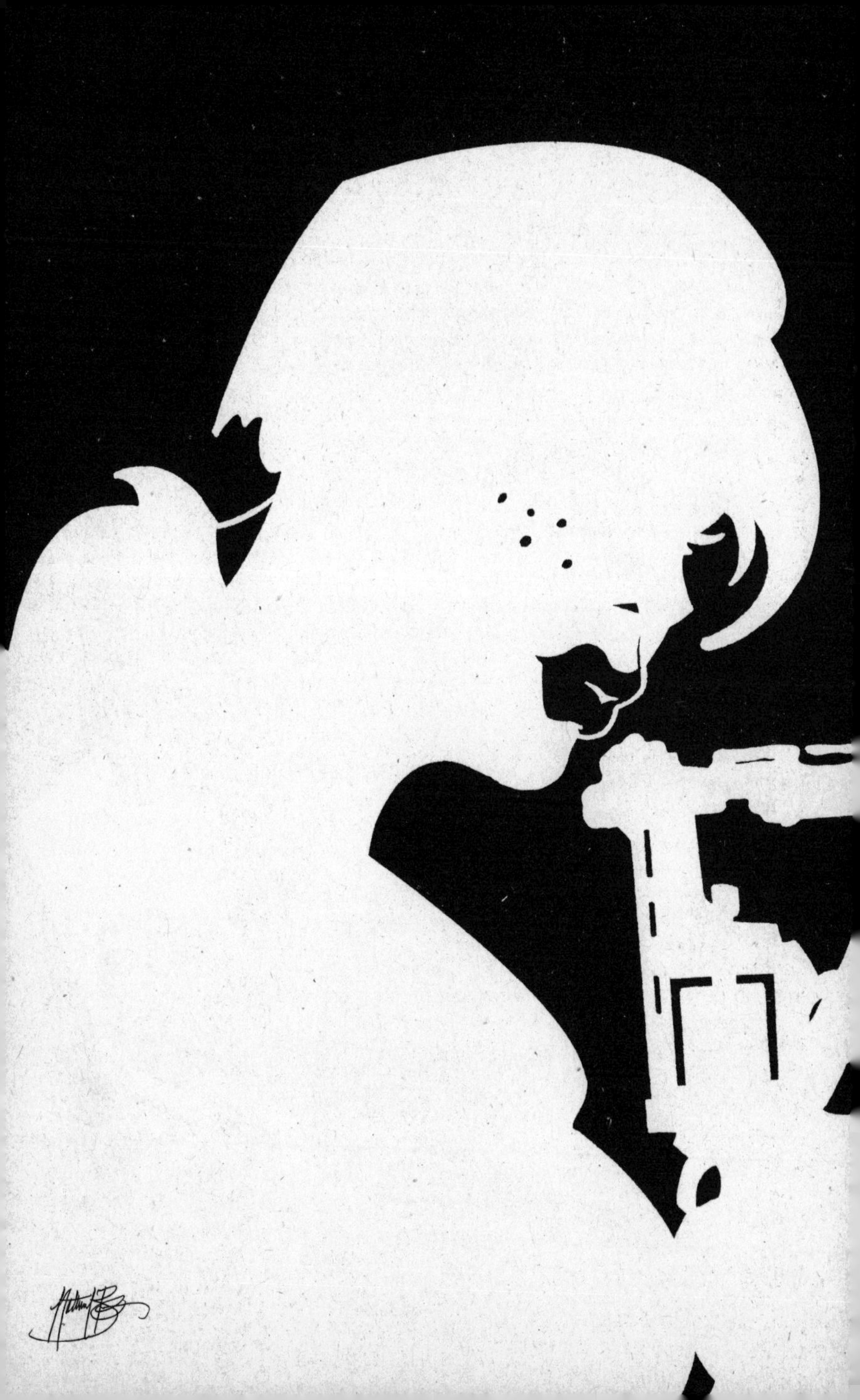

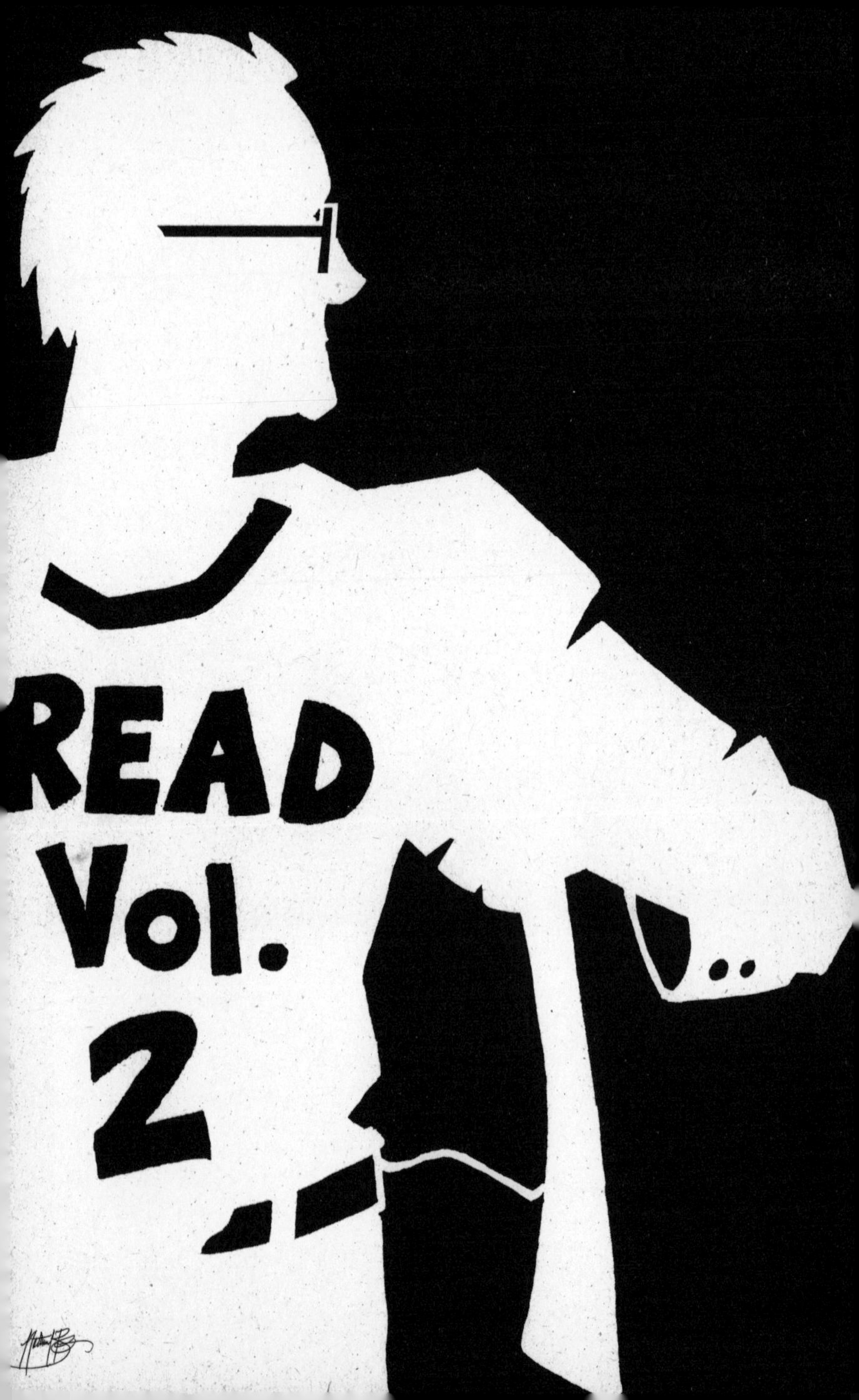
READ Vol. 2

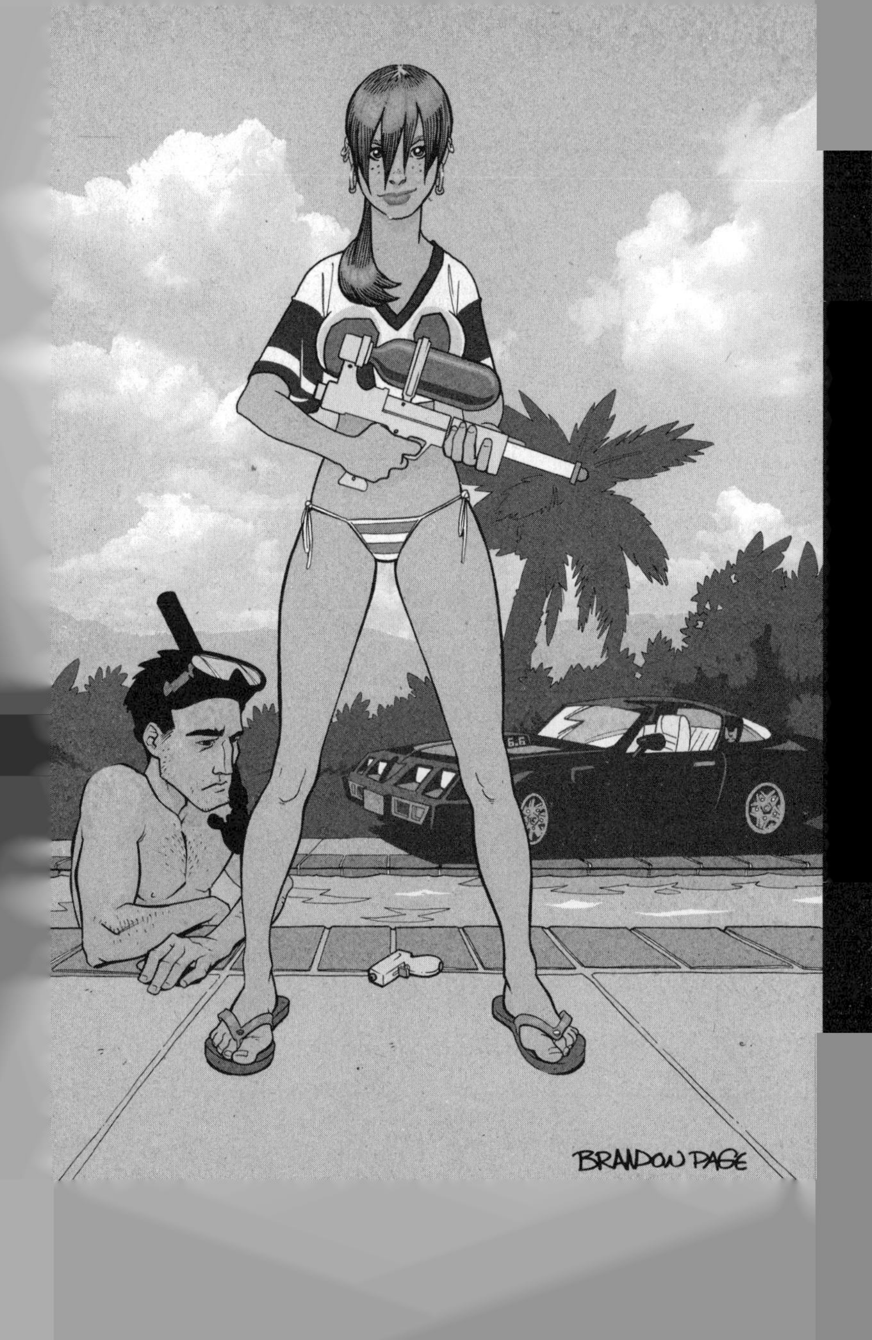
BRANDON PAGE

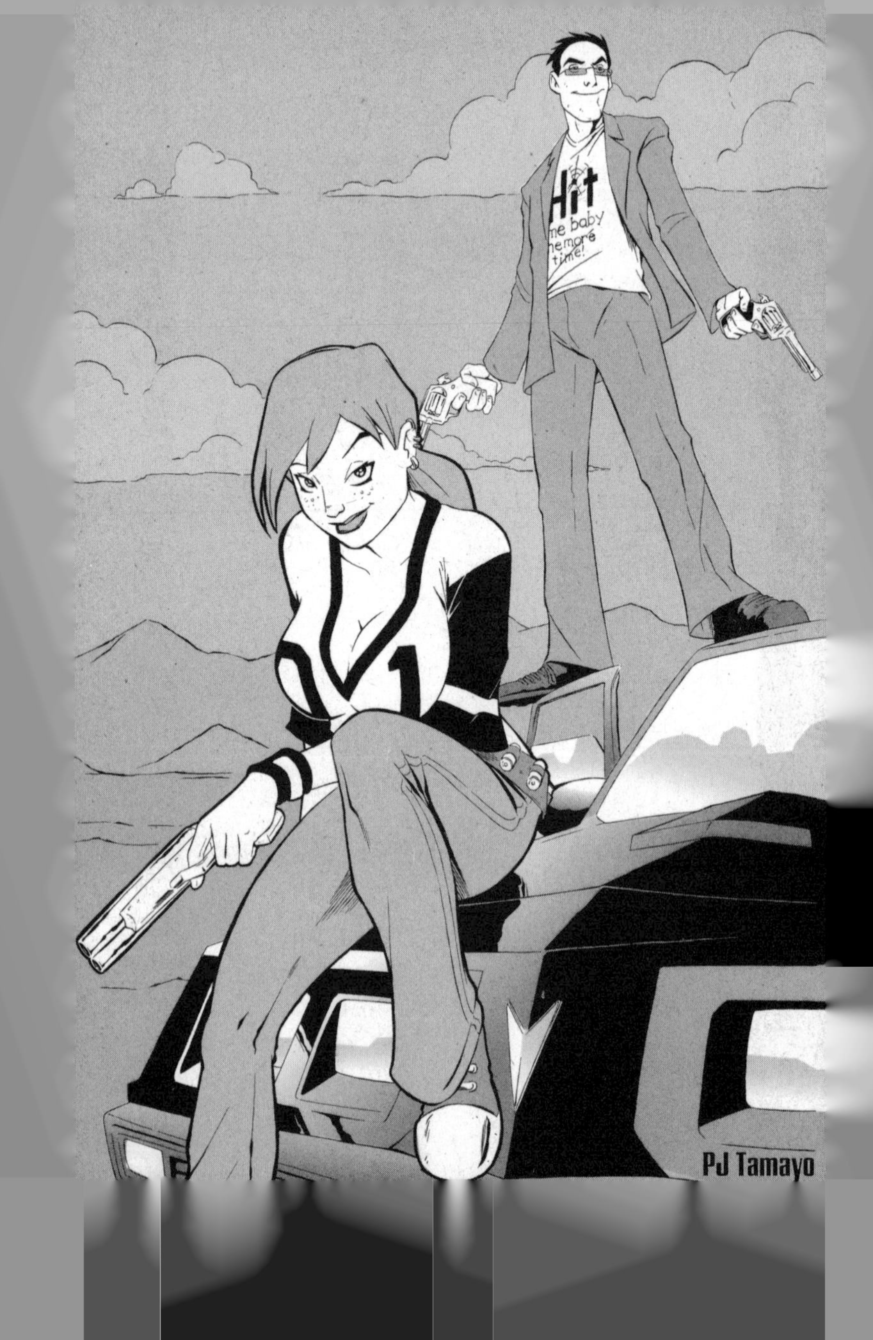
Hit
me baby
ne more
time!
PJ Tamayo

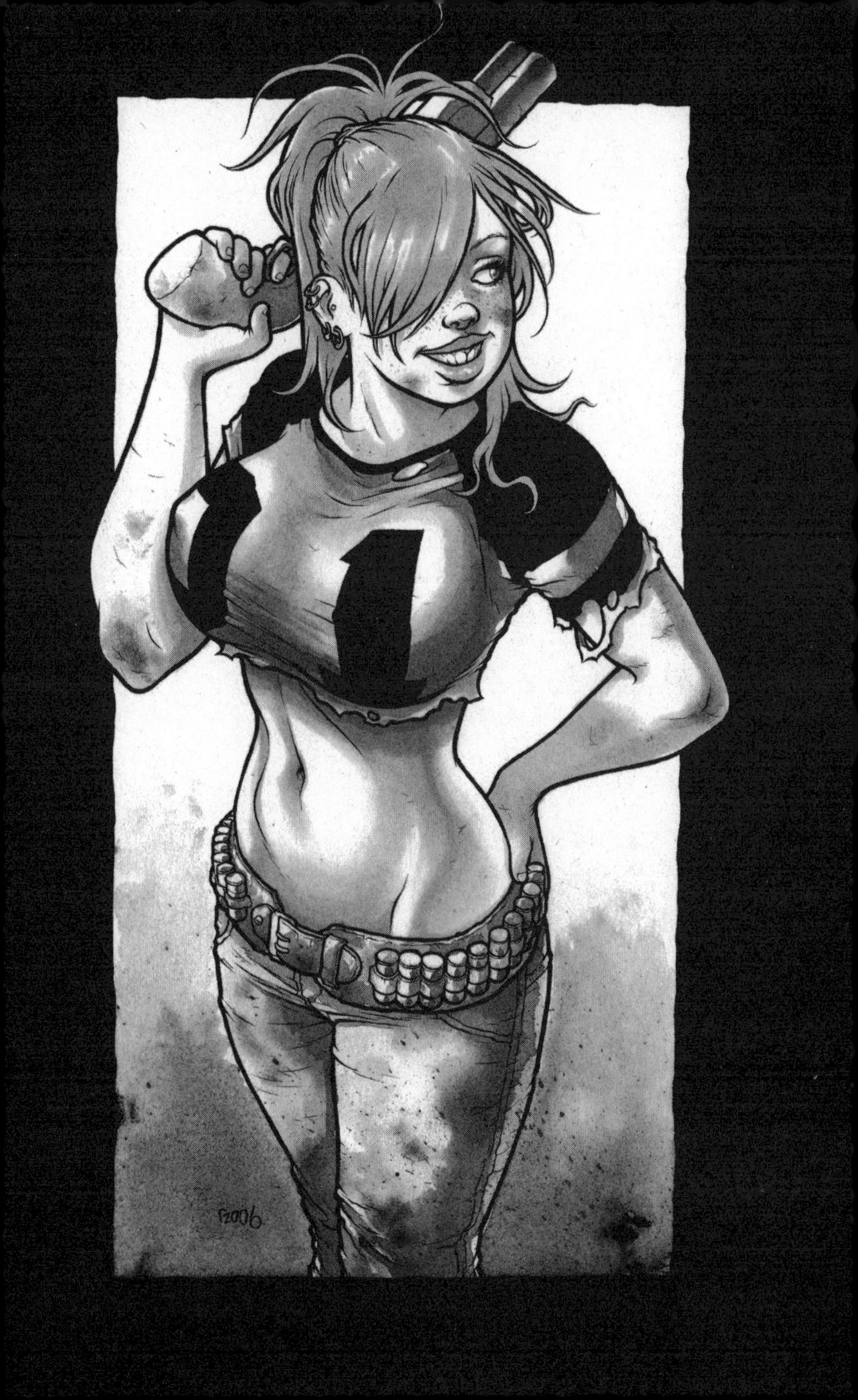

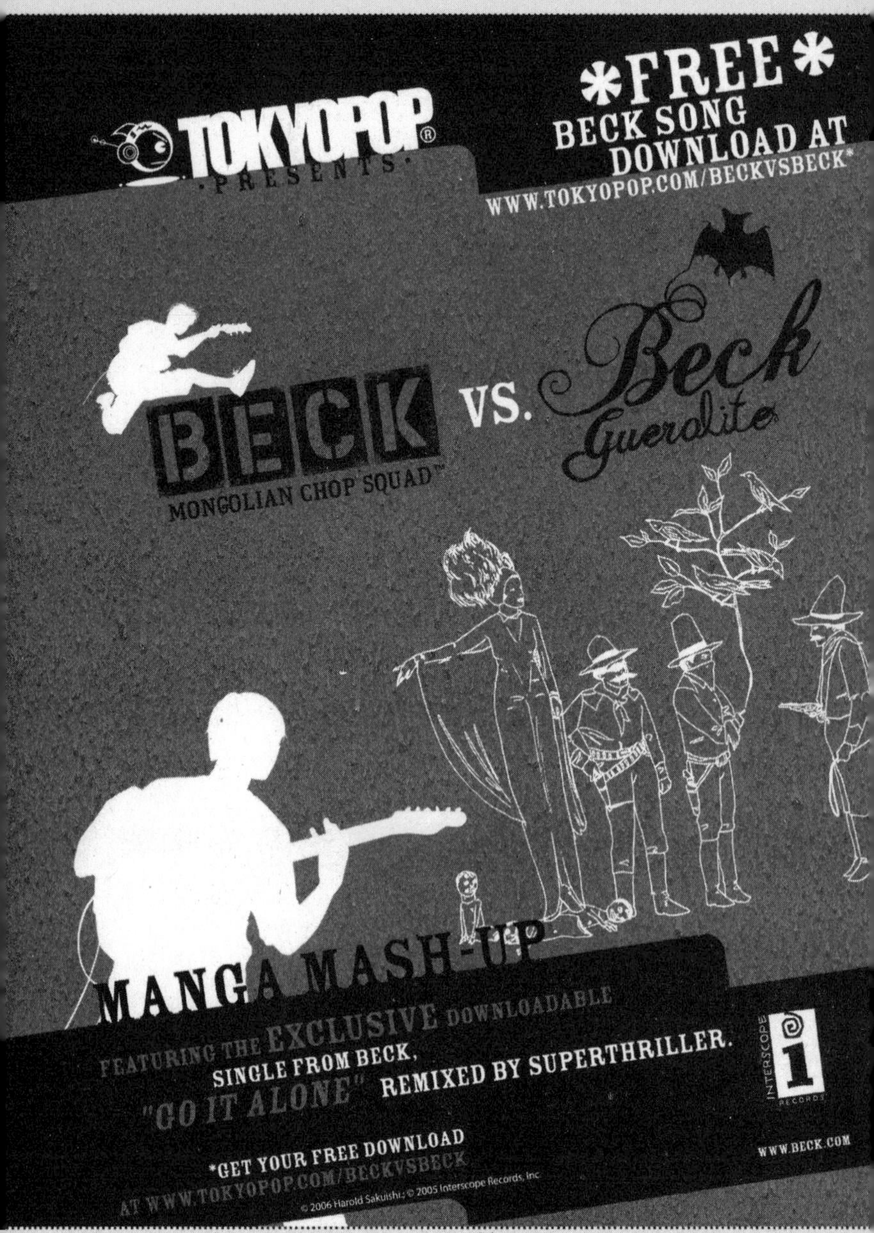
TOKYOPOP®
PRESENTS
FREE
BECK SONG
DOWNLOAD AT
WWW.TOKYOPOP.COM/BECKVSBECK*
BECK
MONGOLIAN CHOP SQUAD™
VS.
Beck
Guerolito
MANGA MASH-UP
FEATURING THE EXCLUSIVE DOWNLOADABLE
SINGLE FROM BECK,
"GO IT ALONE" REMIXED BY SUPERTHRILLER.
INTERSCOPE RECORDS
WWW.BECK.COM
*GET YOUR FREE DOWNLOAD
AT WWW.TOKYOPOP.COM/BECKVSBECK
© 2006 Harold Sakuishi; © 2005 Interscope Records, Inc